THE SECRET LIFE OF PUPPETS

Bruno Schulz and a simulacrum, from the Brothers Quay, *Street of Crocodiles* (1986). Courtesy Stephen and Timothy Quay.

VICTORIA NELSON

THE SECRET LIFE OF PUPPETS

HARVARD UNIVERSITY PRESS

CAMBRIDGE, MASSACHUSETTS, & LONDON, ENGLAND ■ 2001

Printed and bound by CPI Group (UK) Ltd, Croydon, CR0 4YY

Library of Congress Cataloging-in-Publication Data

Nelson, Victoria, 1945–
The secret life of puppets / Victoria Nelson.
p. cm.
Includes bibliographical references and index.
ISBN 0-674-00630-5 (alk. paper)
1. Science fiction—History and criticism. 2. Science fiction—Religious aspects.
3. Puppets in literature. I. Title.

PN3433.6 .N45 2001
809.3'8762—dc21
2001039088

CONTENTS

Laurie Simmons, "The Music of Regret IV." Courtesy Laurie Simmons.

The problem with displacing the supernatural "back" into the realm of psychology . . . is that it remains precisely that: only a displacement. The unearthliness, the charisma, the devastating *noumenon* of the supernatural is conserved. One cannot speak in the end, it seems to me, of a "decline in magic" in post-Enlightenment Western culture, only perhaps its relocation within the new empire of subjectivity itself . . . But the effect was to demonize the world of thought. We have yet to explore very deeply the social, intellectual, and existential implications of the act of demonization.

—Terry Castle

PREFACE

The turn of the millennium found Western societies experiencing a curious reversal in the roles of art and religion. Whereas religion up to the Renaissance provided the content for most high visual art and literature, art and entertainment in our secular era have provided both the content for new religions and the moral framework for those who practice no religion at all. Even as serious literature and art are conventionally supposed to provide a sense of "transcendence," invented cosmogonies and pantheons from the humble genres of science fiction and fantasy now serve as the inspiration for many New Age religions. In this book I focus on the way the larger mainstream culture, via works of imagination instead of official creeds, subscribes to a nonrational, supernatural, quasi-religious view of the universe: pervasively, but behind our own backs. Consuming art forms of the fantastic is only one way that we as nonbelievers allow ourselves, unconsciously, to believe.

Shakespeare's worldview of the Renaissance—the worldview that holds there is another, invisible world besides this one, that our world of the senses is ruled by this other world through signs and portents, that good and evil are physically embodied in our immediate environment—is alive and well today in science fiction and supernatural horror films that build on a three-hundred-year tradition of the secularized supernatural and behind that on the millennia-old beliefs Western culture shares with older societies around the world. The inherent Platonism of cybertheory has given an added boost to a recent gradual transformation of mainstream culture in which ancient themes are being actively revived in aesthetics and philosophy.

The intertwined chapters of this book are intended to be a series of provocative sketches, not a finished mural. In them I attempt to uncover the premodern assumptions still operative in what we imagine to be the rational and scientific perspective we use to assess reality. A subtle paradigm shift, I would like to suggest, is now under way: Western culture is on the verge of adjusting its dominant Aristotelian mode of scientific materialism to allow for the partial reemergence of Platonic idealism. Far from being a new event, this kind of Zeitgeist rollover happens regularly in our culture. The last major turn took place in the seventeenth and early eighteenth centuries, when the Platonism of natural philosophy and the Christian cosmos gave way first to the Protestant Reformation and the scientific revolution, then to Enlightenment rationalism, and ultimately to empirical materialism.

In the current Aristotelian age the transcendental has been forced underground, where it has found a distorted outlet outside the recognized boundaries of religious expression. As members of a secular society in which the cult of art has supplanted scripture and direct revelation, we turn to works of the imagination to learn how our living desire to believe in a transcendent reality has survived outside our conscious awareness. We can locate our repressed religious impulses by looking at the supernatural in fantastic novels and films, where it is almost universally depicted as grotesque and demonic, not benign and angelic—a paradox that developed out of very specific cultural developments of the sixteenth and seventeenth centuries. We can locate our unacknowledged belief in the immortal soul by looking at the ways that human simulacra—puppets, cyborgs and robots—carry on their role as direct descendents of graven images in contemporary science fiction stories and films. Most of the evidence comes from American popular entertainment, but it's in European high literature of the fantastic, too—a curious split whose historical roots I explore.

I begin by tracing the survival of the ancient notion of the underworld after the Renaissance: how it first became attached to the form of fantastic art called "grotesque" (from *grotto*, or cave), and how the entire discredited worldview of Platonism eventually came to be linked with the underworld and the demonic grotesque, a connection that persisted after the Reformation in literature (and, in this century, film) of the fantastic. From the real gardens of Renaissance Italy to its representations in twentieth-century literature and film of the Old and New Worlds, the grotto remains the physical point of connection to the transcendental in the Western imagination.

The roots of this Renaissance worldview lie in the Mediterranean world of the second to fourth centuries C.E., where the matter-spirit split central to Western culture was forged in the syncretic mix of religio-philosophical schools and sects that included Neoplatonism, Hermeticism, Gnosticism, and Christianity. The paradoxical link between human simulacra and the idea of soul also begins here, in these ancient schools and in the automated moving and talking holy statues featured in many theurgic sects. From this starting point in Late Antiquity I survey the history of puppets, mannequins, and mummies as fictive characters and holy objects in Western culture from the Middle Ages through the twentieth century. I examine selected European Romantic and post-Romantic literary works of the nineteenth and twentieth century—by Kleist, Hoffmann, Leopardi, Rilke, and the Polish Jewish writer Bruno Schulz—that revived the ancient paradox of spiritualized matter by identifying human simulacra (the dead or inanimate) with the soul (the immortal or animate).

From the nineteenth century through approximately the year 1990, the supernatural suffered a more restrictive fate as a literary subject (though not in popular religion) in the United States than it did in Europe, where it remained a strong presence in high avant-garde literature. Consigned to the burgeoning American pulp industry of the nineteenth century, the fantastic blossomed in science fiction, horror literature, comics, and ultimately film. I compare H. P. Lovecraft, the quintessential American pulp chronicler of the supernatural grotesque, with Bruno Schulz and the famous schizophrenic memoirist Daniel Paul Schreber as a way of considering issues of high and low art, madness and mysticism, and thwarted transfiguration in the naive Expressionism of their curiously similar "psychotopographic" works.

Using the ancient model of cosmography developed by Ptolemy, I map the psychotopography of the Platonic otherworld in its displaced materialist incarnation as a hole in the sky, a hole in the globe, and a hole in the head in nineteenth- and twentieth-century literary works and film. Other shorthand attempts in both high European art and popular American film and literature to reconcile the matter-spirit dichotomy that I examine include the plot structure that reveals the supernatural as either a delusion or a reality and the ancient notion of an original "angelic" language. I also survey the reversed migration of religious content from works of fantasy and science fiction into practicing cults, including the new cosmogonic myths in which extraterrestrial "aliens" have supplanted the old deities.

Frances Yates and other scholars have described the mnemonics systems of the ancient world that were revived and transformed in the Renaissance. I examine their new life in an aesthetic cult of esoteric memory practiced by a range of modernist masters including Proust, Joyce, and Nabokov. In the last decade of the twentieth century, the cult of memory resurfaced in cybergames and virtual reality models. I examine allegory (a genre closely linked to the ancient art of memory and the Platonic cosmogony) as a reemerging art form—in high art as well as cybergames—with a new audience as large and populist as it enjoyed in the European Middle Ages. In the early twentieth century, allegory was subjectivized via the newly identified psychological function of "projection" into a homocentric reframing of the premodern notion of a cosmos possessing material and invisible "correspondences"; Expressionism and Surrealism both based their aesthetics on the notion of an identity between internal and external realities. Since 1990, a new wave of secular allegorizing reinforced by Platonizing cybertheory has emerged. I examine this "New Expressionism" in the works of the British novelist Will Self and the Danish director Lars von Trier within the historical context of twentieth-century Expressionism, old and new.

The resurgence of contemporary literary and philosophical Neoplatonism (in conjunction with the characteristic low-art storytelling genre of Late Antiquity, the Greek romance) is also presented here through the oppositional lens of the ardent Aristotelian Umberto Eco. In defending the fortress of his faith against the barbarian hordes of Platonism, to which he assigns the generic label Hermeticism/Occultism, Eco draws an unfavorable comparison between our society and the syncretic culture of the second-century Mediterranean world. As a semiotician, he embodies the traditional twentieth-century schoolman's resistance to transcendentalism and the religious impulse in any form. Though he misidentifies the enemy by equating deconstructionism and other postmodern schools with Neoplatonism, Eco has correctly anticipated the paradigm shift now under way.

This shift is perhaps most vividly illustrated by contemporary incarnations of the Western puppet-soul as robot, android, and cyborg in horror and science fiction films, representations that reflect a radical change in mood after 1990 and the reemergence of the benign supernatural from the shadow of the demonic grotesque. Using a series of turn-of-the-millennium New Expressionist Hollywood films devoted to the unlikely subject of demiurgy, finally, I attempt to show the ways in which cybertheory and our perceptual framing of virtual reality as a literal "otherworld" have brought us full circle to that ideal of Renaissance Hermeticism and Neoplatonism propounded most famously by the natural philosopher and heretic Giordano Bruno: the divinization of the human.

Of the world known by the ancients—

That it seemed more in keeping with the range of human intelligence.
That it is because they knew better than we do how to envisage all
things in a manner appropriate to placing them in their minds.
That our minds are still astonished by our new discoveries and that
instead of detaching ourselves from this affectation we affect a type of eloquence
that continually strengthens it within us . . .
That the mind must dominate everything and that when it is
dominated this means it is in the wrong place.

—Joseph Joubert

Orco's mouth at Bomarzo. Photo by Eugenio Battisti, courtesy Francisco Battisti.

Where there are no gods, demons will hold sway.

—Novalis

ONE

GROTTO, AN OPENING

Suppose: a humid July morning in Bomarzo, Italy. You stand among the ruins of Count Vicino Orsini's sixteenth-century statuary gardens, the Sacro Bosco or Sacred Wood. Directly ahead on the overgrown hillside, past the sleeping Psyche, the elephant crushing the Roman soldier in its trunk, the harpy, and the sphinx, looms the enormous stone face of Orco, the ogre. Inside its gaping maw is a door. Pause at the threshold under the motto *Ogni pensiero vola* ("Every thought flies"). Remember that even the great Leonardo hesitated, at the entrance to a similar grotto: "After having remained at the entry some time," he wrote in his *Diaries*, "two contrary emotions arose in me, fear and desire—fear of the threatening dark grotto, desire to see whether there were any marvelous thing within it."

Walk into Orco's mouth anyway (as Leonardo did); discover it is not a bad place. There is a stillness, an expectant stillness, in the cool air of this artificial whitewashed cavern that its Renaissance builders designed to look like a crude initiatory cave from their pagan past. By their way of thinking, you are no longer in a realm where the conventional rules of nature apply. Here in the grotto you are inside a magical simulacrum of the universe, in Naomi Miller's phrase a "heavenly cave," halfway to the classical underworld.

Say, as is likely, nothing much seems to happen. Step out of Orco's mouth into a hot summer day and be struck by Socrates' admonition that the world, ordinary life, is the real cave; by contrast *this* is what heaven feels like. Then find you have snagged your shirt on some inconvenient outcropping back there in the grotto and the zigzagging cotton thread is drawing after it a whole forgotten way of looking at reality, the same way of looking so eagerly revived by the Christians who built this and other grottoes all across Italy and the rest of western Europe a millennium after Christianity itself had suppressed the pagan cults that inspired them.

Unlike the history of most great aesthetic movements, the birth of the Western grotesque is easy to pinpoint. When Italian antiquarians excavated the Roman emperor Nero's Domus Aurea outside Rome in 1480, they had to dig so far down to reach it that they called its rooms and corridors *grotte*, from *crypta*, a Latin borrowing from Greek meaning "hidden pit" or "cave." On the interior walls of the sunken palace they found murals depicting strange hybrid monsters of a style in vogue in the first century after Christ—a style Horace had mocked in *Ars Poetica* for its fantastic juxtapositions (a horse's neck with a man's head, a woman's body with a fish's tail) as "dreams of a sick person's mind."

Once uncovered from Nero's *grotte*, this visual conceit of the early Roman empire was immediately taken up by Raphael and other Italian painters at the turn of the fifteenth century. The mode *alla grottesca* swept across Europe and the grotto itself became a staple of every nobleman's garden. A century after the Domus Aurea excavations, the grotto or artificial cave had become nothing less than the "place of birth and death, passing away and rebirth, descent and resurrection," a highly charged microcosmic container of selected physical objects that drew down the arcane energy of counterpart Forms in the superior world. Out of the same kind of syncretic mix-and-matching that had been practiced in the late ancient Mediterranean world, these decorations from the walls of a Roman palace combined in the Renaissance matrix with Platonic, Neoplatonic, and Christian lore (not to mention a considerable tradition of monsters and fancies from medieval tradition) to create a new art form and emblem for the universe. Now Montaigne could label himself a "grotesque" writer, and an adjective created for a specific style of visual art had been stretched—just as the "modernist" and "postmodernist" labels were to be in the twentieth century, and with equally jumbled results—to describe a much broader aesthetic sensibility.

For another two hundred years after Bomarzo, grottoes replete with automata, water organs, and fantastic statuary proliferated in the gardens of Western Europe, culminating in such self-conscious eighteenth-century productions as Alexander Pope's studio at Twickenham, an underground passage cum atelier bedecked with mirrors, seashells, and false stalactites where Pope heroically communed with his muse despite his severe arthritis, which the damp cavern adjacent to the Thames must have unbearably provoked. But the perception-altering powers of this chamber, its ability to make one feel one had entered a different reality, still shines through in Pope's enthusiastic description: "When you shut the doors of the Grotto, it becomes on the instant, from a luminous Room, a *Camera obscura;* on the Walls of which the Objects of the River, Hills, Woods, and Boars, are forming a moving Picture in their visible Radiations."

Grottoes have long been out of fashion in the modern era, but what we continue to think of as *grotesque* has not. This style of art—in John Ruskin's definition still faithful to Horace, composed of "two elements, one ludicrous, the other fearful"—remains linked with caves and the underground by what seems an accident of linguistics and spatial association, but in fact evokes a tradition that was very old not only in 1480 but in the first century C.E. as well. The tradition of caves as the antechamber of the classical underworld, the land of the dead, a halfway point from which to contact the gods in their separate reality, was firmly entrenched from archaic times. Before the advent of what Peter Kingsley has dubbed the "aetherial" model of Plato's cave (a World of Forms preceding and informing the shadowy reality we perceive through the senses), pre-Socratic Greek philosophy was rooted in a tradition of seeking wisdom in the darkness, not the light, via dream incubation in caves. Initiates who slept in these sacred places journeyed to the realm of the dead in hope of meeting a divinity who would become their friend and mentor. Unlike Parmenides and Empedocles, whose cults, like many others in the ancient world, offered the cave as a place of healing and connection to a transcendental world outside the senses, Plato would present the cave as a parable for the limitation of perception derived solely from sensory experience—hence a place the exceptional person is obliged to escape from if he is to perceive truth.

It is worth returning to the famous passage in *The Republic,* so often alluded to, so rarely read firsthand, to ponder the allegory that would long rule Western culture. "Imagine men to be living in an underground cavelike dwelling place," Socrates begins his illustration of the "effect of education and its absence,"

> The men have been there from childhood, with their neck and legs in fetters, so that they remain in the same place and can only see ahead of them, as their bonds prevent them turning their heads. Light is provided by a fire burning some way behind and above them. Between the fire and the prisoners, some way behind them and on a higher ground, there is a path across the cave and along this a low wall has been built, like the screen at a puppet show in front of the performers who show their puppets above it . . . See then also men carrying along that wall, so that they overtop it, all kinds of artifacts, statues of men, reproductions of other animals in stone or wood fashioned in all sorts of ways, and, as is likely, some of the carriers are talking while others are silent.

From this complicated theatrical image Socrates proceeds to his point:

> Do you think, in the first place, that such men could see anything of themselves and each other except the shadows which the fire casts upon the wall of the cave in front of them? . . . such men would believe the truth to be nothing else than the shadows of the artifacts.

But what would happen if one of these men were freed? First, Socrates says, he would see the fire, then the real objects instead of their shadows, and would thus be at a loss to explain what they were. Next, implicitly, he would discover that these objects were no more than artifacts and statues, human-made representations. Then, "dragged by force up the rough and steep path" into the sunlight, this man "would no longer be able to see a single one of the things which are now said to be true," and a slow period of adjustment to the reality of the "world above" would follow—first shadows, then reflections, then "the things themselves" that exist in this upper world.

Six centuries after Plato, the belief in an eternal higher reality hidden behind the transitory and misleading shapes of a mortal lower existence still pervaded the ancient Western world's Hellenistic cults, philosophical schools, and new religions, most notably Christianity. According to the second-century C.E. sage Bolos of Mendes (also known as Democritos), the dual cosmos is a living organism; every atom of the material world is duplicated in, and bound to, the other world by a complicated but exact set of affinities; reality is hierarchical and flows downward from the divine level in a "great chain of being" of increasingly inferior manifestations. The Alexandrian Neoplatonic philosopher Plotinus (205–270 C.E.) further refined the model into a hierarchy of microcosm to macrocosm in which our world of the senses is an exact if imperfect copy of the perfect world, as we ourselves are an imperfect copy of its creator. More than a millennium later, the grotto builders of the Italian Renaissance still shared many of the tenets of this cosmogony with their classical forebears; those they did not receive from medieval tradition, often through translation from the Arabic, they revived from newly discovered Greek and Latin manuscripts. In his *Heptaplus* (1495), the Florentine theologian Pico della Mirandola could reconcile Plato and Genesis in essentially the same Neoplatonic framework: "Whatever is in the lower world is also in the higher world, but in a more superior form; similarly, what is found in the higher world can also be seen in the lower one, but in a deteriorated condition and with a somewhat adulterated nature."

Fast-forward a mere half-millennium to the present day, however, and we find the old Platonic cosmos universally regarded as a quaint construct utterly dead to all but scholars—a magnificent "history of a failure," in Arthur Lovejoy's words; a lingering set of occult superstitions, in Umberto Eco's. The two-world construct that put a creator in the higher world and creation in this world was secularized into the modern two-level model that M. H. Abrams described as "subject and object, ego and non-ego, the human mind or consciousness and its transactions with nature." We believe in only one world now, the world our senses perceive, and within this world we maintain the old duality at the material level by means of the Cartesian distinction of mental versus physical substances. As proud inheritors of a rational scientific tradition that asserts it has permanently vanquished its predecessors, we have completely distanced ourselves from any conscious grotto connection, either to the forgotten classical underworld—in Kingsley's words, the "dark place of wisdom . . . the supreme place of paradox where all the opposites meet"—or to Plato's World of Forms or Ideas carried on in the Neoplatonized Christianity of our cultural ancestors and still preserved (with rather the custodial air of museum keepers) by the contemporary Christian churches.

But the underworld is not really dead. Neither is the overworld. The distance from Plato's cave to Kafka's burrow is, like the mathematical paradox of a good Hellene like Zeno, immeasurably wide and immeasurably small at the same time. The old notion of the microcosm and the macrocosm, the physical world as a double-reflecting mirror between our psyches and a transcendental other world, is more deeply embedded in us than we imagine. Think of the lowest level of the parking garage in the last ten action films you have watched, always the site of danger and discord, where the hero or heroine is stalked and attacked by the villain, where a tumultuous car chase ends in wholesale destruction. Or the mysterious regions under the subway in these movies, where the ancient world's dead souls are manifest as hordes of the homeless. Or the labyrinths these movies always position under their fictive Chinatowns. Or any number of alternate or secondary worlds that the science fiction genre has given us, including the caverns of the mysterious planet in the movie *Alien* (1979), filled with the sinister pods that infect the crew of the visiting space freighter *Nostromo* with the aggressively destructive organism that kills every living thing it inhabits. Or the statement, repeated in one form or another in almost every virtual-reality fiction or film, that what we see around us is an illusion created to mask a very different reality that lies either below or above us.

Our culture has a long history of pushing discredited religion and science alike off their former pedestals and recycling them in works of the imagination. Throughout the Christian Renaissance, the notion of a *mundus subterraneus*, a world existing under the surface of our planet, became an acceptable geographical secularization of Western antiquity's underworld, earning a prominent position in the atlases of learned eminences like Athanasius Kircher. As we will see in Chapter 6, however, after the scientific revolution of the seventeenth century followed by the first polar expeditions, the *mundus subterraneus* could no longer be accepted as a real physical location and was transformed through a series of interesting steps into a fictive transcendental-psychological locus in literature and film.

The scientific revolution was itself built on the sixteenth-century Reformation, which had imposed limits on the old Christian cosmogony that were to have far-reaching consequences. Most significantly, the new Protestant dogma had fixed the "cessation of miracles," in D. P. Walker's phrase—and hence the direct intrusion of the supernatural into human lives—back to the year 600 C.E. The repudiation of miraculous events and other intrusions from the higher world, including ghosts, became not simply the dividing line between the new mainstream Protestant culture and the older Catholic belief but a marker of piety as well. Keith Thomas relates a telling anecdote of early seventeenth-century England: "When Sir Thomas Wise saw a walking spirit in the reign of James, the local archdeacon was inclined to think it might have been an angelic apparition. But the theologian Daniel Featley firmly declared that it must have been an evil spirit because it was well known that good ones could no longer be expected to appear." Henceforth any instance of supernatural intervention—that is, of the influence of an assumed invisible world on our world of the senses—would be seen as the work of the Devil.

So dramatically was the line drawn between acceptable religious belief and the perils of the supernatural, now reframed as magic and witchery, that three hundred years later we still subscribe, in an unacknowledged way that surfaces mainly in what might be called the "sub-Zeitgeist" of our popular culture, not to a strictly materialist viewpoint but rather to one that implicitly upholds the supernatural as a demonized realm. Likewise, once Protestant Christianity had internalized the influence of the invisible world and restricted it solely to religious experience, the physical world became the only legitimate subject of scientific study and knowledge was balkanized into areas of specialist expertise. By the time of the Jesuit natural philosopher Athanasius Kircher (in Joscelyn Godwin's words, the "last man to know everything"), the Renaissance man of knowledge had split into three mutually exclusive figures: theologian, philosopher, and scientist. A shadowy fourth figure, the magus—the creator of "magic," from the Greek word for the Zoroastrian priests of old Persia, always the heretic in Western Christian culture but heir of the Late Antique Neoplatonists, as was his marginally more respectable cousin the medieval alchemist—found his role as manipulator of the forces of nature usurped by the scientist.

Some of the magus's fading energy would also transfer to secular artists and writers as they moved to greater cultural prominence during and after the Renaissance. Later, as rationality and human-sourced consciousness were instituted as absolute measures of reality in the French Enlightenment of the eighteenth century, that same conflation of iconoclasm and empiricism which had rejected the Platonic universe also banished from mainstream intellectual discourse the circumscribed remnant of celestial cosmogony that Protestant Christianity still retained.

This splintering of disciplines may partially account for the curious way the Western popular imagination chose to assign the roles of good and bad magus after the Renaissance. The good magus role, with its benign demiurgic powers first divorced from divine inspiration, then aestheticized and psychologized, was ultimately absorbed into the figures of the artist and the writer; the bad magus role, with its supernatural powers linked to the dark grotto of the underworld, was absorbed into the figure of the scientist. In the newly valorized aesthetic dimension of Western secular intellectual culture, the act of high artistic creation came to be regarded as the *summum bonum;* in popular entertainments, meanwhile, the act of scientific creation—in a trend bookmarked by Christopher Marlowe's *Dr. Faustus,* Goethe's *Faust,* and Mary Shelley's *Frankenstein,* and this long before the H-bomb—has been almost universally depicted as malevolent. The natural philosopher turned scientist is typically shown as a power-mad, misguided tinkerer, and the fact that the scientist is now perceived as possessing the only credible connection to the supernatural (by virtue of mysterious powers exerted over the natural world) has much to do with this stereotype. The figure of the "mad scientist" did not arise, as is commonly believed, from a mistrust of the new empirical science's stupendous achievements, good and bad, but rather from a much older mistrust of those who mediate with the supernatural outside the bounds of organized religion. Now as then, it represents a disguised fear of sorcery.

The same paradigm shift that banished both the underworld and the overworld as "real" locations, meanwhile, was simultaneously opening up possibilities of nontranscendental worlds other than our own. The theory of the plurality of material worlds (including inhabited ones), advanced by philosophers as diverse in their views as Giordano Bruno and René Descartes, was well entrenched by the end of the seventeenth century. These developments helped push the disallowed transcendent dimension into newly labeled territories of the imagination and fantastic literature, such as the formerly celestial realm of "outer space." During the nineteenth and twentieth centuries, as Western culture moved gradually into its present postreligious intellectual stance, the supernatural was increasingly consigned to popular entertainments, where it carried on in its circumscribed role. The underworld especially, in combination with its antechamber the grotto, continued to provoke both attraction and repulsion, requiring only minor updating to retain its ancient role as the setting for violent confrontation and/or profound communion with that aspect of the super- or anti-natural we still broadly label the "grotesque."

In modern times, this means that the grotto has also carried the extra burden of the unacknowledged and unacceptable divine. Once perceived as *awe filling*, the transcendent gradually shrank in our awareness after the seventeenth century into something more weakly and secularly *awful*—a process structurally analogous to the earlier co-option by Christianity of pagan gods into devils, as indeed the neutral Hellenistic spirits syncretically dubbed *daimones*, or daemons, became the *demons* of the early Christian church.

As the supernatural itself was displaced out of Protestant Christian religious discourse and into the imaginary, the experiences of redemption and personal transformation once confined to religious practice also began to shift into the aesthetic experience. In his preface to *The Birth of Tragedy*, the consummate modern philosopher Nietzsche proclaimed (and later retracted) that art in our times has become "the highest human task, the true metaphysical activity of man"—an aesthetification Jorge Luis Borges gleefully took to its *reductio ad absurdum* in "Tlön, Uqbar, Orbis Tertius" when the philosophers of his parallel idealist world flatly declare that "metaphysics is a branch of fantastic literature." The arts, now regarded as homocentric secular territories ruled entirely by the human imagination, have come to serve as a kind of unconscious wellspring of religion instead of the other way around. Most obviously, the precepts of many marginal religious cults derive from science fiction and fantasy films. Less obviously, the rest of us also seek from the arts what we once sought from religion, from the cultish worship of "stars" at one extreme to the genteel passion for extracting moral exempla from novels at the other. (In the latter case, the desire to glean information from fiction on how to live one's life is often fueled by the secret hope of "transforming" it.) The perception that art possesses salvific properties has resulted in what the critic Leo Bersani once dubbed a falsely inflated "culture of redemption" in which art's value and authority derive from its perceived ability to master and redeem human experience—precisely the task it inherited from religion. As part of the new prominence of human subjectivity after the Freudian revolution, Western intellectual culture would similarly displace the transcendental impulse into the psychological and the biological, and most especially sexuality, during the twentieth century.

With the transcendent wedded to the demonic at the deepest level of the post-1700 Western Protestant imagination, it is no surprise that the supernatural grotesque is currently alive and flourishing—both as imagined territory and as aesthetic style—in all types of literature, film, and mass entertainment. Perhaps the best examples of this sensibility are provided by those writers who obsessively imagine physical grottoes as mysterious loci of psychic or spiritual transformation. The two great Western grotto chroniclers of the twentieth century were Franz Kafka and E. M. Forster. In contrast to the ornate extravagances of the Renaissance, the heavenly caves constructed by these two high-art modernists (underground and also, in Forster's case, underwater) hark back to the oldest realm of the pre-Socratics. Rude openings in the earth, they are either entirely unaltered by human hand and thus "natural" (Forster) or excavated by an unnamed creature with a human consciousness and an animal's habits (Kafka).

In the pivotal incident of Forster's novel *A Passage to India* (1924), European and Indian visitors alike are swallowed up in the terrifying impersonality of the Marabar Caves:

> Bending their heads, they disappeared one by one into the interior of the hills. The small black hole gaped where their varied forms and colours had momentarily functioned. They were sucked in like water down a drain . . . And then the hole belched and humanity returned.

In the space of this paragraph—and tantalizingly out of our readerly sight—the two Englishwomen (both refined practitioners of Anglicanism) have had a catastrophically ambiguous experience inside the alien grotto, an experience that they translate into strikingly opposed perceptions: Adele perceives an assault, which she can only interpret as coming sexually from another human, the Muslim Aziz; Mrs. Moore falls prey to either a spiritual insight or a spiritual infection that simultaneously kills her and (in the perception of the Hindus) reincarnates her as a demigoddess. For both, the grotto's potential for violence and an ambiguous transcendentalism has been fully realized.

Forster's pre-1914 "The Story of the Siren," in contrast, is set squarely in the physical and cultural territory of Western religiosity. In a single bravura emblem the story's opening establishes a radical perspective from which to view the rationalized, intellectualized Christianity that is our culture's official gatekeeper to the other world:

> Few things have been more beautiful than my notebook on the Deist Controversy as it fell downward through the waters of the Mediterranean. It dived, like a piece of black slate, but opened soon, disclosing leaves of pale green, which quivered into blue. Now it had vanished, now it was a piece of magical india-rubber stretching out to infinity, now it was a book again, but bigger than the book of all knowledge. It grew more fantastic as it reached the bottom, where a puff of sand welcomed it and obscured it from view. But it reappeared, quite sane though a little tremulous, lying decently open on its back, while unseen fingers fidgeted among its leaves.

The superficially distorting but subliminally clarifying context of the underwater transcendent allows us and the narrator a brief but tantalizing glimpse, via a so-called optical illusion (actually the resonance between the microcosmic physical and the macrocosmic spiritual worlds), into the ecstatic and awe-ful possibilities of this religion, possibilities that are quickly extinguished by a reverse metamorphosis back to a "sane" and sentimental framework complete with deliberately kitschy "unseen fingers."

Inside the defining context of Capri's Blue Grotto, this "world of blue whose floor was the sea and whose walls and roof of rock trembled with the sea's reflections," where "only the fantastic would be tolerable," the local boatman now recounts the tale of a mysterious female god whom the Christian priests have confined in the sea. Because they forgot to bless themselves before entering the sea, his brother and a young woman were among the unlucky few to have "seen the Siren" under the water—yet another ambivalent experience of the transcendent that has rendered them mute outcasts who eventually find each other. The village priest murders her to prevent the couple's child—Savior or Antichrist, depending on one's perspective—from being born; the brother flees to America. But, the boatman reports, someday a child will be born "who will fetch up the Siren from the sea, and destroy silence, and save the world!" Just as he makes this astonishing prophecy, "the whole cave darkened, and there rode in through its narrow entrance the returning boat" full of chattering tourists. In the Blue Grotto as in Plato's cave, the shadows of mundane reality are powerful enough to obliterate the tantalizing reflected glimpses of a transcendental world.

We can recognize in Forster's fable the tendency of many late nineteenth- and early twentieth-century Western writers and scholars to disguise their religious instincts (from themselves as much as from others) within an intellectual quest to discover a surviving pagan or indigenous authenticity. The object of this fervent scholarship, whether the god Pan or the Green Knight, was always half-consciously represented by these commentators as an ineffable that-which-cannot-be-named even as they maintained their objectivity, never owning to a secret and powerful desire to worship what they sought. Yet Forster is also able to parody this impulse, both in the device of the little book for tourists that describes the Siren in sentimental terms and in the narrator's own fatuous and condescending initial response, and thus he is able to incorporate a more self-conscious awareness of his own ambivalent pull toward ecstatic religion than his scholar peers—the Jessie L. Westons and Roger Loomises struggling with the "Grail problem"—were able to do.

This trend of displaced scholarly cultism peaked in the pursuit of what might be called the "colonized transcendent"—that is, the twentieth-century Western fascination with the religions of pretechnological cultures around the world, which amounted to an allowable means by which to experience vicariously one's inclinations toward the holy. Though (to put it mildly) such romanticizing efforts provided a much-needed corrective to the cultural imperialism that preceded them, many anthropologists and their audiences did not always appear conscious of their own underlying pull to *believe,* rather than simply understand, the religious systems of the "natives" under their scrutiny. As long as we maintain that the gods belong to someone else, the religious impulse stays safely exoticized in the realm of the other, the not-us. But much as we might like to ignore the fact, the gods are ours.

Where Forster is explicit and polemical, Kafka is implicit and ambiguous. "The Burrow" is the first-person account of a creature we would be wrong to assume is human, though it thinks and feels like one. This burrower inhabits an elaborate underground lair it has constructed and enlarged from the meager tunnels of previous animals. Its two great obsessions, territoriality and freedom, are perversely opposed to each other; its overriding fear is of the intrusion of other animals into this space with malign intent. Caught in the great secular undertow of the twentieth-century West, this story has been submerged, as it were, beneath a flood of metaphorical interpretations, from that of a man exploring the labyrinth of his subconscious to the artist's relation to his creation. Yet the most striking impression "The Burrow" produces in a reader is that of *being an animal*—a sensitive, articulate animal, but still an animal, driven by deep instinctive needs to hunt and kill, to defend a lair (not a nest; sexuality is rigorously excluded) from "greedy muzzles," and, if need be, to "leap on" any intruder, "maul him, tear the flesh from his bones, destroy him, drink his blood, and fling his corpse among the rest of my spoil."

One of the great Renaissance interpreters of the Neoplatonic tradition, Giordano Bruno, maintained that *gnosis*, the mystical act of knowing God—and in the process becoming God—is an Ovidian transformation of the soul that comes through the metamorphosis into animal form that occurs during sleep and dreaming (hence the god of sleep, Morpheus, whose name embodies the experience). The same sense of *being an animal* informs "The Metamorphosis," in which Kafka's narrator Gregor awakens from an Ovidian "night of troubled dreams" transformed into a giant insect who has a human's need for romantic love, an insect's appetite for food—but again, strangely, neither species' appetite for mating. This is a belief contemporary Westerners once again tend to relegate reflexively to the exotic territory of "indigenous spirituality," where it is ubiquitous. Something in the subliminal experience of "The Burrow"—a tale lodged squarely inside our own modern culture—also suggests this radical notion, the paradox that the animal's instinctive knowledge may be a pathway to something not of this world.

To Kafka's twentieth-century burrower, however, the upcoming encounter with the unknown typically evokes not awe but that corollary of the demonized supernatural, dread. Into the burrow—whose "stillness" the narrator constantly extols—intrudes the "almost inaudible whistling noise" that dominates the last third of the story. The burrower believes this sound to be the call of a predator, but it has an eerie quality as well, presaging an impending reckoning far beyond the ordinary. No living creature naturally produces the steady whistling noise that the Greeks called *trismos*, but folklore and Western antiquity say that it is a sound reserved exclusively for dead souls. (Chapter 5 will examine the American horror writer H. P. Lovecraft's elaboration of the same motif.) Merging with the echo in Forster's Marabar Caves, the dreadful expectation this combined noise arouses amounts to our secular, unmediated, *gut* perception of "that which cannot be named."

To the grottoes of Forster and Kakfa can be added an anomalous work by Graham Greene. In Greene's remarkable long story "Under the Garden" (1963), Wilditch, a middle-aged man dying of cancer, is moved to visit the estate where he spent his summers as a boy. Here, in a complexly layered remembering, the man recalls having had, as a seven-year-old, an extraordinary adventure deep in a tunnel under the roots of an ancient oak in the improbable company of a two-hundred-year-old man on a toilet seat and his female consort. In classic grotto fashion, this underworld that the old pair inhabit is a halfway point between the upper world and a grander, more mysterious region below. The two grotto denizens show the boy a heap of jewelry and golden objects stuffed away in a cardboard box and tell him in gnomic terms about the two worlds, above and below. Finally the boy announces to the old man that he is returning to the upper world to search for the old man's daughter, known only by her hilariously suggestive honorific title "Ramsdale Beauty Queen." This is an entity we have no trouble recognizing as Venus-Aphrodite, the powerful erotic principle that has smitten the boy on the spot and will rule him all his life.

The old man grants young Wilditch a golden chamber pot as a souvenir ("You've got to have something when you start a search to give you substance"), but the old woman tries to stop him—a hint of an embodied mother complex here—and the boy drops the chamber pot as he makes his escape. This archetypal blunder makes the boy (his name "Wilditch" redolent of the medieval *Homo ferus*, the "wodwose" or wild man of the woods) unable to translate the spiritual gift the old man has given him into its equivalent in the conscious, material world of the senses above ground. As a grown man he never quite locates the Ramsgate Beauty Queen or much of anything else in his journey through life—and what he now finds, under the oak, is merely an old tin chamber pot that "had lost all colour in the ground except . . . a few flakes of yellow paint." In a transformation much like the one the Deist Controversy notebook undergoes in Forster's story, the brightness of the numinous, from the limited perspective of the mortal life Wilditch has led outside its grace, looks like nothing more than faded bits of paint on a chamber pot.

All manner of stories within stories, versions of stories, unfold in "Under the Garden," and the work itself, one strongly suspects, is Greene's own "cover story"—as Wilditch likens the bowdlerized version of "pirate treasure" he concocted for the school magazine to stories told by Resistance fighters to the Nazis to protect the real story. "Under the Garden," in fact, is a *samizdat* document unique in Greene's oeuvre, an elaborately coded religious allegory, *Pilgrim's Progress* artfully disguised as an enigmatic little modernist fable. Defying and satirizing literal allegory—a form vital to the Platonic worldview, as I will show in Chapter 8—yet deeply invested in its values, the story is carefully constructed to protect its author, a sophisticated soul only too aware of the mockery he would suffer were the code broken and the story read correctly. Greene knew very well that it was acceptable to write, in realist terms, about priests losing their faith and assorted other secular moral issues, but not to explicitly present the supernatural as "real." Instead he carefully framed these nesting stories as recounted by a character whose memory or reliability is subject to question. Those of a mind to read the message of the golden chamber pot would do so, while those blind to this level would have plenty of satisfying false trails to follow: Freudian issues of "toilet training," the Oedipus conflict, life's limited outcomes compared with the dreams of childhood, and so forth.

Works such as these have coexisted within a cultural and critical perspective that has mostly ignored or dismissed their transcendental dimension. Paul O'Prey interprets the fumbled gift of the chamber pot as follows: "On the one hand, as part of the religious theme it can be taken as a parody of the Holy Grail. On the other hand it represents the transformation of experience into art in the hands of the novelist. However, the novelist is not an alchemist and cannot change base metal into gold, as [Wilditch] had tried to do. He has a responsibility to the truth of experience and should not pretend that a painted tin chamber-pot is a fabulous 'golden po.'" Similarly, Michael Sheldon dismisses the story itself as "a childhood dream which had scrambled and exaggerated various bits and pieces of reality," and locates the true meaning of Greene's "encoded message" in the gardener's potting shed on the original family estate, where the writer had tried to hang himself as a boy. The possibility of a religious message communicated in a supernatural rather than moral manner embarrasses both writers almost as much as it did the narrator's mother, who feared the boy's first version of his adventures betrayed a religious inclination.

"Under the Garden" and "The Burrow" have been sensitively interpreted by Wendy Lesser, whose *episteme* observation that the two levels of reality, literal and symbolic, are curiously inseparable in both stories hints at more. Lesser intuitively senses precisely what most commentators fail to understand about allegory in the context of the premodern worldview it belongs to: that an element in one level of reality, however we define that level, does not *stand for* an element in another level; under the element's original terms, both manifestations are to be regarded as equally real. That precondition of this literary form, however, has enormous implications that twentieth-century secular Westerners, cut off at the neck from a good portion of their own religio-philosophical tradition, were reluctant to explore. The greatest taboo among serious intellectuals of the century just behind us, in fact, proved to be none of the "transgressions" itemized by postmodern thinkers: it was, rather, the heresy of challenging a materialist worldview.

And few did. Overall, the prototypical twentieth-century critical position on the supernatural in art—and by extension its post-1700 vehicle of choice, the grotesque—is well represented by the condescension of a commentator like Bernard McElroy, who unwittingly replicates the classic colonial anthropologist's position when he states that "the grotesque does not address the rationalist in us or the scientist in us, but the vestigial primitive in us, the child in us, the potential psychotic in us." Staying strictly inside a materialist worldview, the major contributors to a twentieth-century theory of the grotesque—Mikhail Bakhtin, Wolfgang Kayser, and Tzvetan Todorov—likewise grant it only an aesthetic, not a religio-philosophical dimension.

Whereas literary critics aestheticized the transcendental, psychologists subjectivized (and often pathologized) it. No one, for example, has written more brilliantly than Kenneth Gross about puppets and other human simulacra in the *episteme* context of the aesthetic "imaginary." It might be argued that the great Western critical voyage of discovery over the last century has been that of reinterpreting all phenomena of the universe within a secularized psychological framework. And it has been an immeasurably exciting journey, once Sigmund Freud identified this territory and then, as it were, explored and mapped it. Freud psychologized and secularized the transcendental by advancing the notion of homocentric subjectivity—that we project inner psychic content onto the world around us in structurally the same way that God was formerly supposed to have projected his reality onto us. For Freud, psychic reality is a different realm from material reality and this reality is ruled by the unconscious, an autonomous inner grotto inaccessible to consciousness except through dreams.

Besides the profound contribution of a theoretical framework within which to study inner processes, through his emphasis on sexuality as a kind of secular "first cause" Freud also performed the intellectual equivalent of restoring the old fertility cults to a measure of respectability in a mainstream culture deeply imbued with Christian asceticism. We do well to recall, however, another remark made by Borges about his metaphysicians: "They know that a system is nothing more than the subordination of all aspects of the universe to any one such aspect." The psychologizing of high intellectual culture by Freud and his successors traversed a full arc in the twentieth century. (The recent preeminence of "desire" in the vocabulary of academic discourse is a good example of the slightly overblown late stage in the history of an idea.) It is just at this point, when a movement has reached its maximum level of cultural influence, that the opposite way of looking at the world begins to reemerge, against considerable opposition. The Freudian revolution is a revolution no longer, but that does not mean it has become something to be overturned itself. We are in a better position than our ancestors to integrate the wisdom of the transcendental if we make use of the profound wisdom of the psychological, and the constantly shifting interface between these two realms is the major focus of this book.

Most other modernist and postmodernist commentators, following Freud, have focused exclusively on the psychological dimension of the "uncanny," literally that which cannot be "kenned" or known by the five senses (though by linguistic reversal both "canny" and "uncanny," in English as in German, are equally associated with magical powers). They have taken as a given Freud's famous definition of the uncanny or *unheimlich* as primarily a resurgence of primitive "discarded beliefs" (omnipotence of thought, fulfillment of secret wishes, return of the dead, and so on)—beliefs, that is, in the supernatural—that cause us to doubt the absolute standard of material reality. The uncanny in literature, Freud says, draws on a much broader range of effects because it lacks the reality testing we can supply in real life (a notion to be explored further in Chapters 3 and 7), but the larger truth is that via the "exception" of the uncanny we have given the arts the freedom we don't give ourselves to violate the assumptions of our materialist worldview.

Freud's contemporary Rudolf Otto placed the uncanny within this larger context. Religious feeling, Otto said in *The Idea of the Holy*, is "awe" when confronted by the divine, a more primitive version of which is "the 'demonic dread . . . with its queer perversion, a sort of abortive off-shoot, the 'dread of ghosts.' It first begins to stir in the feeling of 'something uncanny.'" Freud believed the feeling itself was real but the stimulus imaginary; Otto asserted that the feeling was a low-grade type of religious response to a transcendental or numinous reality. Whichever interpretation one opts for, aesthetically induced demonic dread of the sort Freud describes—the feeling aroused by stories of the supernatural grotesque, the dread we share with the burrower when the whistling begins—is finally all that we superstition-free rationalists possess of the numinous.

Yet the fact remains that Kafka, Forster, and Greene belong to a small minority of practitioners of high art. Today the supernatural grotesque is most readily found in popular entertainments—and in this venue, at the turn of the new century, it is undergoing a profound shift. With caveats for the complex relationship between market-manipulated media culture and mass response, in certain ways popular entertainments more than high art act as a kind of sub-Zeitgeist that is constantly engaging in a low-level discourse on intellectually forbidden subjects—philosophy's disavowed avant-garde, as it were. Because the religious impulse is profoundly unacceptable to the dominant Western intellectual culture, it has been obliged to sneak in this back door, where our guard is down. Thus our true contemporary secular pantheon of unacknowledged deities resides in mass entertainments, and it is a demonology, ranging from the "serial killers" in various embodied and disembodied forms to vampires and werewolves and a stereotypical Devil.

At the same time, however, this demonology is the only avenue open to the transcendental. "You can raise issues in the horror genre that you can't raise so easily in other types of films," a Hollywood screenwriter once ingenuously explained, adding, "Characters can talk about the existence of God in a horror movie, whereas in other films that would be incredibly pretentious." Ironically, because of the old Reformation link between Catholicism and the supernatural, the only means for defending oneself against the Devil in these narratives is always represented as a potpourri of faux rituals rendered in Latin or Greek and always erroneously attributed to the Catholic Church, to the unending aggravation of that church's worthies, who might be less upset if only they reflected on the unavoidable implication—that the Protestant mainstream unconsciously perceives its own rituals as utterly inadequate for warding off demons.

But the real reason behind our secular fascination with the demonic lies at a deeper level than the fact that the Protestant/materialist/scientific perspective routinely brands the supernatural (and hence the transcendental) as superstition. It is likewise not, as a Christian fundamentalist would have it, that those who lack religion are the Devil's playthings. A more urgent need is present here. As the brilliant maverick Otto Rank observed in his long-overlooked *Psychology and the Soul:* "We still hold to . . . a naive belief in immortality, but we do not do so consciously, like people in the animistic era: We are shamed and deny it . . . The human psychological universal that has been passed down is after all the soul, our soul-belief—the old psychology we believe in at heart but keep out of mind in modern psychology."

To give a secular explanation for our fascination with the supernatural grotesque—for just as Freud secularized the old metaphysics, it seems a fitting tribute to apply the dynamic he first identified to discover and recover what got left behind—it is because our culture's post-Reformation, post-Enlightenment prohibition on the supernatural and exclusion of a transcendent, nonmaterialist level of reality from the allowable universe has created the ontological equivalent of a perversion caused by repression. Lacking an allowable connection with the transcendent, we have substituted an obsessive, unconscious focus on the negative dimension of the denied experience. In popular Western entertainments through the end of the twentieth century, the supernatural translated mostly as terror and monsters enjoyably consumed. But as Paul Tillich profoundly remarked, "Wherever the demonic appears, there the question of its correlate, the divine, will also be raised."

The displaced religious impulse surfaces elsewhere not as the demonic but rather as an overvaluing of the object beyond its intrinsic function in our lives. Craving its holy objects, its temples, its roadside shrines and absolutions, we have let the transcendental in distorted form invade art, the sexual experience, psychotherapy, even the quasi-worship of celebrities living and dead. But as the art historian Michael Camille acutely observed, of pious medieval Christians' attempts to justify their love of Greek and Roman art as motivated solely by aesthetic appreciation: "The aesthetic anaesthetizes. It annihilates function, taking the object out of the realm of necessity into the disinterested contemplation of the subjective viewer's consciousness . . . As opposed to religious modes of apprehension that attempt to penetrate 'reality' in ritual action and symbolic codification, the aesthetic framework takes things out of their context, stabilizes them on the surface. What better way might the power of ancient pagan deities be neutralized than by viewing them through the ideology of the aesthetic, as 'art.'"

In our officially postreligious intellectual culture, we miss the idols, too, and we have similarly aestheticized them. Just as the mad scientist figure carries the negative but still highly charged projection of the holy man who would otherwise have no place in our living culture, the repressed religious is also visible in representations of puppets, robots, cyborgs, and other artificial humans in literature and film. It endures as a fascination with the spiritualizing of matter and the demiurgic infusion of soul into human simulacra—a fascination that manifested itself, in the twentieth century, both in avant-garde theater and in popular entertainments (comics, films, and cybergames). These simulacra, from killer puppets to indestructible cyborgs, came to carry the burden of our outlawed but tenacious belief in the holiness of graven images, and behind that in the immortality of the human soul, for complex reasons that will be explored in the next chapter. Later chapters will also feature the many and various *grotte*, all inhabited by horrors, of H. P. Lovecraft, granduncle of American late twentieth-century sub-Zeitgeist popular horror culture. We will see Forster's watery underworld again in such works as Lovecraft's "Shadow over Innsmouth" and in Stanislaw Lem's *Solaris*, about an oceanic world that is able to read the minds of its human visitors and send back simulacra of their deepest desires.

The grotto locus of violence and the supernatural was translated in early American and Japanese genre movies into the place the monster comes from: the underwater grottoes of the creature from the Black Lagoon and the H-bombed Pacific atoll that spawned Godzilla. During the twentieth century, as we will see, the otherworld increasingly relocated itself from below to above, from underground and underwater to outer space and virtual reality. At a subliminal level untouched by our conscious stance of estrangement from the supernatural, the empirical reality of space travel powerfully reinforced the demonic underworld of the dead (read: malignant aliens) in our imaginations, just as the empirical reality of electronic communication dramatically reified the more benign overworld of the Neoplatonic theurgists. Within the euphemistic construct of "science" fiction, the machine (as "spaceship," "time machine," "transcender," and most recently computer) is the enabling conceit that gives us as rationalists permission to journey to the transcendental otherworld as a fantasy experience without having to acknowledge a direct contradiction to our worldview.

If the postmodern indeed turns out to be the premodern, as Lawrence Weschler provocatively implies in *Mr. Wilson's Cabinet of Wonders*, we now stand at the threshold of a paradigm shift whose scope is equivalent to that of the seventeenth century. But this shift finds us standing at the threshold with Leonardo, not Francis Bacon, since the upheavals in philosophy and aesthetics currently under way in the West—those overthrowing modernism and postmodernism alike—draw heavily from the premodern image of a living cosmos. Over a span of three hundred years, we have maintained our connection to officially vanquished notions, principally via the arts, in unconscious ways. But now this worldview is being explicitly revived in the new technologies of cybernetics, with the paradoxical result that the widespread use of Platonic metaphors such as "virtual reality" to describe computer-generated images as if they "lived" in a tangible place has carried us deeply (backward or forward, according to one's bias) into the Western mystical tradition. This presentation of metaphor as scientific reality—a practice that the philosopher John Searle, casting himself in the role of Samuel Johnson to cybertheory's myriad Bishop Berkeleys, has devoted considerable time and energy to exposing and refuting—represents not so much a "willing suspension of disbelief" (in Coleridge's words) as an eager if unconscious reversion to beliefs embedded in our culture that we have never completely surrendered.

Giordano Bruno believed that meditating on phantasma activated by images or symbols (mentally induced events that were more real to people of his age than "fantasies" are to us) produced an imprinting via an "inner light joined to a most profound contemplation" and opened the door for spirits to gain access to the human soul. In a manner similar to Bruno's image-based meditation, the art historian Horst Bredekamp argues that today "highly technical societies are experiencing a phase of Copernican change from the dominance of language to the hegemony of images." In our unconscious conflation of art with the religio-philosophical, it might be said that because too much of our religious nature has become invested in aesthetics, we experience some kinds of art in a crude approximation of Neoplatonic contemplation, a theurgic "drawing down" of spirit that allows us to engage in a form of religious discourse without ever being aware of doing so.

Orco's mouth at Bomarzo, then, is Bakhtin's grotesque gaping mouth, the gateway to the underworld "through which enters the world to be swallowed up." The grotesque is a mode that is first and foremost about crossing into a different and transformative order of reality, and second about the unexpected recombinations of events, objects, species we encounter once we are inside. And for centuries it has been a secular society's only path back to the transcendent. We crawl into the hole—the grotto, the Symmes Hole, the black hole of the cosmos, the hole in our own heads—in the unspoken and often unconscious hope of undergoing deep change. The words used in the English language to describe this alteration—*metamorphosis* from the Greek, *transformation* from the Latin—describe this same experience.

It was Bruno who asserted that metamorphosis into an animal during meditation was the only way to *transcend*, to know God and reach the true level of spiritual enlightenment. To enter the grotto of this sophisticated Renaissance thinker's perspective requires us to give up the unreconstructed Darwinism that most Westerners unthinkingly subscribe to, the perspective that sees this act (which we also regard as completely make-believe or, at best, "psychological") as a metaphorical descent to a lower, more primitive level of being. We must instead try on the surprising premise that such a transformation is not metaphorical but real, a doorway not to the "primitive" but to a higher and more integrated mode of being.

For now, we still enter the realm of *nous* or *gnosis*, of transcendental self-knowledge, in one way only: by going down, not up, and mostly into popular modes of horror and science fiction. The contemporary realm of popular entertainment is our main subterranean entry, the grotto entry, to the boarded-up mansion of sacred awe, where we conduct our primitive discourse on religious subjects—a discourse whose crudeness would horrify our pious ancestors, but nonetheless a discourse—behind our own backs. It is our inheritance (via the German Romantics, who got it from the Renaissance natural philosophers, who found it by foraging in newly discovered classical texts as well as Roman ruins) from the Mediterranean world of Hellenism and Late Antiquity that laid down the parameters and tensions of Western culture as we still know it today.

To go higher, you must first go lower. But *caveat lector:* those in the know view the process as irreversible. What comes out of the hole, the hole of this book that you must crawl into, will not be the same as what went in.

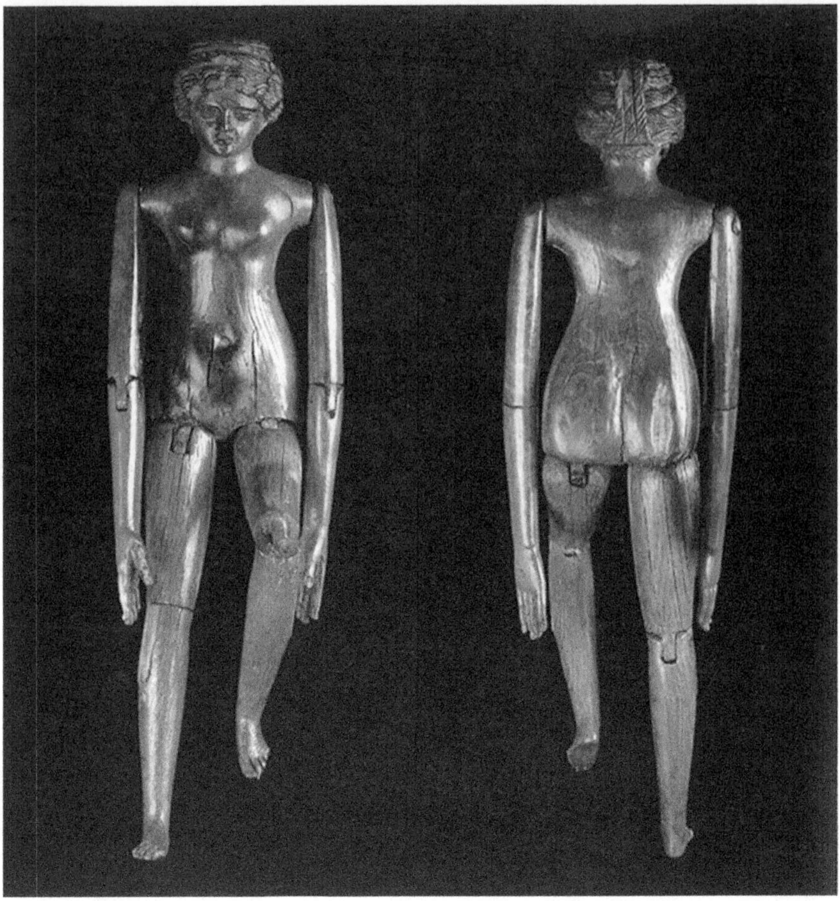

Jointed Roman doll, ca. second century C.E. **Rome, Antiquarium Comunale.**

To speak of a puppet with most men and women is to cause them to giggle. They think at once of the wires; they think of the stiff hands and the jerky movements; they tell me it is "a funny little doll." But . . . these puppets . . . are the descendants of a great and noble family of Images, images which were indeed made "in the likeness of god."

—E. Gordon Craig

TWO

EARLY ADVENTURES OF THE EARTHLY GODS

One March afternoon in the last year of the twentieth century I stood before a glass exhibit case in the "Ice Age" section of the American Natural History Museum on West 86th Street in New York City. The object of my attention was an articulated male figure carved from a tiny collection of mammoth bones. Looking very closely, I could see even tinier holes at all the proper joints, clearly meant for threading bits of twine through to tie them together. Voilà, a Cro-Magnon puppet! And more than fitting, given the Eastern and Central European passion for puppetry and the fantastic, the little man's venue was Brno, in the present Czech Republic: twenty centuries in advance, an ancestor of the great puppetmaster Jan Svankmajer had been laying down the tradition. I was forgetting, however, that the Upper Pleistocene was a time when art served religion, not entertainment. The puppet was a god, or at the least a sacred talisman.

A god. Most Westerners today, looking at a stone Krishna laden with plumeria leis or even, within our own cultural tradition, a wooden Christ bleeding wooden blood and nailed on a wooden cross, find it virtually impossible to experience these human-made images as possessing both life and supernatural powers—as *holy*, a lost field of perception for us. To see them so violates one of the deepest taboos of our empirical-materialist belief system, namely, accepting a vision of the universe that includes both a level of nonmaterial reality and a direct connection to this other level through that which seems most profoundly to negate it: the "dead" inanimate matter of which sacred objects are made. In spite of our worldview's relatively brief tenure of three hundred or so years, we feel an enormous emotional and intellectual resistance toward even imagining, let alone entering authentically into a state of mind that freely grants, such possibilities.

Rather than bolstering our sense of superiority at having so quickly and successfully vanquished a fallacious and outmoded worldview, however, our inability to perform this leap of imagination might suggest to us instead a certain parochialism or limitation inherent in our own viewpoint. When the first department store in Port Moresby, the capital of Papua New Guinea, opened with dress mannequins on public display in the 1970s, citizens rioted because they believed the souls of someone's ancestors were being desecrated. Instead of labeling this reaction as ridiculous superstition ("The heathen in his blindness / Bows down to wood and stone," in the words of Bishop Reginald Heber's famous hymn) or extending rote tolerance toward "indigenous spirituality," is there a way we might actually try to inhabit this venerable viewpoint, to experience what it feels like from the inside? Could we exercise our imaginations in a way that would allow us to feel as such believers did—that we were in the presence of our own souls or those of our closest family members, made external from us and in those objects joined to the transcendental?

But why should we even consider making such a leap? Why, given that from our perspective this is superstition based on a scientifically false assumption about the natural world (and on unprovable assertions about any other world), should we care at all about reinhabiting the old standpoint, which in its most essential nature is still the standpoint of millions upon millions of the world's religious orthodox today? If for no other reason, I would argue, than that the depth of resistance—even anxiety and outrage—we experience at such a request should signal to us that it is an avenue worth investigating. More important, because by doing so we might risk broadening the boundaries of our consciousness, at the very least (speaking in the language of our own viewpoint) bringing into awareness an element of our total mental field that is mostly invisible to us but very much in operation below the surface.

THE TWO WAYS OF KNOWING

Using Foucault's terms as markers, Garth Fowden has pointed out that in Late Antiquity philosophy as *episteme*, the state of knowing, and religion as *gnosis*, the process of knowing, were combined in a system of thinking and perceiving that was both more unified and more variegated than the one we as heirs of the Enlightenment enjoy today. At the end of the eighteenth century, the French aphorist Joseph Joubert still stood close enough to the banished "world known by the ancients" and preserved through the Renaissance to provide a sympathetic and unprejudiced assessment of this lost perspective, whose worthiness he succinctly identified in the passage that serves as this book's opening epigraph. Indeed, "they knew better than we do" how to maintain a balance between the two ways of knowing. "To distinguish between rational and irrational, between the world of the prosaic and that of the gods," the Egyptologist J. D. Ray reminds us, "is not the ancient manner."

Of "the ancients' conviction that human and divine knowledge, reason and intuition, are interdependent" Fowden says: "[It is] a view which continued to prevail in Islam, particularly in Shiite and Sufi circles, but which the Western intellectual tradition has often rejected, decomposing knowledge into independent categories, separating philosophy from theology, and in so doing setting up serious obstacles to the understanding of more unified world-views." Paraphrasing a Hermetic text of the second century—"God offered the souls of men the chance to be baptized in a huge bowl so that those who deserved it might receive the gift of *nous* as well as *logos*"—Fowden suggests that embracing both modes at the same time provides a more comprehensive viewpoint than holding to the strictly rational and quantifiable.

Trying on this perspective even provisionally does not mean abandoning a rational-empirical position; acknowledging the unfavored mode, bathing in the bowl containing that which cannot be perceived by the senses as well as that which can, means rather partaking of both modes without confusing their separate functions and lapsing into the errors of "superstition" on one hand or "heresy" on the other. This is not a backward regression but simply the logical next step in the spiral that we call, in our homocentric way of looking at things, the evolution of consciousness. Over the span of Western culture, as one commentator observes, "the argument has been made that consciousness is the ultimate instance of deciding between right and wrong, true and false, and just and unjust, irrespective of whether it is placed in the faith of God or in the Cartesian *Cogito*, in reason or in the transparency of the individual's self-examination."

Far from being mutually exclusive, *nous* and *logos* share this common denominator of human consciousness, a field that has remained constant while its content and focus have swung like a pendulum between the two modes. For the *gnosis*-oriented authors of the Corpus Hermeticum tractates, consciousness was not only humanity's distinguishing characteristic but the special feature that connected us with the divine. This position was counterbalanced by the materialist views of their contemporaries the Stoics and Skeptics; indeed, many Greeks and Romans of the time openly mocked graven images. And, as Susanna Elm argues, far from being a "decline into belief" as is usually supposed, the radical iconoclasm of Judeo-Christianity, learnedly argued first by the rabbis and then by the early Christian fathers, represented a scientific revolution of rational discourse that supplanted the *gnosis*-dominated cults and religions of Late Antiquity analogous to the iconoclasm of the Protestant Reformation, which performed a similar function in relation to the Catholic Church a millennium later.

In the bitter competition that the two perspectives—those labeled, with varying degrees of accuracy, *gnosis* and *episteme*, *nous* and *logos*, Platonism and Aristotelianism, idealism and materialism, premodern and modern—have always waged to rule our hearts and minds, it can be misleading to equate *episteme* solely with materialism. Much of ancient and medieval medicine and astronomy, for example, was based on closely observed natural phenomena whose rules were logically interpreted within the intellectual construct of a hierarchical cosmos. Nor can the Neoplatonic side be equated solely with irrationalism, as witness the internal rationality of the system of the hierarchical cosmos as emphasized by *episteme* scholars like Arthur Lovejoy.

Platonic *gnosis* would enjoy some twelve hundred years of hegemony after the end of the ancient world, even as pockets of Aristotelian *episteme* flourished in the intellectual realm of Christian philosophers. The Renaissance offered, like Late Antiquity, a rare moment of dueling equals, but on the heels of its attendant separation of reason and imagination (initiated by thinkers like Francis Bacon), *episteme* won out. The subsequent rise of empirical science and the pigeonholing of intellectual disciplines during the nineteenth and twentieth centuries would displace *gnosis* from its role as the prism of truth through which to view the entire cosmos into merely one of many fictive prisms of the imagination within the realm of art. At the present time, *gnosis* stands at a diminished level in mainstream Western intellectual culture while the *episteme* of scientific materialism is at a peak—the exact reverse of the case in the Middle Ages. In short, Westerners of the Old and New Worlds alike live within an Aristotelian Zeitgeist that still possesses a soft underbelly, a sub-Zeitgeist of half-acknowledged Platonic assumptions.

At the heart of the tensions between the two ways of knowing are their profoundly different perceptions of human life as either divided between the two territories of matter and spirit or consisting solely of the former. As discussed in Chapter 1, contemporary Western consciousness, ruled by a strictly materialist *episteme*, allows for only a mental or "subjective" inner world and a physical or "objective" outer world. The hegemony of materialism, however, has had an unfortunate side effect: the loss of that integrated field of perception described by Fowden. What is universally viewed as a triumph over superstition is in fact a more complicated effect. Some powerful fields of consciousness are opened up, but others are put off limits.

Coleridge once said that people are either Platonists or Aristotelians, but in eras when one mode predominates we are not always consciously aware of our true affiliation. A red flag that we are too deeply identified with one mode at the expense of the other is the assumption that the favored mode is both all encompassing and permanently "true." On the contrary, history suggests that such idols of current Western consciousness as the scientific method are no more likely to remain unchallenged or unmodified than their premodern equivalents. In eras of *episteme* such as ours, the general understanding of *gnosis* becomes naive because it is conducted according to the principles of the dominant mode. A scientist's remark, "The story of Jesus' ascension to heaven is ridiculous in the space age," is a classic example of this naivete. In the same way, the understanding of science becomes naive in eras of dominant *gnosis*. Current *gnosis*-inspired conflations of the two modes, such as "creationism" as a scientific description of the material world, muddy the waters even more.

For now, having exiled spirit not just from matter but from our entire worldview, we backers of *episteme* no longer see the many strands of influence that still stretch back to the early history of our culture. One seemingly small thing we have forgotten is that the human simulacrum in particular—whether stationary or moving, two or three dimensional, in its contemporary form of children's dolls and puppets or robots, cyborgs, and the like in popular film and literature—is an object we once worshipped.

From the conventional intellectual perspective of our time we see the puppet, until this century our most familiar human-made artificial human, as a metaphor of the body alienated from and mastered by its operating mind, and the robot as a metaphor of the dominance of the machine over the human, without recognizing the highly conventional flavor of these positions. For the devout of the Mediterranean basin, ca. 300 C.E.—and, in a far less acknowledged way, still for us as their cultural descendants—these human simulacra with articulated limbs (in the form of moving, talking statues of gods, philosophers, or deified rulers) represented exactly the reverse. They were the point of literal congruence between transcendental spirit and physical matter, and thus a great and holy mystery. From this perspective, graven images that humans contrived in their own likeness stood in much closer relation to the gods than their makers did.

This was, surprisingly, a conclusion the German playwright Heinrich von Kleist would also reach some fifteen hundred years later in his 1812 essay "On the Marionette Theater." In this seminal work Kleist has his narrator make the astonishing assertion that no human dancer can equal a puppet in naturalness of movement: "Grace [*Grazia*] appears purest in that human form which has no consciousness or an infinite one, that is, in a puppet or a god." Kleist's very German Romantic fascination with puppets briefly brought back into the Western cultural mainstream the once dominant, now very much marginalized religio-philosophical tradition in Western culture: that no Cartesian boundary between mind and matter exists, and moreover that "dead" inorganic matter and we as sentient, self-conscious beings share a mysterious and direct connection with a second reality that lies beyond the material realm. This belief also stubbornly endures, underground and mostly unconscious, in our secular sub-Zeitgeist of the imagination that lies outside the official territories of both religion and philosophical inquiry.

This, then, will be a discourse on puppets and idols that explores the metamorphosis, over a span of two millennia, of two profoundly religious activities of the early history of Western culture: spiritualizing the material by embalming human bodies, and materializing the spiritual by making human simulacra as physical embodiments of the divine. As these two practices of "ensouling" matter move from religion (the realm of belief) to art (the realm of make-believe or imagination), we will see on one hand the Late Antique mummy transformed in secular works of the imagination from a divine body within an organized religious belief system into a kind of organic demon (homunculus, golem, Frankenstein's monster, genetic clone), and on the other hand the moving, talking Late Antique god statue translated into the automated Neoplatonic daemons of puppet, robot, cyborg, and virtual entity. These invented creatures of our imagination still carry for us, below the level of consciousness, that uncanny aura the unacknowledged "holy" characteristically assumes in a secular context. In the history of puppets and other human simulacra after the decline of religion we can read—in a backward image, like a reflection in a mirror—the underground history of the soul excluded from its religious context in Western culture.

MAKING GOD BODIES

Let us return to that time in our culture's history when the grotto was neither a garden ornament nor a chamber of horrors but a place of worship. This is the world of approximately the first four centuries after Christ, the end of the Hellenistic era shading into Late Antiquity, the last culture of the ancient Mediterranean Western world before the advent of the Christian Middle Ages.

With Alexandria as its hub, the culture of Hellenism incorporated a rich blend of Egyptian, Persian, and other Asia Minor influences within a predominantly Greek matrix. At the close of the first century C.E., Rome conquered Greece and the Greek East, imposing a powerful new framework on the cultural mix. By the third century C.E., the Mediterranean region was home to a range of syncretic philosophical and religious movements; side by side with Judaism, Christianity, and their Gnostic offshoots were Neoplatonism, Hermeticism, Manichaeism, and myriad cults of individual gods such as Isis, Mithras, and Bacchus. Christianity gradually became the official religion of the Roman empire from the third through fifth centuries C.E.—the span of what we call Late Antiquity—then split into western and eastern realms after the fall of Rome in the fifth century. It was this polyglot world of Late Antiquity, not classical Greece or even Rome, from which all later Western culture took its shape and identity.

Through most of the diverse schools, religions, and cults of these times ran a single and (to us) curious thread: the goal of making a human into a divine being. This quest took various forms founded on a shared belief in a many-leveled living cosmos, a belief that recognized no division between organic and inorganic and little between the sensible and the invisible. As we saw in Chapter 1, this cosmographic construct of the Western ancients that endured from the second century C.E. through the sixteenth considered the greater cosmos or *macrocosm* to be a living manifestation of God, not a dead artifact. Humans lived in the smaller cosmos or *microcosm*, the physical world that reflected and was ruled by this divine cosmos—or, as rendered in the succinct shorthand of the Hellenistic science of alchemy: "As above, so below."

Humans in their own bodies were also microcosms or little worlds containing all the attributes of the greater world that ruled them. By *gnosis*, humans could internalize the cosmos and thereby become divine themselves, able to live in both realms simultaneously. Because matter was alive, it could also be spiritualized and made immortal by humans capable of manipulating the highly charged connection between specific material things and their counterparts in the spiritual world.

The key link was the soul, that immortal portion of the human mortal organism connecting each person to the transcendent world. Like the cosmos around it, the soul had two tiers: the *pneuma* or spirit that is also part of God, and the more material *psyche* or soul. (This split in meaning between *pneuma* and *psyche*, which occurred around the second century B.C.E., would influence the subsequent identification of *psyche* in Western culture with individual subjective consciousness as *pneuma* dropped from currency.) The soul originated in the celestial sphere, acquiring an astral body, an ethereal, star-shaped (circular or spherical) covering, as it passed through each of the seven spheres in its descent to inhabit an individual body on earth. Western medicine through the sixteenth century was based on the belief that this invisible astral mantel remained especially susceptible to the stars' influence. After death, the Gnostics believed, the soul rarely ascended back to the world of light on its own; help and support were required to purify it of the sediment absorbed by its astral body before it could return home.

Through all the ancient cults, the spiritualizing of matter—that mystical union of the two levels of the cosmos as it could be made to occur in the individual person, the soul's efforts before and after death to rediscover its divine essence—became the religious goal of these first centuries after Christ. This quest also extended to human-made images that were intended as concrete links to the spiritual. If all things in the material world are simulacra, copies, of the true World of Forms, then statues and people alike (and especially statues if they took the shape of humans) acted not just as passive vessels but as magnets to the energies of the higher world, drawing down the gods' powers and materially embodying them.

The dual goals of Western Late Antiquity's religions—to ensoul matter and to make the human divine—drew from many sources but particularly from Hellenized Egypt and its capital, Alexandria. As the most death-obsessed culture this planet has ever seen, the Egyptians had devised over many millennia a supremely concretist view of the soul. The heart of their intricate religious system (which, mixed with Greek and Roman cults, laid the groundwork for many of the new syncretic religions of Hellenistic and Late Antique times) was the notion of a material soul—an entity that the embalmed mummy did not represent or symbolize (in our worldview's automatic way of supposing) but simply *was*. This idea would be carried on in the Christian notion of Christ's body, a way of spiritualizing matter to which the Gnostic cults, for example, were especially opposed.

Because the Egyptians saw no separation in kind between soul and body, they believed that the physical body of a human or animal could, with human intervention, become an immortal divine body. The god Heka, who was loosely the magic principle itself, "did not fabricate the universe *ex nihilo;* rather, he *reproduced* as terrestrial 'doubles' *(ka*s*)* the acts and *logos* of the demiurge." In the religion of the Old and New Kingdoms, humans consequently had three bodies: the physical body, the double or *ka*, and the personality or *ba;* all three were united after death in the *akh*, a glorified being of light. Mummification preserved the physical body; prayers preserved the spiritual body. Via a false door carved in the inner tomb, the dead person as mummy moved freely between this world and the next while his spirit resided at the same time in funerary statues, which were regularly washed in the Nile and anointed with oil. This identity of matter and spirit is emphasized in the Book of the Dead, which flatly states that the dead person turns into the god Osiris "not in some invisible way or in the way of an analogy, but through the actual concrete operations of the mummification of the corpse."

For Homer and the archaic Greek culture on the other side of the Mediterranean, body was a plural construct just as it was for the Egyptians, but the early Greeks considered the human body to be the mere shadow of the divine model. Both realms of the cosmos, natural and supernatural, were thought to manifest materially, but not in the same way. The human body was a "sub-body," plural and ephemeral compared with the divine super-body of the *athanatoi*, the immortal gods, whose "radiance," in Jean-Pierre

Vernant's elegant words, "robs it of visibility from an excess of light in the way that darkness causes invisibility through a lack of light." Centuries later, Plato would extend this notion by contrasting the mortal world of the senses with the immortal World of Forms, making the human soul distinct from the body and a kind of intermediary between the two worlds. His student Aristotle, in contrast, defined the human soul or mind more particularly in terms of its material function; for Aristotle the "body-mind" was a single entity. (These opposing constructs, the idealist body-versus-soul and the materialist body-mind, established early on the *gnosis-episteme* divide in ancient Greek culture.)

In the *Timaeus*, Plato posited still another intermediary, a being he called the Demiurge (literally "artisan" or "public worker"), who was the craftsman-creator of the visible world. Demiurgy or world creating would be taken up as a potent concept throughout the late ancient world: it was a role Christians assigned to God as Logos, and the Gnostics and Manichaeans, sticking more closely to Plato, to a lesser deity (evil, in the Gnostics' view). The demiurge was also the figure widely used in Late Antiquity to explain how humans came to have a soul; as the Divine or Original Human, a preexisting transcendent being who stood as an intermediate between God and humans, the Anthropos was a macrocosmic human who inhabited the perfect World of Forms and spoke its Perfect Language before he was incarnated and, in the words of the third-century alchemist Zosimos, "thrown down into matter." Because the divine spark of the Anthropos is in every person, our goal as humans is to climb back up the hierarchical ladder of the cosmos and—if we are holy enough—realize the perfect world while we are still alive and in our bodies.

This Divine Human and soul-carrier was called Adam Kadmon by Jews; Jesus Christ, the Second Adam, by Christians; the Anthropos or Vir Unus ("One Man") by Hermeticists; and a "great light-man" by Gnostics and Manichees. All these religions had a story about how the Divine Human, God's intermediary and demiurge, came to create mortal humans on earth. The following is a summary of the Corpus Hermeticum version, told to the narrator by an "enormous being completely unbounded in size" named Poimandres ("Mind of Everywhere"):

> Mind, the father of all, who is life and light, gave birth to a man like himself whom he loved as his own child. The man was most fair: he had the father's image; and god, who was really in love with his own

form, bestowed on him all his craftworks . . . Having all authority over the cosmos of mortals and unreasoning animals, the man broke through the vault and stooped to look through the cosmic framework, thus displaying to lower nature the fair form of god. Nature smiled for love when she saw him whose fairness brings no surfeit . . . for in the water she saw the shape of the main's fairest form and upon the earth its shadow. When the man saw in the water the form like himself as it was in nature, he loved it and wished to inhabit it . . . Nature took hold of her beloved, hugged him all about and embraced him, for they were lovers. Because of this, unlike any other living thing on earth, mankind is twofold—in the body mortal but immortal in the essential man.

We humans are simulacra of this Primal Human, just as our world of the senses is a simulacrum of the World of Forms. Through self-knowledge or *gnosis* we can once again attain the light and the eternal life possessed by the Anthropos, this "essential man."

But is the great mystery of instilling life and motion an ability reserved for the gods, Hellenistic priests and philosophers wanted to know, or can humans replicate the process? The part of us that belongs to the Anthropos or Divine Human is precisely our soul, the part that gives us godlike powers. Exercising these powers was a logical extension and yet a further Hellenistic refinement on Plato's entity, and it was expressed in the widespread obsession with the religio-magical ritual practice of *theurgy* (literally, "god making"), the drawing down of the divine into the material world and the simultaneous raising up of the human soul during life to the transcendental level. The theurgist was a priest who could tap into divine powers to purify himself. In this dual procedure—the *imitatio dei* by *generatio animae*, in Moshe Idel's paraphrase, the "attempt of man to know God by the art He uses in order to create men"—Hellenistic adepts confidently and nonblasphemously manipulated matter with the goal of giving it both life and a soul.

The belief that humans could manipulate the universal life force in this way was evident in the second-century Greek Magical Papyri, which contained many sympathetic spells for giving life to physical objects, both formerly animate (mummified birds, human skulls) and manufactured (rings, statuettes). Within the construct of a layered animate universe—in which even objects like magnetic stones "breathed," and thus naturally possessed life—reciting an incantation was a "sympathetic" tool whereby the theurgists from their inferior position in the microcosm could harness and control the powers of the macrocosm. And from the Egyptians seems to have come the first record of the next logical step—graven images that moved and spoke. (The pharaonic word for sculptor was *s'ankh*, "he who makes life.") "The most accurate description of a Near Eastern temple," said Ioan Couliano, "is a playhouse with gods." These gods, moreover, "were mere statues only to the untrained observer; not so for the hordes of shaven-headed priests who attended them, fed them, bathed them, and took them out for strolls." Animated by magic spells, the figurines came alive to do their duties and tend to the aristocrat's mummy, their movements visible to initiates but not to outsiders.

Animated idols were both numerous and notable in the Hellenistic world, as John Cohen has vividly described: "At Antiu, the birthplace of Hierapolis in Great Phrygia, there are statues that walk from place to place; and melodious voices from virgins of stone fill the temple at Delphi . . . The statue of Memnon, when struck by the rays of the rising sun, emitted sounds like those given by the string of a lyre." During Mithraic rites, Aion, the lion-headed gatekeeper of heaven, belched flames from his jaws. Statues were filled with sympathetic herbs and plants, then brought to life, at which time they often lit up first, then laughed or smiled, or (most important) began prophesying. Live birds were sacrificed to a statuette of Eros so that it took on their breath; "once activated, [the statuette flew] off on its various missions" as its activator's *paredros* or supernatural assistant. Statues of gods often appeared in dreams to offer advice. According to Artemidorus, the great second-century dream commentator, to dream of a statue was to dream of a god, and even the very act of dreaming about it served to bring the statue to life.

The making of mummies remained the ultimate expression of the notion that humans could imitate the gods' powers of creation. The embalmers themselves, through the magical powers they channeled from the gods, were credited with transforming the mortal organic body into an immortal being. Long after the decline of the old religion, mummification flourished in Hellenized Egypt among Greek and Roman settlers, who had their portraits painted and fastened to their mummified bodies in an echo of the old hope of flesh made immortal.

The ancient Egyptians had further believed not just the bodies of living organisms and statues but chemical substances themselves were inherently divine; even metals embodied the gods. In the divinity of chemicals as in the Egyptian notion of creating an "eternal indestructible resurrection body for the dead," we see the origins of the Hellenistic science of alchemy, in which radical divinizing changes could be made to happen in the soul of the alchemist simultaneously with his or her objects of experimentation. "Matter now contains the secret of the incarnated divine man," Zosimos maintained. "Only if the alchemist has through meditation established a relationship to his inner self, that is, to the Anthropos in matter, can he produce the right kind of transformations."

A classic union of *gnosis* and *episteme*, alchemy was both an experimental science and a religious practice. The first stage in the alchemical process, the *nigredo* or blackening of the metal, reproduced the original chaos of the universe, Aristotle's *prima materia.* Then, by successive operations that drew on the sympathetic links between high and low, the demiurgic alchemist could speed up the divine act of creation and push the piece of matter "up the hierarchical ladder," thereby changing its color—regarded as a primary, not secondary property of matter—until the rainbow display known to later alchemists as the *caudo pauvonis* or peacock's tail signaled the first color transformation, from black to white, that would ultimately result in the divine metal, gold. At the same time an analogous divinizing process was taking place within the alchemist's own psyche. This dual resurrection of the body (of the metal and of the human operator) culminated in a material-spiritual event variously concretized as a stone statue or "Philosopher's Stone" or a child/homunculus ("little man," as also *mannikin*). In the kind of paradox for which alchemy was famous, the statue or homunculus, the "living" stone, represented the end, not the beginning, of the process.

Already present here is the paradox that Kleist was to puzzle over in his famous essay: what seems on the surface like a hollow shell, the antithesis of life and a parody of its expressive nature, in some ineffable way embodies its deepest essence. Embodying the adepts' spiritual transformation, this statue functioned as their externalized soul (or, in the language of the old religion, as their *ka*)—the union of soul and body in the figure of the proto-Adam or Anthropos, the Divine Human.

In later centuries alchemy retained this dual function as "a way to explore interiority, the subject's own psyche," in the *episteme* analysis of Kenneth Gross, who has also noted the same inner-outer congruence in the puppeteer's relation to his puppets, "the paradox whereby manipulators, defrauding objects of their right not to be alive, are themselves transformed by the life they invent." For Westerners from ancient times through the Renaissance, moreover, a statue or other human-made image was not regarded as an entity divorced from nature by human artifice, but rather as a natural object on a par with a seashell or seed. The sacred dolls found in Roman burials of young girls were, says Maurizio Bettini, an "economic way to describe the way divine energy energizes matter . . . an image ready to become a person, closer to the realm of being than the realm of signs." The wooden doll pictured at the opening of this chapter, found in the tomb of a young Roman noblewoman of the second century, was supposed to be dedicated to the goddess Venus on the eve of her wedding. Whether idols themselves or human likenesses, these statues and figurines, like embalmed bodies, seem closer to the divine body than does a living human body because their static, unchanging nature imitates the permanence of the immortal.

Animated statues played a special role in Neoplatonism, the ruling school of Late Antiquity—a reworking of Platonic philosophy that, though pagan, deeply influenced the early Christian fathers in its more theoretical forms and thereby exerted a strong influence on medieval and Renaissance Christian philosophers. Its first synthesizer, the third-century Egyptian-born philosopher Plotinus, argued against the extreme world-reviling dualism of the Gnostics and for the inherent unity of the physical and invisible worlds. Objects in the natural world, he believed, could be receptacles for the World Soul, as Jeremy Naydler paraphrases:

> Not only could a physical image (whether two- or three-dimensional) provide the "body" for an already existent spiritual entity, but images could also become the physical base for "thought forms" that were called into existence through their being represented on the physical plane. In this case the images carved on funerary stelae, painted on tomb walls or in papyrus texts, had the effect of activating in a higher dimension their spiritual counterparts . . . The image, by invoking the essence of the substance imaged, was itself magically transformed from being mere image to being an image infused with the spiritual substance it portrayed. At the same time, it became absorbed into this spiritual substance on a spiritual level, and thereby gave access to it.

For the later fourth-century Neoplatonists of Alexandria such as Porphyry and Iamblichus, god statues were a particularly powerful connection to the spiritual world because "every ritual action done on the physical level, every form created, every word spoken or written, acted as the magnet to which its spiritual counterpart was irresistibly pulled." The Emperor Julian was initiated into the "mysteries of theurgy" in an underground chamber cum grotto in Ephesus, where Maximus, a disciple of the later Neoplatonists, brought to life a statue of the goddess Hecate. Porphyry mentions images made to receive aerial daemons through the magical use of smoke; one theurgist even conjured the soul of Plato as a "luminous disk."

In such sacred texts as the *Chaldean Oracles*, a second-century collection of magical spells prized by the Neoplatonists, the highest purpose of theurgy was not to draw the god down but to "help the human soul escape its bodily prison and rise up to divinity." In this "theurgical elevation" the soul of the theurgist was thought to separate physically from the body; the ascent to heaven during life was thus regarded as a spiritual discipline requiring more than simple acts of conjuring.

Out of the rich cross-fertilization of Hellenistic religious sects and philosophical schools emerged an interconnected cluster of Alexandrian spiritual practices that was closely associated with Neoplatonism. The philosophical tenets of this school, known as Hermeticism or Hermetism, survive in a series of loosely connected master-student dialogues from the second century known as the Corpus Hermeticum, though scattered other dialogues have been found, for example, among the Nag Hammadi Gnostic texts. A blend of Egyptian and Greek myths, these tractates set forth opportunities to "realize" the soul for those following the path of Hermes Trismegistus ("Three Times Blessed")—the name of an Egyptian king attached to a seer cum god who was a conflation of Mercury/Hermes, the Greco-Roman god of healing and knowledge, and Thoth, the Egyptian god of knowledge and guide to the underworld.

The Hermetic framing of the soul-body relationship differed from the severe dualism of both orthodox Neoplatonists and the Christian fathers whose framework is the dominant intellectual legacy of Western culture—a dualism that Descartes would transfer structurally intact from the celestial to the material in the seventeenth century. Though elements of dualism are present in the often contradictory dialogues of Hermes, following Egyptian tradition they offered cosmic union as a resolution to the polarities of life-death, body-soul, earthly-divine—and Christian mystics would implicitly adopt this model in the notion of the *unio mystica* of the human soul with God. Hermeticism thus offered a more hopeful view of this life than the "radical" dualism of Gnostic and Manichaean belief, in which only death and separation from the prison of the body and the evils of the material world could bring the soul into itself.

In the Hermetic model, God made "soul-stuff," a kind of plankton soup or "scum," out of which, in a quasi-alchemical operation, the human soul emerged as "subtle, pure and transparent matter." For the followers of Hermes, ascension to divine status via this soul composed of rarefied matter was a real possibility—after much conscious interior effort—in the midst of earthly life. It was precisely the material quality of the soul that allowed this to happen. As the prayer in *Asclepius*, a Latin translation of a Hermetic text, has it: "We rejoice that you have deigned to make us gods for eternity even while we depend on the body."

Like the Neoplatonists, the Hermetic initiates would have regarded the human simulacrum as not just a passive vessel but a *magnet* for attracting these powers, and so they practiced theurgy just as the Neoplatonists did. In a famous passage of *Asclepius*, the deity Hermes Trismegistus—and because of his divinity he would almost certainly have been visualized by listeners or readers of this tractate as a statue—instructs his grandson Asclepius in the differences between heavenly gods, made by God himself, and earthly gods (that is, idols), made by humans: "Our ancestors . . . discovered the art of making gods. To their discovery they added a comfortable power arising from the nature of matter. Because they could not make souls, they mixed this power in and called up the souls of demons or angels and implanted them in likenesses through holy and divine mysteries, whence the idols could have the power to do good or evil." Because they are human-made, Hermes says, the "earthly and material gods" are inferior to the heavenly gods and show human emotions such as anger. Nonetheless, the powers of these "statues ensouled and conscious, filled with spirit and doing great deeds" were formidable indeed: they "foreknow the future and predict it by lots, by prophecy, by dreams and by many other means; [they] . . . make people ill and cure them."

Yes, but—our skeptical voice of *episteme* must finally interject—just how was this wonder of living statues manifested in the material world of cause and effect? Confirming our worst suspicions, exhibit A is a first-century

C.E. bust of Epicurus with a hollowed-out center culminating in a discreet hole in the great philosopher's mouth, which the scholar Frederik Poulsen concludes was made for a tube through which a priest, crouched behind a wall, could speak, allowing the head to act "as a veritable oracle, with a voice which would sound to an emotional mind both mysterious and weird." From the standpoint of *episteme*, the fact that these all too human-made mechanical devices (a number of which survive) undeniably provided the *generatio animae* at once cancels out the validity of the supernatural experience; indeed, Poulsen subtitled his report "A Chapter in the History of Religious Fraud."

To its practitioners, however, ventriloquism of the kind demanded by the bust of Epicurus would not have been a ruse at all, but rather a tool by which the priest possessed by the god could give utterance to the god's words through the statue. That their belief in the experience of divine possession, even as they manipulated the statues, was genuine and not the cynical fakery assumed by modern researchers is demonstrated by the example of the fifth-century Alexandrine philosopher Heraiskos, whose perception (according to the commentator Damascius) was so finely tuned that he

> had a natural gift of discernment in regard to sacred images, whether they were alive or not. The moment he looked at one, if it was alive, he felt a stab of peculiar feeling go through his heart: his soul and body were both agitated, as if he were divinely possessed. If, on the other hand, he felt no such emotion, the image was a lifeless one, destitute of any divine spirit. It was in this way that he knew, by what may be truly called a mystical union with the deity, that the awful image of Aion was inhabited by the god whom the Alexandrines worshipped, and who is Osiris and Adonis in one.

As for animating the statues, we have the testimony of practical texts by the second-century Alexandrian inventor Hero on how to construct moving god images and other automated devices. Using ingenious machines powered by steam or sand, Hero and his mentor Ctesibios devised a host of mechanical marvels, including rotating statues, singing mechanical birds, and automated miniature puppet theaters. The intricate mechanism operating one of these little theaters, as described by J. G. Landels, is an apparatus that "moves forward on wheels [away from the proscenium] and stops in the right position; figures then revolve or move about, doors open and close, fires burn up on tiny altars, and so on. At the end it moves back out of sight."

Though Hero's theater was used for religious purposes, evidence suggests that simulacra used purely for entertainment had been around almost as long as the god statues. Few markers survive that indicate, for any culture, the exact historical moment when the techniques for constructing holy idols were transferred into nonreligious entertainments, or whether, indeed, the two always coexisted. We would expect that the ancient Greeks performed this characteristic separation at the same time that they distinguished drama from purely religious ritual. Even though very few mentions of puppets as secular theatrical devices are present in surviving Greek and Roman literature, the writings of ancient philosophers contain a sprinkling of metaphorical references to the *neurospastes* (literally, "string pullers"). In Chapter 1 we saw the image of a puppet used by Socrates in *The Republic* to explain the deceptive appearances of material reality. Plato also uses it in *The Laws* as a way of explaining how humans, as the gods' puppets ("put together either for their play or for some serious purpose—which, we don't know"), are pulled in various directions by their desires but must strive to go in the direction of that cord which represents the common good.

This emblem of the human simulacrum as an inferior entity manipulated by a superior entity would endure as the primary mainstream emblem of Plato's body-soul relationship throughout later Western culture (and it would be transposed and materialized by Descartes to body-mind in the seventeenth century). The second-century Christian theologian Tertullian pronounced that "the soul moved the body, and its exertions on the inside became visible outside in the same way that the movements of the puppet on the surface are manipulated from the inside." In his treatise *De providentia*, the fourth-century Neoplatonic philosopher and Christian convert Synesius of Cyrene (later Bishop of Ptolemais) drew a sophisticated comparison between the effects of God's unremitting influence on humans and puppets that "still jerk after the hand that controlled them has stopped working the strings."

In contrast, the once equally powerful pagan and Neoplatonic-Hermetic emblem of the human simulacrum as embodied divine force and manipulator of the world around it would be banished only to resurface illicitly inside and outside the official territory of religion. By the end of the fifth century, the god statues of Mediterranean Late Antiquity were literally toppled by Christianity, now the dominant religious bureaucracy knitting together the far-flung regions that were the former Roman empire. (The main reason pagan statues were routinely mutilated was that they were commonly perceived as being alive; this seemed to be the only sure way to kill them.) Of the earlier Judaic idol-smashing chronicled in the Hebrew scriptures, Kenneth Gross notes: "Iconoclasm depends on the fantastic insistence that those termed 'idolators' are merely fetishists, that they worship the sacred object, the graven or molten image, as itself sufficient. The biblical discourse of iconoclasm does not see the image as something animated through its participation within a larger ritual praxis and mythology, as the partial vessel of a divine reality larger than itself." In the same way, the early Christian church needed to make the idol "both dead and demonic" while still reserving some powers of enchantment for itself. Augustine in *The City of God* attacked the Egyptian influence and specifically the practice of animating god statues, which, in the words of another Christian chronicler of the time, constituted "idolatry practiced with soulless matter."

Physical desecration of cult statues, of course, did not eliminate the powerful impulse to idolatry, even among the Christian faithful. Some of this impulse would find its way into officially sanctioned religious practice via the worship of relics and saints, whose images would be carried through the streets on festival days just as the statue of Amun had been displayed in Thebes during the festival of Ipet in Egypt's Old Kingdom. But a second and underground trend, new in the history of Western consciousness, would also begin. Over a long historical period, transcendental forces once perceived as external would slowly be internalized to those areas of human perception labeled the "imagination" and the "unconscious." The "low art" of secular entertainment would come to fill the vacuum left first by the expulsion of god statues and later by the expulsion of religious experience itself from the main currents of Western intellectual culture. Ultimately art and science (as well as human consciousness itself) would replace religious worship as unacknowledged venues for the drawing down of the divine and the raising up of the human. After the year 1700, Western artists and writers would continue to express, though often in an unconscious manner, hidden and increasingly taboo notions of immortality, divinity, and the incorruptible body. In the never-erased Platonic sub-Zeitgeist cult of idolatry, the human simulacrum would carry our denied transcendental double and serve as a vehicle for displaced god and human soul alike.

Homunculus, as Mercury, developing in the alchemical glass vessel. From Altus, *Mutus liber* (1677).

Zeal-of-the-Land Busy: First I say unto thee, idol, thou hast no calling.

Puppet Dionysius: You lie, I am called Dionysius.

Leatherhead: The motion says you lie; he is called Dionysius i' the matter, and to that calling he answers.

Busy: I mean no vocation, idol, no present lawful calling.

Puppet Dionysius: Is yours a lawful calling?

Leatherhead: The motion asketh if yours be a lawful calling?

Busy: Yes, mine is of the spirit.

Puppet Dionysius: Then idol is a lawful calling . . .

Busy: . . . I call him idol again. Yet, I say, his calling, his profession is profane, it is profane, idol.

Puppet Dionysius: It is not profane!

Leatherhead: It is not profane, he says.

Busy: It is profane.

Puppet Dionysius: It is not profane! [etc.]

—Ben Jonson

THREE

THE PUPPET TRACTATES

As a child, the great Goethe had a puppet theater, given to him by his grandmother, with which he played furiously and to which scholars attribute the early inspiration and training for his adult career as a playwright. We also know that he was taken to puppet performances of a popular story, known throughout Europe and the British Isles, about a prideful professor who sells his soul to the Devil in exchange for magical powers. Attached to a historical figure of the late fifteenth century, this legend of one "Johannes Faustus" was first published in chapbook form in Germany in 1587; Christopher Marlowe used the English translation as the basis for his play *The Tragical History of Doctor Faustus*, first performed in 1604. Traveling actors and puppeteers took Marlowe's drama back to the continent, where it proliferated in countless versions that were widely performed through the end of the nineteenth century.

Goethe was to spend sixty years of his life, on and off, composing his own version of the tale of a brilliant scholar who makes a pact with the Devil to gain supernatural powers over the natural world. Like Marlowe's Faustus, Goethe's Faust could theurgically animate phantasms for his emperor's pleasure; Mephistopheles in turn animates an "idol" of Helen of Troy for Faust's erotic pleasure. And in the phantasmagoric *Faust II*, the good doctor's assistant Wagner, himself now promoted to professor, has created "Homunculus," a miniature alchemical golem, in a glass beaker. This "dainty little man," who possesses the Anthropos trait of complete memory of the world's history (a microcosmic counterpart to the perfect knowledge Faust craves), lights the way inside his phosphorescent test tube as he accompanies Faust and Mephistopheles on a flying cloak to classical Greece, where he will undergo a ritual alchemical dissolution in the sea.

By this time in Western culture, animating a human simulacrum was a radically different act than in Late Antiquity, when imbuing matter with spirit and thereby defeating death had been a goal enthusiastically pursued by cult priests, theurgists, and alchemists. By the late sixteenth and early seventeenth centuries, pious Late Antique theurge and Renaissance magus alike had been transformed, via the figure of the original Faustus, into a blasphemer. Marlowe damned his Faustus but Goethe spared his; the next development in making god bodies would shift the target of the transgression from God to the newly conceived "laws of Nature," and the scientist perpetrators would come to be labeled "mad" instead of bad. Mary Shelley's Dr. Frankenstein revived a golem-corpse to face only the creature's revenge, not theological retribution. As an old-fashioned Fluddian natural philosopher, Faust had started to lose his resonance as a Christian antihero by the turn of the nineteenth century and was ripe for replacement by a modern specialist like Frankenstein—even if the latter's powers, as a careful reading of Shelley's 1818 novel shows, are very alchemically framed.

How did this complicated historical reinvention come about? How did the various double-headed traditions—of idols and puppets, sacred art and popular entertainments, the *via positiva* and *via negativa* of mystical theology—come to split and rejoin in our imaginations in such entirely new ways?

AFTER ANTIQUITY

Let us follow the further adventures of the earthly gods after the end of the ancient West. There were still a high road and a low road, and we will follow the low road first. The "low" tradition of puppets as we commonly think of them—popular comedic shows put on by traveling players—is absent from the Western European historical record between the years 400 and 1200, though such entertainments undoubtedly existed. Not until the sixteenth century were public marionette performances frequently mentioned, in particular the "Pulcinella" shows that swept out of Italy to conquer Europe and the British Isles, where Pulcinella became the famous

Punch of Punch-and-Judy fame (Judy would make her first appearance in the eighteenth century).

In England puppets were known as "motions" and puppeteers as "motion-men" or "motion-masters." Puppet shows had long been a tremendous popular favorite at great fairs, as depicted in Ben Jonson's *Bartholomew Fair* (1614), which provides a nice sub-Zeitgeist moment of high-low convergence when the puppeteers Leatherhead and Filcher demonstrate how they convert highbrow classical stories like that of Hero and Leander to "a more familiar strain for our people" via a puppet play madly fractured between Greek myth and the argot of the London streets.

Late Antiquity's high traditions of religious images and scientific innovation, meanwhile, had been kept alive in the Arabic and Byzantine cultures after the collapse of the Roman empire. (A distant echo of Hero's automata is audible in the mechanical birds of "hammered gold and gold enamelling" in Yeats's "Sailing to Byzantium.") Throughout the Middle Ages in Europe, a muted Neoplatonic-theurgic element would survive in two areas outside the church: nonreligious automata and folklore around constructed or resurrected human bodies. Michael Camille has pointed out that the considerable medieval fashion for automata—both real constructions and those imagined contrivances mentioned in romances such as the Arthurian cycle—involved the familiar but now forbidden fascination with the theurgist's imitation of God's powers as creator. The phenomenon of oracular statues and busts, so prevalent in Late Antiquity, also survived as a folk tradition in the Middle Ages: Pope Sylvester II was rumored to consult such a "talking head" on difficult matters of theology, as were the monk Roger Bacon and the Dominican friar and natural philosopher Albertus Magnus. References in medieval English miracle plays to "gods on strings"—true marionettes now?—date from 1200, and the occasional contrived wonder is noted, such as a crucifix in Boxley, Kent, whose eyes and head were made to move by the monks at significant moments and puppets used by pre-Reformation English priests to enact the Passion.

All these automated marvels stood outside theologians' long-standing but losing battle against idolatry in the form of image and statue worship within the church. Over the long span of the Christian Middle Ages, a sharp distinction had been drawn between the contrived mechanical wonders wrought by humans and the authentic wonder of *mirabilia*, God's true miracles. Churchmen persistently attacked the heretical popular belief that, in one clerical commentator's words, "the factitious gods or statues, idols and images made by man into which the splendour of divinity is poured or impressed by celestial spirits or the heavens and stars and thus with observations of the hours, constellations when the image is cast, engraved, or fabricated." Nonetheless, Christian image making itself remained a highly charged and implicitly theurgic activity for medieval artists. Camille notes that until the twelfth century, when religious sculpture underwent a revival, the prohibition on idolatry had virtually extinguished the making of three-dimensional images for over a millennium. Open worship of saints' images and relics was subsumed within the church. The *ex voto* practice, which persisted in Europe well into the twentieth century, even allowed the devout to offer life-sized statues, made of wax or other precious substances and fashioned in their own likeness, as a way to sacrifice themselves symbolically to God. In 1600, Max von Boehn records, one church in Florence held no fewer than six hundred of these simulacra and innumerable smaller ones.

As the Middle Ages waned, so did, noticeably, the perceived sacrilege in animating the inanimate. The fascination with automata would flower more freely in the humanistic matrix of the Renaissance, when traditions of talking or living statues were ornamentally featured in the secular revival of the Greek and Roman myths. (When Shakespeare transposed Ovid's story of Pygmalion to *A Winter's Tale*, its continuing popularity may have been linked to the fact that in the original tale a sculptor's creation, not a theurgist's holy idol, was brought to life; thus no blasphemy was implied.) Elaborate automata, including artificial humans, were an increasing feature of spectacles, masques, and other elite entertainments. In *The New Atlantis* (1603), Francis Bacon featured an imaginary "house of Solomon" stuffed with perpetual motion machines, clocks, and mechanical moving creatures of all sorts. Not coincidentally, real automata were a standard feature of many European grottoes, which "were viewed as anthropomorphic 'wombs' where metals became by a kind of natural alchemical action more highly developed, as though in an underground laboratory." One Heidelberg grotto of the early seventeenth century featured an elaborate mechanism—of an automated Galatea moving back and forth on the waves before the giant Polyphemus—that its creator, Salomon de Caus, had modeled after instructions provided in Hero's *Pneumatica*.

Along with the talking statues and other automata in the secular realm, Christian belief in the resurrected human body as a form of spiritualized matter lent a kind of philosophical support to the renewed fascination with alchemical homunculi, golems from the Jewish tradition, and pieces of Egyptian mummies to which magical powers were ascribed. Ronald Gray has usefully identified three variations on this model of the human-made human (and potential Divine Human): (1) the entity with life but no spirit, (2) the entity with spirit but no body, and (3) the entity with a body but no life. These simulacra we would now classify as "organic" in contrast to the mechanical or "inorganic" automata, but such a distinction did not exist in our culture until after the seventeenth century. Up to that time, metals were thought to change, grow old, and die just like the bodies of humans and animals, with the consequence that early machines were perceived in continuum with, not opposition to, fleshly bodies.

Alchemy reinforced the belief that matter not only was alive but had a soul as well, and that what was being transformed in the imprisoned matter of the alchemical crucible during the Work, as it was called, was also being transformed in the person of the alchemist/theurgist/magus. The homunculus or little man born in the alchemical vessel was allegorized as a baby (or a dove, or other creatures) in alchemical diagrams—that was, in fact, considered to be its form in the upper world—but in the material world it consisted of a combination of metals that the alchemist hoped to divinize into the immortal substance gold. Even as skepticism was growing—in *The Alchemist* (1610), Ben Jonson had excoriated the low-level counterfeiters who pursued a false dream of material gain—alchemy reached its peak in the early seventeenth century, after which time it began its transmutation (as its *episteme* heirs would insist) from misguided superstition into the gold of the empirical natural sciences as we know them today.

Medieval Jewish mysticism had an even more dramatic tradition of spiritual regeneration through creating an artificial human. In Late Antiquity the Jewish rabbis had known of the rituals for bringing statues to life, and these merged with the syncretic tradition of the Adam Kadmon/Divine Human. In the late Hellenistic midrash tradition, says Moshe Idel, the artificial human, created from dust and brought to life with a magic inscription of Hebrew letters stuck in its mouth, possessed "within himself the entire range of creation, and therefore it is parallel to the divine creation of the world." These theurgic and idolatrous tendencies resurfaced in the early twelfth century, when Abraham ibn Ezra in Spain interpreted the golden calf as a legal way to bring down astral powers into matter. The thirteenth-century mystic Abraham Abulafia emphasized that "the real creation was the spiritual one, which transcends the finite realm of production of bodies"; the maker would receive an "influx of wisdom," revelation from God. In the mid-fourteenth century, the Jewish scholar Alemanno, thought to be the teacher of the Christian natural philosopher Pico della Mirandola, combined ancient Hermetic practice with the precepts of alchemy to undertake experiments whose goal was to produce a double manifestation of the Adam Kadmon in creator and created alike.

As early as the thirteenth century in Europe, these high learning traditions had produced a popular counterpart in the legend of the "golem," a word that means "unformed" or "amorphous" in Hebrew. (Gershem Scholem reports its use as early as the second and third centuries, when the ancient midrashes referred to Adam as God's golem, a living being that filled the universe.) By the time the famous story of the golem of Prague was attached to the sixteenth-century historical figure Rabbi Loewy, however, the older mystical tradition of achieving true contact with God by making a micro-Anthropos was rapidly being supplanted by the widely disseminated popular story of a monster wreaking havoc on a city. The folklore scholar Jakob Grimm provides a late (1808) but comprehensive description of this legend:

> After saying certain prayers and observing certain fast days, the Polish Jews make the figure of a man from clay or mud, and when they pronounce the miraculous Shemhamphoras [the name of God] over him, he must come to life. He cannot speak, but he understands fairly well what is said or commanded. They call him golem and use him as a servant to do all sorts of housework. But he must never leave the house. On his forehead is written *'emeth* [truth]; every day he gains weight and becomes somewhat larger and stronger than all the others in the house, regardless of how little he was to begin with. For fear of him, they therefore erase the first letter, so that nothing remains but *meth* [he is dead], whereupon he collapses and turns to clay again.

Here, as in folklore and popular entertainments of the next two hundred years, the expanding size of this imaginary human simulacrum would continue to reflect his ancient stature as the macrocosmic Adam (and the hidden sub-Zeitgeist desire that he regain this preeminent standing). One of several implicit reasons that all such creatures inevitably shake loose their traces and revolt against human control in these fictions even today is precisely that the Divine Human is not bounded by the laws of this world; its magus creator is presented as having drawn down energies from a level of reality where the laws pertaining solely to the lower world do not apply.

As the oldest Western form of Divine Human, finally, mummies had been collected whole and piecemeal from tombs and sarcophagi by Arab alchemists for more than a millennium. Because of their blackened exteriors, these looted mummy parts were thought to be made of tar, prized as a curative in European medicine. From this mistaken identity the medieval Latin word *mumia* (from Arabic *mumiya*, or bitumen) became linked to the Egyptians' embalmed corpses. Demand for the product became so great that "mummy factories" routinely churned out fakes using the bodies of prisoners or slaves. In the sixteenth century, Paracelsus was still using ground *mumia* in his universal elixir for prolonging life, for he regarded this substance as the Divine Human itself, the microcosm inside immortal humans that corresponded to the celestial macrocosm. Paracelsus also linked his "mysticall Mummies," as his admirer Robert Fludd called them, to the alchemical production of the homunculus.

Although theurgic magic survived in these scattered forms during the Middle Ages through Arabic texts and the alchemical tradition, it was not until the end of the fifteenth century that the founding works of Neoplatonic and Hermetic philosophy again became available to Europeans. Just two decades before the "grotto" murals of Nero's palace were uncovered outside Rome, Cosimo de Medici had commissioned the scholar Marsilio Ficino to translate into the vernacular the major Platonic and Neoplatonic texts (including all the Neoplatonist demonologies of Porphyry, Proclus, and Iamblichus) along with the newly discovered Corpus Hermeticum collection. Significantly, the idol-making passage in *Asclepius* became a central text for Ficino and other Renaissance thinkers. Even as "the wisdom of Hermes" gradually became a tag for all manner of esoterica from the end of Late Antiquity through the Middle Ages, the roots of Renaissance philosophy and magic alike lay in the Neoplatonic, not the Hermetic, literature.

Ficino was a practicing theurgist whose goal was to tap into the higher cosmos via its links in this world, and his life's mission was to frame Plato as a religious writer whose theories worked in concordance with Christian theology. As D. P. Walker explains, this ancient philosopher played a tradition-breaking role in the minds of Ficino and his contemporaries: "Seen through such a screen [the later school of Neoplatonism], Platonism could not possibly be, for Renaissance thinkers, a secular, religiously neutral, innocuously natural philosophy, as, in the large areas of logic and natural science, Aristotelianism could claim to be. It taught a theology and a theurgy; it was either a rival religion to Christianity or the two must be somehow fused together." With this fusion established, Ficino could safely affirm in *De vita coelitus comparanda* (1476): "Plato is right in his concept of the world as a machine constructed in such a way that celestial things have, on earth, a terrestrial state, and likewise that terrestrial things have, in the heavens, a celestial dignity." That concept, in Ficino's view, validated "the principle of magic, which enables men to attract to themselves celestial presences by means of inferior things utilized at opportune moments and corresponding to higher things."

A millennium of Christian culture, however, had wrought a major change in the Neoplatonic magic rites. Now, instead of attempting to ensoul an actual statue or holy image, Ficino *visualized* key emblematic images—such as a statue of Saturn made entirely of sapphire or other personifications of planets—and by this demiurgic act of imagining believed he could endow these images with the requisite divine energy. In this process the human mediator's own role was significantly increased from that of middleman theurge to god-imitating demiurge, not only bringing the images to life inside himself in a form of "inner sculpting," but (skirting the narrow line between Christianity and sorcery) giving them external form as spirits as well. Operating from the same principle as the alchemists, Ficino, like Giordano Bruno after him, regarded the act of *imaginatio* as a physical activity that produced tangible results, a kind of subtle body rather than immaterial phantoms—that is, just the holographic phantasms that Marlowe and Goethe would later have their Faustus/Faust magus create.

Under the nominal rubric of Christianity, these precepts of Neoplatonism and Hermeticism flourished in fifteenth- and sixteenth-century Western Europe, creating a religio-philosophical matrix of reference that allowed a philosopher such as Tommaso Campanella, for example, to pronounce that the universe was "a statue, an image, the living temple and book [codex] of God." As late as 1622, the alchemist Johann Daniel Mylius could complain, about his efforts to produce the Philosopher's Stone, which he equated with the risen Christ or Second Adam: "For it is more difficult to make a man live again, than to slay him . . . it is a great mystery to create souls, and to mould the lifeless body into a living statue."

Declaring that the universe we perceive with our senses is nothing but a "simulacrum of primary nature," Giordano Bruno combined theurgy with the ancient memory techniques recorded by Suetonius and Cicero that will be examined in Chapter 8. By reciting the idol-animating passage from the Hermetic *Asclepius*, Bruno intended to call down astral powers into mnemonic statues that he visualized in a mental topography dictated by the classical memory system. Once magic had animated these inner images, he meditated on them with the goal of sympathetically siphoning off their powers and making himself an equal of the gods. Deeply immersed in the Jewish mysticism of the cabbala, Bruno syncretized the traditional cabbalistic divinization of language and the alphabet in his three-pronged *cabala-filosofia-teologia.* Elevating images, the "language of the gods," over the inadequacies of written language, he believed that his brand of Neoplatonic meditation forged a transcendental link between metaphysics and art. "It follows," Bruno pronounced, "that philosophers are also painters and poets, poets are painters and philosophers, and painters are philosophers and poets."

Just such a conflation, secularized and for the most part unconscious, was already taking place as Renaissance artists along with growing numbers of the new scientists absorbed some of the aura formerly granted only to holy men of God. It would be a common Romantic complaint, as voiced by Achim von Arnim, that the Reformation "took the mystery from the priesthood and gave it entirely to science." But artists and writers, by analogy, also created new life and assumed demiurgic powers over their new territories, and the Romantics would likewise anoint themselves, in the form of William Blake's "Poetic Genius," as the new priests.

Even by Bruno's day, however, followers of Hermes who strove too blatantly to fashion themselves into Divine Humans did not deceive the keepers of orthodoxy when they stopped being philosophers and reinvented themselves as magi. Giordano Bruno was branded a heretic and burned at the stake in 1600.

THE DIVINE MACHINE

The year of Bruno's death marks a halfway point in the process of internalizing and subjectivizing the transcendent within Western society, a process that would be further hastened by the iconoclasts of the Protestant Reformation, whose radical position was well illustrated by the pronouncement uttered in 1584 by an English Puritan preacher, William Perkins, that "a thing conceived in the mind by the imagination is an idol." Zeal-of-the-Land Busy's earnest disputation with a puppet in Jonson's *Bartholomew Fair*, quoted at the chapter opening, presents a fair parody of this extreme dogma. Since the puppet Dionysius is at once simulacrum of a pagan god and theatrical effigy/idol, it is no wonder that Busy abhors his "treble squeaking" as "the chariot wheels of Satan." Significantly, Perkins's declaration resembles his contemporary Bruno's position in suggesting that, for good or ill, humans do possess the magus's god-imitating powers within themselves.

This drastic reinterpretation of reality as a material world in which one's only transcendental link to God is internal, I would argue, marks the real dividing line in Western culture. The turning point was not, as usually believed, that between the ancient world and the Christian culture that grew out of it, nor that between the Middle Ages and the Renaissance, nor that between preindustrial and industrial society, but rather that between Western culture up to the seventeenth century and what came after. The sixteenth-century Protestant Reformation and the concomitant elevation of human reason as the ultimate arbiter of reality by philosophers such as Bacon and then Descartes laid the groundwork for the exploration of empirical reality unfettered by *gnosis* dogma that produced the scientific revolution and its technological consequence, the industrial revolution. The combined impetus of this sequence of realignments, all of which began to take their present shape in the seventeenth century, conspired to produce a more profound shift in the Western worldview than anything in the preceding three millennia.

In that critical century, battlefield for the clash of what Keith Thomas aptly described as the "Neoplatonic versus Aristotelian views of the properties of matter," the Aristotelian view won, effectively removing *gnosis* belief in a supernatural world with causal and moral links to the material world as a cornerstone of Western intellectual culture. Just as Francis Bacon had sounded the death knell of alchemy a century earlier when he declared an object's color to be an external trait of appearance and not a manifestation of inward essence, once the Protestant reformers purged idol-worshipping and the magical from religious ritual (as the early Christian fathers had done before them) Europeans gradually became, in Thomas's words, "reluctant to believe that physical objects could change their nature by a ritual or exorcism and consecration." If, as the Protestants decreed, miracles no longer happened, it followed that neither was there any legitimate access to the Platonic otherworld outside the individual's own inner relationship to God. Taken to its logical conclusion, this reasoning would eventually undermine Christianity's own truth claims as well. (It is tempting to speculate that the enormous rise in witchcraft prosecution during the late seventeenth century occurred out of the simple need, on both sides, to provide the still-widespread belief in the supernatural with some kind of outlet, even an unsanctioned one.)

At first the new scientific empirical discoveries seemed to validate the old notions of the congruent great and little cosmos. The Cambridge Platonists, for example, continued to assert that the physical world embodied the World Soul, and in Chapter 6 we will see how Thomas Burnet materialized this notion in his views of the planet Earth. By the end of the seventeenth century, however, alchemy had begotten modern chemistry purged of the notion of the divinity of matter, and by the eighteenth century—with the further elevation of human-sourced reason by the French Encyclopedists—the reversed swing of the pendulum was well under way. Isaac Newton recorded alchemical and astrological calculations while he was identifying gravity—this example has become the standard chestnut for summing up his era's contradictions—but science had also divorced natural occurrences such as earthquakes and plagues from any causal links to the supernatural. In the eighteenth and nineteenth centuries, the internalization and secularization of the transcendent would culminate in the intellectual event that Terry Castle has described as the complete "absorption of ghosts into the world of thought."

But as researchers like William Harvey were busy transferring the transcendent properties of the soul into the material properties of blood, and philosophers like Descartes were transferring these same qualities into the material properties of mind, what was happening to the notion of the soul itself? Among many other places, I will argue, it went—much as the soul of the dying serial killer Charles Lee Ray leaps into a handy "Good Guy" doll in the movie *Child's Play* (1988)—into that newly valorized human creation the machine, and specifically into mechanical artificial humans as imagined in literary and theatrical works over the next two centuries.

Understanding the disguises of the supernatural in Western culture after the year 1700 means looking most of all at the larger idea of the machine and the mechanical—of which category the human automaton is only a single example, but a very crucial one. To avoid the taint of idol making, the new applied sciences required theological justification, which could be found in the following demiurgic reasoning as summarized by Horst Bredekamp:

> Since man had been created in the image of God, he had the duty to emulate the divine mechanic and create objects . . . Machines could help humans return to Eden . . . Since life in its highest form was defined since Plato's time as the ability to move independently, the creation of movement became the decisive criterion.

Bredekamp argues that during the Renaissance machines were viewed both as living entities and as sculptural descendants of classical art ("not in contradiction to each other but as a progression"), but by the eighteenth century "mechanics was conceptually and actually disengaged from the realm of the tradition of antiquity and art." Halfway between the old and new sensibilities, Renaissance machines like those of Jacques Besson were seen to run according to the old principles of correspondence in the sympathetic universe. As I will explore in later chapters, a great deal of this early fusion of *gnosis* and *episteme* lingers in our continuing awe-ful regard for what we imagine to be the infinite capabilities of the machine.

It is difficult for us now to picture a time when the independent territory of *imagine*—a realm neither material nor transcendental, and completely distinct from that of *believe*—was not freely available. As C. S. Lewis once pointed out, "we are apt to take it for granted that a poet has at his command, besides the actual world and the world of his own religion, a third world of myth and fancy. The probable, the marvellous-taken-as-fact, the marvellous-known-to-be-fiction—such is the triple equipment of the post-Renaissance poet." Lewis locates the origins of this "third world" of the marvelous as far back as the third century C.E., when writers like Marianus Capella pickled the fading pagan gods and goddesses in allegory, thereby preserving them for an exuberant revival in the Renaissance,

> when they could wake again in the beauty of acknowledged myth and thus provide modern Europe with its "third world" of romantic imag-

ining . . . No religion, so long as it is believed, can have that kind of beauty which we find in the gods of Titian, of Botticelli, or of our own romantic poets. To this day [Lewis was writing in 1936] you cannot make poetry *of that sort* out of the Christian heaven and hell. The gods must be, as it were, disinfected of belief; the last taint of the sacrifice, and of the urgent practical interest, the selfish prayer, must be washed away from them, before that other divinity can come to light in the imagination.

But during this mass migration of former citizens of the territory of *believe* into the new territory of *imagine*, I would argue, the disinfection process was anything but complete.

In the *imagine* realm that Lewis's third world of fantastic literature occupies, the scientist character, the negative magus who destructively manipulates the arcane forces locked in matter, is a familiar figure. Less familiar but more foundational in our imaginations is an enduring post-1700 belief in the divine and infernal powers of the machine itself. The urge to divinize did carry over, unacknowledged but intact, even as its focus radically shifted—from Apollo and Venus to Robby the Robot. Via the unconscious displacement of the transcendental impulse into fantasy, the machine has served for almost four hundred years as the principal Trojan horse for the supernatural in our rationalized existence.

After the Renaissance, the banished Platonic worldview would be reinvented within the arts, the only realm in which our empirical worldview allows us to "suspend disbelief" in the laws of physical reality while reading, watching, or looking at works of the imagination. The internalization of the supernatural as secularized "fantasy" meant that corresponding literary genres sprang up in which the old worldview could still be represented. By the nineteenth century the supernatural had been excluded from most high art, but it proliferated in such popular entertainments as ghost stories and Gothic romances, which in turn led to the next century's science fiction and fantasy genres. As acts of god making and the spiritualizing of matter were transplanted into this literature, however, the resulting divine body, alchemical product of the fusion of its creator's thought processes with the material at hand, was no golden child or luminous disk but a monster. Offspring of the demonized supernatural, the human-made simulacrum of the nineteenth and twentieth centuries is either an innocent turned vengefully destructive, like the creature Mary Shelley fashioned for her Dr. Frankenstein, or, in its later sub-Zeitgeist transformations, an entity of unmitigated evil—most typically, the soul of the "serial killer" animating the body of a doll or inhabiting virtual reality. Not until the close of the twentieth century would the mad scientist's sympathetically deformed *ka* show signs of changing back into a being of light.

THE NEW IDOLS

A scattering of Western European writers of the nineteenth and early twentieth centuries imagined human simulacra—in the form of mummies, dummies, and marionettes—from the vantage of *gnosis* rather than *episteme.* Their works offer us brief but vivid glimpses of the complex historical transfer under way in which ideas about the transcendental soul attached to the human simulacrum were shifting from the context of the sacred into secular culture.

Why look at discourses *about* puppets and other human simulacra rather than at puppets in performance? Because even as puppet shows retain their timeless theatrical charm, imagined puppets carry a stronger charge of the "uncanny" or suppressed holy. The simulacrum has always traveled both a high road and a low road in human culture—as highest form of worship and as lowest form of entertainment—but it is a peculiarity of Western culture of the last three hundred years that the two roads have joined into one that runs, as it were, below sea level. Once the human likeness was no longer worshipped, it became an idea, not an idol, partaking of the insensible territory "imaginary" instead of the insensible territory "holy." Beneath these meditations on simulacra, however, lie the same half-conscious assumptions that animate the terminators, replicants, and virtual entities who are their twenty-first-century descendants.

Our commentators, who might be styled as old-fashioned natural philosophers now exiled to the smaller territory of aesthetics, are the three Romantic contemporaries Heinrich von Kleist (1777–1811), E. T. A. Hoffmann (1776–1822), and Giacomo Leopardi (1798–1837) along with their twentieth-century heirs apparent Rainer Maria Rilke (1875–1926) and Bruno Schulz (1892–1942). It is significant that all but Rilke cast the core passages of their essay-fictions as dialogue, a classic vehicle of *gnosis* rather than *episteme.* Dialogue, as Tullio Maranhao has noted, is antithetical to scientific thinking because it emphasizes process over essence and amounts, in fact, to an "anti-epistemology" that inevitably "undermines the stability of the categories of knowledge."

These puppet tractates, however, do not follow the dialogue model most familiar to us—that is, the Platonic debate involving more or less equal "encounters among souls"—but echo instead the Late Antiquity master-disciple exchanges like those of the *Asclepius*, in which the wise man may also turn out to be a god. Obsessing as they do on the superhuman powers of human simulacra (or, in Leopardi's case, of reanimated corpses) the dialogues of our commentators come across as disguised or sublimated religio-philosophical tractates much in the spirit of the Corpus Hermeticum. Meanwhile their great subjects the god-dolls live on in the popular entertainments of the present day so well known to us all—the mummy from ancient Egypt revived to wreak havoc; the doll or mannequin come to life through the efforts of a charismatic creator or soul-bestower; the puppet turned robot-android-clone-cyborg seeking humanity and immortality at the same time.

Kleist and the Dancer's Soul

Nowhere is the destabilizing action of dialogue more clearly at work than in Heinrich von Kleist's essay "On the Marionette Theater," written as an occasional piece for the *Berliner Abendblatter* (December 12–15, 1810). A discourse on the externalized soul couched in the metaphors of eighteenth-century mathematics, optics, and Newtonian physics, this essay has been the target of countless interpretations that have dubbed it anything from a veiled critique of human actors on the Berlin stage to an expression of sublimated narcissistic rage. Its similarity to both Platonic and Hermetic dialogues has also been noted. The beginning of the nineteenth century had seen a *gnosis* revival in the form of the aesthetic movement called Romanticism, once aptly dubbed "spilt religion" by T. E. Hulme. Kleist, along with other German Romantics, was consciously reviving much of the philosophy and religion of Late Antiquity in reaction to eighteenth-century rationalism and Neoclassicism; his debut piece in this new journal two months earlier had been a mock "Zoroaster's Prayer."

Kleist gives us his central premise immediately, placing us without preamble at the heart of the high road–low road puppet conundrum. Strolling in the park, his first-person narrator encounters a "Mr. C.," principal dancer at the opera, who describes being irresistibly drawn to the puppet shows in the marketplace and asks the narrator if he hasn't been struck by the graceful movements of the wooden figures.

To understand just how radically contrarian this aesthetic judgment would have been to Kleist's erudite readers, it is helpful to remember that by the nineteenth century puppet shows were widely attacked in the same way that comic books, video games, and action movies are today—for crudity, obscenity, violence, and setting an overall bad example for the young. Despite the fact that puppetry enjoyed great popularity in eighteenth-century Europe, by the time of Kleist's essay they were regarded as the basest form of public entertainment. Mr. C., however, aims his analysis of the lowly figurines resolutely upward by proceeding to a quasi-scientific explanation based on the notion of a "center of gravity":

> Each movement, [C.] said, had its center of gravity: it would suffice to control this within the puppet; the limbs, which are only pendulums, follow mechanically of their own accord—without further help . . . The line which the center of gravity has to follow is indeed quite simple and in most cases, he believed, straight. In the cases in which it is curved, the law of its curvature seems to be at least of the first or at most of the second order; even in the latter case the line is only elliptical, a form of movement of the body's extremities (because of the joints) which is most natural, so this hardly demands great talent on the part of the operator.

The line of reasoning in this brilliantly rendered but kinetically fantastic explanation takes yet another left turn, delivered by Mr. C. (who will be given several other memorable punch lines in the course of the essay): "Seen from another point of view, this line could be something very mysterious, for it is nothing other than the *path taken by the dancer's soul.*" Far from being a mechanical operation, he says, manipulation of the puppet would require total identification of operator and puppet: the operator himself would have to dance.

Moreover, says C., a properly made puppet could perform a dance more gracefully than the most skilled human dancer because it would lack the human flaw of "affectation," a quality of self-conscious playacting that moves this very concretized "soul," which he describes as *vis motrix*, "force of motion," away from its proper site, the center of gravity. C. points mockingly to various well-known dancers whose souls, at dramatic climaxes in various ballets, appear in the "small of the back" or the "elbow"—thanks to an unappealing combination of the forces of gravity and self-consciousness. (The latter sin, acquired when humans ate from the Tree of Knowledge, causes this dislocation.) Since primal innocence cannot be regained and "Paradise is locked," C. continues, "we have to travel around the world to see if it is perhaps open again somewhere at the back."

Besides being unself-conscious (hence in a state of pre-Fall primal innocence that humans have lost), C. goes on, puppets are essentially weightless. They need the ground only to boost their momentum, whereas humans require it to "recover from the exertions of the dance, a moment which is clearly not part of the dance." To the narrator's continued objections that no puppet could equal the grace (*Grazie)* of the human body, C. delivers, as it were, the *coup de grace:* "It would be impossible for man to come anywhere near the puppet," he declares. "Only a god could equal inanimate matter in this respect; and here is the point where the two ends of the circular world meet."

The narrator now interrupts with a long digression about a young man whose self-consciousness in attempting to duplicate a spontaneous movement permanently ruined his youthful grace. C. responds with his own experience as a skilled swordsman in Russia, drawn into a mock duel with his sword against a bear. Because the bear's eye, says C., was "fixed on mine as if [he] could read my soul in it," he was able to anticipate C.'s every thrust and distinguish the genuine ones from the feints. From this tale C. derives his, and Kleist's, final moral:

> We see that in the organic world, as reflection grows darker and weaker, grace emerges more brilliantly and commandingly. But just as the section drawn through two lines suddenly appears on the other side of a point after passing through infinity, or just as the image in a concave mirror turns up before us again after having moved off into the endless distance, so too grace itself returns when knowledge has gone through an infinity. Grace appears purest in that human form

which has either no consciousness or an infinite one, that is, in a puppet or in a god.

When the wondering narrator inquires if, in this cycle of consciousness and unconsciousness, humans must eat the apple again to return to the primal state of innocence, C. triumphantly affirms that this paradoxical and perverse act must happen: it is, he says, the "last chapter" in the history of the world.

What exactly is to be made of all this? "Real" puppets, of course, do not operate more gracefully than humans. As well as a frustrated theurge, we may also see Kleist as an early proponent of what Sherry Turkle has called (after George Bernard Shaw's version of the Pygmalion legend) the "ELIZA" effect in the current "culture of simulation," which prompts us, for example, to perceive real animals as less "realistic" than animatronic animals in film. The "*opacity* of the machine," Turkle says, causes us to view it in a psychological way and thereby make the unconscious leap that closes "the gap between what actually can be done and what we *imagine* can be done." As will be discussed in Chapters 11 and 12, this has become a governing mechanism in our perception of what the technology Platonically dubbed "virtual reality" can do. In Kleist's case, it could be argued, this very opacity of the marionette allows him to see it in a spiritual way.

In *Discourse on Method* (1637), the practicing scientist René Descartes had followed the new spirit of his time by declaring that the body is like a machine "which, having been made by the hand of God, is incomparably better structured than any machine that could be invented by human beings." By reviving the ancient animistic notion that all matter has its own soul life, Kleist turned Descartes's position on its head. Grace or *Grazia* in the sense in which Kleist uses the word has a Christian connotation—a state, if you will, of "weightlessness" that emanates from the transcendental world—that is best expressed not by the human alone but in this externalized soul embodied as the puppet. And this notion, conceit, belief of Kleist's, expressed in a short essay on a low art form, would exert an impact on writers and poets far out of proportion to its ostensible subject over the next two centuries.

Hoffmann: The Turk Talks

Kleist's fellow Romantic E. T. A. Hoffmann was one of the first to register some of the implications of his contemporary's essay. Enthusiast of puppets and automatons (like Goethe, he had puppets, and even as an adult he would often bring them out for guests), composer, and supreme innovator, Hoffmann was also the bearer of what is, on the surface, a more immediately familiar notion of the human simulacrum—that of the "soulless" automaton that falls far short of its human model. By virtue of his very fascination with puppets and mechanical androids that pass for human, however, Hoffmann kept alive the debate over the presence of souls in matter in the new intellectual environment of the nineteenth century. The entire worldview of Hoffmann's stories, for that matter—with their alchemical manipulations, metal queens, and talking vegetables that marry humans—remains that of the old living cosmos, the nostalgic worldview of Romanticism that coexists in a certain tension with his views on the sinister imitation of the human by the puppet-machine and is reinforced by the fact that the automaton usually brings about the destruction of the human's hopes and sometimes the human himself.

But even this position contained its own theurgic element because Hoffmann like no other writer would fix in our consciousness the idea of the human simulacrum as a projected double or *ka* "that comes into being," in John Cohen's words, "by the fission of its creator's personality." When a Hoffmann automaton comes to life, it contains the essence of its creator in a true father-child relation and is often passed off as a biological child. Hoffmann's puppetmeister-theurge-fathers are always sinister, unpleasant, tricky characters, in contrast to his beautiful and usually female mechanical creations—though the latter are seen as "disagreeably perfect" in a different way than their creators are disagreeably imperfect. Hoffmann's paradigm of the inhumanly beautiful puppet/simulacrum as victim of its parent the puppetmaster would endure through literature of the nineteenth century into the present day.

Hoffmann's major philosophizing about automata is to be found in the two stories "Automata" (1814) and the more famous "The Sandman" (1816–17), which was deeply influenced by Kleist's essay and in turn deeply influenced Sigmund Freud. In formulating his definition of the uncanny, Freud quoted his colleague Ernst Jentsch's statement: "In telling a story, one of the most successful devices for easily creating uncanny effects is to leave the reader in uncertainty whether a particular figure in the story is a human being or an automaton." "The Sandman," which Jentsch cited as a prime example of this effect, features a set of intertwined negative father figures and the prototypical Hoffmann automaton, an attractive young woman who lures the hero away from his true love to infatuation and doom. Every time mechanical Olimpia utters a metallic "Ah! Ah! Ah!" Nathaniel "imagines a profound harmony, "his own heart's voice speaking to him." His human lover Clara meanwhile speculates that the soul "projects these phantoms into the outer world and is constantly attracted by the fatally deceptive images which it created"—a modern twist on Hoffmann's part that steers the story toward the subjectivizing homocentric psychological and away from the notion of an animated being.

The rambling tale "Automata" contains two concentric stories featuring two pairs of male student protagonists, Lewis and Ferdinand, who are not at all different in class and temperament from Kleist's two disputants (all are versions of the prototypical German Romantic male couple, a twentieth-century example of which will appear in Chapter 7). In the inner story Lewis declares that he hates automata, "which can scarcely be said to counterfeit humanity so much as to travesty it—mere images of living death or inanimate life," whereas Ferdinand says the automaton's most striking quality is the "spiritual power" of its insight into humans. Over and over, the inferiority of the mechanical and artificial is stressed—in music, movement, and (always) soulfulness.

The true core dialogue of this multilayered fragment of a story, however, does not take place between Lewis and Ferdinand but rather between these two students and an automaton called the Talking Turk, a carnival attraction to which people direct questions about their lives. Hoffmann represents the Talking Turk as an oracular fortuneteller like the divinely charged talking statues of Late Antiquity, but the students speculate that the automaton is somehow able to mirror back the deepest knowledge of the person posing the question. (When William Butler Yeats consulted an oracular automaton known as the "Metallic Medium" in the early twentieth century, let it be noted, he expected its wisdom to come from a source external to his own psyche.) On this model the Talking Turk correctly interprets Ferdinand's question about personal happiness and responds with the dire news that the next time he sees the woman he loves will be the moment he is lost to her forever.

The Turk's response convinced Ferdinand that "this strange intelligence . . . beholds that germ of the future which is being formed within us in mysterious connection with the outer world, and knows what will happen to us in the far future." Here the "fission" effect of the double is not that between simulacrum and creator but—as with Nathaniel and Olimpia in "The Sandman"—between the simulacrum and those humans it encounters in the world, a considerably different proposition. Whereas Olimpia's springs and wires are revealed, however, the Turk retains his mystery. The underlying suggestion that a mechanical object can "read the soul" of a human contradicts all the surface statements about the automaton's inadequacies and leaves us with the strong feeling that Hoffmann is closer to Kleist in terms of ensouling the inanimate than he would have us (or himself) believe.

Leopardi's "Mysticall Mummies"

In 1827 the Italian poet and essayist Giacomo Leopardi brought out his collected *Operette morali*, a philosophical discourse presented as a series of imaginary dialogues between such entities as the Sun and the Moon, Plotinus and Porphyry, and so on. In the "Dialogue between Frederick Ruysch and His Mummies," Leopardi imagines a scene between the famous seventeenth-century Dutch anatomist (1648–1731) who invented (we should say reinvented) the embalming process and some of the subjects of his skill. Ruysch is also remembered today for his spare-time hobby, allegorical *tableaux morts* constructed of skeletons of human fetuses set in decorative landscapes made of gallstones, artificially preserved veins and arteries, and other body pieces. For a Late Antique person, particularly an Egyptian, Ruysch's artistic efforts, meant to deliver a moral on the brevity and vanity of life, would have been nothing less than desecration—a reaction they still arouse today from public censors.

In his dialogue, Leopardi focuses not on these *memento mori* of Ruysch's but rather on the recipients of the anatomist's improved embalming methods. By styling them as mummies, Leopardi is consciously linking these modern preserved corpses not only with the fabled art of the ancient Egyptians but also with the divine *mumia* of alchemists like Paracelsus. Cleverly joining the old science and the new, Leopardi animates his chorus of the revived dead to engage in a discourse on what it is like to die. Uncanny this encounter certainly is, but Leopardi grants Ruysch, as a proper scientist of the new era, a notable absence of religious awe in the presence of the resurrected dead. Leopardi's Ruysch is the magus seeking knowledge from these entities he has "created" through his embalming methods, but he is not the bad-mad magus-scientist: although Ruysch wonders at first, in alarm, if they are vampires, the mummies do not turn on him and attempt to destroy him.

In their opening song, sung at midnight on the day when the great mathematical year ends (the propitious moment when, according to Cicero, the universe completes its vast orbit and the dead speak), the mummies lament that they understand life no better now than they understood death when they were alive. They are alive only for a quarter of an hour, and—like Hoffmann's Talking Turk and other entities from the oracular tradition—they can speak only in response to a question. Ruysch, surprised they've been able to come back in this way "simply because I preserved them from decomposition," quizzes the mummies on how it feels to be dead. Since death means the extinction of feeling, they answer, there is no pain at the point of death. Ruysch objects that surely the forcible separation of the soul from the body must be a violent event that produces extreme suffering. No, say the mummies; it's an easy entry and an easy departure. And that is all. There is no talk of Christian resurrection, no expressed concern with an immortal body. Leopardi's risen dead are neither evil nor fear-inducing; at the most they are merely plaintive. When their fifteen minutes are up, they go back very gently into their good night.

The great *episteme* revelation for Leopardi's contemporaries in this tractate is that the physical experience of death is pleasurable, not painful. Just as with Hoffmann's Talking Turk, however, the mere fact that Leopardi himself, standing behind the character "Ruysch," has animated these soulless mummies raises more questions than his mummies have answered. In the interest of affirming a materialist vision of death, he has nonetheless chosen to bestow a kind of temporary soul or *vis motrix* on the mummies. The energy Leopardi as artist-theurge grants his corpse-simulacra reflects a kind of primitive animism of matter completely detached from religious belief and hints at the broad-based animism of objects that would obsess both Rainer Maria Rilke and Bruno Schulz almost a century later.

Rilke's Disappointing Dolls

In the essay "Doll: On the Wax Dolls of Lotte Pritzel" (1913–14), inspired by an exhibit of life-size adult dolls he had seen in Munich as well as the Kleist essay, Rainer Maria Rilke confronts the frustrating paradox of graven images that will *not* come to life. Noting as a casual given that most inanimate objects "eagerly" absorb human tenderness ("a violin's devotion, the good-natured eagerness of horn-rimmed spectacles"), he laments the fact that the childhood fusion with the self-object doll is a barren union that promises everything and delivers nothing. "You doll-soul," he exclaims in this monologue addressed to an idol that does not reply, "not made by god, you soul, begged as a whim by some impetuous elf, you thing-soul exhaled laboriously by an idol and kept in being by us all." As children, he says, we invent a soul for the doll, but ultimately the doll makes the child feel cheated, "unmasked as the gruesome foreign body on which we squandered our purest affection." By the end of childhood "we could not make it into a thing or person, and in such moments it became a stranger to us," and so the doll-soul and its possibilities die for good. Rilke suggests that this kind of infantile wish-animism is doomed to wither in the object once it has died within us.

The same is not true of the puppet, however. Rilke expresses his hope that this simulacrum will prove to be a potential soul vessel in the fourth Duino elegy, where he builds explicitly on the paradoxes Kleist set forth in "On the Marionette Theater":

> when I am in the mood
> to wait before the puppet stage, no,
> to watch it so intensely that, in order
> finally to compensate for my watching, as puppeteer
> an angel must come to set the puppets in motion.

Or, as Harold Segel has elegantly paraphrased this passage: "Once the self is overcome, one stands before the possibility of a heretofore unrealizable interaction of the material world, represented by the puppet figure, and the transcendent world, represented by the figure of an angel . . . the path to harmonize the world." The puppet-angel conjunction is in fact Rilke's solution to the mute and fruitless idolatry of childhood, a state of innocence to which, like the Garden of Eden, we cannot return.

Rilke continues:

> Angel and puppet. Now we will have a play.
> Now will there come together what we always
> Divide because of our presence . . .
> Now will the angel perform over us.

To achieve the loss of ego necessary to experience the true *unio mystica*, the conjunction of the visible and invisible worlds, he says, we must do precisely as Kleist's Mr. C. suggests—bite the apple again and re-lose our innocence. For Rilke, however, this loss of ego may represent not, as Louis Sass argues about Kleist, the subject-object fusion that is "an obliteration of all individuating self-consciousness," but rather a more sophisticated state of integration, "a higher self-consciousness that is, at the same time, a higher self-forgetfulness," the true Paradise on earth.

Bruno Schulz and the Tailors' Dummies

Often likened to Kakfa—with whom he shares principally a fondness for metempsychosis and a childhood in the same Austro-Hungarian cultural matrix—the Polish-Jewish writer Bruno Schulz (1892–1942) must certainly have drawn inspiration from the essay by his literary hero Rilke. Schulz's dolls also disappoint, though in a different way: their potential for secondary life is extinguished by the inertia of the material, in the form of thwarted human desire. Schulz propagates a kind of pantheistic cabbalism within the German Romantic tradition; as an anti-Gnostic more exaggeratedly Hermetic than Kleist, he asserts that not spirit but matter itself—an animistic collective soul distributed equally across all objects in the landscape—is trapped here on earth. "Have you heard at night the terrible howling of these wax figures, shut in the fair-booths," he asks us, "the pitiful chorus of those forms of wood or porcelain, banging their fists against the walls of their prisons?" Not just mannequins but all material objects in this world live and feel, and we humans treat their feelings far too cavalierly—we cannot, for example, imagine the pain of various grains of wood yoked together in a chair or in other artificial and arbitrary forms we humans impose on them, which is also our own tragedy: "Weep, ladies, over your own fate, when you see the misery of imprisoned matter, of tortured matter which does not know what it is and why it is, nor where the gesture may lead that has been imposed on it for ever."

Schulz's first collection of stories, *Cinnamon Shops* (1934), retitled *The Street of Crocodiles* in its English translation, creates a phantasmagoric cosmos out of his childhood experience featuring the recurring figures of a mad father and an all-powerful servant girl, Adela. In these stories Schulz lays out his main metaphysical proposition, which is deeply Platonic: that what we mistake for objective reality—that is, the empirical world of the senses—is always trembling on the point of disintegration. "Reality," says Schulz, "is as thin as paper and betrays with all its cracks its imitative character."

His great disquisition on the union of spirit and matter takes place in a group of four mock expositions, collectively entitled "Tailors' Dummies," which assert that inanimate objects—as illustrated by the dressmaker's mannequins in the family attic—possess a life and spirit of their own. Schulz casts his Father character, whom he likens repeatedly to an automaton, as his latter-day magus and "heretical Demiurgy." Father serves as Schulz the ventriloquist's own puppet mouthpiece in discoursing like a good Hellene about the self-animating properties of matter: "Matter has been given infinite fertility, inexhaustible vitality, and, at the same time, a seductive power of temptation which invites us to create as well . . . Matter is the most passive and most defenseless essence in the cosmos. Anyone can mold it and shape it; it obeys everybody." God is the Demiurge or Platonic craftsman or shaper of matter, and we humans crave the same creative powers for ourselves. But, says Father, "Demiurge, that great master and artist, made matter invisible, made it disappear under the surface of life. We, on the contrary, love its creaking, its resistance, its clumsiness."

As the focus of Father's eloquent harangue, the tailors' dummies lack mobility like Leopardi's mummies, but more strikingly they also lack speech. Mute, headless, but still powerfully female, they function as primitive secular idols. The fact that Father talks constantly and neither the tailors' dummies nor the servant Adela says a word makes these two disquisitions monologues on the surface. At a deeper level, however, the real dialogue is conducted with the forces of materialism that Adela embodies and enforces. It is a dialogue of imagination pitted against physical acts: Adela's response is always pure action, through which she defeats the not-so-all-powerful word; though she does not speak, she *moves.* In her mute power Adela seems golemlike, an animated extension of the idol-mannequins.

When Father pronounces his grandiloquent intention "to create man a second time—in the shape and semblance of a tailor's dummy," Adela instantly takes up her adversarial role:

> Just as my father pronounced the word "dummy," Adela looked at her wristwatch and exchanged a knowing look with Polda. She then moved her chair forward and, without getting up from it, lifted her dress to reveal her foot tightly covered in black silk, and then stretched it out stiffly like a serpent's head . . . Adela's outstretched slipper trembled slightly and shone like a serpent's tongue. My father rose slowly, still looking down, took a step forward like an automaton, and fell to his knees.

By this single act she has turned Father into the dummy, enslaved to a domineering female eros, effectively canceling the delicate sublife of the spirit Father is attempting to tease out of matter.

The world created by imagination loses as the matter-ness of matter triumphs: Schulz the artist elaborated this motif in his numerous drawings celebrating erotic fetish. His best-known portfolio of engravings—entitled, not by coincidence, *The Book of Idolatry*—restages the moral of the tailors' dummies tractates again and again: humble men prostrate themselves at the feet of all-powerful women as the transcendent migrates into another favored realm of displacement, that of extravagantly suffocated sexual fantasy. These images illustrate the repetition compulsion of genre formula that will be explored in Chapter 5; to look at one drawing this way means not to examine it deeply but simply to experience the compulsion to look at more images cast in the same mold.

With Schulz and Rilke we leave the puppet-idols poised at the brink of a new adventure in the world of secular entertainment. By the later nineteenth century, Hoffmann's stories about mechanical automata had been widely disseminated in the ballets *Coppélia*, *Tales of Hoffmann*, and *The Nutcracker*, and the earthly gods were ready to undergo an astonishing technological upgrade in the avant-garde and the popular arts alike.

Angel and puppet: *now* we would have a play.

Marvel comic book cover, 1974. ™ and © Marvel Characters, Inc. Used with permission.

The [high] fantastic tradition is not, in the country of Edgar Allan Poe, as rich as one might believe it to be.

—Maurice Lévy

The American occult is the intellectual life of the common people.

—Paul Bray

FOUR

THE STRANGE HISTORY OF THE AMERICAN FANTASTIC

Before the play begins, we must take a short trip across the Atlantic with Bruno Schulz. The journey of this chapter requires a sketch map, up to about the year 1990, of the larger category of fantastic literature and its diverging fates in Europe and America. On this map we will follow a complex series of migrations: between one continent and another, between high art and low art, between art and religion.

Fantastic—incorporating elements by turns supernatural, antirepresentational, and grotesque—is the term that best describes C. S. Lewis's third world of the marvelous, born in the Renaissance and revived during the Romantic era as an aesthetic revolt against the eighteenth century's rising Aristotelianism. The Romantic storytelling mode, whose model was set by the stories of Hoffmann, flowered in America in the work of Edgar Allan Poe, whose *Tales of the Grotesque and Arabesque* (1839) and subsequent stories of murder, detection, and premature burial exerted in turn a dramatic and enduring influence on the literature of continental Europe that far exceeded his impact on the serious literature of his own country. Over the course of the eighteenth and nineteenth centuries a second variant of fantastic literature, the Gothic novel, together with its stepchild the Victorian ghost story, became perhaps the first fictional literary form to penetrate popular culture.

The line between high and popular art has never been a distinct one, either in America or in Europe; they have functioned as a continuum, interconnected and fueling each other while crossing class, cultural, and geographical boundaries. The Faust legend, as we saw in Chapter 3, ricocheted from popular legend and puppet show to high drama and back to puppet show. The ballad "Riddles Wisely Expounded," as Tristram Coffin recounts, was "a British broadside [that] was freely translated into German by Herder, used by Goethe in an opera [*Die Fischerin*], retranslated into English, and thence went back into oral tradition to be picked up a half-century or more later in Maine." Before the nineteenth century arrived, America had its own domestic and richly diverse tradition of secular fantastic story in the form of Puritan "providences" (anecdotes that defied the ban on the miraculous by illustrating God's will at work in everyday life); tall tales (noted by Tocqueville); African conjure stories; and marvels and scandals retailed in a burgeoning mass press of newspapers, magazines, and chapbooks.

This rich storehouse of popular story and religious narrative, as David Reynolds has demonstrated, provisioned the great works of Melville, Hawthorne, Poe, Dickinson, Emerson, and others during the early nineteenth-century cultural moment known as the American Renaissance. In this "crucial watershed moment between the metaphysical past and the secular future, between the typological, otherworldly ethos of Puritanism and the mimetic, earthly world of literary realism," Reynolds comments, Emily Dickinson "discovered psychological, metaphorical reapplications of traditional religious forms and images. Poe progressed from early imitation of popular religious styles . . . to a nonreligious aesthetic which equated poetic effect with supernal beauty." The Transcendentalists were serious Neoplatonists; even the most casual reading of Emerson reveals very little daylight between his "Over-Soul" and Plotinus's World Soul. Walt Whitman's pronouncement "The priest departs, the divine literatus comes" was a fitting slogan for the first great flowering of American literature.

The postindigenous society known as "America" had begun, of course, as a religious idea initiated by English Puritans in the pivotal seventeenth century, and since these ideological beginnings it has remained a culture periodically swept by religious fervor and revivalism. The Great Awakening in the mid-eighteenth century was followed by at least three more, according to Robert Fogel: the second, at the turn of the nineteenth century, would spill over into the religio-philosophical event of Transcendentalism in high culture as well as countless popular manifestations, including the Spiritualist movement, Theosophy, and new religions and cults such as the Mormons, the very Gnostic Christian Scientists, and the Shakers. The third Great Awakening, Fogel says, occurred between 1890 and 1930, and we are still in the midst of the fourth, which began in the 1960s.

All this religion making took place in a cultural matrix that ultimately produced what Harold Bloom has called the "American Religion": a Gnostic strain idiosyncratic to this country, exemplified in Southern Baptism, Pentecostalism, and especially Mormonism, that mandates "self-divinizing" via the individual's direct encounter with the holy. Joseph Smith described his holy adventures novelistically in *The Book of Mormon* to produce, as John L. Brooke has shown, a distinctive Americanizing of late Renaissance theology that joined aspects of Hermeticism, Gnosticism, alchemy, and popular magic to produce a "fully developed" alternative to Christianity. And Smith, Bloom notes, linked his story to the Old Testament prophet Enoch, transformed in the angel Metatron, "giant in size, radiant with light . . . a preexistent cosmic anthropos, at once God, angel, and man." Shakerism was likewise a seventeenth-century English autodidact's replica of Gnosticism. (As we will see in Chapter 7, the content of American fantastic literature and film migrated back into new popular religions in the twentieth century.)

Even though the country had a rich supernatural—even apocalyptic—tradition in its popular religion, however, other cultural influences would severely limit the presence of the transcendental in the mainstream intellectual culture of the new republic, which was secular by state decree and pragmatic by virtue of its pioneer roots. This exaggerated split personality—an official Aristotelian culture containing a popular, often clandestine Neoplatonic subculture—is noticeable even in the American Constitution, with its unique aura of an untouchable, autonomous Divine Machine fashioned theurgically from the mechanistic rationalism of the eighteenth-century founding fathers. The result is a wildly contradictory cultural persona composed—as Reynolds emphatically characterizes it—of equal parts "*outward innocence and inner demonism.*"

In the twentieth century, fantastic literature would have sharply divergent fates in America and Europe. The Old World saw a resurgence of the fantastic in high culture: European antirepresentational literature, especially in France and Germany, served as vehicle of the continental avant-garde art movements such as Surrealism and Expressionism, as we will see in later chapters. In the United States, meanwhile, the supernatural with its distinctive post-1700 grotesque baggage became confined almost entirely to popular cultural forms. The sophisticated literary experimentation that continued through the rest of the twentieth century in continental Europe had no substantial counterpart in American high art. The fantastic would be defined solely in terms of content and framed as a tradition of "entertainments," the minor work of major authors, as it had traditionally been for Washington Irving or early Romantic imitators like Charles Brockden Brown, followed by Edith Wharton and Henry James a century later. With two exceptions—the maverick Ambrose Bierce and the master Henry James (whose *Turn of the Screw*, as discussed in Chapter 7, took the Gothic mode to its modernist apotheosis)—the Romantic/Transcendental that flourished briefly after Poe in Nathaniel Hawthorne's allegories and Herman Melville's epic romances had sunk from view in this country by the close of the nineteenth century.

At the same time, however, the currents of the popular sub-Zeitgeist were flowing even more strongly. Cheaper printing methods, along with the widening literacy of a growing national population, produced a flood of pulp periodicals devoted to the genre forms of detective stories (the form Poe himself is credited with inventing), cowboy stories, and horror and ghost stories. By the turn of the twentieth century, pulp fiction was about to embark on its own American Renaissance, a trend that is beautifully embodied in the work of two persons: Hawthorne's own son Julian, whose prolific output of fantasy, romance, and crime stories often appeared in the pulps, and H. P. Lovecraft, the horror writer of the 1920s and 1930s who remains Poe's only true literary heir in his own country.

Even more primal in the American sub-Zeitgeist than pulp fictions were the comic books. The mythic element in this huge cluster of story cycles about heroes with superpowers derived from the otherworld—Superman, Batman, Spiderman, and all the others—was not drawn from folklore or ancient myth but is completely original to its creators in the twentieth century. The comic book superheroes and superheroines possess all the powers pertaining to beings of the superior World of Forms, minus the obeisance to a Supreme Being—a state of affairs that suggests that these Divine Humans live in a higher-world democracy in which their only true counterparts are the supervillains they must battle. Under what the cartoonist

Jules Feiffer once wittily dubbed the "Minsk Theory of Krypton," these American Anthropoi were principally the creations of the Eastern European Jewish immigrants pouring into the country from the 1890s on. (Of what he considers the "ultimate assimilationist fantasy" about the benign alien possessing extraordinary powers, Feiffer says, "it wasn't Krypton that Superman really came from, it was the planet Minsk or Lodz or Wilna or Warsaw.") In the 1980s comic books began to be translated from children's reading and matinee serial fare to the medium of adult mass movies. Comic books themselves had always attracted a shifting adult readership—from the crude pornography of the earliest forms through the counterculture comics of the 1960s to the sophisticated "graphic novels" of the 1980s, such as *The Nightwatchman*, written by Alan Moore and drawn by Dave Gibbons, which feature an exaggerated cinematic style.

By the mid-twentieth century, the ghettoization of the American fantastic, first in pulp magazines and then in films and comic books, was complete. The domestic American fantastic (whose current hypostases include role-playing games, video games, and interactive Web entertainment as well) is now confined principally to three distinct popular genres: science fiction, horror, and fantasy. Meanwhile the form of realism, whose conventions of plot and characterization were well established by the end of the nineteenth century, has enjoyed, and continues to enjoy, its reign as the dominant mode for cultured American readers. In essence, what is labeled "serious" American prose fiction has remained mostly a static form for a century and a half.

How are we to explain this long love affair with realism, a mode of representation as artificial as any other, and no more "real"? One popular theory attributes it to the preeminence of journalism in this country and the circumstance that many serious writers, the iconic exempla being Mark Twain and Ernest Hemingway, began their careers as journalists. We should not use a symptom to explain a symptom, however. Within the post-Romantic, post-Transcendental rationalist Anglo-American philosophical and literary tradition, America is noted for its even more determined elevation of the pragmatic even as it also boasts the most outrageous sub-Zeitgeist of mass entertainment and cultic religions on the planet. The worship of the fact, of solid documentable information, is a reality of mainstream American culture. The religion of the empirical carries with it the strong impulse to rationalize the irrational, to dethrone and "manage" it—a tendency detectable even in Poe, who was, on the surface, an indefatigable ratiocinator not merely in his detective stories but in, for example, his prominent positioning of the bust of Pallas Athena in "The Raven." In his imaginative works, however—and this is a quintessential American contradiction—Poe always sabotaged his own rational constructs. As we will see in Chapter 7, the goddess of reason and wisdom is no match for a greasy-feathered black bird and the ancient tradition he brings with him through the window.

And it was not the influence of journalism that brought about the alteration of the English and Scottish ballads in their new home in America. In the migration of traditional folksongs to the rural United States, ghosts, elves, and goblins for the most part vanished; the American variants of these ancient songs contain far fewer elements of the supernatural. Fairy knights turned into cowboy drifters; an encounter between a knight, a giant, and his magic boar became a comic tale of a frontiersman killing a wild pig; and so on. This same process of rationalization and localization also took place in the British Isles as part of the social and economic transformation wrought by the industrial revolution and the complex transition from oral folk culture to mass popular culture, but the de-supernaturalizing of the old folklore during the nineteenth century is much more drastic and immediately visible in the United States, which lacked both a feudal past and the Walter Scott–driven impulse to Gothicize it.

Yet even though the supernatural was dramatically reduced in American ballads compared with their mostly Scottish sources, a subcategory of ballads about visitation or abduction by spirits (mostly angels) did flourish, though they were often not recorded by folklorists because of what was deemed to be their religious sentimentality. (On this groundwork the motif of the "extraterrestrial" would flourish in the next century.) A comparable censorship was maintained until recently in the venerable *New York Times* bestseller list, to which Christian apocalyptic fiction—which sells the most books of all in a country whose previous bestsellers of several centuries were the Bible, Milton's *Paradise Lost,* and John Bunyan's *The Pilgrim's Progress*—was only added in the year 1999.

The re-supernaturalizing of America's popular culture during the twentieth century stands in striking opposition to the secularizing, anti-transcendentalizing impetus of its high art. We can see the latter effect nicely embodied—if I may be permitted to use a first-generation citizen of

Polish Jewish extraction as an example—in the works of a single migrating author, Isaac Bashevis Singer. In the first portion of his career, while he still lived in Warsaw, Singer wrote fantastic tales of the *shtetl*, of witches, demons, revenants, and imps. After his flight to the United States in 1935, he produced a second, American oeuvre—sophisticated, sardonic tales of erotic encounters—that he immediately and dramatically purged of the fantastic.

Now it might be argued that the cataclysmic historical events in Europe, not the benign Enlightenment influence of Thomas Jefferson and the founding fathers, were the alchemical vessel that transformed Singer from a mystic folklorist into a bleak and mordant observer of erotic survivors, real-life revenants, *Landsmänner* from Galicia who sit in the Golden Cafeteria in Brooklyn, swapping domestic war stories of desperate lives. In his story "The Last Demon," Singer has his imp declare that all demons perished in the Katzets. Yet it is strikingly obvious that in America Singer went through his own micro-Enlightenment, drastically relocating and secularizing the source of what might be called "wonder"—that is, the supernatural, the irrational, the grotesque juxtaposition of forms and defiance of natural laws. No longer did he attribute this quality to external reality, as supernatural creatures or magical acts, an integral part of a coherent religious universe and a manifestation of God's inscrutable will; once in America, he situated wonder within the human temperament, characteristically expressing itself in the spontaneous, perverse, unpredictable course of amorous adventures.

Most mortals have difficulty holding citizenship in two realms of sensibility at the same time. If the American high-culture republic of the imagination characteristically rationalizes and pragmatizes, then novels of realism, serving as a kind of documentary adjunct to life, are the logical extension of this tendency. When Isaac Singer became an American, he renounced as well his former allegiance to his countryman and fellow fantasist Bruno Schulz's "republic of dreams." In place of imps and other supernatural creatures a series of "penitents" emerged, worldly erotomanes obsessed with (and never quite succeeding in) regaining Paradise by a reversion to Orthodox piety.

Just past midcentury, American literature witnessed another of the recurring revolts against its Aristotelian superstructure, a manifestation of the same latent mystic urge that had also fed into American Transcendentalism. During the fourth Great Awakening of the 1960s, ecstatic religion, communalism, utopianism, and related ideas spread through a relatively broad sector of the population just as they had a hundred and twenty years earlier. Briefly it seemed as if this new Transcendentalism, besides spawning a huge subgenre of Tolkien-derived fantasy novels along with visionary New Age tracts, might even work its way directly into serious literature. A native sort of highly intellectualized fantastic literature had already begun to develop in the works of John Barth, Donald Barthelme, and Thomas Pynchon along with such mavericks as John Hawkes, William Burroughs, Richard Brautigan, and Joseph Heller. Mainstream writers like John Cheever had introduced a modest vein of fantasy in their works, perhaps echoing the earlier forays into that region by F. Scott Fitzgerald (notably "A Diamond as Big as the Ritz"). These efforts, however, were still very much in the category of "entertainments," minor works by major writers; almost by definition no major native-born American writer of the twentieth century could be a fantasist. In a very different vein from Singer, another naturalized exile from Eastern Europe, Vladimir Nabokov, performed highly antirepresentational antics even as he worked within superficially realist conventions, exerting a profound stylistic influence on American writers and readers of the 1960s and 1970s. Nabokov's aesthetic Platonism, meanwhile, went unnoticed.

The mighty Mississippi of American popular culture had been fed early in the century by European Expressionism via art films and their American stepchild *film noir* (created in large part by émigré directors), a migration that will be examined in later chapters. Eastern European literature, theater, and film, meanwhile, had also provided some impetus for the small groundswell of antirealism during the 1960s: as they were exposed to the fantastic element in the work of high European directors like Bergman and Fellini, young Americans of this generation also took in the theater of the absurd and the experiments of such directors as Jerzy Grotowski and such Polish, Czech, and Russian films as Sergei Paradjanov's *Shadows of Forgotten Ancestors* (1964) or Jan Svankmajer's animated films or Wojciech Has's version of Jan Potocki's *The Saragossa Manuscript* (1965).

Through the 1980s echoes of this early schooling in the fantastic still popped up in unexpected places: the main character of Maxine Hong Kingston's quirky novel *Tripmaster Monkey* (1989), for example, is Whitman Ah Sing, a Chinese-American would-be beatnik of the Sixties obsessed with the plot details of *The Saragossa Manuscript.* Eventually, however, the spontaneous social and artistic upheavals of the 1960s transformed themselves into a variety of individual social movements—the women's movement, the ethnic minorities movements, the gay rights movement—that slowly instituted some very broad populist changes in American society (a transformation, it should be noted, that occurred under and despite increasingly conservative political administrations during the 1970s and 1980s). And it was here that the fantastic began to reappear, but only in the circumscribed modes of the "colonized" and exotic transcendent.

There was one area in which the educated American reader in the last two decades of the twentieth century could both accept and expect the antirepresentational or the fantastic, and that was as imported exotica: Latin American magic realism as exemplified by Gabriel García Márquez or the Central and Eastern European fantastic as represented by such writers as Milan Kundera as well as the obvious Kafka. To a lesser extent the fantastic was allowed in domestic writing either explicitly or implicitly labeled "ethnic": Toni Morrison could write a novel, *Beloved,* about a ghost, or Kingston could draw on Chinese legends (with the occasional Polish accent), because initially both writers were still regarded as the Other, not as the We, by the bulk of their mainstream middle-class white readers. The same could be said of any number of other ethnically identified writers, from Native American to Hispanic to Filipino. There is the obvious explanation that non-European cultures preserve richer traditions of the supernatural; at the same time, however, one senses the tendency of the publishing industry—not the writers themselves—to commodify these traditions as markers of ethnicity. (After 1990 categories of the "allowable" transcendent would began a subtle shift; see Chapter 9.)

Yet even as American theater and art continued to move in more experimental directions, the breadth and extent of the social rebellions of the 1960s and their aftermath worked to subvert the initial surge of avant-gardism in American fiction. In the long term, these social changes actually helped reinforce realism as a prevailing literary convention through the beginning of the 1990s. Of the innovators of that decade, only Thomas Pynchon (whose contribution to the polar romance mode will be explored in Chapter 6) continued to break new ground. How did this happen? The modest blossoming of experimentalism in American high literature, it might be argued, faded in the face of the pressing need, during the early 1970s, to identify and manage social change via fiction. With the preexisting bias toward the empirically verifiable fact creating a powerful backward pull into realism, the resulting plethora of socially emblematic novels were attempts to organize, explain, describe, and ultimately control the events of this confusing time.

And so there were novels about the transformed experience of women; novels about divorced families and stepfamilies; novels about minority experience, historical and contemporary; novels about the place of homosexuals in society. In fact, a whole new literature of realism had to be created to reexamine and redescribe social relationships, to imagine a new, enlarged society and thereby smooth the integration of these potentially explosive tendencies into mainstream American culture. Writers of the 1970s such as E. L. Doctorow who did attempt to introduce a mythic element into their work found their imaginations failing them and fell back, in a typically American way, on an uneasy hybrid of fiction and historical fact. Hailed as an innovative form, the docufiction—whether historical, as with Doctorow, or contemporary, as with the works of Norman Mailer and Truman Capote—still rested squarely within the conventions of journalism and realist fiction.

For a broader view, it is important to look at how the displaced longing for the transcendental functions in the larger framework of a mercantile society like ours, which values art primarily when it manages to achieve the status of economic commodity (or, failing that, of some readily promotable adjunct of national or cultural identity). This is a subject on which Walter Benjamin had something worthwhile to say: that the Patron to whom twentieth-century artists must make flattering obeisance is the middle class. Paradoxically, in literature this obeisance is also (and especially) performed by works of fiction depicting poverty, violence, exotic cultures, and the like, all of which serve as Object to the Patron's Subject. Literature subsidized by the middle class must appeal alternately to its voyeurism and its narcissism. Here is your mirror, and there is your shadow; both images serve the literate consumer's needs.

The aesthetics of the "culture of redemption," to use Leo Bersani's useful coinage, are thus particularly validated and reinforced by the conventions of realism. The market, after all, is essentially commissioning its self-portrait. Just as it is a touch classier to own a painting of oneself than a photograph, so does a fiction that presents a recognizable likeness flatter in a way a case study, a mere recital of facts, cannot. A piece of literature tailored to render faithfully the concerns of the day and mirror the lives of its readers "saves" those lives—a neat piece of secular religiosity—by transmuting them into art. By the very act of fictionalizing an ordinary life, art adds the ineffable dimension, the bogus promise of transfiguration; it efficiently organizes things-as-they-are and redeems them by that organization.

A WALK DOWN CROCODILE STREET

An instructive parable of the ways in which the fantastic tradition, so deeply influenced by Poe, reentered America via Eastern Europe is the example of Bruno Schulz, Isaac Singer's contemporary and our puppet tractate author of Chapter 3. Of the works of this Galician Jewish artist, writer, and high school teacher, two collections of stories, some essays and reviews, a few fragments of fiction, and a sizeable number of drawings survive. World War II ended Schulz's life, brutally—he was shot down on the street of his native Drohobycz by a Gestapo officer—and scattered the remainder of his manuscripts. Yet his small body of published work has managed, these five decades later, to seep into the consciousness of a handful of American writers and a larger number of readers in interesting ways.

Schulz's reputation in America grew slowly. His first collection of stories, *Sklepy Cynamonowe* (Cinnamon Shops), first appeared in English translation in the United Kingdom and was published in the United States in 1963 by Walker and Company. It is a wonderful if accidental irony of Schulz's publishing destiny that this book's retitling in the English-speaking world as *The Street of Crocodiles*—done because the book was printed in Poland to save money and the title *Cinnamon Shops* was on the communist authorities' proscribed list—represents a subtle shift of emphasis that directs our eyes away from the sweet-smelling spice shops in the old quarter of Drohobycz to that shady, ephemeral new sector where "Pseudo-Americanism" reigns supreme in a "rich but empty and colorless vegetation of vulgarity."

The Street of Crocodiles was to gain no significant notice until its reissue a decade later in the Penguin paperback series "Writers from the Other Europe" under the general editorship of Philip Roth. Publication in this series was crucial to the book's subsequent distribution and modest succès d'estime. In a 1977 *New York Times* review Cynthia Ozick—of whom more shortly—dubbed Schulz "one of the most original literary imaginations of modern Europe." Voicing the impact of his dark sensibility on the congenital optimism of the American reader, Ozick cited Babel, Schulz and Kafka and asked, almost in outrage: "Why should these cultivated Slavic Jews run into the black crevices of nihilism, animism, hollow riddle?" During the same year three of Schulz's stories—"Loneliness," "Sanatorium under the Sign of the Hourglass," and "Father's Last Escape"—were published in the *New Yorker*, further legitimating his mainstream status.

In 1978, following the paperback success of *The Street of Crocodiles*, Walker and Company published for the first time the translation of Schulz's second book of stories, *Sanatorium pod Klepsydra* (Sanatorium under the Sign of the Hourglass), which promptly appeared in the Penguin paperback series the following year, this time with an introduction by John Updike. Thus, and supplementing the indefatigable international efforts of his Polish editor, Jerzy Ficowski, two eminent American writers, Roth and Updike, played a critical role in the introduction of Bruno Schulz to American readers. Polish émigré literary figures such as Jan Kott, Ewa Kuryluk, and Stanislaw Baranczak did further service as Schulz's cultural mediators in America.

How did an esoteric fantasist manage to gain a toehold in a foreign literary culture known for its century and a half of virtually unquestioning loyalty to the tenets of realism in high art? Certainly not by the resemblance of his works to those of anyone known to American readers—the non-Yiddish-speaking Schulz's stories are, for example, utterly different from Singer's *shtetl* wonder tales in drawing virtually nothing from traditional Jewish folklore; his Neoplatonic-cabbalistic mythos is a strikingly original invention; and though his literary feats of metempsychosis include the conversion of a human into a cockroach, Schulz's sensibility is also utterly removed from that of his slightly older contemporary Franz Kafka of Prague. What Schulz fits perfectly, however, is the category of European high-art grotesque. In accordance with Arthur Clayborough's succinct definition of the grotesque as the "combining of heterogeneous forms," the literary equivalent of Horace's "hybrid monsters," the juxtaposition of discordant images (and even clauses) in writers like Schulz and his contemporary the early Surrealist Raymond Roussel becomes a way of breaking down an empirical perception of reality.

Roussel's tactic, Michel Foucault says, was "to join beings across the greatest distances of the cosmos (the earthworm and the musician, the rooster and the writer, the heart of a loaf of bread and marble, tarot cards and phosphorus); to join incompatible elements (the water line and the thread of material, chance and the rules, infirmity and virtuosity, puffs of smoke and the mass of a sculpture)." Schulz joins opposite concepts or images in much the same way. In "The Comet" a character turns into an insistently ringing doorbell; in another story the same character is transformed by a long illness into the rubber tubing of an enema bag. Of Schulz's cultic animism of everyday objects, John Updike argues, "Personal experience taken cabbalistically: This formula fits much modern fiction and, complain though we will, is hard to transcend. Being ourselves is the one religious experience we all have." At the same time Updike cannot ignore the perfervid, compensatory intensity of these images: "Limited, in a scientific age that has redefined verification, to incidents he has witnessed, to the existence he has lived minute by drab minute, the writer is driven to magnify, and the texture of magnification is bizarre." Schulz, we will see, is a perfect example of a *gnosis* sensibility laboring outside the framework of traditional religion and striving—at times too hard—to find a home in an *episteme* age.

Because no equivalent mainstream category exists in the United States, Schulz's high-art supernatural grotesque could be grandfathered in as literature of exotica, subcategory imported. Eastern European fantastic literature and South American magic realism have been granted entry to the mainstream canon because their antirealistic vision can be clearly labeled "alien" in cultural as well as literary terms. In fact, the terms under which Schulz's work received a favorable endorsement from American literary culture highlight the often arbitrary and superficial ways in which authors are transplanted into another language and culture. Americans are great packagers, and literary figures are no exception to this compulsion. The first packaging category is premature death: since the Romantic era an artist whose life is dramatically cut short tends to exercise a stronger appeal on the reader's imagination than those with the good fortune to lead long, uneventful lives.

Next, by extension—even though Schulz's surviving fiction predates the events of World War II and is utterly removed from its issues—comes the category of Holocaust literature. Jerzy Kosinski's *The Painted Bird* (1965), cast as a kind of Boschean nightmare, was the first of such works Americans encountered that was neither a sober work of realism nor a memoir of the Anne Frank type. That novel paved the way for later works in translation, from Tadeusz Borowski's *This Way for the Gas, Ladies and Gentlemen* (1967) and other antirealistic literature of the Holocaust to novels by the Israeli authors Aaron Appelfeld and David Grossman (who used Bruno Schulz as a character in his 1989 novel *See Under: Love*). The Holocaust became an acceptable area for the fantastic in the English-speaking world if only because the experience of the camps defied one's sense of what could happen in real life. American and English writers were thereby given a limited mandate to use the fantastic mode in their own works on that subject, as witness the popularity of D. M. Thomas's *The White Hotel* (1981) and—in an interesting example of crossover from the always hardier American popular sub-Zeitgeist culture of the fantastic— of *Maus I* (1987) and *Maus II* (1991), Art Spiegelman's comic book memoir of his parents' experience at Auschwitz, cast as a cat-and-mouse fable.

Finally, an author can be assimilated more easily by a literary audience if he or she is explicitly linked with one or more prominent colleagues or forebears. In Schulz's case came the inevitable comparisons with Kafka, though in both aesthetics and sensibility Schulz, who had read deeply in German literature and also wrote at least one long story in that language, stands far closer to Hoffmann and the German Romantic grotesque. Both the link with Kafka and the simultaneous refutation of that link have been features of Schulz's reputation virtually from the time his first book of stories was published in Poland, and this ambiguous connection was continued in America to good effect in a comment by Isaac Singer, quoted on the cover of the paperback edition of *The Street of Crocodiles*, that Schulz "wrote sometimes like Kafka, sometimes like Proust, and at times succeeded in reaching depths that neither of them reached." In his perceptive introduction to *Sanatorium under the Sign of the Hourglass*, John Updike took up Singer's Kafka-Proust comparison, refuted it with qualifications, and likened Schulz instead to Jorge Luis Borges as a "cosmographer without a theology."

By the end of the 1980s, Bruno Schulz had gained an American audience. When the collection *Letters, Drawings and Selected Prose* appeared in 1988, reviewers treated Schulz as a major international literary figure—though always, significantly, describing him as "unknown" and "neglected." The truly neglected, of course, are not reviewed on the front pages of the *Times Literary Supplement*, the *New York Times Book Review*, and the *New York Review of Books*. It is important, nevertheless, that they be conceptualized as such when they are discussed in these venues, for this is possibly the most effective packaging category of all.

Since Schulz gained his entree, however, his influence on American writers and readers—like that of other Eastern European fabulists—has been perhaps more subtle and more extensive than we might gauge merely from the testimony of the literary reviewing industry. In an attempt to incorporate an alternative vision into the relentlessly pragmatic aesthetics of their own literary culture, a few American writers and filmmakers have experimented with explicit imitations and homages relating to the Central and Eastern European fantastic. While remaining committed realists in their own fiction, for example, Roth and Updike shared a strong fascination for the idiosyncratic figures of this more or less Slavic, more or less Jewish literary territory—Roth for Kafka and Updike for Nabokov and Schulz—that led them to try their hand in the mythic, antirepresentational mode.

Roth, whose brief flirtations with the fantastic are reminiscent of Schulz's own guilty attraction to the Street of Crocodiles, gave us, in a 1972 entertainment, a professor of English who has turned into an enormous female breast. The cause of this transformation is a mystery, but the professor offers his doctor one hypothesis: "It might be my way of *being* a Kafka, being a Gogol, being a Swift. They could *envision* those marvelous transformations—they were artists. They had the language and those obsessive fictional brains. I didn't. So I had to live the thing." In this open imitation of "The Metamorphosis," Roth's competitive narrator tries to claim he's gone farther than the great artist: "So I took the leap. Beyond sublimation. I made the word flesh. I have out-Kafkaed Kafka. He could only *imagine* a man turning into a cockroach. But look what I have done."

This playful work is clearly intended as a tourist excursion into the fantastic; for a more thoroughgoing example of influence, we must look to the fictions and essays of Cynthia Ozick. Via the connecting link of Jewish folklore and cabbalistic tradition, Ozick brings a masterly prose style and a highly original imagination to bear on the problems of transposing materials of the Eastern European fantastic into the context of her own deeply American vision. A remarkable long story called "Puttermesser and Xanthippe" (1982), second in a quintet of stories sharing the same main character (published together in 1997 as *The Puttermesser Papers: A Novel*), deserves our attention first. Though Ozick had read Schulz before writing this tale of a female golem created by a woman, the overriding influence is clearly that of the Hebrew scholar and cabbala authority (and, at the same time, upholder of *episteme*) Gershom Scholem. Whereas Schulz's mannequins in his stories on tailors' dummies are not golems (though they partake, as we have seen, of the underlying principles of this tradition), Ozick draws directly from folkloric conventions of the organic artificial human. Unlike Schulz's dummies, her golem or "female moloch" is a double, a personal ally, not an object. But like Adela, the golem eludes control.

Ruth Puttermesser, a lawyer working in the bowels of New York City's municipal bureaucracy, has just been demoted in a shift of political favors among higher-ups. Alone, forty, powerless, childless and regretting her childlessness, she returns to her shabby apartment one day to find an unfinished-looking creature made of clay lying in her bed. On the creature's tongue is a piece of paper printed with the three Hebrew letters *Ha-Shem*, "the Name"—Ozick's pious euphemism for the four letters of the Tetragrammaton, the Name of Names traditionally written on this paper that, indeed, brings the golem to life when Puttermesser pronounces them.

As a patriotic American Puttermesser at first objects vehemently to the golem's presence, protesting that she

> was no mystic, enthusiast, pneumaticist, ecstatic, kabbalist. Her mind was clean; she was a rationalist . . . She was not at all attached to any notion of shade or specter, however corporeal it might appear, and least of all to the idea of a golem . . . What transfixed her was the type of intellect (immensely sober, pragmatic, unfanciful, rationalist like her own) to which a golem ordinarily occurred—occurred, that is, in the shock of its true flesh and absolute being.

In Puttermesser's view, Rabbi Judah Loew of Prague and the other legendary golem makers were not "misty romantics" but "scientific realists" who had come up with the golem as a sensible way of protecting Jews against violence and persecution in an atmosphere of rampant urban corruption and decay. Therefore, our good Yankee decides—and quite in line with Gershom Scholem's rehabilitation of this tradition—there is nothing in the least irrational about owning a golem, and she is able to admit for the first time that she made the creature herself, out of the dirt in her potted plants.

Before long the mute golem, who communicates on scraps of paper and has named herself Xanthippe (because "Xanthippe alone had the courage to gainsay Socrates"), has given Puttermesser a "PLAN," a vision of Paradise Ozick tells us is traditionally associated with golems—but in this case, for the high-minded rationalist Puttermesser, her golemic double has come up with a blueprint for civic reform, a vision of a new Manhattan rising from the ashes. Elected mayor of New York on an independent reform ticket thanks to the golem's relentless talent for organization, Puttermesser is able to transform the city into a place of peace and beauty. Inevitably, however, things go awry; Xanthippe, growing physically ever larger as golems must, cannot keep her sexual appetite under control, and scandals proliferate. In the end Puttermesser is obliged to perform the reverse rite that returns the golem to earth. Xanthippe ends up as a large mound of geraniums in Central Park, and we are left with Puttermesser to contemplate the possibility that too much Paradise is also a kind of greed.

In contrast to this story—but with some noteworthy parallels as well—Ozick's novella *The Messiah of Stockholm*, published in 1987, is a self-conscious homage to Schulz. One of his many self-portraits serves as the frontispiece, and the novella is dedicated to Philip Roth. The book's epigraph is Schulz's description of the animism of matter and "secondary creation" in the "Tailors' Dummies" stories:

> "There is no dead matter," [Father] taught us, "lifelessness is only a disguise behind which hide unknown forms of life. The range of these forms is infinite and their shades and nuances limitless. The Demiurge was in possession of important and interesting creative recipes. Thanks to them, he created a multiplicity of species which renew themselves by their own devices. No one knows whether these recipes will ever be reconstructed. But this is unnecessary, because even if the classical methods of creation should prove inaccessible for evermore, there still remain some illegal methods, an infinity of heretical and criminal methods."

As we saw in Chapter 3, this madman's assertion could be placed without a single alteration in the mouth of a fourth-century Alexandrian theurge. In its prominence here, however, the statement is transformed into Ozick's ironical comment on the "tertiary creation," drawn from Schulz, that her novella represents.

The protagonist of *The Messiah of Stockholm* is a down-at-heel Swedish book reviewer, Lars Andemening, whose face bears the "unfinished" look, significantly, shared by Puttermesser's golem. An orphan, he chose his name, he tells us, from the dictionary—and I, consulting the same Swedish-English dictionary Cynthia Ozick herself no doubt did, can tell you that "Andemening" means "spirit" or "inward sense." Moreover, "Lars," though a common Swedish male name, may contain some distant echoes of the Latin *laris*, or household deity, one of those small but powerful statues presiding over the pagan Roman hearth, or even one of the earthly gods that the Corpus Hermeticum describes. This self-created human nourishes the secret conviction that he is the son of Bruno Schulz, smuggled out of Poland as an infant to stay with relatives of his mother in Stockholm.

Obsessed with a possible real-life lost manuscript of Schulz's (enigmatically entitled *The Messiah*), Lars through his confidante, a German bookseller named Heidi, is put in touch with a mysterious young woman with the evocative name "Adela," the Schulz family servant in real life and Father's prime obstructer in Schulz's tales. Claiming to be Lars's half-sister through Schulz (her mother, she says, was his student and model), Adela produces a handwritten copy of what she claims is *The Messiah*, which she allows Lars to read.

As her story within a story, Ozick now describes an invented Messiah in the spirit of Schulz, but one strongly rooted in her own imaginative universe as well. The Messiah, she tells us, is a universe called Drohobycz that is inhabited not by humans but by idols: idols of all sorts, "plump Buddhas," "mammoth Easter Island heads," "large stone birds." Since there are no humans in Drohobycz to worship the idols, they must worship and sacrifice to one another. This practice leads to chaos, and the idols burn one another up in a "frenzy of mutual adoration." At this point the Messiah itself arrives—an entity "alive, organic, palpitating with wild motion and disturbance—yet not like a robot, not like a machine." It emerges from the empty cellar of the Drohobycz synagogue, where formerly a very old man named Moses the Righteous One slept on a huge bundle of hay.

The idols believe the Messiah is composed of this very "hay" (cabbalistic pun intended), but, says Ozick, of course it is not: it most resembles a marvelous Book, fashioned of humble materials and possessing winglike flippers displaying a strange cuneiform script that makes them resemble tattooed petals. This curious artifact gives birth to a small bird bearing a strand of the precious hay whose touch dissolves humans and idols alike into sparks, scouring Drohobycz of everything and leaving "empty shops and empty houses, and the flecks of sparks fading to ash."

In her essays Ozick has shown herself, after the bidding of the Second Commandment, an ardent smasher of idols, which she defines as "anything that is allowed to come between ourselves and God. Anything that is *instead of* God." She has stated that "the chief characteristic of any idol is that it is a system sufficient in itself. It leads back only to itself. It is indifferent to the world and to humanity. Like a toy or like a doll—which, in fact, is what an idol is—it lures human beings to copy it, to become like it. It dehumanized . . . Every idol is a shadow of Moloch, demanding human flesh to feed on . . . When art is put in competition, like a God, with the Creator, it too is turned into an idol." Idols are the creations of human beings; they are, in a word, no more than golems, and subject to the terrifying limitations of these creatures. Who would be so foolish as to worship a golem? In *The Messiah of Stockholm* Ozick appears to be smashing the incipient Neoplatonic "idolatry" that Schulz engages in—not simply the female molochs that are the tailors' dummies but his blasphemous assumption that as an artist he operates as a demiurge capable of divinizing an infinitely malleable imaginary universe. To worship the products of art, Ozick says, is to worship toys.

On close inspection, Ozick's hypothetical Messiah thus proves to be an alternative Gnostic-Jewish universe in which she has created—her caveat on demiurgy notwithstanding—a set of mythopoeic symbols drawn in equal parts from folklore, cabbala, and her own imagination. The "huge bundle of hay" on which the archetypal patriarch sleeps in the cellar of the Drohobycz synagogue—itself suggestive of a collective Jewish unconscious—bears some resemblance to *H'* (pronounced "hey"), the first letter and abbreviated form of Ha-Shem, "the Name." Mimicking the human tendency to confuse the concrete and material with what lies behind them, the overliteral idols naturally mistake the hay for God Himself. But Ozick suggests that the Messiah is not a Divine Human but a Divine Book, a living entity that breathes, flies, has a life of its own. We might suppose this tattooed, beflippered being to be none other than the mysterious concept of Torah, no static text but a living system that expands and replaces itself, an organic process of self-renewal that goes on even to the present day. The small bird it spawns (surely Noah's dove?) has a bit of the magical hay in its beak that turns the idols to dust in a satisfying Fourth of July finale, a display of cabbalistic *scintillae*, or sparks of the divine light.

In her 1977 review of *The Street of Crocodiles* Ozick had this to say of Bruno Schulz's animistic universe presided over by a profane "Demiurgy" that forms and deforms the *prima materia:* "What is being invented in the very drone of our passive literary expectation is Religion—not the taming religion of theology and morality, but the brute splendor of rite, gesture, phantasmagoric mortification, repugnance, terror, cult. The religion of animism, in fact, where everything comes alive with an unpredictable and spiteful spirit force, where even living tissue contains ghosts, where there is no pity."

Yet even as she repudiates it, in other areas Ozick's thinking shows profound similarities to Schulz's. In an essay entitled "The Mythologizing of Reality," Bruno Schulz had pronounced: "We usually regard the word as the shadow of reality, its symbol. The reverse of this statement would be more correct: reality is the shadow of the word. Philosophy is actually philology, the deep, creative exploration of the word." Ozick echoes this profoundly Platonic assumption in more conventionally cabbalistic terms—that is, the idea of language as a mystic code in which every word and even every letter partakes of arcane meaning—when she has her protagonist speculate, in a previous Puttermesser story, on the "stunning mechanism" of the Hebrew verb: "Three letters, whichever fated three, could command all possibility simply by a change in their pronunciation, or the addition of a wing-letter fore and aft. Every conceivable utterance blossomed from this trinity. It seemed to [Puttermesser] not so much a language for expression as a code for the world's design, indissoluble, predetermined, translucent." Here Ozick seems to be granting the Hebrew language, in itself and without mention of a divine source, demiurgical powers of secondary creation; philosophy has indeed become philology. This notion of the Perfect Language, magical artifact of the World of Forms, we have seen already and will meet many times again in the course of this book.

Is Ozick's magic flying tattooed Book, then, a reformed and sanitized monotheistic vision she bestows on Schulz, is it meant as further criticism of Schulz's heretical animism, or does it constitute a new heresy in itself? A more informed religious perspective than mine must answer this question.

Nevertheless, Ozick's "secondary" Messiah allows her to give a profoundly moral resolution to what she considers the central dilemma of Bruno Schulz's cosmos—and, by extension, to defuse the intensity of the spell Drohobycz's second creator has cast on Lars (and possibly on herself). After Lars reads the amazing document that tells of these wonders, he decides it is a forgery and impulsively burns the manuscript. Somehow, though, this ambiguous experience has the effect of transforming him and the other "refugee imposters." Though the true identities of all the characters remain shifting and ephemeral, slowly Lars's own idolatry subsides and he adopts a more "normal" life.

There is a sense, finally, in which *The Messiah of Stockholm* may be slightly overheated in its rhetoric and trivialized by its frame of a literary treasure hunt—why is the child's dream of a "lost" something always more enticing than what survives?—played out in the dubious shadow of the Swedish Academy and its Nobel Prize, also the object of Lars's uncritical worship. But the layers and undertones of authorial invention, the rich density of Ozick's style and what might be called her metaphysical intelligence make this novella a remarkable achievement: not a literary jest, like Roth's version of Kafka, but a work deeply integrated into her major artistic themes.

Bruno Schulz's second major American redactor consists not of one person but two. These are the Brothers Quay, twins living and working in England, whose 1984 puppet film *Street of Crocodiles* draws on the central images of the stories to re-represent the magical, industrialized Gothic universe of Schulz's Drohobycz. With nothing whatever in it identifiably "American," this nonlinear narrative is a virtually perfect re-creation of eastern European style and mood. Using headless mannequins, dolls with glowing eye sockets, a red-haired Bruno puppet, and repeating and uninterpretable ritual movements performed by inorganic objects that have come perversely and obscurely to life, Timothy and Steven Quay have, like Ozick, forged their own brilliantly original variation on Schulzian themes.

Via the Quays, whose films are widely shown in college art film houses as well as on television by (among others) the performance artist Laurie Anderson, Bruno Schulz in a small way entered the American youth pop subculture. This mass exposure may explain why a young blonde woman dressed entirely in black came up to me after a reading in Tucson to declare unequivocally that Bruno Schulz was her hero. I like to think that this adulation would have given Schulz, had he lived to hear it, a lot more pleasure than a mere literary prize. And it gives rise to a final, irresistible speculation: What if Schulz himself, his complex resistance to leaving his native turf overcome at last, had washed ashore in America instead of meeting his dark fate at home? Because we are a country of immigrants and unexpected destinies, Americans are very much given to wondering about such possibilities. Philip Roth once beautifully imagined an exile's fate for Kafka in America: in 1942 he is none other than the fifty-nine-year-old Hebrew teacher of the precocious Philip, whose imitations of the shy, withdrawn former lawyer convulse his friends. In this alternative universe, Dr. Kafka dies at the age of seventy in a local sanatorium; because there is no Max Brod in Newark, New Jersey, his papers disappear and there is no author Franz Kafka, either.

This scenario possesses an eerie and easily transferable accuracy: in Roth's spirit of *imitatio*, I give you Bruno, slaving away the war years in the art department of a Newark—or Brooklyn—public high school, heading for the same septuagenarian's oblivion. But wait. The ladies of the local B'nai B'rith decide to hold an art show to raise money for war relief. The modest high school teacher donates a sheaf of drawings, some of which are rather daring, but since the artist is a refugee himself and the cause is a good one, they are accepted. The officials of Newark/Brooklyn, however, do not take such a benign view of "The Book of Idolatry." The exhibit is closed, the exhibitors charged under the obscenity statutes. In the wake of the enormous publicity generated by the scandal, various alert national magazines quickly translate and publish Schulz's Polish tales; at the war's close, Maurice Girodias buys the rights to publish the drawings in France.

By such devices Schulz's international reputation is made—a good thirty years ahead of schedule, and with its possessor alive and fully able to relish it. Except, in this not so very alternative universe, Schulz would have found himself presented by his American packagers not as Kafka's nephew but as a dashing, naughty figure rather on the order of Aubrey Beardsley, a droll eroticist who scribbled quaint little *feuilletons* in his spare time. And in this de-formation of his identity Bruno Schulz might have uncovered the same truth Vladimir Nabokov was to meet a few years later—that in America an artist's path to fame lies only down Crocodile Street.

Meanwhile, not as antirepresentational high art or literary fiction but in all the garish store displays on this same American boulevard of trash, the realm I call the sub-Zeitgeist—that strange disposal area of paperbacks, comic books, movies, video games, and the World Wide Web, not quite folklore and not quite consumer product, where the slickest and the most rejected leitmotivs in our culture flourish side by side—the homegrown supernatural in America continued to proliferate like a happy weed.

Hollywood films after the year 1970 (in another ripple effect of the Golden Age of the psychedelic-mystic 1960s) began to follow the lead of the unabashedly mythic American comic books in dispensing altogether with the temporizing influence of Pallas Athena. Previously, even in the pulps, the fantastic was frequently explained as a delusion, or a dream, or the attempt by one character to trick another character into believing he is losing his mind. American movies of the post–*Star Wars* era, in contrast, display a series of interesting, sophisticated, ironic images. The decade of the 1980s saw, for example, an angry Babylonian god trapped in a New York apartment refrigerator, without benefit of rationalizing frame, in Ivan Reitman's *Ghostbusters* (1984), written by Dan Ackroyd and Harold Ramis; it saw the postmodern mannequin-dead in Tim Burton's *Beetlejuice* (1988), written by Burton and Caroline Thompson; it saw the Jan Svankmajer and Brothers Quay flavor of the same director's story of the tragic metal-boy *Edward Scissorhands* (1990), written by Michael McDowell. Shapeshifting and trans- and de-formation were increasingly common features, though mostly with the typically American emphasis on the technological rather than the metaphysical dimension of these phenomena.

By the beginning of the 1990s, American genre literature of the fantastic had become, through films, a popular and acceptable mainstream mode with an enormous and enthusiastic audience among younger Americans of both sexes. Doris Lessing, who crossed the line herself in the 1980s from realistic fiction to a series of science fiction and fantasy novels, pointed early on to this great underground shift in taste: that a substantial portion of younger people in English-speaking countries no longer read realistic literature, that science fiction of the 1940s and 1950s was a new and significant wrinkle in traditional storytelling, and that the chasm between older and younger audiences was absolute. This is a huge gap in reader sensibility that critics of high literature and mass culture alike still do not take into account, failing to recognize that for a very large and intelligent audience science fiction, horror, and fantasy are not a failure to acquire culture but a deliberate aesthetic choice. To most of these young people the doors of the treasure house of realist literature, a realm they perceive as one of stale and precious autobiographical journalism, are closed.

In this *fin-de-siècle* vacuum of literary experimentation, featuring a highly materialist, representational aesthetics firmly committed to holding the mirror up to nature on one hand and a thriving comic book/paperback/movie/Web subculture of the supernatural on the other, what sorts of high-art works should we be looking for? By the end of the 1980s a few small but significant signs of change were pointing in Platonic directions that will be explored in later chapters. One humble but telling extratextual signpost uniting the two American literary sensibilities—realist/high and fantastic/low—can be noted here. In a characteristically confusing mix of high-end marketing tactics and sub-Zeitgeist sensibility, it was constructed anonymously by commercial graphic artists brought in during the 1980s to ramp up the jacket art of literary novels in America in much the same way that talented young filmmakers were subverted to MTV.

The result, in both cases, was works whose look, if not content, was often surprisingly avant-garde. (Before, between the dignified typography and/or middlebrow kitsch of trade publishers and the low-budget black-and-white modernist asceticism of avant-garde publishers like New Directions, there had been little to choose from.) A trendy farce about divorcing television personalities sported a portrait of the duo, riven by a single arrow, worthy of Max Ernst; the cover of a collection of *Bildungsroman* stories by an up-and-coming young writer boasted a striking upside-down photographic image, reminiscent of Man Ray, of a figure diving out of, rather than into, the water; and so on for endless variations. But a reader could most emphatically not judge the books in question by their jackets. In their aesthetic assumptions these newly sophisticated, exaggeratedly antirealistic covers were diametrically opposed to the works they illustrated; in visual and metaphysical adventurousness they were light-years ahead. During the next decade this trend continued, and intensified, in the ever more commercialized and consolidated world of literary publishing.

What to make of this comical discontinuity between image and word, between the aesthetics of the cover and the aesthetics of the fiction inside? Something new was clearly happening in our uncertain millennial age, and typically it was starting in the visual arts. "Postmodernism" has become a generic catch-all label for anything new, but the movement itself has always been a backward commentary on the past, not a viable future direction. The correct term here is New Expressionism, and we will meet this sensibility in its first post-1990 incarnations in later chapters.

In the best tradition of that movement, meanwhile, these jacket wrappers are still laboring to transform their unpromising contents. In time, when they have worked their full osmotic influence, the metamorphosis will be compete and Americans will have a new kind of imaginative literature, one that embraces high and low in the spirit of the American Renaissance. At the new century's beginning, after many young Americans of the 1990s traveled to Prague, Budapest, Warsaw, and Lodz to study art and film at a very favorable rate of exchange, our countryman Poe, in a much mutated form, has been brought home with them from his European exile at last. A premature burial, indeed.

"I looked out over the squalid sea of roofs below me." From H. P. Lovecraft, "The Shadow over Innsmouth" (1936), illustration by Frank A. Utpatel. Courtesy Brown University Library.

"Radiates, vegetables, monstrosities, star spawn—whatever they had been, they were men!"

—H. P. Lovecraft

FIVE

H. P. LOVECRAFT AND THE GREAT HERESIES

The real story of Edgar Allan Poe's journey home begins in the early twentieth century with the works of his much-maligned grandnephew (and exact contemporary of Bruno Schulz), the New England horror writer H. P. Lovecraft.

"Four Corners" is a bit of generic roadside slang for that fixed point in the landscape where a quaternity of boundaries meet. There is a similar nexus within the human psyche where three territories rigorously fenced off from one another by post-1700 Western intellectual culture—philosophy, religion, psychology—converge with a fourth, the secular territory of *imagine.* Only a handful of literary maps to this inner "region of the Great Heresies," as Schulz dubbed it, were drawn during the past century of modernism-postmodernism. Those I wish to examine here belong to Lovecraft, that consummate grotto chronicler, with cartographic glosses provided by Schulz and a notable madman named Daniel Paul Schreber.

THE OUTCAST OF THE UNIVERSE

"I know always that I am an outsider; a stranger in this century and among those who are still men." So speaks the reclusive narrator of Lovecraft's story "The Outsider," which reaches its climax in the split second when this nameless character understands that the horrific shambling creature approaching him down the hall of a strange castle is an image in a never-before encountered object: a mirror. A century earlier, the outcast of Nathaniel Hawthorne's "Wakefield," a man who abandoned wife and home for a twenty-year exile from the quotidian, had always the option, in his voluntary limbo apart from humanity, of returning to "normality." This was an opportunity that Lovecraft, a writer some of his followers consider the heir of Hawthorne, Melville, and Poe, never viewed as available to him.

Howard Phillips Lovecraft was born in 1890 in the port city of Providence, Rhode Island, the only child of a silver salesman who was declared legally insane when Howard was three. Five years later the father died, in an institution, of paresis (the medical diagnosis of tertiary syphilis), and Howard and his mother moved in with his wealthy maternal grandparents for the rest of his childhood and early adolescence. The family fortunes collapsed at his grandfather's death when Howard was fourteen, after which the young Lovecraft lived a secluded life with his mentally disturbed mother. He withdrew increasingly from the world; ill-defined health problems in childhood and a self-described nervous breakdown during adolescence allowed him to skip regular school attendance, and he did not attempt college. During World War I, at age twenty-seven, he tried to join the Rhode Island national guard, but he was rejected after his mother intervened with authorities. His mother was institutionalized in 1919 and died in confinement two years later. Shortly thereafter Lovecraft contracted a brief, unsuccessful marriage with Sonia Greene, an older woman who was an admirer of his stories, and they settled in Manhattan. Within two years they separated; he returned to Providence to live with an elderly aunt. In 1937, at age forty-seven, he died of intestinal cancer.

During his short life Lovecraft produced the body of horror stories and novellas (some sixty-eight of his own composition, plus poetry and nonfiction) for which he is famous. He was as well an avid "amateur journalist"; a participant in a large informal network of aspiring writers who published their own magazines and corresponded through national clubs; a prolific letter writer (over 5,000 pages in typescript survive); and a reviser (for tiny sums) of other people's manuscripts. As a result, besides Lovecraft's own work there is a corpus of mediocre stories, under the names of other authors, that also bear the Lovecraftian stamp. The identities of Lovecraft and his "host" writers in these tales are so merged that, as with one of Lovecraft's own monsters, it is impossible to tell where the body of one leaves off and that of the other begins. A similar fate awaited some of Lovecraft's unfinished stories after he died, when August Derleth and other writers engaged in "posthumous collaborations" based on notes Lovecraft had left or simply used Lovecraft's unique fictional universe as a matrix for their own tales.

The stories—Lovecraft's own and those he ghostwrote—were published in the pulp magazines that are the Ur-source of twentieth-century American popular literature and film. In part because his work appeared in these venues and never in established literary journals, Lovecraft is traditionally regarded as a marginal figure outside the canon of serious American literature. The best-known high-critical judgment was passed by Edmund Wilson, who declared, "The only real horror in most of the fictions is the horror of bad taste and bad art." In spite of a surge of critical interest that began in the 1970s, the mainstream American assessment of Lovecraft's stories remains the same: it is fodder for young adolescent males, what older brothers read aloud to their younger brothers in hope of frightening them out of their wits.

Lovecraft's chief literary influence, the author he venerated as his "god of Fiction" in much the same way that Bruno Schulz revered Rilke as his literary father, was Edgar Allan Poe. Like Poe, Lovecraft produced tale after tale of monsters erupting from the regions of *Unrat* in defiance of his own staunchly held materialist views. An erudite autodidact, he adopted both the style and the rationalist stance of the Enlightenment; like Schulz, he also drew heavily from the Aesthetic tradition of his birth decade. This tension between eighteenth- and nineteenth-century worldviews and literary styles within a single twentieth-century writer is one of the special charms of Lovecraft's stories.

Other strong influences on Lovecraft's work were the fantasists Lord Dunsany and Arthur Machen, whose presence (especially Dunsany's) dominates his stories virtually from the day he began reading them until the point, a few years later, when he smoothly integrated some of their features into his own inimitable style and voice. In "Supernatural Horror in Fiction," a lengthy essay written and frequently revised between 1925 and 1927, Lovecraft sketched the development of the Gothic in the kind of careful detail that shows his high awareness both of the tradition and of his own place in it.

The deeper source of inspiration for Lovecraft was no literary forebear but rather, as it was for Bruno Schulz, his own childhood dreams and obsessions. Schulz once wrote to the playwright S. I. Witkiewicz of a few key images from childhood, such as the figure of Death in Goethe's "Erlkönig," that set the tone for his creative life: "These early images mark out to artists the boundaries of their creative powers. The works they create represent drafts on existing balances. They do not discover anything new after that, they only learn how to understand better and better the secret entrusted to them at the outset." Lovecraft's formative images were creatures he called the "Night Gaunts," which began appearing in the six-year-old's dreams after the death of his grandmother, as he wrote to a friend:

> I began to have nightmares of the most hideous description, peopled with *things* which I called "night-gaunts"—a compound word of my own coinage (perhaps the idea of these figures came from an edition de luxe of *Paradise Lost* with illustrations by Doré, which I discovered one day in the east parlour). In dreams they were wont to whirl me through space at a sickening rate of speed, the while fretting & impelling me with their detestable tridents.

Lovecraft asserts that the terror these creatures evoked in him made up the principal impetus for his fiction—though we may ask whether these male demons are related to a child's loss of a grandparent, as he stated, or to the more profound loss by degrees of his father, first to insanity and then to death.

A typical Lovecraft story (for intertwined reasons of genre and individual psychology we can talk about a "typical" Lovecraft or Poe story, but not a "typical" Schulz story) involves an encounter between a studious, celibate, introverted male protagonist and a deformed or formless, intensely repulsive, and terror-inducing male creature (labeled "indescribable," "unnameable," or "unspeakable" but in fact drawn in loving, obsessive detail). This confrontation with the antinatural or supernatural "thing-that-cannot-be" triggers in the protagonist either insanity or physical disintegration into a loathsome alien form—outcomes, as we will see, that are structurally identical.

In a Lovecraft story this intrusion of the impossible into the world of the senses—in stark contrast to the often playful shapeshifting in the tales of Bruno Schulz—is an occasion of terror as opposed to wonder, irony, or delight. Psychological possession is also presented as yet another form of the dreadful conquest of the human by the inhuman. Both types of invasion usually happen in the context of family via the ill-advised actions or genetic predisposition of an ancestor. The protagonist (who is also often the narrator) discovers he is related by blood to, or descended from, the horror. This realization either triggers or is coincident with his own regression into the antihuman Form. By story's end he either is mad (and, conventionally, writing from an asylum) or is engulfed and metamorphosing into an alien creature himself.

Beneath the simple narrative pattern Lovecraft created an elaborate cosmogony of extraterrestrial beings—what his fans dubbed the "Cthulhu mythos," after one of the principal gods of this demonic hierarchy, who lies in a state of suspended animation in his ruined city deep beneath the Pacific Ocean. There are also Azathoth, the blind idiot god, his servant Nyarlathotep, and Yog-Sothoth, a mediating entity who wanders in space and assumes various loathsome forms. These entities inhabit a plane of being in which natural laws as we know them are abolished; the Lovecraftian universe that surrounds (and whose inhabitants sometimes invade and overwhelm) our narrow sublunary life is cruel, meaningless, and profoundly antagonistic to humans.

A paramount feature of the stories is setting. The city of Providence and a highly Gothicized New England past served as Lovecraft's *locus inspirationis* in the identical way that the Galician town of Drohobycz was the womb of Schulz's imaginings. Onto this real-world topography Lovecraft grafted imaginary rural areas (always described as "degenerate") as well as towns, principally Arkham, home of the fictional Miskatonic University, which he modeled on Salem, Massachusetts. Sorcerers and the occasional witch (women characters are sparse in the stories) represent token nods to the more notorious aspects of New England's Puritan past, but these figures seem perfunctory next to his true and deeply original subject, the misshapen horrors from "beyond the stars." Lovecraft also invented a number of occult works to which the stories make constant reference, most notably a mysterious book called the *Necronomicon*—always with the adjective "dreaded" appended—written by the "mad Arab" Abdul Al-Hazred. Lovecraft's repeated citations of these works allowed him to construct a formal framework of spurious scholarly authority that equally bestows credibility on and contrasts starkly with the anarchic, uncontained de-formity of his creatures.

A model story is "The Dunwich Horror," a tale of the twin offspring of a mating between an entity from outside space and time and the daughter of a decayed backwoods family. The more human twin, Wilbur Whateley, grows into a golemic creature eight feet tall who is partly human above the waist, a fabulous monster below. Caught breaking into a university library in quest of forbidden Hermetic lore, he is attacked by dogs and disintegrates into a "sticky, whitish mass" on the floor. His invisible brother, in desperate flight to the realm of their father, Yog-Sothoth, materializes briefly on a hillside as something resembling a gigantic octopus with half a man's face, yards wide, then vanishes in a bolt of lightning, leaving behind a horrid stench. A Miskatonic professor explains to the terrified locals that the thing

> was mostly a kind of force that doesn't belong in our part of space; a kind of force that acts and grows and shapes itself by other laws than those of our sort of Nature. We have no business calling in such things from outside, and only very wicked people and very wicked cults ever try to . . . It grew fast and big for the same reason that Wilbur grew fast and big—but it beat him because it had a greater share of the *outsideness* in it. You needn't ask how Wilbur called it out of the air. He didn't call it out. *It was his twin brother, but it looked more like the father than he did.*

This last sentence, in Lovecraft's italics, ends a story that suggests a demonic parody of the Christian sacrifice and ascension. But what, exactly, is the nature of the "outsideness" in which Wilbur and his invisible twin participate?

FACTS IN THE CASE OF DANIEL PAUL SCHREBER

"Madness," Gérard de Nerval once declared, "is the desire to be recognized by an ideal other who functions as a transcendental Being." Wilbur's outsideness consists, in one of its intersecting Four Corners, of that cluster of abnormal mental and emotional attributes which our ancestors called demonic possession, our great-grandparents called *dementia praecox*, and we call psychosis in its various forms.

Some biographical similarities between Lovecraft and Schulz are relevant here. Both were, as children, profoundly influenced by the image of the engulfment of the child by malevolent, stereotypically Romantic supernatural male figures: Erlkönig and Night Gaunts, respectively. They were also, not coincidentally, ardent letter writers, in a quantity—in Lovecraft's case, certainly—far exceeding that of their literary works. The fiction of both was intimately linked to, and grew out of, their correspondence with friends. Schulz's stories had their inception in his letters to a woman friend, Debora Vogel; Lovecraft's story writing also evolved to a large degree out of the personal relationships he was able to establish in letters.

This seemingly idiosyncratic and private approach to the creative process has deep roots in the Romantic tradition. (Its rationale is perhaps most persuasively presented by their literary great-uncle Heinrich von Kleist in his famous essay "On the Gradual Formation of Ideas in Speech," in which he argues that it is necessary to be writing to a single sympathetic person, well known to the author, to provoke inspiration.) On a more mundane level the letter writing was also symptomatic of the profound emotional isolation in which both Schulz and Lovecraft lived, prolonging their childhood in the bosom of the family of origin throughout their entire adult lives, bound by choice as well as duty to neurotic households peopled with elderly relatives, craving yet rarely allowing themselves any release from the cage of aging natal family.

Above all, both Schulz and Lovecraft were the children of psychotic parents. Lovecraft's father developed what was probably an organic psychosis caused by tertiary syphilis; by the time of her hospitalization his mother was clearly suffering from a paranoid psychosis of some kind (there is no evidence that it was also paresis). And the symptomatology displayed by the Father figure in Schulz's stories strongly suggests that his actual father, Jakub, was schizophrenic, or at least by some measure psychotic.

As a means of gaining access to the symbolic language of these two writers—in both cases that of the quasi-religious grotesque—I want to suggest that the life problem that replicates itself so characteristically throughout their works, and particularly Lovecraft's, unmistakably involves psychosis, but (and this is an important distinction) it is the teasing, tantalizing prospect of and proximity to psychosis, not the condition itself. What is the difference between a person describing his own madness and a writer obsessed with the notion of containing and controlling madness through art? C. G. Jung made the distinction neatly when he described James Joyce and his schizophrenic daughter as "two people going to the bottom of a river, one falling and the other drowning." In fact, however, three categories, or states of mind, can be distinguished: psychosis *in medias res*, psychosis recalled from a later perspective of relative sanity, and latent psychosis distanced and controlled, but never completely banished, by means of the containing narrative structure of a composed "fiction."

The first state is that of a person living through a psychotic episode, one who cannot mediate his madness but is totally identified with it. The second state is madness viewed in hindsight, after the episode has passed—a rather darkly Wordsworthian mode that Theophile Gautier, describing his friend Nerval's *Aurélia*, dubbed "the memoirs of Insanity dictated to Reason." The third state characterizes writers like Lovecraft, who, even as they describe in figurative terms the process of going mad (often, one suspects, with little conscious knowledge of what they are up to), remain themselves unpossessed—that is, to use their own symbolic terms, still present in body, space, and time.

The Saxon judge Daniel Paul Schreber (1842–1911), in contrast, wrote as one who had passed through the transcendentally deforming experience and then returned, if only temporarily, to describe it in the language of human sanity. Schreber produced a remarkable document, *Memoirs of My Nervous Illness* (1903), that owed its initial notoriety primarily to Freud's use of it, in a 1911 paper, to theorize about the link between homosexuality and paranoia. Later Freudians and other commentators have since investigated Schreber from a staggering variety of theoretical perspectives. From our post at the Four Corners, however, Schreber's universe shows striking similarities to Lovecraft's invented one, and particularly to the recurring Lovecraftian theme of physical invasion by (or generation from) an alien male entity, an act of violation that forcibly triggers a profane metamorphosis in the helpless human victim.

Lovecraft was intrigued by Freud's theories as a bolster to his own oft-asserted belief in scientific materialism but was disinclined to apply them directly to life or literature. Though he may have read Freud's paper on Schreber, it is highly unlikely that Lovecraft knew of Schreber's memoir, which was not translated into English until 1955. The similarities between Lovecraft's and Schreber's created realms, I believe, arise from Lovecraft's inner intuitions and not his reading, just as Schreber's own peculiar cosmogony of solar rays derives from the nature of his psychotic compulsion as well as from the knowledge of Zoroastrianism and other Late Antique religions he undoubtedly possessed as a cultivated German reader of the late nineteenth century, when the scholar Max Müller was publishing his voluminous series "Sacred Books of the East."

Schreber believed that the souls of men, and especially his own, existed in unending and excruciatingly painful "nerve contact" with one another and with God, as a consequence of the mutual attraction between impersonal divine rays and individual human nerves. The continual bombardment by God's rays he has endured since the onset of his illness, Schreber tells us, has devastated him; voices from inside told him that this crisis was precipitated by an act of "soul murder," committed against the Schreber family either by his psychiatrist Dr. Flechsig or by one of Flechsig's forebears. Flechsig himself now constantly violates other people's nerves and invades their thoughts; he has this power because souls have much weaker characters than living men do. Most of Flechsig's soul now resides inside Schreber, whom the unremitting contact with the divine rays has transformed into a woman, both sexually and in the sense of a passive receptor.

Schreber's paranoia is perfectly matched in Lovecraft's vision of the malign intentions of the creatures who live outside space and time. These "Great Old Ones" came to earth long before men existed and were, says Lovecraft in "The Call of Cthulhu," "not composed altogether of flesh and blood. They had shape . . . but that shape was not made of matter. When the stars were right, They could plunge from world to world through the sky; but when the stars were wrong, They could not live. But although They no longer lived, They would never really die . . . They knew all that was occurring in the universe, for Their mode of speech was transmitted thought. Even now They talked in their tombs." In this classic paranoid construct featuring "ancient and elaborate alliances between the hidden outer creatures and certain members of the human race" and "*nonhuman creatures watching us all the time*," the human victim inevitably succumbs. Yet even though his protagonists can never resist the murderous Dionysian call of the Old Ones (Lovecraft had read his Nietzsche), their creator locates himself squarely on the metaphorical side of "sanity" that the rigid structure of his stories provides.

Neither Lovecraft nor Schulz, as far as we know, ever experienced a psychotic episode; the evidence for Lovecraft's early "breakdown" is sketchy. The recurring images in their works suggest rather that engulfment by powerful and (in Lovecraft's case) extremely negative unconscious forces remained a possibility over which their restless consciousnesses constantly circled without ever actually touching down. This crucial distinction is mirrored in the literary category in which each of our authors has placed his works: Schreber is writing a self-described nonfiction memoir, Schulz a fictional "autobiography" (which he further describes as a "spiritual genealogy" of an invented "mythic family tree"), Lovecraft simply fiction. Yet all three, in their way, are realists, as committed to truthful representationalism as a Zola or a Dreiser. They are faithful documentors of the interior reality they directly experience, autobiographers of the deepest level of their psyches.

THE PSYCHOTOPOGRAPHIC IMAGINATION

One of the most distinctive features of psychosis is its dynamic of externalization. Madness is experienced as being *enacted on* the subject from without; a person perceives his own unintegrated psychological contents as outer-world creatures and demons who threaten to engulf and physically destroy him. The barriers between inner and outer, subject and object, dissolve so entirely that no boundary remains to protect the ego from the onslaught of this projected unconscious material. "No wall however thick," Schreber complained, "no closed window can prevent the ray filaments penetrating in a way incomprehensible to man and so reaching any part of my body, particularly my head." When the inner life of the psyche is allegorized so concretely, the outer world of objects becomes a perfect mirror in which to view the fragments of one's projected soul.

In literary works we are accustomed, after John Ruskin, to branding this universe of subject merging with object as pure pathetic fallacy. A Victorian rationalist's "fallacy," however, represents what had been for premodern Westerners a profound organizing principle of the universe. Viewed in this framework, the outer landscape does not simply mirror our inner feelings; rather, in the tradition of Neoplatonic natural philosophy, the human soul, the *parvus mundus,* contains within itself the heavenly macrocosm. Each mirrors the other and reverberates at the points of coincidence, and behind both is posited a deeper transcendental reality.

To these interior psychic regions as we find them projected onto an outer landscape I would like to give the name *psychotopography.* A psychotopographer is the artist who devotes herself to describing—with varying degrees of awareness about the true nature of the subject—the images of these inner regions as she discovers them in an imagined exterior landscape. Working backward from the sum of these details, the reader gains a picture not of what lies without but of what lies within. In art that has a psychotopographic dimension every object, every cloud in the sky, every piece of furniture, even the ground itself is a piece of psychic matter that we perceive to be extruded from the main character or narrator (and by extension from the author himself, consciously or unconsciously). The contents of the psyche are cast like a net in ever-widening circles, first onto immediate surroundings—furniture, rooms, houses—then onto the larger natural landscape, finally even onto the globe itself.

This literary mode is found in twentieth-century Expressionism, principally in the visual arts, as a studiedly *naïf* attribution of human feelings to objects in the outer world. Within this aesthetic framework, as one commentator has noted, "the environment, whether city or nature, is conceived as the places where subject and object meet . . . a creature or object into which the creative self is intuitively projected and whose topographic situation orders and conditions the structure of the poem, novel, play or painting." Expressionism in turn represents a resurrected Romanticism of the sort reflected in Philipp Otto Runge's famous remarks to Ludwig Tieck:

> I think that I know now approximately what you mean by landscape. Throughout ancient history the artists have always striven to see and express the workings of the elements inherent in the natural forces . . . The essence of landscape would be expressed by the very opposite idea, namely, for man to see himself, his habits and his passions embodied in flowers, plants, and other natural phenomena. When looking at flowers and trees, I become increasingly aware that each contains some human quality, thought, or feeling, and I am sure that this must reflect the state of Paradise.

Further back, this sensibility has strong morphological links to the Neoplatonic cosmos of Late Antiquity. In the early Gnostic cults, Giovanni Filoramo tells us, to know meant to "be transformed through enlightenment into the actual object of knowledge"; the Romantics secularized this epiphany and priestified the artist to make the literary act "become the encounter with the Absolute, and its result a revelation."

As a literary device (as well as a ubiquitous metaphor of dreams), the house—as Gaston Bachelard has told us and as is reflected in the old English kenning for body, *lifhus* or "life house"—is perhaps the most familiar of all psychotopographic loci. In Schulz's story "Father's Last Escape" the components of Father's face dissolve into this immediate domestic environment: "His features were already dispersed throughout the room in which he had lived, and were sprouting in it . . . The wallpaper began in certain places to imitate his habitual nervous tic; the flower designs arranged themselves into the doleful elements of his smile, symmetrical as the fossilized imprint of a trilobite." In the fragment "Autumn" Schulz says, "Man's house becomes like the little stable of Bethlehem, the core around which all demons, all spirits of the upper and lower sphere, condense." The rooms in a Schulzian house, moreover, proliferate and multiply; they have no fixed identity or even quantity. Such a disturbing lack of fixity in the house of the psyche may well have been, coincidentally, the source of Schreber's anxious concern about the physical layout of the clinics in which he was housed (whose floor plans he includes in the *Memoir*) and his occasional conviction that he was in a room that "does not tally with any one of the rooms known to me in Flechsig's Asylum."

What the psychotic experiences as direct, unmediated hallucination, the writer obsessed with psychosis imagines as psychotopographic metaphor. Lovecraft's house of the psyche is more conventionally Gothic than Schulz's. It is, like Schreber's, an architectural and geologic metaphor of consciousness (historic, material) grading down to the unconscious (prehistoric, transcendent). In "The Rats in the Walls," the American narrator's ancestral English home, Exham Priory, is described as "architecture involving Gothic towers resting on a Saxon or Romanesque substructure, whose foundation in turn was of a still earlier order or blend of orders—Roman, and even Druidic or native Cymric, if legends speak truly."

Beneath this structure lies a subterranean chamber deeper than the deepest known Roman vault. Rats seem to be crawling from these lower depths, whose passages show signs of having been "chiseled *from beneath.*" A search party, dispatched to investigate, ultimately discovers, in a "twilit grotto," a sea of gnawed human bones; in this place humans from time immemorial had been bred in pens, butchered, and eaten by succeeding generations of the depraved family. What lies still farther below? Says the narrator, the last descendant (shortly to go mad and begin eating the other searchers): "those grinning caverns of earth's center where Nyarlathotep, the mad faceless god, howls blindly in the darkness to the piping of two amorphous idiot flute-players." Like Poe before him, Lovecraft, touching down at the bottom of his psyche, fictionally anticipates death and chaos in the encounter with the unconscious.

In a tragic echo of "The Rats in the Walls," Schreber experiences the onset of his all-too-real psychotic breakdown in what he perceives as a constant rustling of mice in the walls in his bedroom. Schreber enters his madness in a kind of historic and collective topographic plunge from conscious to unconscious functioning: "It was as though I were sitting in a railway carriage or in a lift driving into the depths of the earth and I recapitulated, as it were, the whole history of mankind or of the earth in reverse order; in the upper regions there were still forests of leafy trees; in the nether regions it became progressively darker and blacker." For Schreber as for Lovecraft, the nether regions of the psyche constitute a vile dictatorship of absolute demonic possession; to surrender to their seductive charms is to court soul murder of the most immediate and literal sort.

Bruno Schulz, in contrast, finds the downward journey into the grotto of self satisfying and engrossing. Blackness, idiot gods, and Ultimate Chaos don't lie at the end of his trail; for Schulz the unconscious is the source, the taproot, for all creativity and life: "Here at the very bottom, in the dark foundations, among the Mothers . . . Where would writers find their ideas, how would they muster the courage for invention, had they not been aware of these reserves, this frozen capital, these funds salted away in the underworld? What a buzz of whispers, what persistent purr of the earth!" And what lies even farther below? In the depths of the grotto unconscious lies collective mythology, where the individual spirit, traced to its roots, "merges into mythology, to be lost in the mutterings of mythological delirium." Schulz adds: "That is the ultimate depth; it is impossible to reach farther down."

Whether they experience it positively or negatively, however, all three authors agree that the deepest level of the psyche—in psychotopographic terms, the map's edge or the end of the known universe—is the point at which we enter a completely different reality operating outside the conventional laws of the known world. They assert that the self makes this journey, a grotesquely ecumenical *itinerarium mentis ad Deum*, by moving regressively *down*, the *via negativa*, rather than progressively *up*, the mystic's *via positiva* and the soul's traditional direction. And finally, according to their joint testimony, three kinds of transformations concretely enact the journey into the transcendental world of madness: bodily deformation, the decomposition of human speech, and the collapse of time and space.

THE DE-FORMING OF BODY

"The grotesque body," Mikhail Bakhtin wrote, "is a body in the act of becoming. It is never finished, never completed; it is continually built, created, and builds and creates another body." Tobin Siebers, pointing to what he calls the "great writers of the metamorphic tradition—Ovid, Shakespeare, Gogol and Kafka," notes that E. T. A. Hoffmann in particular "employs a bizarre anti-Darwinism in which humans mutate into plants." Hoffmann's governing principle of metamorphosis, which draws heavily from the alchemical tradition (another syncretic thread, as we have seen, that links Romanticism and twentieth-century fantastic literature to the philosophical legacy of Late Antiquity), is shared by Schulz and Lovecraft, in whose imaginations transformation of shape occurs as a kind of profound regression into lower forms of life, vegetative or animal.

For Bruno Schulz, all form is inherently unstable: "Shape does not penetrate essence, is only a role to be adopted for the moment, an outer skin soon to be shed . . . The life of the substance consists in the assuming and consuming of numberless masks. This migration of forms is the essence of life." Objects, household objects especially, burst into life whenever the writer turns his attention to them, as if these unstable forms require only the gaze of the observer as the catalyst for transformation. Following the rules of their own profane mythology, Schulz's human characters metamorphose into enema tubing, doorbells, cockroaches, dogs, piles of ash.

In the "Tailors' Dummies" stories, we have seen that Schulz casts his Father character in the role of a latter-day magus, a "heretical Demiurgy" and craftsman of secondary creation who announces the genesis of his true *generatio aequivoca*, namely,

> a species of beings only half organic, a kind of pseudofauna and pseudoflora, the result of a fantastic fermentation of matter. They were creations resembling, in appearance only, living creatures such as crustaceans, vertebrates, cephalopods. In reality the appearance was misleading—they were amorphous creatures, with no internal structure, products of the imitative tendency of matter which, equipped with memory, repeats from force of habit the forms already accepted.

One species of Lovecraft's creatures shows the same imitative characteristics and lack of internal structure as Father's alchemical creations. The "Shoggoths," Lovecraft tells us, created by the "Old Ones" to mediate with humans, are "formless protoplasm able to mock and reflect all forms and organs and processes—viscous agglutinations of bubbling cells—rubbery fifteen-foot spheroids infinitely plastic and ductile."

Whereas Father's monsters are playful human-made golems, well under his control and not at all demonized, Lovecraft's pseudoforma and pseudoflora are menacing, revolting forms that are decidedly outside his protagonists' control: "When Danforth and I saw the freshly glistening and reflectively iridescent black slime which clung thickly to those headless bodies and stank obscenely with that new, unknown odor whose cause only a diseased fancy could envisage . . . we understood the quality of cosmic fear to its uttermost depths." Elsewhere Lovecraft describes the Shoggoths as "slopping," "slobbering," "greasy," and "green, sticky spawn of the stars." An aura of sexual squeamishness and repulsion hovers like a low and unattended fog around these descriptions; sex is *the* major unaddressed issue of Lovecraft's work, displaced in an uneasy fusion with the transcendent into monstrosity.

To the Schulzian and Lovecraftian pseudoforma Schreber adds his own theory of demiurgic creation:

> For years I have experienced direct genesis (creation) through divine miracles certainly on *lower animals* and I still experience it around my-

self hourly. I have thus gained the certain conviction that *spontaneous generation* (parentless generation, *generatio aequivoca*) does in fact exist; not, however, in the materialistic sense which in natural science is connected with these terms . . . here it is used in the totally different sense that the coming into existence of such life is due to the purposeful manifestations of divine power of will or divine power of creation.

Schreber directly experiences a hallucinatory altering of his own body as well as of the bodies of the living creatures around him, which are there because God created them specifically for him. In this supercharged interior "holy landscape," he believes himself to have been impregnated, much like Spenser's sleepy nymph Chrysogyne in *The Faerie Queene,* by God's solar rays. He undergoes his most profound bodily change, from male to female, and also experiences a shrinking in size; his penis retracts, and various inner organs—heart, stomach, gullet, and intestines—are distorted or eliminated entirely by the rays. Schreber is further convinced that he has a second, "mentally inferior" body. Outside his own deformations is a category of creatures he calls "fleeting-improvised-men," or "humans produced by miracle," representing humans disembodied into souls.

Carlo Ginzburg notes the widespread Eurasian folk belief that anything modifying the image of the whole human body is a way of expressing "an experience that exceeds the limits of what is human . . . Anyone who goes to or returns from the nether world . . . is marked by asymmetry." In stories such as "Dreams in the Witch House," Lovecraft attaches tremendous violence as well as terror to the breakdown of form, echoing Henri Bergson's suggestion that "plasticity of the human form . . . is not a physical, but a metaphysical attribute connected to *violence.*"

Lovecraft also gives metamorphosis a considerably more demonic twist, reserving his greatest powers of eloquence to capture the sense of a deformed biology that lies, as he characteristically insists, beyond the reach of human language or perception—though, as the following description of the naked Wilbur Whateley demonstrates, he's always game to try:

Above the waist it was semi-anthropomorphic; though its chest . . . had the leathery, reticulated hide of a crocodile or alligator. The back was piebald with yellow and black, and dimly suggested the squamous covering of certain snakes. Below the waist, though, it was the worst;

> for here all human resemblance left off and sheer phantasy began. The skin was thickly covered with coarse black fur, and from the abdomen a score of long greenish-grey tentacles with red sucking mouths protruded limply. Their arrangement was odd, and seemed to follow the symmetries of some cosmic geometry unknown to earth or the solar system. On each of the hips, deep set in a kind of pinkish, cilated orbit, was what seemed to be a rudimentary eye; whilst in lieu of a tail there depended a kind of trunk or feeler with purple annular markings, and with many evidences of being an undeveloped mouth or throat.

Lovecraft, no minimalist, renders the dreaded physical metamorphosis of human to inhuman in gloriously overblown excess (this passage carries on another half page), thereby sealing his doom with the reader of orthodox tastes. Lovers of the baroque, however, may have a different reaction.

We may wonder if actual memories or overheard stories of Winfield Scott Lovecraft's death from syphilis, the sexually transmitted disease whose physical marks were lesions, eruptions, tubercles, bubos, and gummas of the most horrific sort, may have impressed themselves on his sensitive son. Whether or not Lovecraft's father's neurosyphilitic psychosis manifested such bodily symptoms as well, an avid lay reader—as Lovecraft was, in a wide range of subjects—who looked up "paresis" in the medical textbooks of the early twentieth century would have encountered graphic photographs of real-life deformities the horrific magnitude of which most certainly defies description. It is hard not to believe, viewing these anonymous and pathetic images of suffering, that one has located the originals of Lovecraft's pustulating horrors.

Lovecraft's monsters, in fact, are always hybrids, embodying Wolfgang Kayser's definition of the grotesque, after Horace, as a "monstrous fusion of human and nonhuman elements." Produced as they are by the sexual union of human and otherworld entity, their lack of sexuality—or rather, the monstrous incomprehensibility of their sexual parts—is a key aspect of their horror.

Despite the opposing affects of dread and joyful wonder that Schreber and Lovecraft on one side and Schulz on the other attach to the process of metamorphosis out of the human, all three strongly associate deformation of shape with genealogy, the family tree. Schulz declared he had invented a "spiritual genealogy," exalting family to the level of myth "just as the ancients traced their ancestry from mythical unions with gods"; the transformations Father and other characters (usually relatives) endure in Schulz's stories occur within this insular family matrix. Schreber, in what was probably a displacement from his overbearing father, the child pedagogist Moritz Schreber—who before his death was subject to "hallucinations with a pathological urge to murder," in his son's words—attaches his own soul murder and bodily distortions to a feud between prior generations of his own family and that of his doctor.

Lovecraft's obsessional interest in family past rather than future, forebears rather than offspring, typically manifests in his narrators' discovery of a genetic relation between themselves and a nonhuman ancestor whose fate and form they must inevitably assume. In a brilliant echo of the amphibious Nantucket of *Moby-Dick*, the men-fish inhabitants of a seedy port town in "The Shadow over Innsmouth" share a characteristic "Innsmouth look" that bears the mark of "biological degeneration rather than alienage." The sea creatures have told their human allies that everything living came from the water and would return to the water; if the humans mated with them and went back to the water, they would never die. A kind of profane immortality, in other words, can be achieved by moving *down* the evolutionary scale. In the modern Darwinian, not premodern, context, this is a dark emblem. The "shadows" that populate Lovecraft's titles are intimations of another reality, but they are shadows of demonic Forms. (As Melville himself succinctly put it in his story of the great whale: "Reversion—or the soul's undoing.")

"Biological degeneration" in Lovecraft's stories is thus a figuring of the parental madness backward through the family tree as well as a psychotopographic rendering of regression into the separate reality of psychosis and/or physical disfigurement. (Lovecraft consistently referred to the onset of his father's psychosis as "a complete paralysis resulting from a brain overtaxed with study and business cares.") A full awareness of Winfield Scott Lovecraft's syphilis would certainly have instilled in the son a deep and legitimate fear that he had inherited the disease.

More than simply physical inheritance is involved in the dynamic Lovecraft presents in these stories. The fact that he depicts only members of inbred, isolated families mating with monsters also suggests a materialization of the psychological dynamics of incest, the inversion and perversion of family that simultaneously combines biological and psychological regression. Schizophrenia, often found in children of socially isolated families with an overly dominant parent, might be considered the psychological analogue of physical incest, representing as it does an early psychic engulfment by the parent and a consequent failure by the child to differentiate from the family nucleus. Schreber's overriding sense of invasion, which he projects onto the figure of his doctor as well as onto God (structurally equivalent father figures, as shown in his revealing remark: "God is incapable of judging me correctly"), as well as the extreme and unrelenting violation of interpsychic boundaries, is a pervasive theme in the testimonies of schizophrenic clinical literature.

DECOMPOSITION OF LANGUAGE

"What does language communicate?" asks Walter Benjamin, who promptly answers himself: "It communicates the mental being corresponding to it." In the psychotopographic universe language is also subject to transformation, and its disintegration from a vehicle for recognizable human communication into something "other"—both divine and demonic—also signals the shift into the transcendental world of merged subject and object.

Once again, as we examine possible sources for the cosmogonies of Schulz, Lovecraft, and Schreber, eerie parallels emerge from two radically separate contexts: Neoplatonic/cabbalistic language theories and the linguistic concretism characteristic of schizophrenia. According to the syncretic principles formulated in Late Antiquity, developed and extended in medieval Jewish cabbalism, and revived by Christian Hermeticists during the Renaissance, humans have lost the ability to understand God's divine language, the pre–Tower of Babel *lingua adamica*, the Perfect Language spoken by the Divine Human, in which a name concretely *is* the idea of its object. In seeking to recapture this ontological link between being and language, the late sixteenth-century mystic Jakob Boehme declared that the *Natursprache*, God's original language, could be perceived in a trance, but that God was also literally embodied in the words of human language as manifest in intricate schemes involving heart, breath, and utterance. For Boehme, the cosmos-binding attributes of language were accessible to the individual worshipper; spoken words could be *ausgesprochenes Wesen*, a vehicle for the immediate experience of transcendence during the inward journey to God. The articulation of vowels and consonants during prayer was a tangible act of unity with God, with the mystic event occurring concretely in the mouth of the speaker and thereby drawing down the divine into the ordinary world.

Just such a merging of signified and signifier in language is a widespread clinical symptom of schizophrenia. In the latter condition, however, it indicates severe confusion and a breakdown in analogical thinking. A person experiencing a schizophrenic psychotic episode often perceives figurative language in literal terms and is incapable of separating the symbol from the object it stands for. For this reason clinicians have traditionally used as a primary diagnostic indicator the inability to interpret metaphorically a proverb such as "A rolling stone gathers no moss". In the breakdown between internal and external boundaries, schizophrenics also typically hear voices they do not identify as their own—auditory hallucinations that clinicians believe are physically produced by their "hearer," who is activating his own speech muscles without emitting audible sounds. Whether the schizophrenic perceives these voices as coming from inside or outside, however, he experiences them as other, alien, invasive. Or as Schreber put it with terrifying succinctness: "I am exposed to acts of bellowing."

Some schizophrenics report that the voices speak in an alien language that only the afflicted person is able to understand. Here Schreber presents a perfect psychotic parody of Boehme's angelic language, for the voices he hears speak in the "nerve language" in which God communicates with souls. This tongue, which Schreber also calls *Grundsprache* ("basic language"), he describes as a "somewhat antiquated but powerful German" in which many words have reverse meaning ("poison" means "food," and so on). A principal feature of the nerve language is that, as with God's rays, the voices use it to bombard a defenseless Schreber day and night. In the microcosm of the human psyche the cosmos-uniting attributes of Boehme's angelic *Natursprache* have become the cosmos-disintegrating forces of Schreber's demonic *Grundsprache*. This crucial difference between the language of mystics and that of psychotics was identified precisely by Michel Foucault in his gloss on the magical language of Raymond Roussel (yet another schizophrenic, and a contemporary of Lovecraft's as well as Schulz's): "The cruelty of this solar language is that instead of being the perfect sphere of an illuminated world, it divides things to introduce darkness into them."

In a striking parallel to Boehme, Schreber believes that the psychosis can be thwarted physically at the site of utterance in the vocal cords of the larynx, the point where language converts from a private to a social act and where, for Boehme, divine and human unite. The voices torment Schreber by delivering fragments of the same sentence hundreds of times a day. Though cursing and obscenities also serve, Schreber's best defense against this onslaught is to finish the fragments, compulsively, with grammatically complete phrases; doing so destroys the rays in his mouth. It is Schreber's profound conviction that conquering nerve language by speaking in complete sentences "is the *ultima ratio* for preserving my house," a means by which to stay at least half sane and stave off total possession. (We may note that Nikolai Gogol, who did go mad, though he was not yet mad when he wrote "The Overcoat," gave his character Akaky Akakievich the distinctive trait of expressing himself only in "prepositions, adverbs, and particles which have absolutely no significance whatsoever. If the subject was a very difficult one, it was his habit to leave his sentences quite unfinished." A dangerous habit, as Schreber would have advised him.)

For Bruno Schulz, words as well as bodies are subject to transformation backward into essence, and in some ways what happens to language is a more critical transformation for him than what happens to the body. As we saw in Chapters 3 and 4, Schulz in his essays and stories reveals himself as an ecumenical cabbalist who avers that "reality is the shadow of the word" and that the study of the universe is a "philological, not a philosophical" endeavor: "The primeval word was a shimmering aura circling around the sense of the word, was a great universal whole. The word in its common usage today is only a fragment, remnant of some former all-embracing, integral mythology. That is why it possessed a tendency to grow back, to regenerate and complete itself in full meaning." In the Neoplatonic-cabbalistic framework language does not represent nature, nature represents language; it is only one of the many masks the Ur-words adopt in the world of our senses. Though language is the ordering principle of the cosmos, Schulz perversely sees the breakdown of language—and by extension of the cosmos—as desirable, because it allows us entry into that other realm, the magical preexisting world that lies beyond, behind, and under words.

Lovecraft similarly believes in a transcendental realm "beyond words" (though not a desirable one). The most obvious mark of this belief is his trademark use of the adjectives "indescribable," "unspeakable," and "unnameable"—in their lower-case manifestation a secularization of the divine "name that cannot be pronounced"—to render his things-that-cannot-be. By the standard conventions of literary style, of course, frequent recourse to this mode of nondescription is considered very bad form, and Lovecraft was often taken to task for it. Lovecraft himself was well aware of these criticisms. In a story called, with deliberate irony, "The Unnameable," he has a character chide the protagonist, a stand-in for himself, that

> my constant talk about "unnameable" and "unmentionable" things was a very puerile device, quite in keeping with my lowly standing as an author. I was too fond of ending my stories with sights or sounds which paralyzed my heroes' faculties and left them without courage, words, or associations to tell what they had experienced. We know things, he said, only through our five senses or our religious convictions; wherefore it is quite impossible to refer to any object or spectacle which cannot be clearly depicted by the solid definitions of fact or the correct doctrines of theology—preferably those of the Congregationalist, with whatever modifications tradition and Sir Arthur Conan Doyle can supply.

The two characters are, appropriately, sitting in a cemetery during this conversation; the story concludes triumphantly with the doubting character quite literally scared out of his wits—and, by extension, his rationalist stance—by an apparition in a nearby cursed house

On a deeper level, Lovecraft depicts the journey to the other reality in much the same terms as Schreber experiences it—in the actual loss of ability to speak human language that his characters frequently experience, and their subsequent involuntary conversion to a demonic language. Lovecraft's version of *Grundsprache* is Aklo, the language of the demiurge Cthulhu and his minions, which he reproduces in words, phrases, and—once—a sentence (*Ph'nglui mglw'nafh Cthulhu R'lyeh wgah'nagl fhtagn*, "In his house at R'lyeh dead Cthulhu waits dreaming"). A common representation in a Lovecraft story is of a cultivated male English-speaking voice either juxtaposed with or declining into a buzzing nonhuman noise "like the drone of some loathsome gigantic insect" that produces in the listener a "feeling of blasphemous infinity." (One also thinks irresistibly of Gregor Samsa's insect language, incomprehensible to humans.) The narrator, if overwhelmed, ends by either talking in this demonic Ur-language or describing his surrender to the forces that rule the other reality in exalted, quasi-religious terms.

The main character of "The Rats in the Walls" undergoes his linguistic regression in the grotto deep below his ancestral home, surrounded by the sea of gnawed human bones:

> No, no, I tell you, I am *not* that daemon swineherd in the twilit grotto! It was *not* Edward Norrys' face on that flabby, fungous thing! . . . Curse you, Thornton, I'll teach you to faint at what my family do! . . . 'Sblood, thou stinkard, I'll learn ye how to gust . . . wolde ye swynke me thike wys? . . . *Magna Mater! Magna Mater!* . . . *Atys* . . . *Dia ad aghaidh's ad aodaun [. . .] agus bas danach ort! Dhonas's dholas ort, agus leat-saw! [. . .] Ungl . . . ungl . . . rrlh . . . chchch . . .*

These remarks may be glossed as modern English, Elizabethan English, Middle English, Latin, Celtic, and Aklo. The story is a bit of a cheat, since the narrator tells it in perfect English from the stereotypical vantage point of the madhouse, having been restored to "form" solely by the conventions of the popular genre Lovecraft is working within.

For Schulz, the journey to the fourth dimension can occur through cracks in syntax. There is also a sense, as we have seen, in which it takes place on the level of syntax itself, as in the grotesque layering of realities and yoking of incongruous associations that closes Schulz's long story "The Comet": "Sometimes [Father] opened the door of the flue and looked grinning into its dark abyss, where a smiling homunculus slept forever in its luminous sleep, enclosed in a glass capsule, bathed in fluorescent light, already adjudged, erased, filed away, another record card in the immense archives of the sky." In this bewildering conflation of inner and outer realities, Father has been using a microscope to observe a comet in the chimney, which transforms under his alchemical gaze from piece of Gruyere cheese to human brain to embryo. The final shape-shift to "record card" in the "archives of the sky" completes a cognitive disjuncture at a level of imagistic sophistication more complex than the literal-minded Lovecraft can offer us.

Lovecraft and Schulz both represent auditory hallucinations as externally real occurrences in their fictions. Where Schulz is aesthetically entranced by this otherworld flood of speech and refers glowingly to the subterranean "buzz of whispers" and "persistent purr of the earth," Lovecraft and his characters, like Schreber, shrink from the "subterrene voices of intelligence shouting monotonously in enigmatic sense-impacts indescribable save as gibberish." In folklore such distortion of voice or language has traditionally been a distinguishing feature of the otherworld and, in premodern Western culture, of dead souls. Against Schreber's "bellowings" and the "thunder croakings" and "croaking, baying voices" of the Whateley offspring in a story like "The Dunwich Horror," for example, can be set a range of mythic parallels from Greek antiquity. Maurizio Bettini has noted the "squeaking, gibbering" voices of the dead in the *Iliad*, a cacophony associated with bats, and the statement by Eusthathius, in his commentary on the *Odyssey*, that "mythically *trismos* [whistling] got chosen for souls because they were deprived of articulated speech and only made noise" (recall the whistling in Kafka's "The Burrow" from Chapter 1). The presence of this strong tradition implies at the very least that the internal experience of schizophrenia replicates, in ways we do not yet understand, a culturally consistent representation of the supernatural and not merely, as Louis Sass asserts in *Madness and Modernism*, a distinctively twentieth-century sensibility of Apollonian alienation.

Lovecraft and Schreber are clearly much more caught up in the disintegration of spoken, not written, language than the more typographically oriented Schulz. Lovecraft renders the process of transmigration into the other world more or less consistently as the decomposition of human speech into the language of the beings beyond time and space. In some Lovecraft stories the Old Ones communicate by telepathy rather than uttered speech. Telepathy considered as a purely psychological construct amounts to a dissolving of boundaries between one human being and another, producing an inchoate merging in place of true contact. Language, a social act, is thereby reduced to thought, a private inner act that functions as a vehicle of invasion, not of communication and relationship—precisely the effect of psychic violation that Schreber describes in the constant assault he endures from his inner voices. In terms of a primal undifferentiated universe, telepathy allegorizes as well the engulfing parent from the perspective of a passive child.

"Syntax," the scholar James Russell has noted, "is a deep part of what makes us human." For a shaky and disintegrating self, the ordering framework of language as a social act whose rules we share with those around us functions as a stabilizing psychotopographic container. As an affirmation of sanity Schreber strives heroically to keep within the bounds of conventional language. Both Schulz and Lovecraft also take pains only to describe, and not to replicate in the texture of their writing, the kind of disjuncture that might lead them to a truly unmediated encounter with the Perfect Language. Though Lovecraft reproduces words, phrases, and whole sentences in the Aklo language and Schulz tries to break down conventional associations of images, both stay firmly rooted in the syntax and vocabulary of their native human languages, English and Polish—a comforting family matrix of its own, and the base to which they invariably return no matter how attractive the world beyond ordinary human communication becomes.

TIME, SPACE, AND SOME GREAT HERESIES

In the fictions of Schulz and Lovecraft as well as Schreber's account of his madness, the twin events of disintegration of body and language also mark the shift out of the boundaries of space and time. As Schulz said, "The discrepancies of time, place and person are irrelevant to the psyche," a statement that perfectly captures the twentieth-century high-art interiorization of the Platonic otherworld. From the point of departure in consciousness there is a move downward into unconsciousness and ultimately, at the bottom of the psyche, into transcendent reality. But this interior destination, for the psychotic sensibility, means hell rather than heaven.

The science fiction writer Fritz Leiber suggests that Lovecraft, who so emphatically declared himself a materialist, was in fact one of the first horror writers to abandon conventional objects of supernatural terror (the Devil, ghosts, vampires, ghouls) and locate dread in the new postreligious universe of scientific materialism. Even as Lovecraft vowed his own allegiance to this worldview, he also believed the cosmos to be "something fundamental & boundless & static as a whole, & utterly outside the realm of such things as time, space, direction, purpose, or consciousness." And even as he insists that the Old Ones are not supernatural beings but "alien life forms" consonant with scientific materialism, in his fiction Lovecraft represents the world of the senses as an illusion behind which lies a "truer" but more terrible realm outside time and space. A character in "Beyond the Wall of Sleep" asserts: "From my experience I cannot doubt but that man, when lost to terrestrial consciousness, is indeed sojourning in another incorporeal life of a far different nature from the life we know.

Sometimes I believe that this less material life [of dreams] is our truer life, and that our vain presence on the terraqueous globe is itself the secondary or merely virtual phenomenon."

Humans, in Lovecraft's view, stand in constant danger of eroding or reverting (never "ascending") into this fourth-dimensional realm of altered forms. This is no world of Perfect Forms but, as he says in another story, a misshapen realm of terror and chaos: in speaking of the architecture of the city of the Great Old Ones, he declares that its "*geometry* was *all wrong*."

In "Beyond the Wall of Sleep," the narrator is able to experience the other world telepathically, by means of a machine wired up to a dreaming madman. Here Lovecraft has recourse to a literary cliché so congenial to contemporary sensibility that it must be identified explicitly as a piece of ontological flummery: using a Divine Machine as a psychotopographic locus of visionary and mystical powers. This convenient "rationalization" of the supernatural enabled Lovecraft, like many writers before and after him, to maintain an official stance as a rational materialist while delving into completely contradictory realms. Through the handy intervention of the machine, Lovecraft's narrator learns from the madman's dreams that each person has a "waking self" and another "real self" that roams space and time freely, without restraint.

Bruno Schulz characteristically frames the decomposition of time and space within the psychotopographic metaphors of the seasons and day/night: "On such extramarginal nights that know no limits," he says in the fragment "Autumn," "space loses its meaning." In "Night of the Great Season" he invents a thirteenth month. The story "Sanatorium under the Sign of the Hourglass" (where the Father character ultimately becomes an inmate) creates a kind of anti-town and anti-landscape, as insubstantial as "billowing, stealthily moving clouds," in which "whole chunks of time are casually lost somewhere; control over the continuity of the day is loosened until it finally ceases to matter; and the framework of uninterrupted chronology finally ceases to matter." Once we have entered this realm of "pre-image" via "liberating metamorphosis," once we have "removed the bottom of the eternal barrel of memories, of an ultra-barrel of myth," we have "broken into a prehuman night of untamed elements, of incoherent anamnesis."

Daniel Paul Schreber, having dwelt in his own life in the sanatorium under the sign of the hourglass, was equally committed to the notion of a "realer"—and more horrific—transcendental world outside time and space.

Schreber's inner universe is consistently ordered according to the cosmogony of premodern natural philosophy; there is little difference, for example, between his self-described "cosmogenic theory" of divine rays and the Hermetic-Gnostic vision, promulgated in the Renaissance from Ficino to Robert Fludd, of a physical universe in which, according to a Corpus Hermeticum treatise from the second century C.E., there is "a community of actions among the hierarchies whose operations are like rays of God . . . and the operations work through the world and work upon man through the physical rays of the cosmos." Schreber's account of the transmigration of souls to other planets and of an explicitly Zoroastrian upper God (Ormuzd) and lower God (Ariman) might be regarded as the ultimate Gnostic text in which the individual becomes the special, albeit not particularly *favored*, object of the deity's attention: "God entered into exclusive nerve contact with me, and I thus became the sole human being on whom His interest centres."

Schreber is not the only modern Western psychotic in the literary record to have been overwhelmed by Hermetic visions of the macrocosm. One of many such examples is Gérard de Nerval, who saw (he tells us in *Aurélia*) "a great conspiracy afoot among all animate beings to restore the world to its primordial harmony":

> All things live, function, relate to one another; the rays of magnetism emanating from myself or from other individuals pass without impediment along and through the endless chain of created things; they form an invisible network which covers the whole globe, and detached filaments of them make their way by degrees to the very planets and stars. Captive for the time being on the earth, I am in touch with the sun, the moon and the stars, who share in my joys and my sorrows!

Such testimony seems to lead us toward a conclusion that schizophrenia may include as one of its characteristics a fairly orthodox Neoplatonic worldview with religious overtones that parody the mystic's revelation experience. Schreber himself was emphatic on the subject: "A person with sound nerves is, so to speak, *mentally* blind compared with him who receives supernatural impressions by virtue of his diseased nerves."

Schulz and Lovecraft echo, at a greater distance, this representation of psychosis as simultaneous possession by spirits and initiation into the secrets of the hidden universe. Whereas Schulz might be labeled a Hermetic cabbalist and Schreber a solar Zoroastrian, Lovecraft is—as Barton Levi St. Armand has correctly labeled him—a Gnostic dualist. Lovecraft turns the dark vision of Gnosticism on its head, however, in his insistence that not physical matter but the preexisting Forms themselves are evil and demonic; we leave this world to cleave with them to our eternal damnation. Such a position, to put it mildly, represents "materialism" of a rather qualified sort. Even though Schreber typically, like Lovecraft, identifies himself as a rationalist and adamantly denies he was ever a religious believer, he insists that "the most gruesome time of my life . . . was also the *holy* time of my life." Both men in a sense were involuntary mystics catapulted against their will, via their pathology, into the transcendent.

This neglected angle of entry into the Four Corners, in which the secular and relatively new field of psychology touches on the older religious dimension of hierophany and the soul, obliges us to reflect again on the historical shift of attitudes, now a virtually unconscious reflex in all intellectual endeavor, that exiled the transcendental from the mainstream of Western thinking. At the level of language this transition is embodied in the shift in meaning of the term *psychosis*, which meant to the Greeks of Late Antiquity the movement of the soul, or the principle of life generally (compare the Latin synonym *animatio*, or "animation"). In the transition from "soul" to "self" traced in Chapter 2, the concept of the soul, known as the *pneuma* or *psyche* in antiquity, was increasingly absorbed into the psycho-physiological vocabulary of Western medical science after the seventeenth century as both terms became attached to the body and the mind (Descartes's "physical substance" and "mental substance," respectively).

By the nineteenth century, *psyche* referred to one's material self and *psychosis* (first employed as a psychiatric term by Ernst Feuchtersleben in 1854) had been transformed into pathological movement, or agitation: in the OED definition, "mental illness that includes hallucinations, delusions, loss of contact with external reality." The stage was thus set for the coup de grace at the turn of the twentieth century, when, in Otto Rank's words,

> Freud essentially eliminated the soul. By acknowledging the unconscious, he acknowledged the realm of the soul; but by his materialistic explanation of the unconscious he denied the soul. Consciousness,

> obviously, contains *something* more, as well as something different, than just the data of the external world. Freud attempted to explain this "something more" out of the unconscious; but he takes the unconscious itself again to be merely a reflection of reality, a remnant of the external world. But the unconscious, too, contains more than past reality; it contains and encompasses something unreal, extra-sensory, which from the start was inherent in the concept of the soul.

Of Schreber's elaborate belief system with its capricious deity, omnipresent miracles, and hierarchies of souls, Freud commented simply that the rays "are in reality nothing else than a concrete representation and external projection of libidinal cathexes." Psyche was now a fully materialized entity.

Yet we ignore or rationalize the spiritual dimension at our peril. Schreber's psychotic universe is noteworthy precisely because, in what was already a predominantly secular era, it contains a crucial component of religious experience: terror and awe. Tobin Siebers has observed that, in our secular age, "the desire to supplant sacred terror with psychological pathology is a common reaction to the supernatural." Yet until 1623, when the Church banned the further representation of monsters in sacred art at the Council of Trent, the supernatural grotesque had always been an important feature of Christian art, a recognized "sacred language" in and of itself revealing a reality beyond the natural. David Williams has noted that "Christianity, as a rational, philosophic religion, required a deep symbolic encoding of the mysterious and mystical truth of the grotesque and the fantastic, on the one hand to prevent its degeneration into magic and, on the other hand, to elevate it to the full intellectual reality of the allegorical."

In the twentieth century the narrow field of the literature of the fantastic, with its strong undercurrents of pathology, reproduces ambiguous fragments of that experience. Georges Bataille said, "Those arts which sustain anguish and the recovery from anguish within us, are the heirs of religion." In the vacuum left by the exile of the soul, a French commentator on Lovecraft, Maurice Lévy, has noted, like many others, this strange—one wants to say "unholy" as well as *unheimlich*—link between literature of the grotesque, personal pathology, and the mystic religious experience: "Driven by a myth—a necessarily *oriented* structure, based on the quest for and the revelation of the sacred—horror can only be expressed by and in sacrilege; the impious cults, hideous ceremonies, blasphemous rites . . . which tell a reverse history of salvation . . . To formulate sacrilege is somehow to recover the meaning of the sacred." If the Godhead in orthodox religion must always find some representation as Monster, as Slavoj Zizek asserts, the post-Christian monster is an equally necessary appendage of the Enlightenment: as soon as Kant's pure Subject appears, says Zizek, there is also the *Ding an Sich*, the void that cannot be grasped, an empty space of thinking where the monster—that is, the inherently unstable element—appears. In this way the grotesque tradition, with its now-tattered link to a sense of the divine, continues to fulfill its ancient function.

The grotesque, however, makes up only half—the dark half—of the complete religious experience. As Wolfgang Kayser noted, the grotesque truly "instils fear of life rather than fear of death." What it noticeably lacks is the experience of bliss, grace, divine joy. When the union of human and more than human occurs as a merging of subject and object in the compromised context of a psychotic episode, the field can only bear a blighted fruit. The inner worlds of Lovecraft and Schreber are full of fear and suffering, painful metamorphoses, debasement: transformation minus transfiguration.

If psychotics might be considered failed mystics, it is not the absence of a communal framework of shared religious belief or philosophical speculation that betrays them—madness, after all, was equally well known in the Christian Middle Ages as well as across cultures—but rather the encounter with their deepest psychic wounds, the fatal flaw that first lures them into the region of the Great Heresies and then overwhelms them. As a refiguring of the wound in allegorical terms, the transcendental experience draws the psychotic further and further away from a human, conscious integration of his own suffering. Episodes of false grandiosity are quickly followed by crushing despair. No healing occurs as a result of the compelled inner journey, only a perverse urge to repeat one's submission to it. If Jakob Boehme was, as he is sometimes styled, a master of the inward journey, then Daniel Paul Schreber was its slave. (I will return to this theme in Chapter 7.)

Still, as Moshe Idel remarked of Bruno Schulz, the shared malaise of this trio, however inseparable from their individual pathologies it may ultimately be, can be considered not simply "symptomatic" in a clinical sense but a microcosmic reflection of a deeper metaphysical unrest, a tragic, half-articulated awareness "that avenues once open are no longer accessible to man." Like Wilbur Whateley in "The Dunwich Horror," they are seeking, and failing to find, the invisible twin without whom the kingdom of heaven cannot be reached.

FORM AND FORMULA

Lovecraft, at some level highly aware of the duplicitous nature of the psychotic's downward journey, intuitively sensed (probably rightly) that the Gnostic epiphany of *knowing*—being "transformed through enlightenment into the actual object of knowledge," as Giovanni Filoramo puts it—was more than his conscious ego could handle, that any fusion with the transcendental object would be fatal to his sanity. The encounter with the horror at the center of self had, consequently, to be avoided at all costs. In the following warning we read Lovecraft's strategy for managing the uncontrollable uprushings of the psyche: "It is absolutely necessary, for the peace and safety of mankind, that some of earth's dark, dead corners and unplumbed depths be let alone; lest sleeping abnormalities wake to resurgent life, and blasphemously surviving nightmares squirm and splash out of their black lairs to newer and wider conquests." Or, as one of his characters says elsewhere, "The most merciful thing in the world, I think, is the inability of the human mind to correlate all its contents."

Just as psychosis itself might be said to represent the psyche's symbolic defense mechanism for avoiding the direct experience of unbearable pain, both Schulz and Lovecraft use a considerable array of literary devices as defense mechanisms to disarm psychosis in their works. In Schulz's stories the madness of the Father character is expressionistically rendered in his loss of boundaries, his shape-shifting; we feel a kind of sympathetic aesthetic relish for the psychic transformations and growing alienation of this creature gradually dwindling away from his humanity. Pain and suffering are distanced and subsumed into two-dimensional affects flaunted by a quasi-heroic figure in whom the son as artist seems to have merged with the chaotic disintegrating paternal presence. Of this representation, however, John Updike has astutely noted:

> The many metamorphoses of Schulz's fictional father-figure, culminating in the horrifying crab form he assumes in [the story "Father's Last Escape"], the sometimes magnificent delusional systems the old man spins, and the terrible war of diminishment versus enlargement in the imagery that surrounds this figure have their basis in an actual metamorphosis that must have been, to the victim's son, more frightening than amusing, more humiliating than poetic.

And even though Schulz has generously bestowed on Father his own role as "Demiurgy" of the secondary creations of the imagination, the teller of the stories remains an omniscient, nonparticipating observer on whom Father's dangerously disintegrating representations have no visible effect.

Lovecraft's rendering of the same Ur-dilemma, the loss of a father to a terrifying and dehumanizing transformation, is at once more immediate and less accessible. His policy of strictest containment, even as it seems to be superficially overturned time and again in the dark outcomes of his stories—in which at least one sacrificial victim is inevitably served up, stripped of human shape, speech, and identity, to the Great Old Ones—Lovecraft in fact enforces at the level of narrative structure. At first his representations seem straightforward enough. The prospect of metamorphosis, whether physical or psychological, fills his characters—and us as readers by extension—with terror, disgust, and loathing. At the same time, however, his stories evoke the same low-level terror over and over again without taking his readers any further toward resolution or any deeper into self-awareness. The madness is tightly locked into the formulaic structure and metaphoric level of these stories, and consequently it remains an enchanted beast that can never have its curse lifted, can never be humanized, by the insights of art.

In Chapter 4 I drew a distinction between the separate fates of popular and high forms of fantastic literature in the Old and New Worlds. This separation of category is crucial to an understanding of how we as readers experience H. P. Lovecraft in contrast to writers like Schulz or Kafka. The fact that popular genre literature lacks the sanction of traditional high-culture critics does not prove ipso facto that it possesses subverting virtues; there are very good reasons to have reservations about these literary modes, and there is, in fact, a level on which Edmund Wilson's judgment of Lovecraft is not entirely off the mark.

The basic distinction is between a reading experience that is complete in itself and another kind of reading experience that provides a catharsis of sorts yet carries within it the compulsive demand to be repeated. After reading *Moby-Dick* a reader does not feel compelled, in a week or two, to seek out another adventure story with whales in it. Reading Henry James's *Turn of the Screw* or a tale by Singer, Schulz, or Kafka does not trigger an insatiable hunger for more stories about demons real and possible or men turning into insects. These works are self-fulfilling in some mysterious way; they are inherently satisfying in themselves and can, in time, be reread with even deeper appreciation for their levels of meaning. Reading a murder mystery, in contrast, or a ghost story or a romance—all the genres whose readers are accurately described as "addicts"—is in essence engaging in a *Wiederholungsdrang*, the repetition compulsion that Freud identified as a trait of certain neuroses. After finishing the work, such a reader is moved not to reread it (specific works in these genres tend to have a one-time reading function only) but to read another of exactly the same kind, new content cast in the same unchanging form. Even to read a story by Poe, Lovecraft, or any of the great Victorian or Edwardian ghost story writers is to embark on an endless cycle in which the true catharsis seems oddly displaced, moved forever forward into the future as the reader "devours" story after story.

Why is this so? One answer is obvious: the stories of Kafka, for example, do not replicate a single narrative movement; they contain nothing formulaic or "typical," as Lovecraft's stories do, in their plot or characters. But the truth lies deeper. W. H. Auden provided an important clue when he said, "The identification of fantasy is always an attempt to avoid one's own suffering: the identification of art is a sharing in the suffering of another." If this is a true statement—and I believe it is profoundly true—what is there in the avoidance of suffering that offers such a compulsive attraction, such a hook? In Lovecraft's work and horror stories generally, the repetitive element is an experience of inchoate terror that is packaged into a familiar, predictable, and highly structured plot in such a way that the reader is teased with the tantalizing prospect of utter loss of control, of possession or engulfment, while safely contained within a formalized, almost ritualized narrative. In their inexorable journey from symptomatology to the revelation of male homosexuality, it must be noted, many of Freud's own case studies partake of these same dynamics—temporarily reducing the writer's anxiety, one suspects, while avoiding a direct encounter with its source.

Reading (or writing) a horror story, then, might be considered a similar experience to what Lenore Terr and other psychiatric researchers now call the "posttraumatic games" that children who have been kidnapped, raped, or otherwise mistreated typically invent. That is, while often repressing a direct memory of the event, such children play games that symbolically reproduce the dreadful experience. Because they make no conscious connections, however, the wound is never healed by this enactment; it is only unconsciously displayed over and over again. In the same way, representations of terror-inducing entities and situations fulfill the compulsion to experience a familiar yet disconnected sense of being overwhelmed—a rewounding in the name of healing that never arrives at its goal. Because both writer and reader dare not come too close to the true wound at the core of their being—it is *too* terrifying—they are cursed to reenact its effects compulsively, and the psychic experience, like the game playing, remains a completely unconscious act.

Projection itself—the central device of all modern psychotopographic art, high or low—represents (in the psychological quarter of the Four Corners) an attempt by parts of the personality to communicate with one another through internal defenses erected within the psyche. (For the Neoplatonic perspective on projection, see Chapter 8.) The paradox is that this effort to communicate must be forever thwarted by the very nature of its form, which demands constant repetition with no resolution. An affect that is personified as an Other, in the real world or a work of literature, is calling attention to itself, wants the conscious psyche to notice it. The very fact that it *is* the Other, however, means that the projection stays intact; no true recognition occurs.

Popular ghost and horror stories, which keep their projections entirely intact, offer no identification with suffering, no understanding of its source. They merely replicate in the reader the emotional aftershocks of psychic trauma (dread, terror) in a manageable form while the source of the suffering remains untouched, unlived, and unmastered. To read a genre story is to participate in a Sisyphean reenactment that is not the kind of complex, deeply identified reexperiencing a reader undergoes with the works of a writer like Kafka. Thus a world of difference lies between, on one hand, watching a movie called, perhaps, "Invasion of the Giant Cockroaches"—one's heart thumping with terror as the enormous menacing insects attack a town, tiny citizens fleeing in all directions, a few crushed to death—and, on the other, waking up one morning with Gregor Samsa after a night of troubled dreams. In the second case, the deeper problem that both these works in their own very different ways take up, namely, the inner monster that belongs first to us, however much it also belongs to the outer cosmos, is identified with and *lived* from the inside out, not experienced as an invading Other.

Before this begins to sound too much like moralizing, it is important to acknowledge the deep human craving, a craving that far transcends pathology, for Story in its most primal form. "People must have conversation, they must have houses, and they must have stories," G. K. Chesterton flatly declared in his classic "In Defence of Penny Dreadfuls," adding for good measure: "Literature is a luxury; fiction is a necessity." Of the pleasure produced by "degrading high literature," Bakhtin says, "All that is high wearies in the long run." High art–low art is a symbiotic, mutually reinforcing continuum, not a dichotomy—a continuum on which it is possible to go too far in either direction. Too much cerebration without the spine of Story means a basic emotional bonding with the work never takes place, but a reader will also drown in too much formulaic tale telling.

As the film scholar Russell Merritt has observed, the fantastic is the one genre that uniquely negotiates the twentieth-century dialogue between high and low art, and story is their common denominator. The person who watches "Invasion of the Giant Cockroaches" will very probably, the next week, go to see "Attack of the Fungoids." But this person may well be reading "The Metamorphosis" at the same time (witness Wittgenstein and his pulp detective fiction). It could be argued that this instinctive craving for repetition is exactly the experience of listening to a traditional folktale, that something inherent in formulaic structure triggers the desire to repeat the experience. Though they share with folktale a characteristic naive replication of plot and character type, however, the modern written mass genres are highly specialized forms that embody highly specific psychological Gordian knots. In the murder mystery, for example, I suspect we see the simultaneous ritualized reenactment, and warding off, of a vast repressed and unconnected rage. Identification is absent in the repetition compulsion of formulaic narrative. In Freud's quest to make homosexuality the virtually universal answer to the "question" posed by the pathology of his male patients, we see repetition compulsion enacted by its identifier: the need to discover again and again in others what one is not able, at the deepest level, to connect to oneself.

Schulz's universe, emotionally distanced though it is, is built on childlike joy rather than dread at the encounter with the unconscious. So, at the deep level of authorial invention, is Kafka's. Using this distinction as an aesthetic rule of thumb, the difference between Lovecraft on one hand and Kafka and Schulz on the other—bearing in mind that all three are still situated squarely on this side of the fence of sanity from Daniel Paul Schreber—might be expressed as the difference between pathology displaced and pathology partially acknowledged and identified with, therefore transformed.

Maurice Lévy believes that writers like Lovecraft are effecting their own cure, which both parallels and partakes of the religious experience of redemption. The fantastic, he says, "is at once an evasion and the mobilization of anguish": "It is at this deep level that the cure operates: because the sick man recognizes these images of horror as his own, he is in a position to assume them fully and thereby overcome them. To give a material representation to anguish is in itself to be freed from it." The Lovecraft stories, however, provide neither consciousness nor "cure" but a makeshift and compulsive form of anxiety management in which, as Foucault observed of Roussel, "the work bears the burden of resolving in the imagination the problems posed by the illness."

Like all humans, artists show varying degrees of psychological self-awareness. Lovecraft was not the sort of writer, or person, to look at his own stories and say: "Aha! My male creatures are always horribly deformed below the waist, they worship great phallic monoliths dripping with green liquid, and there is never a whisper of sex in my stories! I wonder if there is any connection?" Lovecraft's awareness of the displacement of sexuality in his fictions—like Poe's of his obsessive sex-death nexus—seems nonexistent and consequently untransformed. A core of monstrousness at the bottom of his psyche remains monstrous; his eternally misshapen beasts are never released from the evil spell under which they labor.

But we must also remember that art that incorporates identification does not "cure" its practitioner, either, though it can provide an opening up, a sense of expansion absent in the repetition compulsion of formulaic narrative. (As S. S. Prawer brilliantly observed, there are Tolstoy truths and Kafka truths, and we need both.) Even in its most sophisticated forms, art that is psychotopographic remains profoundly narcissistic and solipsistic. In the end, after this long dive into self, the outer world, the world of the truly Other, begins to pull urgently at the reader. We don't want to stay trapped down under the roots, gasping for air; we know intuitively we must somehow resurface in the human community or die. Often, just when we think he has totally drowned himself in the inner phantasmagoria, Bruno Schulz will make a sudden, unexpected break for the light. In the last scene of the story "Night of the Great Season," even Father finds the products of the imagination hollow and soulless in the light of day. The sun is shining, the shop assistants wake up yawning; upstairs in the kitchen sleepy Adela with her uncombed hair grinds coffee in a mill that she heats up against her body. The cat washes itself in the sunlight. The reader draws a breath of air, and the world becomes a human place again.

Neither Poe nor Lovecraft surfaced to such a vision in their fiction, yet both are important and original American talents. Obsessed by themes whose full dimension he was unable or unwilling to grasp consciously, Lovecraft used his intense sensitivity to his own unconscious uprushings to give modern readers a unique body of work and a new variation on some very old religious and philosophical traditions of Western culture. No other writer has rendered madness as a physical metamorphosis in quite this way, nor produced a demonic cosmography of such intelligent and breathtaking originality. Not the least of his virtues, finally, was personal bravery, the tenacious spirit of the Outsider who managed to win his own mental stability and life as an artist against all odds of upbringing and family circumstance. Howard Phillips Lovecraft's greatest creation was to make himself human.

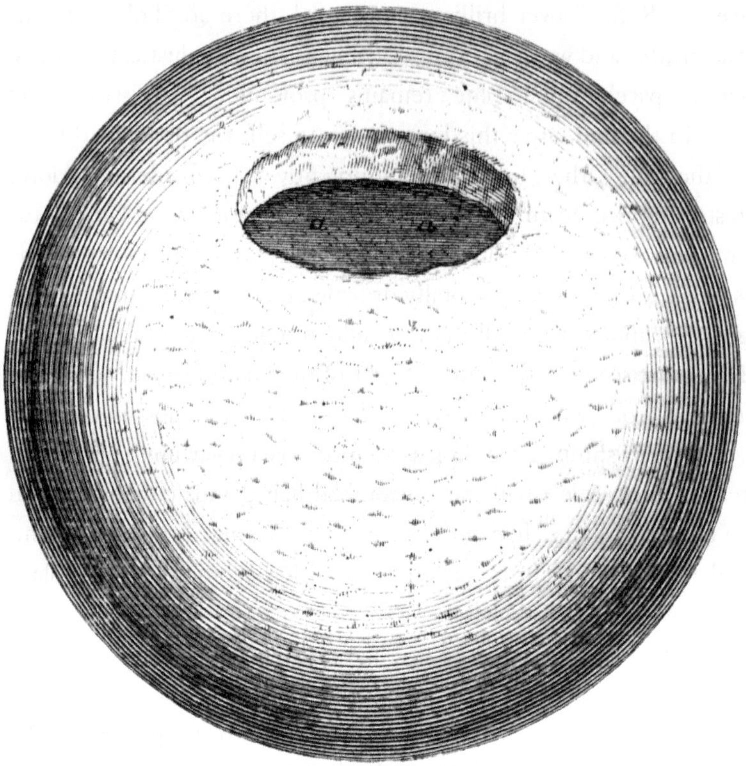

Thomas Burnet's polar hole, out of which the Flood emerges. From Burnet, *Sacred Theory of the Earth* (1691–1692).

Quaesivit arcana poli videt dei.
He sought the secret of the Pole
but found the secret face of God.

—Inscription, Scott Polar Institute, Cambridge

Everyone has an Antarctic.

—Thomas Pynchon

SIX

SYMMES HOLE, OR THE SOUTH POLAR GROTTO

As a child I was home-schooled on an old schooner in various anchorages along the Gulf Coast of Florida. In a corner of our paneled dark mahogany main cabin sat a globe that turned reluctantly on a rusty metal stand. Rubbing my fingers along the buckled seams of the pasted-on sections of world map, I brooded over the shapes of the continents and the way they seemed to match one another like pieces of a giant puzzle. Florida's jagged concave inner curve, if you swept assorted West Indies island bits and pieces along with it, locked boldly onto the north rim of South America, whose eastern edge, like any good jigsaw piece, snapped into place under the jutting bulge of West Africa. Joining the land masses in my head produced in me a pleasure too intense to put into words—as if, inside me, all my own continents had united in a single Gondwanaland.

I didn't know it but I was childishly anticipating, in the early 1950s, the rehabilitation of a then-discredited geological theory. Continental drift is one of those curious instances in which the techniques of empirical science converge with a long-standing human tendency to see inner psychological contents—images of wholeness, and ultimately of the self—reflected back from the larger physical contours of our planet. This identification is an ancient one in Western culture, and it continues to flourish long past its allotted historical moment in science as well as in literature and film of the fantastic.

Representations of the planet Earth as a *topos* of the human psyche derive from the premodern Neoplatonic framework of hierarchies of the living cosmos in which the heavens are mirrored, great to small, in the human body and (especially once its roundness was established) in Earth itself. Microcosm and macrocosm converge in the *rotundum*, the spherical container—cosmos, globe, and human soul. Renaissance natural philosophers drew their notions directly from Greco-Roman cosmology. The cosmos or world soul, according Plato's *Timaeus*, is a perfect living animal, feeding on its own waste, with no need of eyes or ears since there is nothing outside to see or hear, that also happens to possess the perfect form: "a sphere, without organs or limbs, rotating on its axis." *The Republic* presents the cosmos as eight hollow concentric spheres set inside one another like "nested bowls" with Earth at the center. The celestial axis holds the Earth still while the three Fates at the North Pole—apex of the Earth and its interface with the celestial axis and heaven—wheel the spheres and their attached fixed stars around it.

Though the idea of a round Earth would be abandoned for more than a millennium after ancient times, medieval and Renaissance philosophers retained the concept of concentric circles to describe the relationship between our terrestrial regions and the heavens. Meanwhile the Platonic sphere endured in Western consciousness in other forms. It was St. Augustine's famous dictum that the nature of God is a circle whose center is everywhere and whose circumference is nowhere. In alchemy, the dual transformation of matter and psyche occurred, not coincidentally, within yet another perfect sphere—the crucible or *rotundum*, that oval Vase of Hermes which was, by sympathetic connection, the heavenly sphere and a human head as well, embodying the transcendental essence of matter. The Neoplatonic concept of a spherical "astral body" surrounding the soul also endured into the Renaissance, reflecting as well the continuing deep belief in the ineffability of "Roundness." ("Time," Joseph Joubert eloquently pronounced, "does not know where to take hold of it.")

DOWNLOADING THE COSMOS

As the Copernican revolution and the new empirical sciences converted cosmic forces to telluric ones, the focus of attention shifted downward from the celestial and ethereal spheres to the newly valorized elemental sphere in the seventeenth century and Earth became the important level in the geocosmic hierarchy. Ontology begat geology, not cosmology, as all the classical attributes of the cosmic spheres—equator, tropics, and poles—were transferred and laid like a grid onto the *orbis Terrarum*. Ironically, even as the new sciences put the notion of an animate universe under active attack, the old guard found it no strain at all to fit a spherical Earth into the resonating symbolic framework of Pythagoras, Plato, and Ptolemy. For seventeenth-century alchemists—unregenerate Neoplatonists still "comprehending," in Robert Fludd's words of a previous century, "the true core of natural bodies," not just the puny "quantitative shadows" available to our five senses—the globe became yet another level of correspondence in the hierarchy of Hermetic vessels.

Non-alchemists proved equally adept at pouring the old wine into new glasses. Just as the pole star was thought by the ancients to mark a hole in the heavens, the earthly poles were now believed to mark holes in the planet. In his *Mundus subterraneus* (1664), the Jesuit Athanasius Kircher described ocean currents as subterranean waters rushing out of an enormous vortex at the South Pole to converge in a giant whirlpool that sucked them back under in a second hole at the North Pole. In 1692 the astronomer Edmund Halley advanced the theory that the Earth is composed of a series of inner concentric spheres capable of sustaining life. The most fascinating document of the rapidly expiring Platonic natural philosophy of this era, however, is Thomas Burnet's *Telluris sacra theoria* (1689), revised and expanded in an English version, *The Sacred Theory of the Earth* (1691–92). Burnet, master of Charterhouse and a pupil of the Cambridge Platonists Ralph Cudworth and John Tillotson, presented his explanation of the divine plan as manifested in the natural laws of Earth's physical development. Regarded by its author as a devout work of "Christian geology" but by others as highly heretical, *The Sacred Theory* represents a last-ditch effort to bridge the widening gap between the old and new sciences.

Carrying through a tradition of medieval Christian Neoplatonism out of Pythagoreanism, Burnet describes Earth as a "Mundane Egg," with the shell the Earth's crust and its interior the yolk. He posits an historical sequence of three Earths: first, out of Chaos, an original Edenic orb that was a fixed star, a Platonic *rotundum* of unblemished smoothness and regularity; then the present "broken Globe," whose continents, crevices, mountains, and other irregularities are a consequence of its humanlike Fall (a 1600-year process of geological "moral degeneration" in which a flood erupted from waters already lying within the hollow Earth); and finally a

The alchemical globe, nourisher and vessel of transformation. From Michael Maier, *Atalanta fugiens* (1618).

third millennial Earth, restored to a regular surface once more after a universal conflagration, where the resurrected righteous will rule for a thousand years until, after a final epic fire, the planet will metamorphose once again into a fixed star.

It is alchemy as implicit subtext, however, that rules the metaphorical structure of *The Sacred Theory*. In the story of Burnet's planet, whose rivers flow like arterial blood and whose fissures embody moral decay, we see geological, cultural, and spiritual transmutations nostalgically coincide. The cyclic births and deaths of Burnet's first and second Earth are virtually identical with the transmutation process, and the Earth itself makes an ideal crucible. The perfection of this Edenic Earth is ruptured by a Kircherian "Great Abysse" near the Pole that unleashes subterranean waters onto the Earth's surface in an alchemical *dissolutio* resonant with Noah's Flood to produce the split-apart land masses of its present fallen state. After purging in a "*Refiner's fire*," Earth will be transmuted by a *coniunctio* of earthly and divine into its ultimate *lapis* status as a fixed star.

Narratively as well as alchemically, Burnet's geocosmic vision of planet Earth also functions as a kind of microcosmic sacred theory of the psyche. Within the individual human, the apocalyptic sequence occurs as a profound interior transformation of the personality. Much like the tree-cum-Cross protagonist of the Old English *Dream of the Rood*, Earth is a character whose progress we follow in a *Bildungsroman* narrative of high adventure. Its Fall from *rotundum* to "mighty Ruine" mirrors the human misfortune, its continental drift the emergence of the specific personal topography of character that spoils the perfect regularity of the undifferentiated pre-Fall soul. Both self and globe will regain their perfection after the Resurrection. Winding up his story, Burnet bids an affectionate goodbye, as to a familiar figure: "There we leave [Earth]; Having conducted it for the space of Seven Thousand Years, through various changes from a *dark Chaos to a bright Star.*"

The intertwined apocalyptic destiny of self and globe, as we will see, is a theme Burnet's literary heirs in the twentieth century would often return to. At the end of the seventeenth century, however, Burnet as a redactor of the old science was already a marginalized figure. In the next century's perspective, Erasmus Darwin's syncretic conceits in *The Botanic Garden* (1791)—such as his millennial vision of "Nymphs" towing icebergs to the equator to equalize the climates, thereby allowing Earth to return to its Edenic state—would seem even quainter. For eighteenth-century Westerners, alchemy and the sympathetic identifications had been increasingly exiled to the realm of ornamental metaphor and, for wits like Pope, outright satire. Though Neoplatonic metaphors continued to exert a strong influence on the new empiricists and vestiges of the old *Naturphilosophie* would be revived by Goethe, Humboldt, and others well into the nineteenth century, after the Renaissance "the means of internalizing the cosmos," as Ernest Tuveson has said, would be "by the aesthetic rather than natural science." We must look to literary, not scientific, descendants of Fluddian natural philosophy for the continuing identification of self with globe and cosmos.

Out of the same mixture of Christian and classical sources drawn on by the old sciences, however, Western religious tradition already possessed a literary genre of mystical geography. From Dante to John Bunyan, the quest literature of Christianity had always boasted authors who, much like the classical and medieval mnemonists we will meet in Chapter 8, created their own special kind of inner topography. In the concrete allegory of these narratives, outer and inner worlds describe each other; the spiritual journey enacts itself in the physical journey, and vice versa. Unlike the theoretical foundation of natural philosophy, however, the underlying terms of this literary genre were not immediately—and in some cases never—erased by the rapidly changing philosophical, religious, and scientific worldviews after the seventeenth century. From the Romantic era on, the Neoplatonic tradition would be carried on in a distinct group of literary sea and adventure narratives that, while ostensibly imitating the real feats of Western explorers circumnavigating the globe, became vehicles for a new kind of soul quest through the geocosm.

"O vast Rondure," intoned our trusty nineteenth-century Hermeticist Walt Whitman (also known to identify himself as "a Kosmos"):

> Swimming in space,
> Cover'd all over with visible power and beauty!
> O soul, repressless, I with thee and thou with me,
> The circumnavigation of the world begin,
> Of man, the voyage of his mind's return,
> To reason's early paradise . . .

The new secularized quest narratives embodied considerably "more than passage to India," however. Now, as earlier, this spiritualizing of physical geography would require that the journey be undertaken by real people and start at a quantifiable point in time and space in the physical world precisely so as to end up in an internalized soul region outside time and space. Using the topographical allegorizing of the religious narratives, the creators of these fictions would also oblige their readers to employ, within their own interpretative process, the analogic principles of the old discarded science.

For the Romantics and their literary heirs, the artist became Robert Fludd's Pan who fashions a world that is the perfect mirror of his own insides. Coleridge and Poe would *imagine* their journeys in a Neoplatonic demiurgic mode, creating visionary landscapes in the realm of C. S. Lewis's "third world" of fantasy in which elements first are hypothesized, then appear; possibilities are entertained, then materialize. What M. H. Abrams called the Romantics' "habitual reading of passion, life and physiognomy into the landscape," deriving from precisely such older notions of the *imago Mundi* as a mirror of the human soul, contributes the same demiurgic framing to Chapter 5's "psychotopographic" aesthetic, in which, naively or deliberately, writers transferred their inner psychic processes onto an exterior landscape. The Romantic revival of other features of the Neoplatonic cosmos emerged equally in American Transcendentalism, when Emerson could declare both the existence of the "Over-Soul" as pure Mind and nature as a system of "concentric circles"—the circle being, in his view, the "highest emblem in the cipher of the world."

Nowhere is this complicated heritage of the Renaissance more strikingly apparent than in the nineteenth- and twentieth-century Western fictional narratives of journeys to the Poles, and particularly (because of its greater remoteness) to the South Pole. The historical path of this identification follows the same development as that for the Earth generally. "Pole" began as an astronomical term (Greek *polos,* axis or sky; Latin *polus*), first as the entire axis of the celestial sphere, then as the two fixed points in the celestial sphere around which the stars seemed to revolve. By the sixteenth century, *pole* signified the two points at which the earth's axis met the celestial sphere. (Similarly, *Arktos* the Bear, the northern constellation, and *anti-Arktos,* its southern counterpart, gave the Arctic and Antarctic regions of the Earth their names.)

The term *pole* was also extended to each of the two opposite points on the surface of a magnet, which aligns itself north-south. The magnetic poles of the earth are these two points in the North and South Poles, respectively, where the compass needle takes a vertical position. The magnet was a crucial tool for mariners in finding their way (*lodestone,* the old word for magnet, means literally "way-stone"). Thus the Poles, in both their "true" and "magnetic" manifestations, are orienting points. In microcosmic terms, this means they are the orienting loci of the psyche, but by the same token they are also the least known, the farthest from consciousness, the point (inherent in the notion of *polarity*) where the transcendent and celestial spheres have special access to the human sphere. This specialness of the Poles had a precedent as early as *The Republic,* in which Plato also described "openings in the sky" where souls depart after death and "openings in the earth" where they return to be reborn—later identified by the Neoplatonist Porphyry as the northernmost and southernmost points of the zodiac, or the apex and nadir of the heavens.

This association is reinforced in Western fantastic representations across the centuries that present the outer, geographic Poles as either Hells or Edens. In the *Metaphysics* Aristotle situated the Ekumene, the inhabited part of the Earth, in a northern temperate zone that had a southern counterpart, the "Antipodes," on the lower side of the sphere—a region the Pythagoreans had earlier dubbed the "Antichthones" because they believed it to be a separate celestial body, an *alter orbis* completely distinct from our planet. Lucretius and other ancient commentators, however, derided the idea of an inhabited southern area because their position on the sphere (literally "anti-podes") would oblige these people to hang upside down by their feet. Nonetheless, the belief in a large southern land region led Ptolemy in the second century C.E. to posit the "Terra Australis Incognita," a southern continent completely enclosing the Indian Ocean—an hypothesis that would be accepted as geographical fact for the next fifteen hundred years.

The tradition of the Antichthones and Antipodes as a region of reversals *contra naturam* was similarly transferred into medieval Christian geography; Higden's fourteenth-century *Polychronicon*, for example, contains a mappemonde detailing the monsters of the south ("Androphagi, Garamantes, Farici, Virgogici, Troglodytes"); in *Paradise Lost* Milton located a "frozen continent" in Hell. Even as late as the eighteenth century, the Earl of Shaftesbury could comment, about his map of nature: "In the places most remote from man's works and occupations we encounter the manifestation of the divine Mind pure and undefiled." Out of this tradition comes the implicit identification of the Poles with the furthest unknown reaches of the self/world and, for that very reason, with its transcendent center as well. For what is farthest away and most hidden is, paradoxically, always what is most important: the journey to the pole is a journey to the center of the soul.

A mystic or occult notion of both Poles also figures strongly in alchemists' speculations about the resonating inner and outer worlds. C. G. Jung—the twentieth century's only unabashed Neoplatonic philosopher disguised as a psychologist, and not coincidentally a fervent student of alchemical literature—uncovered numerous references to the Poles in the works of the "chemical" philosophers: in the *Museum Hermeticum*,

"Philalethes" asserts that since the magnet has a hidden center which turns toward the Pole, thus "in the Pole is found the heart of Mercurius, which is the true fire wherein its Lord has his rest. He who journeys through this great and wide sea may touch at both Indies, may guide his course by the sight of the North Star, which our Magnet will cause to appear to you." Performing his own twentieth-century downloading of grids—this time into the psychological realm, not the geographical one—Jung interprets this passage as a description of the psyche's irresistible journey or impetus toward wholeness, that is, "the *Deus absconditus* (hidden God) who dwells at the North Pole and reveals himself through magnetism. His other synonym is mercurius, whose heart is to be found at the Pole, and who guides men on the perilous voyage over the sea of the world. The idea [is] that the whole machinery of the world is driven by the infernal life at the North Pole, that this is hell, and that hell is a system of upper powers reflected in the lower." Jung believed the "true nature of the Pole" was "a cross from which the four directions radiate"; that the quest to reach the Pole was symbolic of striving for "wholeness as the goal to which the 'archaic appetite' points, the magnetic north which gives the traveller his bearings on the 'sea of the world.'"

The Rime of Arthur Gordon Pym

In the sharply diverging post-1700 histories of natural philosophy and nautical exploration, we may safely identify a single shared moment of harmonic convergence: Sunday, December 30, 1774, when Captain James Cook in his journey to the Southern Ocean on the *Adventure* reached latitude 71°10′ south. In place of Ptolemy's Terra Australis Incognita and a mystic *circulus australis* there was now a real Antarctic Circle, and a real ship had just penetrated it. Deciding because of the "immense Icefields" that he "could not proceed one Inch farther South," however, Cook concluded there was no southern land mass enclosing the Indian Ocean from the south.

Samuel Taylor Coleridge had read Cook's accounts of his voyages, right along with the little volume of his Neoplatonic muses "Iamblichus, Proclus, Psellus, and Hermes Trismegistus" that he purchased in 1796 and carried everywhere in his pocket. Whereas Mary Shelley would have her golem disappear into the "darkness and distance" of the Arctic, the South

Pole's greater remoteness seduced Coleridge sufficiently to transpose his extensive readings in Arctic literature to the Southern Ocean when he composed *The Rime of the Ancient Mariner*, first published in 1798 in *Lyrical Ballads* and revised in 1800.

Universally recognized as the "travelogue of a spiritual journey," *The Ancient Mariner* is a profoundly alchemical and elemental poem that most closely resembles the medieval dream vision whose landscape provides fixed points for meditation and self-reflection. Coleridge's unique amalgam of physical and soul journey was to set the pattern of the southern journey for his many imitators in Western literature: an archetypal sea trip from a bustling port (consciousness) to Terra Australis Incognita (unconsciousness), where a transcendental encounter takes place that initiates either the integration of the self or the possibility of psychic (and physical) annihilation.

In a not surprising convergence of influences, the poem begins with a quote from Burnet's *Archaeologiae Philosophicae* attesting to the reality of Neoplatonic spirits in the air around us. In Burnetian (or even Miltonian) terms, if humans lost their inner vision at the Fall, a journey to the Pole must involve an initial failure to recognize that the journey has an esoteric as well as an exoteric meaning; and this failure must produce catastrophe followed by suffering and eventual redemption. This is exactly what happens in *The Ancient Mariner:* a man blind to his inner spirit (the albatross) kills it, but is redeemed when he experiences love for God's creatures (the sea-snakes) as his ship or body journeys on the larger Body of the globe, pushed by angelic forces in a harrowing voyage of self-discovery. Ultimately, the "lonesome Spirit from the south pole" guides the mariner's boat back to civilization, where it sinks in a maelstrom, leaving him the sole survivor. (This is a trope that Melville would replicate, along with the encounter with an ill-omened white creature.) The journey to the furthest unknown recesses of the psyche discovers a positive force there that supports the ego's act of self-redemption. We take it as a good psychotopographic sign that the sinking occurs close to the Ekumene, home base in Europe, because that suggests the experience inflicted on the mariner is more accessible to his (and the reader's) consciousness than any action taking place at the Pole itself.

In the two voices of *The Ancient Mariner*—one a kind of pre-Shakespearean sixteenth-century balladeer, the other his Percylike antiquarian commentator of roughly Burnet's time in the next century—Coleridge's obvious strategy, as Jerome McGann and others have shown, is to reproduce not just the flavor of an archaic ballad but a sense, as in the Old and New Testaments, of multiple layers of text. In fact, the poem amounts to a kind of self-contained Burnetian geological process of its own, a little evolving world of complex textual strata. As in *The Sacred Theory*, cultural evolution and personal transformation simultaneously represent themselves and each other in *The Ancient Mariner*. The contrasting layers reinforce our sense of the poem and its craggy fissures as no perfect *rotundum* but a self-conscious and all-too-human Burnetian "mighty Ruine."

When Edgar Allan Poe's *The Narrative of Arthur Gordon Pym* was published in 1838, the same year that the U.S.-sponsored Wilkes expedition departed for the Southern Ocean, the Antarctic continent had still not been reached, and its very existence was uncertain. Poe, like Coleridge, drew heavily on explorers' accounts, but even more heavily on the old notions of the animate universe: in the warm waters he bestows on the Antarctic Ocean we see the classical legends of the warm waters of Hyperborea, the land behind the North Wind. More specifically, he uses the then-popular theories of John Cleves Symmes, an army captain who, projecting the structure of the Ptolemaic cosmos, as the Renaissance natural philosophers did, directly onto Earth, postulated a hollow earth composed of five concentric spheres accessible through holes near the North and South Poles.

Symmes's ideas were dramatized in a curious novel entitled *Symzonia: A Voyage of Discovery* (1820), by one "Captain Adam Seaborn," a nicely allegorical Divine Human sobriquet most likely concealing Symmes himself. Considered the first piece of American utopian fiction, *Symzonia* describes Captain Seaborn's most American determination to discover a "new and untried world" because "the resources of the known world have been exhausted by research, its wealth monopolized, its wonders of curiosity explored, its every thing investigated and understood!" Seaborn navigates his custom-built steamboat to a temperate southern land mass and follows a wide river pouring into a hole at the South Pole to the first of the five layered concentric spheres. In this land (which "out of gratitude to Capt. Symmes for his sublime theory" he names Symzonia) Adam Seaborn finds a perfect democracy of albino humans governed by a council of Worthies and a Best Man.

Symmes's theory of the hollow earth was enthusiastically propagated by his follower J. N. Reynolds, whose treatises on the South Pole were both reviewed by Poe and inserted verbatim into *Pym* (which, as the scholar J. O. Bailey once suggested, might just as easily have been titled *Pymzonia*). Widely disseminated in the early nineteenth century, Symmes's notions passed into popular folklore as the polar "Symmes Hole," a belief that kept its currency among hollow-earth cultists in America and Europe well into the twentieth century. In 1906 a sixteen-year-old H. P. Lovecraft would write a letter to the Providence *Daily Journal* to refute the theory advanced in a new book, *The Phantom of the Poles*, "that the earth is a hollow sphere, with openings at the poles." (It is typical of his contradictory conscious and unconscious agendas that this writer, who prided himself on the rigor of his "scientific materialist" views, went on to create just such a Kircherian globe in his own fictions.) Even after World War II—as Joscelyn Godwin details in his comprehensive study *Arktos*—a considerable popular myth arose that Hitler had survived the war in a subterranean Antarctic labyrinth with a legion of flying saucers at his disposal.

Like Lovecraft, Edgar Allan Poe had his own predilections toward the vortex that made the Symmes Hole a perfect fit with the inner structure of his psyche. For even more than *The Ancient Mariner*, *The Narrative of Arthur Gordon Pym of Nantucket* is an "imagined" story in the full sense of the word. In Poe's only novel action must be imaginatively anticipated before it can be made manifest, events seem only to proceed while the first-person narrator lies in a swoon, and Pym awakens each time to find himself regressed into ever more outrageously claustrophobic and life-threatening predicaments. This repetitive retreat into lowered or obliterated consciousness is a microcosmic journey to his own self's southern Terra Incognita, an endless dress rehearsal of the outer journey that will end so obscurely.

In the macrocosmic terms of the larger narrative, the apocalypse that Pym and his comrades rush toward in their small boat (a structurally equivalent act to that chronicled in his stories "MS Found in a Bottle" and "Descent into the Maelstrom") is also the vortex in the unconscious toward which the conscious ego feels both attraction and fear. The two realms, outer and inner, are congruent and resonate sympathetically. In the symbolic terms of Poe's magic cosmos throughout his literary works, falling into a hole or pit is the transforming moment of death, and this recurring private and personal Symmes Hole becomes the inevitable destination or *telos* in both the smaller and larger predicaments of *Pym*. It is the reason that Poe can provide no depiction of the South Pole itself, or of Pym's reaching it.

Pym presents its own complicated pastiche of textual fragments recounted by at least three narrators, two of whom are unidentified. One anonymous commentator obligingly recaps for us after Pym's own account abruptly breaks off: "'*Tekeli'li!*' was the cry of the affrighted natives of Tsalal upon discovering the carcass of the *white* animal picked up at sea. This also was the shuddering exclamation of the captive Tsalalian upon encountering the *white* materials in possession of Mr. Pym. This also was the shriek of the swift-flying, *white*, and gigantic birds which issued from the vapory *white* curtain of the South."

In his giant white birds Poe is echoing Coleridge's albatross, but he engages a "polarity" as well: the black island of Tsalal that intrudes itself before the whiteness. The commentator, however, fails to mention the most striking manifestation of whiteness, namely the giant "shrouded human figure" with snow-white skin who rises before Pym and his companion Dirk Peters out of the ashy cataract filling the southern polar sky. In Poe, as in Coleridge before him, these mysterious white figures embody the transcendental and unearthly dimension of the southern polar region. In *Pym*, however, does this figure represent the Anthropos, the macrocosmic Divine Human, as Richard Howard has proposed? Or is perhaps the globe itself the true Anthropos here and the giant figure merely its microcosmic equivalent? The enigmatic, open-ended narrative leaves readers looking over the edge of the Great Abyss with no clear view of what lies below.

When Herman Melville drew on *Pym* for *Moby-Dick*, he had been a real-life sailor (if only very briefly), and so his descriptions of the landscape of the Southern Ocean are considerably less shadowy and mythic, more grounded in sensory detail, than those of the armchair sailors Poe and Coleridge. Reversing the pattern set by Coleridge and Poe, Melville's greater involvement in the world of the senses makes his characters' pursuit of the whiteness an outer-world journey first and an inner-world journey by extension. It is no coincidence, consequently, that Melville's Anthropos turns out to be a marine mammal, a creature of the elemental world rather than a daemon of the next sphere up.

As the nineteenth century wore on, the Romantic worldview suffered its own continental drift into, on one hand, the Victorian sentimentality of Arthur Conan Doyle, whose supernatural story "The Captain of the 'Pole-star'" (1883), in which a tormented ship's captain meets his end on an Arctic ice floe while pursuing a white insubstantial female form (presumably the ghost of his dead fiancée back in Cornwall), contains more than an echo of *Pym* as well as of *Frankenstein;* and, on the other, the techno-literalism of Jules Verne in works like *The Sphinx of the Ice-Fields* (1897), which it does seem that Verne composed, as William Butcher asserts, not only to "completely superimpose itself on Poe's [novel] but also to cover it so completely as to virtually block it out." The mysterious Sphinx that Verne's explorers are seeking at the South Pole turns out to be a giant magnet that strips their vessel of all its iron; pinned to the lodestone by a stray musket is none other than the frozen corpse of the explorer Arthur Gordon Pym. This device is typical of Verne's framing consciousness of techno-scientific materialism that would achieve dominance in the next century. Verne, like his closest twentieth-century equivalent, the English writer J. G. Ballard, flirts with the sympathetic connections in his primal topographies, but simply because the narrative stays literalized on the level of physical geography, the deeper possibility of the "journey to the center of the self" remains unconscious.

The Little Apocrypha of Lovecraft, Lem, and Pynchon

Verne's sensibility proved the enduring trend as it helped initiate the popular genre of science fiction, which rationalized the supernatural into the Divine Machine capable of accomplishing feats formerly performed by angels, nymphs, and Neoplatonic daemons. A century after Poe, H. P. Lovecraft wrote as both a child of this materialist movement and a rebel against it. Yet another explicit homage to *Pym*, Lovecraft's South Pole horror novella *At the Mountains of Madness* (1931) renders the human as the geological and architectural, depicting inner psychic processes macrocosmically in the globe itself and the city under the globe's South Pole. The narrator of Lovecraft's tale is a geologist who has brought to the Antarctic a remarkable new drill that can go to unplumbed depths. (In the psychotopographic terms of polar romance this means he is an explorer of unconscious strata of the psyche, or, put in a way Lovecraft might not have approved of, a psychoanalyst.) The expedition uncovers evidence of a lost civilization beneath the Pole whose extraterrestrial builders—the Great Old Ones, star-headed beings from another galaxy—entered the planet via the Antarctic Ocean and built marine cities shortly after the moon was separated from the South Pacific.

The heart of the story is the narrator's exploration of the Old Ones' colossal abandoned underground city below the South Pole. Penetrating the multileveled labyrinth of this *mundus subterraneus* becomes the story's true journey within a journey—its novelty lying in the grotto convention that even as we imagine we have penetrated the farthest reaches of the Underpsyche/Underworld, something yet lies beyond and under, something hostile and deeply threatening to human reason. Like Burnet's fallen Earth, Lovecraft's Pole is a decayed realm. "If we could open the Earth," Burnet said, "and go down into the bosom of it, see all the dark Chambers and Apartments there, how ill contriv'd, and how ill kept, so many holes and corners, some fill'd with smoak and fire, some with water, and some with vapours and mouldy Air; how like a ruine it lies gaping and torn in the parts of it." For Lovecraft this region is likewise "a haunted, accursed realm where life and death, space and time, have made black and blasphemous alliances in the unknown epochs since matter first writhed and swam on the planet's scarce-cooled crust." The cities of the Old Ones, we learn, were gradually destroyed *geologically*, by seismic upheavals, the wearing effect of rivers, and similar telluric events.

This Burnetian process of ruination has its parallel in psychic disintegration within the Terra Incognita regions of the human head, which we penetrate at our peril: the assistant goes mad and the narrator barely escapes with his sanity. Microcosmically, Lovecraft in the person of his narrator is telling us not to push the interior journey too far; there is a fatal structural flaw built into the composition of the planet-psyche. At the very least, only the inaccessibility of certain regions holds in check the sinister transcendent principle that, unleashed, would overwhelm it. Here, finally, the hole at the Pole definitively converges with the proverbial "hole in the head" signifying madness.

After Lovecraft the fantastic polar journey continues to flourish in any number of twentieth-century literary and science fiction works. In the Polish writer Stanislaw Lem's *Solaris* (1961), our globe's macrocosmic frame is transposed to a planet entirely covered by a living ocean, a regularized surface of sentient matter much like Plato's sphere and Burnet's flooded Earth (though its name suggests our own planet's sun and an opposing element, fire). After a century's futile attempts to establish contact with this creature, the story opens as scientists on Earth have beamed X-rays onto the surface of the ocean from the space station hovering above its surface, to surprising effect: the three resident scientists have been visited by simulacra or "Phi-creatures" that are the ocean's living representations of the scientists' secret desires. When Kelvin, a psychologist, arrives from Earth, he is immediately sent the simulacrum of his dead wife—a woman who, it is suggested, killed herself because of his emotional neglect.

But the true landscape of *Solaris*, as Gaston Bachelard has correctly observed of *Pym*, is an inner one: the interface of consciousness and unconsciousness or (in the older terms) the material and the transcendent. In Kelvin's helpless love for his Phi-creature wife and growing contact with his own emotions, this story emblematically represents an overly intellectual consciousness (as the quantifying name "Kelvin" suggests) hovering above an inaccessible unconsciousness that resists control and, sending back as it does inconvenient messages about their innermost psychic contents, shows far greater knowledge of those who study it than vice versa. The scientists are self-deceiving, narrow Cartesian rationalists detached from their own animal and emotional natures who vainly attempt to control and subjugate their split-off desires under the guise of "communication."

As one disillusioned scientist/explorer puts it:

> We are searching for an ideal image of our own world: we go in quest of a planet, of a civilization superior to our own but developed on the basis of our primeval past. At the same time, there is something inside us which we don't want to face up to, from which we try to protect ourselves . . . We arrive here as we are in reality, and when that reality is revealed to us—that part of our reality which we would prefer to pass over in silence—then we don't like it any more.

This, indeed, is the classic postcolonialist argument: if the Western imagination does no more than project its own psychic Terra Incognita onto the rest of Earth, then we correctly regard such accounts of these regions as portraits of an alter ego, not an *alter orbis*. The colonialist's psychotopographic presumption is to seek the Other and find only his own reflection. *Solaris* presents the exquisite joke that, for once, rejected contents of the psyche are projected onto an Other who is having none of it and—to the total psychological undoing of the projectors—reflects these contents right back to them.

Inevitably, the planet Solaris is discovered to contain, Chinese-box style, its own *alter orbis*. As Kelvin and the other scientists move the station toward the planet's southern polar region, they try beaming Kelvin's own brain waves into the ocean. Of this same region an earlier scientist, whose suppressed testimony is preserved only in lost notebooks (significantly nicknamed the "Little Apocrypha"), testifies that he saw the shape of a giant baby produced by the ocean after an astronaut fell in it. Is this, as some hypothesize, the ocean's representation of an artifact of the drowned man's memory? Possibly so, but Robert Fludd had this to say on the subject of "polarity" in alchemy: "The two polar fundamental principles of the universe are *form* as the light principle, coming from above, and *matter* as the dark principle, dwelling in the earth . . . In the middle, the sphere of the sun, where these opposing principles just counterbalance each other, there is engendered in the mystery of the chymic wedding the *infans Solaris*, which is at the same time the liberated world-soul."

The ocean, the erudite Lem may be suggesting, could be producing the possibilities of an alchemical *coniunctio*, the sought-for union of spirit and matter, a Philosopher's Stone of its own. But what, exactly, does the baby, this "child of the sun," consist of? Is it materialized spirit or spiritualized matter? Ultimately Kelvin develops a theory not unlike Bachelard's notion of material imagination as he comes to see the ocean as an "imperfect" or "evolving" god "whose passion is not a redemption, who saves nothing, fulfills no purpose—a god who simply is." In his highly alchemical definition, "this God has no existence outside of matter. He would like to free himself from matter, but he cannot." Hoping to maintain his tenuous connection to transcendence through the strait gate of his now fully accepted love, pain, and loss, Kelvin decides to remain on Solaris.

The mystic geography of Thomas Pynchon's *V.* (1963) is also implicitly based on Renaissance natural philosophy. In one of the novel's intricately interwoven subplots, the English explorer Hugh Godolphin, sent on a routine mapping expedition into the heart of Asia, stumbles upon the land of Vheissu, the first letter of whose name, in this novel's terms, signals its membership in a macrocosmic hidden pattern that shapes human events all over the globe and across history. Vheissu is a phantasmagoric region whose physical features have the magical ability to change color constantly, like a "tattooed skin"; its emblematic indigenous species is an iridescent spider monkey. Haunted by visions of Vheissu, Godolphin journeys to its direct opposite, the South Pole. There, "at one of the only two motionless places on this gyratic world" ("a country," he adds simply, "the demiurge had forgotten"), he discovers, shimmering through several feet of transparent ice, the body of one of Vheissu's spider monkeys.

Besides representing the now familiar millennial convergence of tropics and pole, this image recalls the rainbow display of colors preceding the *albedo*, or whitening, the first major transformation in the alchemical process. Yet we learn that this impossible juxtaposition, "the rainbow-colored spider monkey buried beneath the zero point of absolute stasis," is only a cruel parody of the mystic *unio*. An unnamed "They," says Godolphin, deliberately planted it for him to find, as a "mockery of life," to show that Vheissu was simply an amusing fabrication of theirs. If this is the case, then whose fabricated world do Godolphin and all the rest of us live in?

Another character speculates on the identity of these mysterious demiurges. "A barbaric and unknown race," he says, "employed by God knows whom, are even now blasting the Antarctic ice with dynamite, preparing to enter a subterranean network of natural tunnels, a network whose existence is known only to the inhabitants of Vheissu, the Royal Geographic Society in London, Herr Godolphin, and the spies of Florence." In the elaborate tapestry of *V.*, the rulers of the sublunary sphere are able to elude identification by hiding in a polar grotto below the visible pattern of the natural world. Or conversely, in the familiar "Is it real or am I crazy" conundrum to be explored in the next chapter, they may represent no more than the speaker's own paranoid fantasies.

WHEN THE POLES COME HOME

Warning humans off visiting their Antipodean regions, as Lovecraft and Pynchon both do, may seem a sensible strategy—Coleridge, after all, once said that "it is a false and feverous state for the Centre to live in the Circumference"—but what of the psyche/globe whose fate is to have its poles invade its central regions? Here we see the polar quest diverging into two distinct types of journeys cum inner experience: going to the Pole and falling into the *mundus subterraneus* on one hand and, on the other, having the Poles invade the Ekumene, the center of consciousness, in such a way that the ego experiences either demonic conversion (death or psychosis) or a blissful mystical experience.

Using the macro-micro polar *topos* for very different purposes, two British writers, Leonora Carrington (1917–) and Anna Kavan (1901–1968), employ this second type of mystic journey by sending the ice to their protagonists instead of the other way around. This inversion of the polar ice caps amounts to a translation of the psyche/globe into a transcendent Platonic form that delivers Eden or death, and in both writers' works the globe paradoxically reaches its Burnetian regularized perfection by virtue of the solid sheath of ice encasing it. (The reverse polar apocalypse effect—melting ice caps bringing global flooding and unbearable heat—informs J. G. Ballard's 1963 novel *The Drowned World.*)

In *Ice* (1967) by Anna Kavan (a name its bearer, the former Helen Ferguson, adopted midway through her writing career in homage to Kafka), massive glaciers relentlessly encroach on Earth's temperate zones, possibly as an unexpected by-product of nuclear testing. Kavan's main character is an embodied Coleridgean Life-in-Death—a nameless albino young woman with snowy white hair and skin transparent as glass who moves from one landscape of sadism to another in a world that is dying of frost. The "girl's" mute passivity, we are told, is the result of being bullied by a sadistic mother (as Kavan herself claimed to have been). The male narrator, symbiotic alter ego of the brutal men this woman is in thrall to, pursues her through one vaguely totalitarian state after another in a phantasmagoric narrative in which points of view and lines of narrative are constantly shifting. In simultaneous parallel stories, the brutalized girl is resurrected from death, then flung back to it: *Ice*, like *Pym*, is a roller-coaster ride to death.

Kavan's bleak millennial vision communicates powerful excitement about the coming Armageddon. The destruction of life is represented as an enthralling, highly dynamic process:

> Dazzling ice stars bombarded the earth with rays, which splintered and penetrated the earth, filling earth's core with their deadly coolness, reinforcing the cold of the advancing ice. And always, on the surface, the indestructible ice-mass was moving forward, implacably destroying all life.

The Earth Kavan is describing is a Burnetian sphere; even allowing such an event as "ice stars" pelting the planet with their freezing rays, it would be impossible, in real-world terms, for ice to penetrate the Earth's core and freeze it from the inside out. Rather, Kavan is giving us a pathetic-fallacy description of a seductive, welcomed, apocalyptic death taking place at the center of one person's soul and physical body as well as in the outside world:

> Frozen by the deathly cold emanating from the ice, dazzled by the blaze of crystalline ice-light, she felt herself becoming part of the polar vision, her structure becoming one with the structure of ice and snow. As her fate, she accepted the world of ice, shining, shimmering, dead; she resigned herself to the triumph of glaciers and the death of her world.

Kavan died—from either an overdose or complications of long-term addiction—in 1968, at age sixty-seven.

One may draw the obvious parallels between the street name for heroin, the novel's title, and the destruction of the world represented within it. The world and the woman are the same entity; the body of the planet is her body; man's sadistic misuse of both has resulted in their deaths. Perversely, this is also an erotic fulfillment.

Leonora Carrington's shifting polar caps in *The Hearing Trumpet* (1977) provide a millennial vision as playful and life expanding as Anna Kavan's are death dealing. Carrington, an English painter now living in Mexico whose fiction and art have not received the recognition owed them in the annals of Surrealism, has written an explicitly alchemical adventure in which an elderly expatriate in Mexico, Marion Leatherby, is consigned by her son to a peculiar old folks' home (whose quirky buildings serve as an Expressionist extension of the inhabitants' own psyches) run by a Gurdjieffian tyrant. In the course of the entirely unsummarizable plot Marion and the other old ladies, organized by their secret leader the black servant Christabel, stage a personal revolt, with the macrocosmic result of their invocation of a three-headed Goddess being nothing less than the exchange of the poles with the equator and the release of a winged hermaphrodite called the Sephira (a syncretic version of Isaiah's six-winged seraph, here the result of the union of the Devil with a priestess of the old religion disguised as a nun) from the tower of our heroine's own psyche. In such a cataclysmic manner—as wolves and glaciers joyously invade the tropics—is Marion's initial forlorn wish to visit Lapland triumphantly fulfilled.

Very much in the spirit of Erasmus Darwin's eccentric vision of global equalization (complete with attendant nymphs), Carrington allows the protagonist of this psychic navigation to avoid the perils of both the overwhelmed consciousness (as represented by Poe, Lovecraft, and Kavan) and the colonizing consciousness (as represented by Lem). Here the invasion of consciousness by the remote and rejected regions of the psyche creates an icy Eden instead of Lovecraft's and Kavan's icy Hell. Marion Leatherby stands still while the Poles (herself, or her Self, the innermost core of her being divinized as the Old Woman and representing the true Pole) rise to meet consciousness in an ultimately benevolent encounter. At the climax Marion descends into a *mundus subterraneus* below the old folks' home where she dies and—after an alchemical cooking in a bubbling cauldron/*rotundum* stirred by her alter ego—is reborn a greatly enlarged human. This death and rebirth represent the correct outcome of the alchemical work: the mystic *unio* which results in the shrinking of the Terra Incognita and corresponding enlargement of the "inhabited areas" of the psyche. As self, globe, and cosmos are realigned to reflect the proper balance of power between male and female, consciousness and unconsciousness, Carrington lets her novel's eloquent last sentence aptly sum up the paradox.

Polar romance novels continued to flourish after Carrington and Kavan, though with one exception they cannot be covered here. Within a narrative framework of more straightforward realism, the same strands of thinking are visible in a short vignette in William Golding's trilogy of a converted British warship on its perilous voyage through the South Ocean. In *Fire Down Below* (1989), the concluding volume of this underrated masterpiece—misread by reviewers as, among other things, a "great sentimental journey of the naval kind"—the motley flock of passengers are Gnostic *scintillae Dei* whose microcosmically flickering souls resonate with the smoldering keelson in the bowels of the ship that threatens to rend apart at any moment. At one point before the ship reaches safe harbor in Australia, a calving, spinning iceberg (whose "dull and fitful gleam" the narrator first mistakes for the dawn) manifests as an enormous "cliff" that first appears downhill from the ship, then, impossibly, rotates around it. As, in another optical illusion, the berg seems to rush past the ship (a detail with echoes of the reverse-direction pattern used by Carrington), the narrator tells us he "saw a *melange* of visions in the ice which swept past me—figures trapped in the ice, my father among them." Golding's ship of self has had a quick brush with the capricious Polar Spirit, who obligingly offers the ego/narrator a tantalizingly quick glimpse into the transcendent Narcissus pool of his own unconscious.

The notion of psychological *projection*, our secularized human-centered construction of the old trope of sympathetic correspondences, insists (as we will see in Chapter 8) that the macrocosm reflects the microcosm and not vice versa. This is a development a few of the old Renaissance heretics might well have applauded, if only because it locates the divine, albeit unacknowledged, squarely within the human. In these terms, the inner wastes of Antarctica have provided richly resonating correspondences for post-1700 writers and poets, out of the Symmes Hole of whose imaginations have crawled—among other creatures—the Polar Spirit, a giant shrouded figure, a white whale, a huge magnet, snaillike monsters and their star-headed masters, an enormous baby, a winged hermaphrodite, a victimized albino woman, and a multicolored monkey.

In *The Ice*, his admirable study of the Antarctic, Stephen J. Pyne claims that the era of the polar Gothic ended at the close of the twentieth century: "Once Antarctica and the ocean basins had been generally explored, there were no unvisited geographies within which to set a lost civilization; fantasy writing had to resurrect old problems, tour other planets, or plunge into the depths of the human soul." But even as we see this mechanism working in a novel like *Solaris*, it seems likely that our mapped, explored, satellite-circumnavigated and much photographed Whole Earth will continue to exert its macrocosmic seductions on the human psyche. It has been revived, to name only one example, in the new Earth cults of Gaia; Robert Fludd would not find much to quarrel with in their construct of the ecological food chain, a telluric-projected revival of the Neoplatonic great chain of being, or in the fact that the notorious widening hole in the ozone layer over Antarctica, widely believed in our age to leave humans nakedly exposed to malign ultraviolet solar *radii*, is another perfect replication of Ptolemaic cosmology.

Yes, there is a "real," empirically verifiable hole in the ozone layer, just as there is a "real" atmospheric polar vortex that aggravates it, but the polar hole—like holes in the head and black holes in the cosmos—is also a venerable construct of Western culture. We do well to remember, with

Emerson, that "our globe seen by God is a transparent law, not a mass of facts." Just as the Symmes Hole functioned as a kind of global grotto for our immediate ancestors, its present-day equivalent the ozone hole, that provocative tear in the fabric of the "noosphere," functions as a space grotto in our imaginations. Popular storytelling has fed, and continues to feed, this symbolically rendered need. The two Hollywood film versions of *The Thing*, set in the Arctic and the Antarctic respectively, belong to the category of the Other who emerges from the Pole, the desert, under the sea, and all other regions of inner wilderness outside the realm of consciousness. The 1956 *Mole People*, in which albino descendants of the Sumerians are discovered under a volcano, features a "scientific" introduction by Hollywood's favorite Fifties expert, Professor Frank Baxter, who cheerfully cites Symmes and other worthies in defense of a hollow earth. In Peter Weir's *The Last Wave* (1978), Australian aborigines foretell in their dreams the next great Flood, a cataclysm produced by "giant low pressure from the southern polar regions"; Stephen King's *The Langoliers* (1994) features a planeload of people who leave sublunary space and time when they fly through a polar aurora borealis that mysteriously appears in the midwestern skies; Kevin Reynolds's *Waterworld* (1995) depicts an Earth in which the ice caps melt and the poles reverse to produce a lawless anti-Edenic oceanic planet.

In these formula narratives, the level of the inner psychological journey remains submerged and unconscious, though we sense intuitively that it is there, just as I felt the click! of the uniting continents as a child. A catharsis of this sort stays locked in reflexive instinct, lacking the fullness of discovery that a completely realized work of art allows. Yet humans never cease their efforts to bring about the impossible union. The pull we feel the Polar Spirit exerting on us to go to it, of course, is also our own desire for it to come to us. Even as Antarctica continues to be earnestly depicted in documentaries and news reports as "a continent devoted to science," its less allowable representations flourish in a different territory of the human psyche, a region we have never stopped trying to tow into our temperate zones. For this reason, my last sentence must be Carrington's: If the old woman can't go to Lapland, then Lapland must come to the Old Woman.

Dr. Caligari revives Cesare the somnambulist. From Robert Wiene's *The Cabinet of Dr. Caligari* (1919). Photographed by Benjamin Blackwell for the University of California Art Museum, Berkeley; gift of Robert Shapazian.

"The trouble's not in the mirror—it's in my mind! It must be!"

—Character in the film *Dead of Night*

"Inside his head he heard the stormy crows."

—Howard Nemerov

SEVEN

IS THIS REAL OR AM I CRAZY?

Watching Robert Wiene's *The Cabinet of Dr. Caligari* (1919) on video not too long ago evoked a vivid memory of the first time I saw this German Expressionist classic. It was the year of our Lord 1965, and I sat transfixed in the Unicorn, a tiny firetrap "art film" theater annexed to the long since defunct La Jolla bookstore Mithras. How electrifying to an adolescent who was now a Southern Californian (and Beach Boy fan) were the crooked perspectives of the dark European town, the scenery painted not just with arcane symbols but with *energy lines*—sunlight and shadows! Capping it all was the nifty surprise ending that turns the whole story on its head, exposing it as the fantasy of that most unreliable of narrators, an asylum inmate. It was my first high-art encounter with the "Is this real or am I crazy?" plot, and I was hooked. On the spot *Caligari* joined Akira Kirosawa's *Rashomon* in the handy shorthand lexicon of a would-be teenage intellectual seeking a vocabulary to describe the world—or, to put it in a way well out of my reach at the time, the existence of multiple subjective perceptions of reality.

None of the various explicit premises of *Caligari* involved the supernatural, even if, as we will see, its Expressionist matrix implicitly did. In mainstream Western literature of the twentieth century, empirical reality itself served as the displaced grotto locus of the transcendental. Behind the psychological question, however, the teasing ontological one still lurked: Is there another level of reality beyond the one our senses apprehend? But this question could no longer be legitimately posed outside the two carefully circumscribed territories of *believe* and *imagine*, that is, official religion and the genre worlds of science fiction and horror whose "suspension of disbelief" rules were clearly posted at the door by virtue of their humble aesthetic standing. Taking the Aristotelian standpoint that the fantastic operates only within specified works of the imagination and nowhere else, Tzvetan Todorov addressed this issue in Henry James's *The Turn of the Screw*, where he identifies the fantastic as "that hesitation experienced by a person who knows only the laws of nature, confronting an apparently supernatural event":

> In a world which is indeed our world, the one we know, a world without devils, sylphides, or vampires, there occurs an event which cannot be explained by the laws of this same familiar world. The person who experiences the event must opt for one of two possible solutions: either he is the victim of an illusion of the senses, or a product of the imagination—and laws of the world then remain what they are; or else the event has indeed taken place, it is an integral part of reality—but then this reality is controlled by laws unknown to us.

"Once we choose one answer or the other," Todorov adds, "we leave the fantastic for a neighboring genre, the uncanny or the marvelous."

But what if we choose both? This hesitation, I will argue, can be translated into a permanent stance. Something about the "Is this real or am I crazy?" question must have especially bothered and obsessed us during the psychologizing century if we are to judge by the sheer number of times it popped up in works of art both cartoonish and profound. As we have seen, notions of the supernatural and the human soul underwent a complicated transition in Western culture after the seventeenth century—from external to internal experience and from spiritual, immortal *pneuma* to a personal, mortal *psyche*, respectively. At the same time, however, earlier notions of the soul and divine agency often surfaced in secular literature and poetry in disguised or demonized form and most frequently represented in high art as delusional material arising out of the symptomatology of mental illness. No sensitive reader can miss this striking congruence of the old premodern worldview with quasi-psychotic elements in Western literature of the fantastic from the Romantic era on. The connection is a troublesome one and feeds all too easily into the widespread *episteme* prejudice that religious experience itself, if it dares to claim more than moral precepts, is a kind of pathology.

The core dilemma concealed within the obsessive recurrence of the "Is this real or am I crazy?" motif is the fact that authentic mystical religious experience is not recognized as such in a postreligious intellectual culture and takes up at best a very small corner of our awareness (even as Western societies remain filled, paradoxically, with churchgoing believers). Our worldview has pushed us toward perceiving the experience of rapture as coming from within, not without, Terry Castle says; after the eighteenth century, "one could now be 'possessed' by the phantoms of one's own thought—terrorized, entranced, *taken over* by mental images—just as in earlier centuries people had suffered the visitations of real spirits and demons." As a result, the personal experience of Being—the union of spirit and matter that is the deep perception of the Platonic cosmos—is familiar mainly from accounts of psychotic confusion. We know it as hallucination, not vision.

Among sane nonbelieving Westerners such intimations, so repressed as to be inaccessible to ordinary consciousness, seem possible only when artificially induced by psychotropic drugs. During the drug experience, interestingly, the boundary between our perception of organic ("living") matter and inorganic ("dead") matter customarily breaks down, producing a powerful vision of a cosmos that lives and breathes through every physical object around us—the same perception of "spiritualized" matter we saw reported by Gérard de Nerval as well as Daniel Paul Schreber in Chapter 5. One of many observer accounts of this drug-induced perception came from the investigator Stanislav Grof:

> Not infrequently the LSD subjects experience consciousness of inorganic material; the phenomena they can identify with can range from a single atom to various materials such as diamond, granite, or gold. Sometimes the consciousness of particularly stable and durable substances can be experienced as involving an element of sacredness. Some have described, for example, that from this point of view the granite statues of the Egyptians and the pre-Columbian golden sculptures do not appear as images of deities, but deities themselves; what

was worshipped was the stable, immutable, and undifferentiated consciousness of the material involved.

This empirical rediscovery, as it were, of the *unus mundus* by a generation of drug experimenters during the 1960s and 1970s contributed significantly to the populist revival of American Transcendentalism—or, more accurately, to the fourth Great Awakening—that expressed itself in a profusion of religious groups many of whose adherents came to their new faiths straight from psychedelic experience.

Whether it originates in drugs or in extreme mental disorientation, however, quasi-mystical experience of the sort just described is, as noted, fragmented, distorted, and certainly not the same as the experience of true religious mystics. It is chiefly because of their very intriguing surface similarities and our science-oriented culture's disavowal of the otherworld that we tend to regard the mystic's vision as synonymous with the hallucinations of paranoid schizophrenia, and as equally dysfunctional. It is important to recognize that this conflation of insanity with forms of *gnosis* represents a kind of primitive, undifferentiated confusion in its own right. "As for what we call psychoses," Mikkel Borch-Jacobsen comments, "it has long been commonplace to ethnopsychiatry and the sociology of mental illness to emphasise their cultural relativity: our pathetic paranoiacs and schizophrenics would elsewhere have been sacred or accursed beings—people possessed by the devil, prophets, shamans, 'holy madmen.'" Traditional societies did view shamans much as we view artists, as psychically injured souls the cracks in whose psyches allow divine illumination to shine into our world, and other researchers have noted the prevalence in our own society of strongly held religious convictions among schizophrenics, whose recovery often involves a spiritual awakening and sometimes a new role as religious leader. All societies, however, distinguish between injury and insanity. Lunatics have not been regarded as holy either in the European Middle Ages or among the !Kung hunter-gatherers of Africa; in the traditional way of acknowledging an underlying structural kinship among the various manifestations of this state, such persons have been thought to be possessed by the Devil or an evil spirit instead of (like a true mystic) God or a good spirit.

In refuting Géza Roheim's famous claim that premodern magic practices in the West represented "institutionalized schizophrenia," Ioan

Couliano has pointed out that magic actually represents the older vehicle, since preempted by psychoanalysis, "to establish a peaceful coexistence between the conscious and the unconscious . . . When the dream is envisaged as a phantasmic production stemming from the unconscious, and schizophrenia as a state of confusion between oneiric context and sensory context, we no longer need marvel at the correspondence between the phantasms of schizophrenics and the phantasms brought into play by magicians." The difference between them, in Couliano's succinct words: "Mental illness is a function of disorder; magic is a function of order." If we accept the transgressive premise that a state of transcendent experience, like the state of dream experience, is "real," we can make the same distinction between hierophany and schizophrenic delusion.

TURNING THE ONTOLOGICAL SCREW

In our culture the religio-psychological conflict expressed in "Is this real or am I crazy?" has been taken up by numerous twentieth-century imaginers besides James and the makers of *Caligari*, but mostly at the level of mass entertainment—in any number of science fiction novels and Hollywood films. (By the time I saw *Caligari*, like millions of other young Americans I was quite familiar with the motif via various episodes of Rod Serling's early 1960s television series *The Twilight Zone*.) Such stories (and, as we will see, even the science fiction writer Philip K. Dick's first-person nonfiction expositions) follow one of two revelatory paths: (1) a fantastic series of events, including supernatural phenomena, is revealed to be the delusion of its crazed (and typically incarcerated) narrator; or (2) a fantastic series of events, including supernatural phenomena, is revealed to be a true story whose narrator has been falsely labeled as crazy (and is typically incarcerated).

The first, or *crazy*, revelation plot is the crucial trap door that allows the audience to opt for a "rational" rather than a supernatural explanation—and the tale's real-life author to avoid the heresy of open supernaturalism. This type is considered, in the terms of the *episteme* worldview that most educated Westerners inhabit, to be aesthetically superior and sophisticated to the second type because it accords with what we really believe is true about the world. In high art of the twentieth century (to be distinguished from the self-described "entertainments" of major authors and special cases like Kafka and Schulz), the supernatural or paranormal translates most frequently into delusion or projection—the fumes or waste products of subjectivity, as it were—and no more.

The classic example remains *Caligari*, in which a beginning and ending frame seem (in the context of a plot synopsis, at least) to reduce all the uncanny and gruesome doings of a story steeped in the conventions of German Romanticism to a madman's subjective delusions. Interestingly, the original script by Carl Mayer and Hans Janowitz did not include this frame, which was dreamed up by Fritz Lang, the director initially assigned to the film, and carried through by Wiene, its ultimate director. The final version of the story goes as follows: Sitting in a parklike setting, Francis, a young man, recounts to an older man the curious story of a fair that recently came to their town. Its major attraction is the sinister Caligari and his mysterious assistant the "Somnambulist" Cesare, a puppetlike hypnotized entity whom Caligari sends into the town to perform acts of murderous vengeance. Francis, friend to one of the victims, unmasks Caligari as none other than the head administrator of the local insane asylum, a man obsessed with the crimes of the original Dr. Caligari, an eleventh-century mountebank. Returning to the framing story, however, the narrative delivers its second, more shocking revelation: Francis and the other man are patients at this very asylum. The story closes with the announcement by the benevolent doctor (who up to now, seen through the lens of Francis's tale, has looked quite Expressionistically thuggish) that he will now be able to "cure" Francis.

The echoes of Daniel Paul Schreber's memoir, published just sixteen years before the film was made, are unmistakable in *Caligari.* Schreber, you will recall, identified the director of his own asylum, who was also his attending psychiatrist, as his "soul murderer." As in Schreber's case, the story of the evil doctor is completely undermined by the madhouse frame, for we assume that an inmate's tale equals a madman's tale, hence a delusion. In both instances we are pushed toward the unavoidable conclusion that the storytellers are "projecting" their own inner conflicts onto the very person who is trying to heal their illness—the good doctor himself. But are they really? (The deeper implications of the "Is this real or am I crazy?" frame for the Expressionist aesthetic of projection will be taken up in Chapter 8.)

The second, or *real*, revelation plot, was always present in popular genres. In a move that represented a substantial transformation in cultural attitudes, however, the *real* revelation plot became more prevalent in the second half of the twentieth century. In stories of this type, the label "crazy" is what gets thrown off as the character's vision is vindicated by our understanding that in the story's terms the supernatural is real. A typical example is the sci-fi movie *K-Pax* (2001), based on a 1995 novel by Gene Brewer, about

> a mysterious patient admitted to a mental hospital who falls under the care of an emotionally rigid psychiatrist. At first, the psychiatrist dismisses his patient's wildly complicated yet steadfast belief that he has traveled across time and space from a place he calls K-Pax, a planet whose inhabitants possess remarkable abilities. Determined to prove that the stranger is nothing more than a tragic victim of multiple personality disorder, the doctor soon finds himself doubting his own diagnosis. As the supposed alien interacts with the other troubled residents of the hospital, they undergo wondrous transformations and, one by one, shake off lives encumbered by mental disorders and become happy, functioning people.

Reversing the *Caligari* premise, here the patient's reality is validated and the doctor's interpretation is overturned. Here also, just as in Lovecraft's stories, the journey to the otherworld is conflated with the psychotic experience. Whereas Lovecraft's main characters were driven insane by their contact with the demonic rulers of the otherworld, in this case visitors from that reality (the "extraterrestrial alien" subtype common to the science fiction genre throughout the twentieth century) produce a healing, beneficent transformation in the humans they encounter.

Because it is still not in line with what we really believe is true about the world, however, we tend to give a story that features the *real* revelation plot the rank of second-rate, formulaic art—the genre stamp of popular entertainment, "make-believe" that does not warrant the attention of serious minds. In Chapter 5, however, I argued that what makes a literary or film story formulaic is neither its content nor its metaphysics but rather the psychology of its internal structure, a certain distinctive rigidity that reflects the author's desire to avoid a direct confrontation with the inner conflict fueling the surface action of the story. The formula thus resides not in validation of the supernatural but in the characteristic genre trait of repetition compulsion, that curious granny knot of representation which superficially reproduces the conscious anxieties associated with this conflict without mastering them, thereby obliging both writer and reader to repeat the experience obsessively. Lovecraft teasingly encountered and ducked away from the underlying deep pull of psychosis; the present case suggests a strong unconscious desire to cast off the *crazy* frame and believe in the otherworld, a desire that because it conflicts with our knowledge of the laws of the physical world around us produces this unceasing proliferation of genre works falling on either side of the fence.

For the sole example of a work that avoids the genre fate on either side, we must look back to the subject of Todorov's reflections on the fantastic, *The Turn of the Screw*. Published in 1898, this most famous of Henry James's works is the first-person narrative of a nameless young governess who zealously tries to protect her two orphaned charges from a perceived possession by the sinister ghosts of their former governess, one Miss Jessel, and her lover, Peter Quint. In the final scene, which is also the story's climax, the governess stands triumphant against the apparition of Peter Quint at the window—she senses that Miles can no longer see Quint, as she assumes he previously could—only to lose the boy in a way she had not expected:

> With the stroke of the loss I was so proud of, he uttered the cry of a creature hurled over an abyss, and the grasp with which I recovered him might have been that of catching him in his fall. I caught him, yes, I held him—it may be imagined with what a passion; but at the end of a minute I began to feel what it truly was that I held. We were alone with the quiet day, and his little heart, dispossessed, had stopped.

Did Miles's sudden death release him from possession by spirits or from unbearable hounding by the deluded person in whose care he had been placed? Was it an exorcism or a murder? This tale, whose frame does nothing more than emphasize the good character of a narrator whose sanity/perception of the supernatural is deeply in question, stretches a tightrope between the two alternatives that beautifully allows its readers the choice of falling in either direction. (Its tension also neatly embodies the family psychodynamics of James and his own siblings, reared in hothouse social isolation and producing one individual, his distinguished brother

William, with borderline mystical experience and another, his sister Alice, with borderline psychotic experience.)

For most of the twentieth century, however, a vast majority of this book's readers (myself included) derived intense aesthetic satisfaction from contemplating only the psychological half of its insidious Rorschach duality—namely, the conviction that the heroine had projected her own unconscious sexual repression cum delusion onto the figures of the dead caretakers. By 1921, while acknowledging the primal fear—the sense of *uncanniness*—the story aroused in all its readers, Virginia Woolf could flatly state that "Henry James's ghosts . . . have their origin within us." The psychoanalytic trend would reach its apotheosis in Leon Edel's pronouncement that the governess's "demoniacal and malevolent imagination converts her anxieties and guilts, her romantic-sexual imaginings, which she considers 'sinful,' into demons and damned spirits. In seeking to cope with her own demons she infects those around her—as Hitler, raving and ranting, infected an entire nation with his hysteria."

Having subscribed wholeheartedly to a version of this reading my entire adult life, I had never fully absorbed the implications of its alternative until I read a folklore scholar's comparison of the nineteenth-century American folk ballad "Little Bessie" to Goethe's famous literary ballad "Der Erlkönig" (Bruno Schulz's talismanic song, it will be recalled). In both of these songs a child is seduced by an otherworld visitant (Jesus and the King of the Elves, respectively) not visible to the child's adult caretaker and ultimately follows the visitant into death. Suddenly the second, long-ignored half of *The Turn of the Screw*'s pattern surfaced in my consciousness for the very first time, and it was a genuinely startling moment. *What if the ghosts were real?* And the fact that it is virtually impossible for any Western intellectual of today to entertain seriously such a notion automatically makes this the more interesting possibility to explore.

James was surely aware of precisely how his unforgettable closing scene mimicked that staple of nineteenth-century melodrama, the death of a child—whether spirited away by Gothicized demons in the earlier Romantic days or wafted to heaven on the wings of angels in the Victorian era. As discussed in Chapter 4, this was the one supernatural motif sturdy enough to survive in American folk ballads. It is questionable, indeed, whether James himself or his original audience ever regarded the governess as a nefarious projector of demonhood. Privately he referred to the story as "a fairy-tale pure and simple" and "merely apparitional," and once wrote H. G. Wells that in order to make it succeed as such, "I had, about my young woman, to take a very sharp line . . . I had to rule out subjective complications of her own—play of tone, etc.; and keep her impersonal save for the most obvious and indispensable little note of neatness, firmness and courage—without which she wouldn't have had her data." James concludes, characteristically, "But the thing is essentially a pot-boiler and a *jeu d'esprit*," thus underlining the supernatural dimension while carefully establishing his own aesthetic distance from it.

Even as James wrote other tales in which the spirits of the dead were meant to be taken as real presences, he was always careful to emphasize the preeminence of *imagine* over *believe:* "The charm . . . for the distracted modern mind is in the clear field of experience, as I call it, over which we are thus left to roam; an annexed but independent world in which nothing is right save as we rightly imagine it."

Whatever disclaimers James made, and however consciously or unconsciously he may have communicated sexual hysteria in the character of the governess, *on the story's own terms* no other character appears to contradict or correct her version of the events. What is more, pious American and English readers (who would have constituted the majority of James's audience a century ago) would have spotted immediately not just one but two possible supernatural outcomes, as follows: (1) despite his caregiver's wishful hopes, the possessed and already damned Miles follows Quint the revenant straight to hell (the Erlkönig outcome), or (2) thanks to his governess's dogged protection, Miles's innocent spirit flies straight to heaven (the Little Nell outcome). Only James, as (one is tempted to say) a supremely sensitive channeler of ontological ambiguity, managed to capture perfectly both of these old possibilities as well as the brand-new psychoanalytic one: (3) Miles, possessing no soul at all, neither ascends nor descends to any other reality but expires needlessly and tragically under relentless psychological pressure.

Regardless of authorial or (as critics now say) textual intention, cultural context, and all the rest, the element of the uncanny encompasses far more than either the governess's madness or the prospect of "real" ghosts. The uncanniness lies not exactly in the moment of "hesitation" between a natural and a supernatural interpretation, as Todorov would have it, but rather in the visceral and simultaneous comprehension of both realities, that granted by *episteme* and that granted by *gnosis*, each of which in its own way is truth bearing. To read and reread the final scene receiving first one and then another meaning until both mutually exclusive scenarios are operational is the deeply unsettling kind of repetition only high art can motivate.

Does reality run on a single track? The governess is sure, so is Professor Edel, but anyone who has once deeply inhabited both sides of the Rorschach is likely to find them, maddeningly, possible and impossible at the same time.

"IF YOU FIND THIS WORLD BAD . . ."

> If [the novel *Galactic Pot-Healer*] shows signs of psychosis, & it does—it is not because I experienced & knew God but precisely because I did not . . . Thus in a very real sense my sanity depended on my experiencing God, because my creative life logically demanded it.
>
> —Philip K. Dick

The real Augustine of this discussion, the man whom Stanislaw Lem dubbed a "visionary among the charlatans," must be the late Philip K. Dick (1928–1982), a science fiction writer and self-described "fictionalizing philosopher," who did not merely imagine but lived both sides of the Rorschach at once, confronting in the process the intertwined issues of the supernatural, mystical religious experience, and psychotic delusion in a much more explicit way than James, Lovecraft, or certainly Schreber had done a half-century and more earlier. In many ways as well, Dick is the perfect late twentieth-century bookend to Lovecraft: like Lovecraft, he was a sheltered autodidact who dropped out of high school because of unspecified nervous problems, never attended college, was bound to a possessive but emotionally distant mother, wrote in a popular genre despised by mainstream critics, and was obsessed with chronicling the existence of another reality and its impingement on our own. In contrast to Lovecraft's steady insistence that his fictional cosmos was only that (and depended on being untrue to be fully *weird*), Dick did not resist his real-life visions. He believed utterly in their reality at the same time as he sharply questioned the nature of their genesis within him.

Dick's bewildering and unmediated encounter with the Platonic realm took place in the fateful unit of time he labeled "2–3–74" (February and March of the year 1974). During this life-changing experience, as he recounts at length in many venues, he had the overpowering sensation of being "resynthesized" by an entity he called "the Programmer":

> At the moment in which I was resynthesized, I was aware perceptually—which is to say aware in an external way—of his presence . . . It resembled plasmic energy. It had colors. It moved fast, collecting and dispersing. But what it *was*, what he was—I am not sure, even now, except I can tell you that he had simulated normal objects and their processes so as to copy them and in such an artful way as to make himself invisible within them.

The shapeshifting Programmer, Dick believed, is the physical manifestation of a living cosmos, a meta-organism identical in all its features to Plotinus's World Soul. Dick dubbed his cosmos VALIS, or "Vast Active Living Intelligence System," and like its older Neoplatonic counterparts VALIS had a microcosmic-psychological manifestation as well. None other than Dick's own twin sister, who died of malnourishment when they were infants, embodies the "VALIS mind": "It is female. It is on the other side—the postmortem world. It has been with me all my life. It is my twin sister Jane . . . The other psyche I carry inside me is that of my dead sister." The loss of his sister opened the fissure in his psyche, Dick seems to say, that let in the light of the otherworld. In the same way that Giordano Bruno embodied the cosmos he called "New Amphitrite" or "vast Ocean of soul" as an image of the naked Diana, Dick's VALIS-Jane entity bridges the personal and the Infinite.

But if the shaman's wound, the personal-pathological, is the path to the Infinite, how are we to know if this is the right path and not the delusional one? In his first deep perception of a unity underlying all material things, Dick says,

> I was aware of nothing that was not the Programmer. All the things in our pluriform world were segments or subsections of him. Some were at rest but many moved, and did so like portions of a breathing organism that inhaled, exhaled, grew, changed, evolved toward some final state that by its absolute wisdom it had chosen for itself.

As a result of this experience, Dick was overcome by the classic mystic's conviction that for the first time in his life he had been granted true vision:

> I felt keenly that through all the years of my life I had been literally blind; I remember saying over and over to my wife, "I've regained my sight! I can see again!" . . . I understood that I had not acquired a new faculty of perception but had, rather, regained an old one. For a day or so I saw as we once all had, thousands of years ago.

Recall from Chapter 5 that Schreber also shared this sentiment about the "mental" blindness of ordinary people ("compared with him who received supernatural impressions by virtue of his diseased nerves") as Dick goes on to ask: "How had we come to lose sight, this superior sight? Why is it necessary that we be deceived regarding the nature of our reality? Why has he cloaked himself as a plurality of unrelated objects and his movements as a plurality of chance processes?" He concludes, in a now-familiar echo of *The Republic*, that in our time on earth we humans are stuck in the grotto: "We are dead but don't know it, reliving our former lives but on tape (programmed), in a simulated world controlled by Valis the master entity of reality generator."

Reading deeply in world religious literature, Dick devoted the next eight years of his life to the massive effort of integrating his overwhelming experience intellectually. Much of his inner experience he was able to match with the Christian Gnostics' specific brand of Platonism, a "radical" dualism, as it was once termed, in which humans are, in Dick's words, "pluriforms of God voluntarily descended to the prison world." Between us and the true god stands a creator god or demiurge ("deranged," in the Gnostic way of thinking) who causes us to "forget our divine counterpart while caught in his web." After listing "ten major principles of Gnostic revelation," Dick sounds a Lovecraftian note by adding irrepressibly that "to know [them]"—and he means "know" in its fullest Gnostic sense of *become*—"is to court disaster." (As we will see in Chapter 12, Dick would come to frame his religio-psychological experience almost entirely in the language of cybernetics.)

As a thoughtful intellect struggling to digest what had happened to him, Dick also constantly asked himself the hard question: Had he experienced contact with divine reality or with his own subjective mental disorder? As a reality mostly unshared by the rest of his society, were his hallucinations only that, or were they a kind of Platonic anamnesis, a recollection of the archetypal World of Forms? He grappled endlessly with this question in

Exegesis, a journal he kept every night over the eight years from his mystical experience until his death.

Meanwhile the themes were played out in his many novels, notably *Valis* (1981) and *The Divine Invasion* (1981), which acted as fictional vehicles for the religious and philosophical issues that obsessed him. (The skeptic Thomas Disch, it should be noted, dubbed *Valis* "a memoir of madness recollected in a state of borderline lucidity.") Dick himself retained his sense of humor on the subject; in view of the fact that he consistently heard his "AI" (artificial intelligence) talking to him, one feels he would be amused by a new virtual toy called "Sound Bite," a lollipop that, when put in the mouth, transmits electronic voices through the bone structure of the face so that the voices seem to come from inside one's own head. (See the discussion of schizophrenic auditory hallucination in Chapter 5.)

Was it real or was he crazy? For Daniel Paul Schreber the answers were, respectively, no and yes. For Dick, it was the yes-yes, both-sides-at-once Rorschach, and readers of his *Exegesis* confront a real-life *Turn of the Screw:* Is VALIS a cosmos, a schizophrenic's delusion, or both? Dick's biographer and principal scholar Lawrence Sutin states flatly that this writer's work displays a "brilliant coherence and emotional depth that signal anything but the workings of a madman." Given Dick's full and intricate exposition of his experience, I do not presume to make a judgment, in Sutin's words, "on the basis of a simplistic and patronizing sane/insane dualism." The most telling fact, however, must ultimately be that Dick's visions, though frightening in their intensity in his early encounters, were firmly set on the *via positiva.*

On November 17, 1980, two years before his death from a stroke, Dick recorded in his journal: "God manifested himself to me as the infinite void; but it was not the abyss; it was the vault of heaven, with blue sky and wisps of white clouds. He was not some foreign God but the God of my fathers. He was loving and kind and he had personality . . . He made me aware, then, of the bliss that would come; it was infinite and sweet."

THE FANTASY CULTS

What happens when a vision that begins in the realm of *imagine* ends up in *believe* and an author's own stories and characters become the raw material for rites, ritual, and worship? Philip K. Dick's role as science fiction writer links him to the elaborate folklore of the late twentieth-century science fiction and fantasy domains, in which the line between fan club and religious cult has become interestingly blurred. In the United States especially, many minor cults, some religious and some merely social, have sprung from popular fantasy fictions—novels, films, television shows, even comic books. Lovecraft wrote about a graverobbing Cult of Cthulhu; some of his fans responded with a Cthulhu cult of their own (Lovecraft's grave in Providence, which currently receives between ten and fifteen visitors *per day*, was the object of an aborted dig several years ago). This strange crossover marks a profound reversal from earlier times in our culture, when religion fed art instead of the other way around, and in an odd way it puts us further back yet to the earliest of human times, when all stories were about the gods.

Out of what I would argue was an instinctive longing, by segments of the Western late industrial indigenous tribe, to recontact the transcendent via the medium of Story, C. S. Lewis's "third world" of make-believe began its fairly substantial metamorphosis back into religion as cults and related belief systems during the nineteenth and twentieth centuries. But once the boundary between *believe* and *imagine* is breached, there is no controlling the direction the content is going to travel. If, as Lewis believed, fading gods must be "disinfected of belief" before they can appear in fiction, then novels like *The Last Days of Christ the Vampire* (1987)—about a group of street kids, led by a disaffected Catholic from Lovecraft's own Providence, who uncover the "true story" behind Christianity, as revealed in the book's title—demonstrate how much psychic energy has been siphoned away from official religion, in what Harold Bloom has aptly called our "post-Christian nation," into new myths constructed piecemeal from the content of mass entertainments.

Organized religious groups deriving from fantasy, horror, and sci-fi books and films, such as the Church of Scientology, were given an enormous impetus during the 1960s, a decade when the intertwined phenomena of drug/spiritual experience of the Platonic cosmos translated into a profusion of religious movements known as "New Age" in anticipation of the astrological Age of Aquarius, thought to begin on January 23, 1997. Though many young Americans turned to religions of the East such as Buddhism and Hinduism, the new invented religions boasted the distinctive Neoplatonic/ Hermetic/Gnostic cosmology characteristic of Bloom's

"American Religion" discussed in Chapter 4. The Gaia movement and neopagan cults of Druids, wiccas, and the like have all adopted a pantheistic notion of a living cosmos; related "living planet" cults include the large followings of apocalyptics like Art Bell, a radio show host who tracks earthquakes as a marker of a sentient Earth's dangerously elevated metabolism. Practi-tioners of Jungian psychology, taking Jung's lead, have constructed an interiorized alchemical practice they call "active imagination"; they also practice astrology and have adopted many features of the Neoplatonic/Hermetic worldview.

Because suppressed religiosity and popular entertainments have a symbiotic relationship in American culture, there is ample historical precedent for the current sci-fi cults in the United States. Thomas Disch has argued that Poe's stories "Mesmeric Revelation" and "The Facts in the Case of M. Valdemar," both about souls speaking from beyond the grave, were the fictive sources for Mary Baker Eddy's Gnostic Christian Science on one hand and Madame Blavatsky's Theosophical Society on the other. In turn, some scholars believe, the Theosophical Society laid the groundwork for today's UFO religions by developing "a cosmology that included the notion that benevolent beings from other planets were highly evolved adepts who periodically visit the Earth." The fairy abductions of older European folklore so dramatically purged from American ballads were reincarnated in the twentieth century as UFO abductions; in a seamless transferal from the celestial sphere, outer space becomes the realm whose archons create, control, and destroy Earth and its inhabitants. Extraterrestrials are divine beings, ancestors of the human race; they are also, typically, in the other half of the Rorschach design, Westerners' projected notions of Third World cultures.

The most prominent current UFO religion is probably the science fiction writer L. Ron Hubbard's Church of Scientology. Japan's Aum Shinrikyo (Supreme Truth) cult was based on Isaac Asimov's *Foundation* novels. Surely the most dramatic UFO cult so far, however, is Heaven's Gate, the group that gained world notoriety by their mass suicide of 1997 in Rancho Santa Fe, California. The Heaven's Gaters believed the "Kingdom Level Above Human" or "Next Level" is a physical place that is also nontemporal and noncorruptible. In their quest to shed the encumbrances of the human and return to this transcendent world, cult leaders rewrote the core story of Christianity in a *Star Trek* narrative typical of the UFO religions:

> Two thousand years ago, the Kingdom Level Above Human appointed an Older Member to send a Representative (His "Son"), along with some of their beginning students, to incarnate on this garden . . . While on Earth as an "away team" with their "Captain," they were to work on their overcoming of humanness and tell the civilization they were visiting how the true Kingdom of God can be entered. The humans under the control of the adverserial [*sic*] space races [known historically as "Luciferians"] killed the "Captain" and His crew, because of the "blasphemous" position they held, and quickly turned the teachings of the "Captain" (the Older Member's "Son") into watered-down Country Club religion—obscuring the remnants of the Truth.

Though media consumption by cult members was strictly censored, we know that Stephen Spielberg's *E.T.* and the cult-spawning TV series *Star Trek* were on their video-watching list, and greatly enjoyed.

An equally direct influence came, I suspect, from the Walt Disney movies *Escape to Witch Mountain* (1975) and *Return from Witch Mountain* (1978), based on children's novels by Alexander Key. The first of these Gnostic fantasies presents orphaned twins from a world of light where "everybody has a twin"; their ancestors visited earth millions of years ago but "lost touch with the light" when they started fighting over worldly things and became human. The brother and sister escape from an evil scientist who hopes to exploit their special powers and gather with other children of their kind at the "unique magnetic field" on Witch Mountain so that they may all "come home to the light." Throughout the story purple is the color that guides the children to Witch Mountain, and it is the color of the column of light in which they happily ascend, two by two, back to their own world—an image that irresistibly evokes the purple cloth covering the face of each Heaven's Gate suicide.

Most recently, the World Wide Web—that latest great extension of Crocodile Street and heir apparent of the sub-Zeitgeist—has spawned a plethora of religious groups and cults. This phenomenon has taken place for complex reasons arising from the intrinsically Platonic way in which we perceive this technology (see Chapter 12) as well as from the Web's dynamic capacities for group communication. Total lack of censorship coupled with almost universal access encouraged what seems to have been a long-suppressed explosion of new religious thinking that encompasses equally the human capacity for good and evil; along with ET religions of all descriptions, the Web hosts everything from the Emersonian "First Internet Church of All" to racist-nationalist cults worshipping ethnically "pure" gods.

One striking feature of some of the new sci-fi and fantasy cults and social groups is mastery of a fictive language spoken by nonhumans that was featured in the original work of film or fiction but whose grammar was often concocted after the fact by fans. Scholarly study groups produce grammars and dictionaries of J. R. R. Tolkien's invented "elvish" languages from the good medievalist's *Lord of the Rings* series. Among the initiatory social groups that mimic the imaginary species depicted in the various hypostases of the television series *Star Trek*, the "Klingon" group requires initiates not only to costume and make themselves up as these demonic-looking (though benign) humanoids but to learn to speak a grammatically complete Klingon language developed by fans. Members must perform community service and are often asked to touch babies and bless people in observance of a "good way of life that blesses us all"—a highly significant turn, let it be noted, toward subjectivizing and humanizing the demonic grotesque. A nonprofit Klingon Language Institute on the Web is dedicated to promoting the Klingon language, into which not Satanic spells but the Bible, *Hamlet*, and other works have been translated. In a mark of the effable blend of corporatism and cultism that is American mass entertainment, however, the website (www.kli.org) carefully notes that "Klingon, Star Trek, and all related marks are copyrights and trademarks of Paramount Pictures."

In modern times these invented languages became a way both of proving, in reverse, the reality of other worlds and of living a make-believe life within the container of an author's imaginary "third world." Across the painstakingly constructed grammars of these *Ursprache* hobbyists, however, fall the shadows of Schreber's dark schizophrenic religion and Dick's "infinite and sweet" God alike. Plato had maintained in the *Cratylus* that words do not simply describe, they embody the objects or ideas they stand for. Informing both Christian mysticism and Jewish cabbala, this linguistic Platonism is also widespread across folklore and religion in the belief that anyone possessing knowledge of the language of the *unus mundus*, the primal synesthesic reality where spirit and matter, subject and object, are identical, can wield godlike powers over our lower empirical world of the senses. But as we also saw in Chapter 5, the belief in a primal language derived from the World of Forms can be psychotically manifested as either the "concrete" nonmetaphorical apprehension of the person's native tongue or the experience of a completely alien language. As part of the demonization of the supernatural from the Romantics on, the tradition of the primal language characteristically took a left turn down the *via negativa* into the psychotic mode, in which the primal reality is no longer Paradise but the dreadful world of mental suffering reflected in the demonic languages of Lovecraft and Schreber.

One branch of the old tradition links the Perfect Language to the language of the birds, which St. Francis was said to understand. Older human societies recognized a connection between humans, animals, and a magic language of the original world with the power to shape our reality. Platonically inclined Westerners, raised in an Aristotelian climate that prohibits this possibility (Descartes warned that we should not believe, "as some of the ancients did, that beasts speak"), characteristically seek such lore in the religions of non-Western pretechnological cultures. Yet many past notables in our own tradition were, as Hugh Ormsby-Lennon put it, citing John Webster and Jonathan Swift as well as Jakob Boehme, "fluent in mystical birdsong."

Which brings me at last to black birds. I want to talk about what we imagine happens when modern Western people and black birds start talking to each other. In three stories over the last hundred and fifty years, two literary and one from real life, a black bird appears at the window, is granted entry, and strikes up a conversation with his human host. What does it mean, when such a one flies into your life? Is he real, or are you crazy?

MESSAGES OF BLACKBIRDS

Raven, genus *Corvus*, a.k.a. crow. The word derives, as do the names *rook*, *shrike*, and *thrush*, from the echoic Indo-European root *ker*, indicating loud noises of birds (from which source also come the sound-words *crack*, *burst*, *creak*, *shriek*, *screech*, and *scream*). In the natural world ravens feed on dead flesh, but it is not clear how this fact earned them a close association with the gods. On the god Odin's shoulder, says the Icelander Snorri Sturluson in the prose Edda, sit two ravens named Thought and Memory who bring him news of all they see or hear. For this reason Odin is called god-of-the-ravens. The raven stands either for the Devil or for Christ in Christian allegory. In the secular allegory of the dreaming mind, we might say such birds represent sudden dark irrational thoughts or moods, that insidious melancholia the alchemists dubbed *caput corvi* or "Raven's head" which—seemingly from out of nowhere—alights in, and takes over, human consciousness.

In fact, the ravens come from a distinct Somewhere—namely, that inner realm, once marked out for the gods, which was remapped in the Western world during the nineteenth and twentieth centuries as the narrower territory of psychosis. And most literary testimony suggests, in an indirect but compelling way, that it is not healthy for mortals, first, to receive Odin's messengers and, second, to accept the burden of their message. Exhibit 1 belongs to the imagination of Edgar Allan Poe and his rhyming dialogue tractate "The Raven" (1845).

Poe's famous bird is more a "quother" than a croaker, a Gothic monk in rusty black. He is perched not on Odin's shoulder but on a plaster bust of Pallas Athena, another deity of supernatural intellect. When the narrator asks the bird its name, the latter's *responsus* provokes his wonder even though at first he believes that the mantric term Nevermore has "little meaning—little relevancy" (and we recall the enigmatic cry *"Tekeli'li!"* from the black birds in *Pym).* On discovering that his black bird's message consists *only* of this word, however, he grows obsessed with constructing meaning from it as (yet another) "mesmeric revelation." Obligingly he tailors questions and commands that will fit the terrible reply in the direst way imaginable (Will he embrace Lenore again? Will he be allowed to forget her memory? Get out!), when he might just as easily have used the opportunity to paint himself a moderately rosy future (Will I ever feel depressed again? Will I ever *not* see Lenore again?). By the poem's end, Poe's narrator and the "ominous bird of yore" have achieved a kind of symbiotic union, an unholy partnership that lends the former's death-dealing mood the divine endorsement it lacked before the bird's appearance. Has any other character in literature collaborated on casting his own funerary runes with such macabre relish?

Exhibit 2 is a short story by the Austrian writer Robert Musil (1880–1942), a contemporary of Schulz and Kafka and like them born into the old Austro-Hungarian empire. Here a species distinction is necessary: the bird in question is an *Amsel*, that is, a blackbird, not a carrion-eating black bird, not a *Krähe*, not a *Rabe*, certainly not a Kafka-crow. On the surface, and to its human beholder—and possibly even to the author himself—this blackbird appears at first glance an altogether benevolent little feathered being.

I will briefly summarize Musil's remarkable story "The Blackbird" (1935). Complex in structure and surface detail, it is entirely and tragically simple in meaning—that is, in the underlying psychological dilemma it expresses.

Two old friends, both confirmed rational materialists, meet after many years. On these worldly fellows the author has rather perversely bestowed the names Aone and Atwo, causing the alert reader to recognize at once the presence, as in Herman Hesse's works (though rendered here with considerably more brilliance), of those ethereal scions of German Romanticism—direct descendants of Kleist's Mr. C. and Hoffmann's Lewis and Ferdinand—cerebral middle-aged youths (and, one suspects, serious screwups) whose fierce intellectualism and correspondingly fragile emotional development make them ripe prey for Odin's circling messengers.

Atwo recounts to his friend three mystical and therefore "inexplicable" episodes from his life, as follows.

The first episode. Living with his wife in an anthill of urban bourgeois apartment life, Atwo mulls over a thought that has suddenly popped into his head about his parents—"They have given you life." This primal message triggers a magic night of the soul in which the divine or archetypal seems to be materializing before his eyes. A dark green light fills the room, then mysterious sounds approach, sounds he "sees" leaping off the top of the next building "like dolphins."

In these embodied sounds, which "burst softly against the windowpanes and sank slowly into the depths like great silver stars," Atwo senses something magical and portentous; he begins to undergo a magical transformation himself:

> I lay awake on my bed, but differently than in the daytime; I felt like the figure on its coffin lid. It's very hard to describe, but when I reflect on it it was as if I had been turned inside out. I was no longer a solid, space-filling form, but something like a depression in space. The room was not hollow but was permeated by a substance that doesn't exist in the daytime, darkly transparent and darkly transpalpable—I too was made of it. Time ran in fever-small, rapid pulse beats.

All at once he realizes that the sounds inciting this curious transformation of space and time are a bird's song:

> "It's a nightingale that's singing out there," I said to myself, half aloud . . . "To me!" I thought, and sat up with a smile. "A heavenly bird! So they really exist!" In such a moment, you see, one is ready to believe in the supernatural in the most natural way, as though one had spent one's entire childhood in a magical world. Immediately I thought: "I will follow the nightingale. Goodbye, my love. Goodbye, indeed, love, house, city . . !"

But the bird abandons Atwo, who realizes, in great despair, that it was "only" a blackbird, mimicking a nightingale.

Nevertheless, the blackbird's enigmatic signal causes Atwo's life to flip-flop into its opposite as he heeds the siren call to abandon life. He walks out of his apartment, deserting the wife he loves, his work, all he is familiar with. Explaining why the bird's appearance moved him to take this drastic action, he says simply: "I can only tell you what I took it for when I experienced it: a signal had come to me from somewhere. That was my impression of it."

The second episode. In a mountain trench of the Tyrol during the Great War, Atwo hears the song of the aerial dart—a "thin, singing, simple high sound" that signals a hail of deadly iron rods dropped from aircraft, heading straight for him. At once he knows he's going to die, and that it's a great piece of luck. Feeling himself organically linked to this sound, he is convinced that in the next moment, when the dart pierces his body, he will experience the presence of God in himself. At the last minute, however,

Atwo eludes this second signal from the beyond that wishes to penetrate him.

The third episode. Atwo's mother is dying. He describes her as "a lioness confined in the real existence of a very limited woman," a combination that produces a "character which, when personified in our every day experience, is as incomprehensible as when in fabled times gods assumed the shapes of serpents and fishes"—in this way informing us, without at all being able to acknowledge to himself, that he regards her as semidivine (and is thus a secret worshipper at her altar).

We are being prepared for a deep psychological regression, and that is exactly what happens. His mother's death causes Atwo's emotional alienation from her to vanish: "A hardness that had surrounded me melted instantly away." After returning home to bury both mother and father, he tarries, sitting in the attic of his childhood house reading dusty children's books, sleeping in his old nursery. Under these conditions of extreme infantilization Atwo is ready for the second coming of the blackbird. He hears a magnificent song. Once again mistaking it for a nightingale's, he looks up. The blackbird is sitting in the open window. She speaks words and this time Atwo is able to understand them. She has been on his windowsill before, the bird tells him. He agrees. She says, "I am your mother." Atwo quickly shuts the window to keep the bird with him. Just as he is hunting up a cage, he remembers that this same bird, or one like it, had once appeared to him in childhood at this very window; he had let it in then just as he is doing now.

And so, Atwo sums up his story to his friend Aone, he has lived ever since with the blackbird in his parents' house. Though the blackbird hasn't spoken since identifying herself as his mother, Atwo feeds her worms and is utterly delighted with the bird that came to stay. The consequences to his inner life have been profound: "I can only say to you that I have never in my life been so good a person as I have since I've had the blackbird, though I probably can't describe to you what a good person is."

When his friend asks for the single meaning that connects these three happenings in his life, Atwo responds that if he knew the meaning he wouldn't have had to tell the stories: "It's like when you hear whispering or mere rustling, without being able to tell which it is!"

A reader, however, can distinguish the whispering from the rustling and discover a single, ominous meaning in Atwo's stories. They represent first a gradual, then an utter and abandoned Poelike regression out of adult life into the primal world of eternal infancy, or madness. His messenger-guide to this realm may be interpreted—on the model developed in this chapter—as either a supernatural being, as Atwo himself believes, or a massive, unresolved attachment to his mother that has consistently wrenched him out of his "ordinary" life as a man and back to the timeless world of childhood and its seductive flickerings of the divine. Is it VALIS, or a dead twin sister? In the end the two realities are indistinguishable, and in this case not too hopeful. Goodbye, Atwo.

Exhibit 3 comes from the world of flesh and blood, not literature, and so it may throw some retrospective light on Exhibits 1 and 2. This was an apparition that presented itself to my Berkeley scholar friend many years ago during the darkest hour of her depression. One afternoon as she sat immobile in despair on her living room sofa, an extremely black bird with shining golden eyes lit down on the sofa arm beside her and began to talk. Did those golden eyes have "all the seeming of a demon's that is dreaming"? Did her black bird speak English like Poe's, or German like Musil's, or some other local dialect of the god-language by which the ravens communicate with Odin?

She did not, my friend told me, recognize the words the bird spoke to her, but she knew she could have understood them *if that had been her wish.* But she did not so wish. Instead she got up from the sofa, went to the window (noticing only then that all windows in the apartment were shut and locked), opened it wide and, not uttering a word herself, motioned the black bird out—and he obeyed. She shut the window, relocked it firmly against him. This ejection was a statement and a refusal; it was a message from her for the black bird to take back to Odin, the Devil, whomever, and that message was: I will not be tempted to consort with a god. Then she sat down and waited for the world to show its pleasant face to her again. And in time, she said, it did.

Cesare Ripa's "Memoria." From Ripa, *Iconologia* (1593).

"It's a poor sort of memory that works only backwards."

—Queen to Alice, *Alice in Wonderland*

EIGHT

TWO OLD BIRDS AND THEIR NEW FEATHERS

For Neoplatonists like Giordano Bruno, deep thinking was inseparable from the act of remembering—that is, imperfectly recalling the World of Forms. Behind the sense-based memory of the temporal world stands Platonic memory, or *anamnesis*, perhaps best described by the arch-Hermeticist poet Robert Duncan as

> The great speckled bird who broods over the
> Nest of souls, and her egg,
> The dream in which all things are living,
> I return to, leaving my self.

All knowledge, Plato said in the *Phaedrus*, is an attempt to remember the "blessed and spectacular vision" that the living things of the material world imitate in an inferior way. In characterizing Platonic memory as "the long-term DNA gene pool memory that spans many lifetimes," Philip K. Dick asserted that only anamnesis, "the retrieval of this long-term memory . . . which literally means the loss of forgetfulness," is the kind of memory "truly capable of 'reflecting the divine mind behind the universe' . . . brought into being."

Because transcendental memory is regarded as image based, the ancient visual (and eventually literary) device of allegory was typically used as the medium for "recalling" the ideal in material form. Cesare Ripa's late sixteenth-century allegory of memory, reproduced here, embodies this mental faculty as a middle-aged woman (because middle age, Ripa declares rather dubiously, "is the best age for having a good memory"); the dog, the two-faced bust, and its elephant headdress are further icons of excellent memory from traditional folklore. With this image duly imprinted, let us follow, in the language of former generations, the intertwined histories and curious recent resurgence of those two venerables, *Memory* and *Allegory*.

THE ART OF MEMORY

For many thousands of years, humans have been artificially propping up (and simultaneously weakening, if Socrates was right) their natural capacity to remember. This task has been accomplished by a succession of gizmos—the alphabet, the printing press, the computer—the hardware of memory, if you will, whose net effect has been to separate and externalize the memory function from its human host. Before any of these human-made improvements was devised, however, the ability to recollect was a trained skill of paramount cultural as well as individual importance. In preliterate societies memory was the sole repository of human knowledge and skills from one generation to the next. It also shaped literary form and syntax; from Homer to Australian aboriginals, the need to structure public ceremonial expression by means of rhyme, rhythm, repetition, and other mnemonic devices made poetry the supreme art form of memory.

The Greeks rightly celebrated memory as Mnemosyne, mother of all the muses, demonstrating that memory retained its supreme position as preserver of culture and knowledge even in a society that possessed the alphabet but lacked widespread literacy or means of transmitting the written word. (Though such was the impact of writing among them that, reasoning backward, they used the metaphor of inscribing words on a wax tablet as a way of explaining the process of memory, much as we now like to describe the functioning of our brains in terms of files, databases, and the like.)

But even after literacy, as Frances Yates and subsequent scholars have traced, the Greeks continued to develop what their Roman commentators called "artificial memory," and what we would probably call the software of memory: mental techniques by which orators could strengthen and refine their memories in order to deliver lengthy addresses. In this preeminently psychotopographic process the speaker first internalized in his memory a series of real places (*loci* or *topoi;* the use of the word "topic" for subject matter arose, Yates speculates, from the notion of the mnemonic place). These loci were usually arranged in a real building possessing a convenient abundance of stories, rooms, corridors, and ornaments. Within this memorized architectural space the speaker placed, in a predetermined order, certain striking visual "images" *(imagines)* containing emotional associations, a kind of symbolic code for the sequence of points to be made in the speech. With this twofold act of memorization accomplished, the speaker simply moved through his inner building from location to location in the correct sequence to retrieve the content of his speech as he delivered it.

Though the notion of mentally striding into, say, the Parthenon, up the marble stairs, then hanging a quick right at the second column, all to "access" a bit of information from memory, may strike us as quaint in the extreme, Yates stressed:

> The word "mnemotechnics" hardly conveys what the artificial memory of Cicero may have been like, as it moved among the buildings of ancient Rome, *seeing* the places, *seeing* the images stored on the places, with a piercing inner vision which immediately brought to his lips the thoughts and words of his speech . . . The ancient memories were trained by an art which reflected the art and architecture of the ancient world, which could depend on faculties of intense visual memorisation which we have lost.

By this point in Western history oral prose was memorized by means of imagined sight, not heard sound: in the half-literate societies of Greece and Rome visual images had supplanted the repetitive rhythms of poetry as a primary synesthesic aid to internal memory. In synesthesia, in which the experience of one sense calls up that of one or more others (sound evoking odors, taste evoking colors), we detect the shadow of Plato's World of Forms, the place beyond time and space where all senses have collapsed into a single unity.

The classical memory techniques were preserved into the Middle Ages via the slender thread of a single Latin treatise whose precepts were modified by the medieval sensibility into an adjunct of scholastic training endorsed by Thomas Aquinas and Albertus Magnus. The importance of attaching abstract ideas to concrete images continued to be stressed; visualization, the *oculis imaginationis* or eye of the imagination, was still linked synesthesically with memory enhancement. (Not surprisingly, the memory frame on which images and ideas were attached was typically the interior of a cathedral.) Mary Carruthers has described how the ninth-century architectural Plan of St. Gall served as a meditational "machine" or mentally built structure for monks; the construction of the buildings came later as the *imitatio* of the meditative vision, much as the medieval dream vision narratives provided a psychotopographic landscape with "fixed points for meditation and self-reflection."

Medieval philosophy explained the concept of the unified cosmos, the *unus mundus*, in terms of just this kind of architectural plan: "When God created the world, He first made, like a good architect, a plan in His head—He imagined the world in a plan, and only then did He realize it concretely. So at a certain moment, the world existed—but not yet concretely. It existed only as an image in the mind of God, and it had only potential reality." As we will see in Chapter 12, twentieth-century secular Westerners would draw on this concept of a Platonically preexistent "potential" or "virtual" reality in naming—and thereby unconsciously allegorizing—one of the capacities of computer simulation.

Renaissance philosophers transformed the memory system in the crucible of their newly discovered Neoplatonic and Hermetic texts into a quasi-religion that venerated memory as an organ possessing magical and world-ordering powers. According to the tenets of the new thinking, the whole cosmos could be "memorized" in a much more overt *imitatio dei* and by this act magically incorporated into the human organism. Once again, prime visual artifacts of the collective culture were used as the framework of memory, imbuing it with objective as well as subjective meaning. Rather than using public buildings as their memory frames, however, the sixteenth-century magi preferred to build their own. The Italian Guilio Camillo's "Memory Theater," intended to be a literal microcosm of the universe, was an actual physical structure: a wooden model crowded with images and big enough at least for one or two people to enter. The spectator stood on the stage gazing out at a seven-tiered auditorium encompassing the entire order of the universe. Carved images of the archetypes behind reality (represented mostly by planetary gods) were fastened to each level, with masses of written material stored in drawers under the appropriate image. The purpose of the Memory Theater, as a correspondent of Erasmus reported, was one of comprehension through visualization, so that by standing within this "built or constructed mind or soul" the beholder "may at once perceive with his eyes everything that is otherwise hidden in the depths of the human mind. And it is because of this *corporeal looking* that he calls it a theatre."

Incorporating more radically pagan elements, Giordano Bruno also believed the esoterically trained memory was a godlike vessel for encapsulating the entire universe within a single human mind. As an integral part of his agenda as a self-divinizing theurge, Bruno devised his own complicated system of "magic memory" consisting of an intricate wheel of Egyptian celestial and archetypal images. To participate in the rite of mystic incorporation, the (presumably wealthy) initiate was supposed to stare up at a representation of the wheel painted on the ceiling of his bedroom and commit its contents to memory. In so doing, Yates says, "the possessor of this system thus rose above time and reflected the whole universe of nature and of man in his mind." The essentially magical powers of the memory arts as put forth by Bruno and others also linked them irrevocably with the black art of demon summoning, for it had become a basic tenet of Renaissance demonology that spirits were, in Ioan Couliano's words, mental "phantasms that acquire an autonomous existence through a practice of visualization resembling first and foremost the Art of Memory."

Not coincidentally, just as these Renaissance mnemonists were forming their secret circles of the elect, the role of memory as a bearer of mainstream culture was coming under further assault from the next great technological development in the externalization of human memory: the printing press. The widespread availability of the written word was to catapult the role of memory in Western European culture through another significant change. Like the written alphabet before and the computer to follow, the printing press further transformed the value of natural memory to society, weakening its still primary function as a preserver of information and strengthening its role as an arcane art—but an increasingly secular, not religious, one.

The decline of memory as a magic tool for reinforcing the cosmic order on one hand and as a reliable drayhorse in the service and preservation of facts on the other culminated in its revival during the nineteenth century, in a superficially aesthetic way, as an art cultivated in leisure by poets—a revival that took place, paradoxically, within the framework of written language. In the emerging Romantic sensibility the very act of remembering functioned as a kind of aesthetic trance—Wordsworth's "emotion recollected in tranquillity"—that enabled the Romantic *oculis imaginationis* to look into the past as a way of simultaneously peering into the soul and filtering the impressions rising from it into consciousness.

From this Romantic perspective it is no large step to the two great early twentieth-century memory palaces, Proust's *In Search of Lost Time* (1913–27) and Joyce's *Finnegans Wake* (1939), but particularly the former, that "vast structure of recollection" and secular cathedral whose dogma is an elaborate metaphysics of memory. As an architectural creation Proust's work functions as a psychotopographic storehouse of an entire culture in a way analogous to Bruno's memory wheel or Camillo's theater. There is something of the flavor of the old Greco-Roman system as well: Proust states that the past is "somewhere beyond the reach of the intellect, and unmistakably present in some material object (or in the sensation which such an object arouses in us)." *In Search of Lost Time* cunningly situates key objects of subjective significance within the narrative like Easter eggs, allowing the author to retrieve them one by one, via the senses of sight, taste, smell, and touch, as he strolls along the paths of Combray—with "Swann's way" and "Guermantes way" topographically embodying different times and different lives that the narrator inhabits imaginatively. Walter Benjamin even called for a new "physiology of style" as the only possible analytic tool to apply to the primordial synesthesic unity underlying this work—and could that be much different, on the reader's part, from "corporeal looking"?

Deeply influenced by Giordano Bruno, whose philosophy of opposites he assayed to make one of the governing structural devices of *Finnegans Wake*, James Joyce also produced a microcosmic Memory Theater of his culture. The alchemical process, the gradual transformation out of the chaos of the *prima materia* through the many steps to the Philosopher's Stone, similarly informs this maddening novel steeped in Hermetic lore and the synesthesic sensibility—all in the service of emphasizing the role of the artist as latter-day magus, theurge, and alchemist. For if, according to Bruno, the overriding goal of acquiring and using magic memory is the formation of a religious personality, or the personality of a good magus, capable of being in magic communion with nature—the infinite comprehended in the finite—then in Romantic and Proustian terms the new magus, the occult mnemonist, must be the artist. "Magic memory" in this context becomes a means of ordering the universe according to aesthetic, not religious, principles. In a society with other and more efficient means of preserving information, memory has become the vessel of art, an organizing principle that invests experience with highly charged meaning. Both Proust and Joyce followed this logical chain of association within the confines of a worldview that does not include the transcendent.

But the question must be bluntly asked: "Too much meaning?" Why should the artist, any more than the scientist, carry the extra burden of the transcendent, redemptive or not? To do so risks inflation, and just such overheated ambition intermittently burdens the great works of Joyce as of Proust (and as of Bruno before them, in a different sphere), with a self-conscious grandiosity they cannot fully support. The theurgic experience of divinization, as the marginally more modest (if less mentally stable) Philip K. Dick well understood, must take place in the whole person, not in the scheming ego alone; in the latter case, in Dick's words, "man eats God" instead of the other way around. This is an act that produces spiritual indigestion, not transfiguration.

Where systematic memory training is no longer either available or necessary in society at large, however, a person who naturally possesses an extraordinary memory is a regarded as a random freak, literally a sideshow act, rather than—as he would certainly have been in any preliterate culture—a kind of demigod. When the Russian psychologist A. L. Luria first embarked on his experiments in the 1920s, a newspaper reporter appeared at his laboratory one day asking to have his memory tested. To his confusion Luria discovered himself unable to measure this man's memory: it appeared limitless both in the amount of material absorbed and length of time the material was retained. The subject, one Sherashevsky or "S.", as he is called throughout Luria's classic work *The Mind of a Mnemonist*, could remember any number of words or numbers, in any order, and recite them back perfectly at any given later time without mistake. He never forgot a single nonsense syllable or its correct position in any of the hundreds of mnemonic experiments he participated in.

By means of what specific internal devices was S. able to perform these amazing feats? We find to our surprise that he used a completely spontaneous version of the classical "mnemotechnique": words evoked such powerful visual images for S. that when he was given a long list to memorize he would simply distribute these images in an orderly sequence, usually along a street he was familiar with in real life:

> Sometimes this was a street in his home town, which would also include the yard attached to the house he had lived in as a child and which he recalled vividly. On the other hand, he might also select a street in Moscow. Frequently he would take a mental walk along that street—Gorky Street in Moscow—beginning at Mayakovsky Square, and slowly make his way down, "distributing" his images at houses, gates, and store windows. At times, without realizing how it had happened, he would suddenly find himself back in his home town (Torzhok), where he would wind up his trip in the house he had lived in as a child.

Whenever S. made a rare error of recall, it was invariably a visual error of "perception" as he made his memory promenade. S. explained one mistake: "I put the image of the *pencil* near a fence . . . the one down the street, you know. But what happened was that the image fused with that of the fence and I walked right on past without noticing it."

Though the Greco-Roman techniques of artificial memory involved fusion of the visual with emotional associations carried in the *imagines* selected by the individual, S.'s astounding memory was not simply visual but supremely synesthesic, mixing impressions from all the senses. Sound for S. produced taste, visual, and tactile sensations, and vice versa; because no distinct line separated his sensory perceptions, he floated in an ocean of undifferentiated impressions. A given tone caused him to see a "brown strip against a dark background that had red, tongue-like edges" and to taste "sweet and sour borscht . . . that gripped his entire tongue." Sounds of speech and numbers called up similarly distinct visual images.

Luria's friend and colleague the film director Sergei Eisenstein was fascinated by S. when they were introduced. Writing of S. later in *The Film Sense,* Eisenstein dubbed him "Mr. Memory" after the music hall mnemonist in Alfred Hitchcock's *The Thirty-Nine Steps,* from John Buchan's novel. Eisenstein focused immediately on S.'s "synchronization of senses" as it related to his own refinement of the medieval *oculis imaginationis*—the montage effect in film art, which attempted to touch the viewer's every sense for maximum artistic effect. But the potentially unifying and refining capability of S.'s gift was canceled out by its terrifying indiscriminateness, which struck Eisenstein as deeply as it had Luria. The omnivorous nature of S.'s memory, Eisenstein believed, violated the need for *meaning* of the more sophisticated human functions. For though in a narrow manner meaning was vital to the function of S.'s memory (it was the meaning of individual words that summoned up his vivid images), he was incapable either of selective memory or—a more important function of selection—of forgetting. Jorge Luis Borges captures Mr. Memory's dilemma beautifully in his story "Funes the Memorious." Borges's Uruguayan peasant, a dead ringer for S., possesses an infinitely capacious memory of which he boasts, "I have more memories in myself alone than all men have had since the world was a world." But Funes, like S., is a parody of Aristotelian specificity; he is "almost incapable of general, platonic ideas."

Both Luria and Eisenstein regarded synesthesia as an "atavistic" trait in the Freudian sense: a "primary process" function of early life that is lost by adulthood. S.'s own psychological history, in fact, suggests the Wordsworthian Eden of childhood—that psychological state of permanent transitoriness, of limitless potential (in Kohutian psychoanalytic terms, "global narcissistic perfection," but sounding mighty like the Anthropos), trailing clouds of glory into our puny, time-bound world of separations and distinctions *sub specie aeternitatis.* And so, again via Romantic philosophy, we are back in the old worldview, in which the conflation of senses, like original language, is an integral feature of timeless preexistent Platonic reality—that idea of primal reality which Freud had neatly materialized and internalized into primary process. This lack of definition described S.'s entire life as well as his perceptions of the world and his memory. The absence of ego boundaries ran parallel to his sense of merging into, and identification with, the surrounding landscape. Significantly, landscapes from his childhood were the favorite frame for all S.'s memory feats, a circumstance that tantalizingly suggests not only Romantic parallels but Giordano Bruno's quest for a magic communion with nature as well.

As walking, talking Divine Human or Primary Process, however, Luria's Mr. Memory was utterly incapable of making the infinite finite. S., in fact, was the quasi-allegorical embodiment of what Bruno called the "chaotic Infinite" lacking any human mediation—a kind of blasphemous parody not just of the Anthropos but of Yahweh, who, as cabbalistic tradition states, possesses a memory infallible unto the hundredth generation. Not unlike the tantalizingly similar worldviews of paranoid schizophrenics and mystics, S.'s subject-object conflation is structurally congruent with, but still qualitatively opposed to, that of the Neoplatonic universe. Recognizing this tragic flaw in S., Eisenstein attempted to carve out, via a careful examination of the connection between sensory stimuli and the achievement of aesthetic effect, just that "physiology of style" his contemporary Walter Benjamin was seeking for Proust by pinpointing the difference between the raw synesthesic impressions reported by S. and the images in a work of art: ultimately the connections S. automatically made among the various senses lacked meaning because *they were divorced from emotional relationships* and from the relationships among the senses obtaining, for example, "within a system of images dictated by [a] work of art."

In Eisenstein's terms, the role of Mr. Memory belongs, just as it did in the nineteenth century, not to a profane *tabula rasa* like S. but to the organizer, the discriminator, the meaning-imbuer—that familiar twentieth-century magus figure, the artist. In the hands of the artist, memory regains Bruno's divine framework that gives it *meaning*, so that the most specific detail in the memory landscape draws in the wider net of meaning out of which the most general of truths emerges—the Hermetic-Neoplatonic universe mirrored in a single human imagination.

Almost as if Mnemosyne herself had waved a magic wand over a whole generation of Russian intellectuals, we encounter the unmistakable mark of this peculiar, almost *idiot savant* gift of the synesthesic sensibility linked with demiurgic memory in two notable contemporaries of Luria, Eisenstein, and S. The first, Osip Mandelstam (he who wrote "On my lips like black ice burns / The memory of a Stygian bell"), suggested that the act of remembering, in the hands of the artist, might represent not simply re-creation but an independent act of creation of something utterly new. As Mandelstam put forward, in a supremely synesthesic manner:

> We are all, without suspecting it, carriers of an immense embryological experiment: for the very process of remembering, crowned with the victory of memory's effort, is amazingly similar to the phenomenon of growth. In both of them there is a sprout, an embryo, some facial feature, half a character, half a sound, the ending of a name, something labial or palatal, some sweet pea on the tongue—which doesn't develop out of itself but only answers an invitation, only stretches out, justifying one's expectation.

Similarly, what was arbitrary and chaotic in S. becomes architectural and ordered in Mandelstam's contemporary, the self-described "synesthete" Vladimir Nabokov, whose description of refining his memory during numerous revisions of his autobiography *Speak, Memory* demonstrates how synesthesic recollection can be transmuted, through the compulsive ordering of art, from a nightmare jumble of promiscuous sensory input into a meaning-bearing structure, *ars memorativa* in its highest manifestation:

> An object, which had been a mere dummy chosen at random and of no factual significance in the account of an important event, kept bothering me every time I reread that passage in the course of correcting the proofs of various editions, until finally I made a great effort, and the arbitrary spectacles (which Mnemosyne must have needed more than anybody else) were metamorphosed into a clearly recalled oystershell-shaped cigarette case, gleaming in the wet grass at the foot of an aspen on the Chemin du Pendu, where I found on that June day in 1907 a hawkmoth rarely met with so far west, and where a quarter of a century earlier, my father had netted a Peacock butterfly very scarce in our northern woodlands.

Like S.—and like Proust—Nabokov used as his memory frame the landscape and artifacts of personal past (but, unlike S.'s outpourings, duly invested with form and emotional meaning) rather than those of the general culture. This was the distinctive microfocus of the modernist subjective sensibility, which resonated to individually selected *imagines*—the gleam of a cigarette case, the taste of a madeleine, not the larger social vessel of a forum, cathedral, wheel or theater. (Though Nabokov, a confirmed cabbalist and Platonist like Bruno Schulz, always insisted that "reality is the shadow of the word" and that the word "reality" could only used within quotation marks.)

Until the last decade of the twentieth century, this subjective sensibility was still dominant in mainstream Western culture. For, given the choice of a structure to hang our memories on, what would any twentieth-century European or American of either continent have been likely to choose? Reflecting that century's peculiar perception of itself, we would not have used a public building like the New York Public Library but more likely landscapes charged with completely personal associations. Like the Renaissance alchemists, twentieth-century Westerners perceived culture as personal, not general, in the sense that it was borne principally in the microcosm of the individual's associations and not at the level of social institutions. That vision remained subjective not objective, materialist not mystic; and over such subjectivity that century's works of art characteristically emitted faint, erratic religious signals like poorly tuned battery radios.

But then came computers and their most striking characteristic—a phenomenal storage capacity for information, anthropomorphized as "memory." An enormous part of the computer entertainment subculture has been the interactive games whose visual structure shows a striking resemblance to the old mnemonic arts. In his study of the "metaphysics of information," Erik Davis has identified the demiurgic role of Dungeon Master in the pre-computer role-playing game Dungeons & Dragons as a precursor of the wider phenomenon of the new "ecstatic technologies" and their emphasis on imagined topographies. In visualizing a "secondary world," players followed the Dungeon Master's lead, drawing on assorted backup handbooks and "using an elaborate symbolic machinery in order to solidify and organize the plastic material of the imagination." These role-playing games were transferred seamlessly into the computer along with the "virtual data architectures of the *ars memoria*" in such games as Other Planes and Colossal Caves (a.k.a. Adventure, Zork), where "logical loops and algorithms brought the 'symbolic machinery' of its Secondary World one step closer to natural law."

The "infinite" memory capacity of computers has also worked its way into the sub-Zeitgeist imagination to reemerge in the cyborg character of American science fiction films. A new cybernetic Mr. Memory appears in *Johnny Mnemonic* (1995), from the novel by William Gibson, as a human courier with cybernetic "memory chips" implanted in his brain that turn him into a walking "database" able to carry immense amounts of information. We will see in Chapter 11 how the strong link between infinite memory and the Platonic World of Forms also bestows on these cybernetic puppets the Divine Machine aura of immortality and other godlike powers.

Once again in our culture's history, then, memory is being widely and actively represented as an externalized structure. Today we have transplanted our memories into machines as well as the printed word, made them a present of all our "hard facts" and some soft ones, too. Just as we have grown used to driving cars in place of walking, in the general arena of human life our natural muscles of memory, lacking either a framework of discipline or the need to perform, have further slackened, atrophied; even ancient human memory exercises such as the multiplication tables have been taken over by pocket calculators. Will this latest spurt of mechanization cause natural memory to become cultivated even more avidly as an exaggerated adjunct of the artist? One hopes, now that she has escaped the cork-lined bedchamber of the high arts, that Mnemosyne will simply resume her ancient function as a living visual system, resisting the pull to manifest as yet another instance of the Divine Machine.

OLD ALLEGORY, NEW EXPRESSIONISM

As I will examine in Chapter 12, the mental construct that informs the World Wide Web mimics not only the visual structure of the Renaissance memory palace but many other features of the Neoplatonic worldview as well. The Web is above all a medium uniquely suited to the ancient mode of allegory, a capability dramatically evident in the ubiquitous fantasy role-playing narratives. Erik Davis has pointed out the "first-person allegory" of computer games, in which the player "wander[s] through a rigorously structured but dreamlike landscape patched together from phantasms." A whole new generation of demiurgic simulators has already grown up traversing *Pilgrim's Progress*–style imaginary life journeys onscreen. From John Bunyan's Slough of Despond, in which his hero Christian languishes until a sturdy fellow named Hope pulls him out, it is not a very long step to, for example, the "Swamp of No Hope" in the Web game hosted by an online role-playing group who call themselves the "Outriders of Karana."

Mnemosyne herself, as "Mother of the Muses," belongs to this literary form that arose, just as the *ars memoria* did, in the century before Christ and flourished in the centuries after. Allegory—the aesthetic device of personification, of giving, as C. S. Lewis said, "an imagined body to the immaterial"—is closely tied to the externalized visual structures of mnemonics, in both its ancient and its new cybernetic manifestations, because of its dependence on imaging. It was the appropriate aesthetic vehicle for the syncretic worldview of the late ancient world because it exemplified a basic Neoplatonic premise: in the words of the devout Christian Lewis, "If our passions, being immaterial, can be copied by material inventions, then it is possible that our material world in its turn is the copy of an invisible world."

As a literary or visual device, allegory is also the appropriate mode for combining a physical journey with an inward spiritual one of self-discovery. Angus Fletcher states that the traveler is allegory's natural hero "because on his journey he is plausibly led into numerous fresh situations, where it seems likely that new aspects of himself may be turned up." Recall Coleridge's spiritual travelogue, *The Rime of the Ancient Mariner*, from Chapter 6, or the psychotopographic journey of Greene's hero Wilditch in "Under the Garden." It is precisely the extreme nature of the events the allegorical hero must endure, not the plausibility of their happening in everyday life (a founding principle of the realist aesthetic), that draws our sympathetic identification.

Allegory functions as a simulacrum, equivalent to the puppet-idol, capable of drawing down energies from the World of Forms. In terms of the Neoplatonic cosmos, an artist's or writer's allegorical representation did not use a person or material object to "symbolize" or "stand for" a spiritual truth; rather, it shadowed the idea (not really an "abstraction," which is our homocentric formulation) in a way analogous to the role of the whole sensory world itself in relation to the ideal world. To its intended audience allegory "signified" in the premodern, not the postmodern, sense of the term: that is to say, it *embodied.* An allegorical representation, whether in words or images, was alive with the transcendental energy of the essence it depicted. That is why a Renaissance natural philosopher like Bruno could believe that contemplating images of Egyptian and astrological deities allowed him to draw divine essence from the World of Forms into himself. A viewer or reader of allegorical art or literature did not simply have an edifying didactic experience but experienced direct contact with the transcendental world: the artist as theurge had deliberately constructed this artifact of the material world to resonate with its equivalent in the insensible world.

As a visualizing tool for teaching the spiritual message of Christianity, another consolidating institution in Late Antiquity, allegory was to enjoy an unbroken run of popularity in the West that lasted well into the nineteenth century. Until the seventeenth century it also served as the language of science and philosophy; alchemical texts, for example, universally personified chemical processes as acts between humans (the "king" and "queen" copulating in the bath were the metals gold and silver). But as the worldview supporting allegory was increasingly discredited—by the early seventeenth century, as one scholar has commented, what was allegorical was no longer considered "real"—this mode became an empty shell whose inner substance had been slowly siphoned off. Even as its robust life as a didactic tool in popular religious instruction carried through the nineteenth century in such perennial texts as the Puritan John Bunyan's *The Pilgrim's Progress*, by the dawn of the twentieth century allegory had completely sunk from favor in mainstream literature and art. The modernists who were intuitively constructing memory palaces typically chose to furnish them, as we have seen, with physical objects holding subjective associations, not personifications like Truth, Anger, and Patience. In the critical discussion of that century, symbol was traditionally elevated over allegory because it was regarded as more open-ended than the "authoritarian" one-to-one signification of allegory.

Nonetheless, various avant-garde aesthetic movements early in the century did manage to reinvent the old art form in a disguised and peculiarly twentieth-century manner. By making the invisible visible, manifesting the world inside in the world outside, the Expressionist movement that swept continental Europe in the second decade after 1900 implicitly revived the Romantic-sourced precepts of the Neoplatonic worldview—precepts that their more organized and articulate successors the Surrealists would deliberately and explicitly expound.

Strictly speaking, what we think of as Expressionism began, flourished, and in most important respects ended in Munich during the years 1910–1920. Rather than presenting themselves as a unified movement with man-

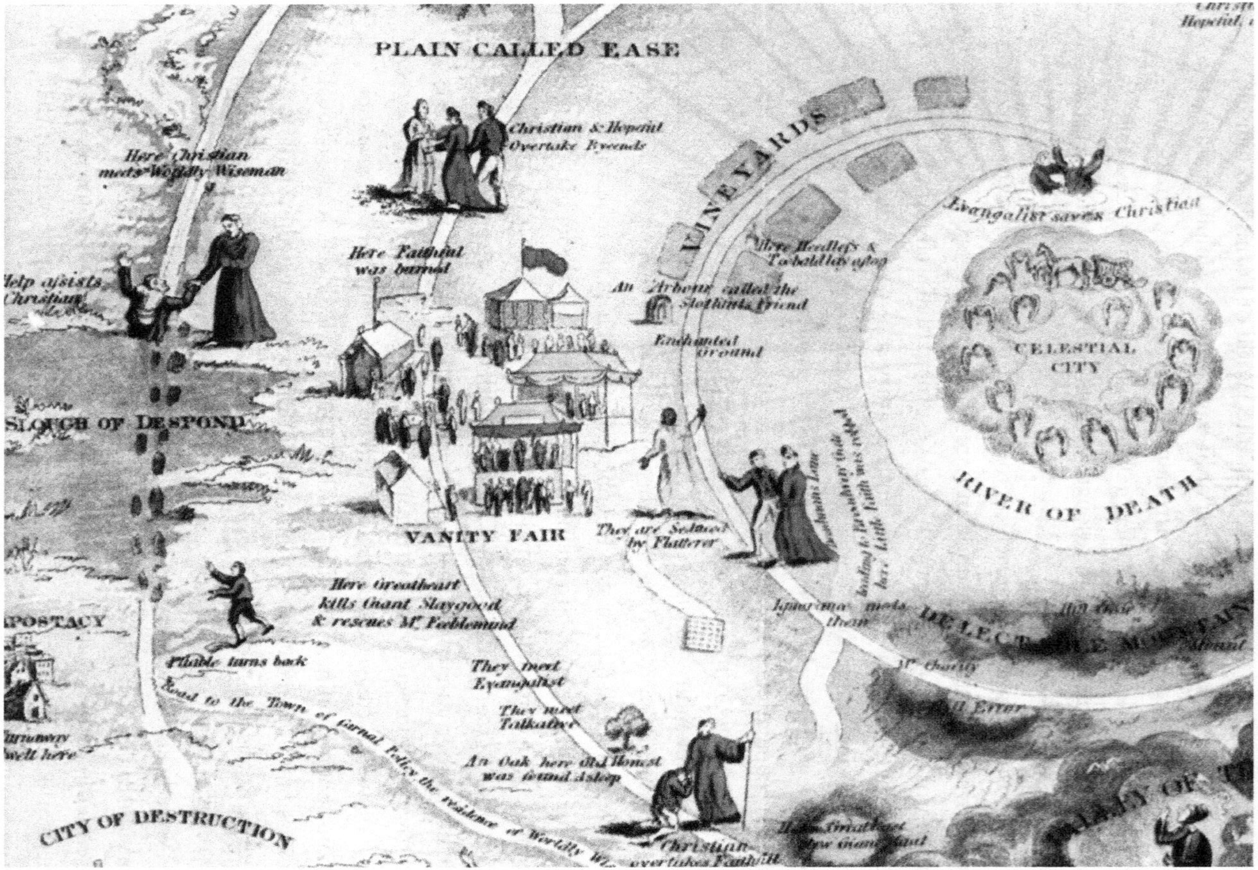

The psychotopography of John Bunyan's *The Pilgrim's Progress.* From an edition published in London by Gall Inglis in the nineteenth century.

ifestos, orchestrated events, and the like, the Ur-German Expressionists, whose numbers included the painters Oskar Kokoschka, Paul Klee, and Vassily Kandinsky along with the poet Georg Heym, were a hodgepodge of irregulars convening in various cafés around Munich. Counting themselves Romantic idealists—in the words of one participant, Ludwig Marcuse, an "apolitical earthquake" in which "the scream drowned out the word"—the Expressionists found drama, both stage and film, to be their true métier. Expressionist stage productions characteristically emphasized the "non-recognition of the empirical world": in one production of *William Tell,* Marcuse noted, the entire polity of Switzerland was "indicated merely by raked steps." Significantly, by casting puppets as human signifiers in sophisticated productions, Expressionist theater also gave our earthly gods their first crossover success from popular entertainment to high art. By 1919, as a late translation into film of a fading visual arts movement, *The Cabinet of Dr. Caligari* was already exaggerating the movement's trademark characteristics. Though later figures such as Otto Dix, Max Beckmann, and others are more familiar to us now as trademark Expressionists, in the 1920s they were already an echo of a sensibility that had been superseded by the more radical and politically engaged movements of Surrealism, Futurism, and Constructivism.

The Surrealists, as a self-conscious and unified school under André Breton, were far more overtly theoretical than the Expressionists even while asserting a deliberate position of anti-intellectuality. They were, in effect, the "postmodernists," the commentators, in comparison with the "modernist" Expressionists, whose content was more subjective and less self-consciously referential to visual arts and literary tradition. As a consequence, even now many Surrealist works remain both easier to "read" simply because they are often commentary—as, for example, Magritte's 1929 painting *The Magic Mirror,* which depicts humans as a microcosmic mirror of the universe by presenting the words "corps humain" inside a mirror frame—and at the same time far more dated than their Expressionist counterparts, which have better withstood the test of time.

The Expressionists shared with one another and with the more overtly organized Surrealists a love of visual distortion—for the Expressionists, the elongation of physical elements; for the Surrealists, the juxtaposition of incongruous elements—that makes their art stylistically grotesque. The two movements also shared one crucial aesthetic goal: that of collapsing the boundaries between subject and object, representing interior human feelings as exteriorized objects in the environment. Carrying on the Romantic inclination for psychotopography discussed in Chapter 5, this defining Expressionist characteristic dovetails neatly with the Neoplatonic identification of the internal and psychic with the external and physical that formed the core of a series of tightly interwoven correspondences between an invisible transcendental level and a visible material one.

In fact, both the Expressionists and the Surrealists had imbibed their premodern sensibility via late nineteenth-century Symbolism from the Romantic movement a hundred years earlier. As part of the general "tellurizing" that took place during the scientific revolution, attributes once applied to God were handed over to "Nature," which was perceived as possessing "immutable laws." In the Romantic revival of what M. H. Abrams called "natural supernaturalism," the sought-for goal became the individual's union with Nature, not with God. From this Romantic foundation the Expressionists represented the union of subject with object in a typically twentieth-century frame: as the encounter of the "total self with the entire world," now typically no longer described as "Nature" but as the "environment," human-made and urban as well as natural.

This act of imaginative merging found an immediate ally in twentieth-century theories of psychology, most especially Freud's notion of *projection*, which entered the common vocabulary as the "attribution of one's own attitudes, feelings, or desires to something or someone as a naive or unconscious defense against anxiety or guilt." In *Totem and Taboo* (1913), Freud declared:

> The projection of inner perceptions to the outside is a primitive mechanism which, for instance, also influences our sense-perceptions, so that it normally has the greatest share in shaping our outer world. Under conditions that have not yet been sufficiently determined even inner perceptions of ideational and emotional processes are projected outwardly, like sense perceptions, and are used to shape the outer world, whereas they ought to remain in the inner world.

By analogy the artist as subject can materialize, make visible, this psychic process by projecting (from Latin *pro* and *iactere;* loosely, "aim and throw") his or her inner "contents" onto the object being created (which is a likeness of an object in the outside world) so that what is interior overlays or merges with the exterior.

Beneath the notion of projection—and behind the Neoplatonic worldview—lies an older identification yet, the cellar below the grotto: the "archaic identity of subject and object" that "still lives at the very bottom of the psyche," that is, the *participation mystique* or boundaryless "mystical participation" identified by Lucien Lévy-Bruhl in which (from our perspective) people in pretechnological societies experienced large parts of their psyche as externalized forces in the environment. As Jeremy Naydler has pointed out, however, our contemporary "self-possessed consciousness" is "a consciousness whose moods, emotions, thoughts, and impulses are regarded as belonging to oneself rather than deriving from gods acting upon—or taking possession of—the soul. The modern belief that the contents of consciousness are subjective in the sense of 'belonging to' the subject who experiences them is the outcome of a historical process that has taken place since ancient Egyptian times." Projection, in other words, is our contemporary homocentric reworking of a much older cosmo- or deocentric notion of the universe found in most pretechnological cultures as well as in earlier Western culture.

Similarly, what we now interpret as a person's subjective psychological complex was formerly regarded as the objective intrusion of a "demon" or evil spirit. "Withdrawal of projection" in psychotherapeutic treatment and exorcism or expulsion of demons in the old belief system amount to structurally equivalent acts. But there is a difference, as Naydler distinguishes: "The argument pursued by C. G. Jung in *Psychology and Religion* and other works required 'the withdrawal of projections' and the 'return to the psyche' of everything of a divine and demonic character fails to take into account the profound metaphysical basis of the ancient 'projections' . . . The ancients did not project their gods onto nature: they apprehended them there."

To find a statement of what projection becomes in the Neoplatonic framework using the new contemporary vocabulary, we need go no further than Philip K. Dick and his conception of the animated universe that he called VALIS: "As to our reality being a projected framework—it appears to be a projection by an *artifact*, a computerlike teaching machine that guides, programs, and generally controls us as we act without awareness of it within our projected world. The artifact, which I call Zebra, has 'created' (actually only projected) our reality as a sort of mirror or image of its maker, so that the maker can obtain thereby an objective standpoint to comprehend its own self."

In this view, in other words, we are God's projections, not the other way around. From that position to the sixteenth-century alchemical tract's assertion "Everything outside us is inside too" to Goethe's late eighteenth-century lines

> In Nature there is everything that is in the subject,
> And something more.
> In the subject there is everything that is in Nature,
> And something more

to Slavoj Zizek's late twentieth-century declaration "The unconscious is outside," we can see in miniature the large-scale changes in attitude toward "subjectivity" in Western culture. And since only the "sourcing" of projection has changed, it might be said that by attributing the power of demiurgic projection to human subjectivity—reversing the "top-down" direction (God-to-human) to "bottom-up" (human-to-environment)—we collectively commit our own culture's intentional fallacy.

At the beginning of the twenty-first century allegory is blossoming as a purveyor of philosophical, religious, and aesthetic truth in the cybernetic framework. Erik Davis describes computer interface languages such as MS-DOS and UNIX as user-friendly "allegories" of the deep computer language (read: Perfect Language) of the binary code that actually powers the machine. All our interaction with computers, he says in a classic Neoplatonic construct, amounts to "iconic simulation" that serves to "pull us further from the binary codespace [read: World of Forms] where the action 'really' lies."

Allegory has begun its move back into the Western mainstream not just in the mass entertainments of computer games and the vocabulary of the new cybernetic sciences but also (as we will see in the next chapter) in a growing body of film and literature that draws more broadly on an Expressionist-based Neoplatonic worldview. The early Expressionists did not explicitly allegorize, but some of their recent successors do—and it is about the most radical aesthetic revolt possible in our time. At the end of the twentieth century, a groundswell in Western literature and film that might be called the New Expressionism—actually, Romanticism in yet another reinvention—increasingly foregrounded the supernatural and a non-materialist worldview. Displaying the characteristic oscillation between Old World high art and New World low art traced through much of this book, twenty-first-century New Expressionism took shape in the *fin-de-siècle* 1990s much as Symbolism, another Romantic-sourced movement, did in the 1890s. The New Expressionism shares many of that movement's precepts, but its first Muse was *Caligari.*

From different ends of the same axis, allegory and projection-based Expressionism feature a sophisticated rendering of the subject-object identifications of pantheism. In the greatest Expressionist dramatic works of the early twentieth century, however, even the rationalizing device that explains a series of fantastic events as simply the "projections" (that is, delusions) of a character was called into question. In the case of *Caligari,* the narrator's point of view seems at first to be completely undermined by its rationalist frame as a madman's tale—that is, the main character's "projection" of his own inner conflicts onto the very person who is trying to heal his illness. But as S. S. Prawer brilliantly expounded in *Caligari's Children* (1980)—which follows the seamless transition of nineteenth-century ghost stories into twentieth-century film—there is room for doubt. To whom or what in this film can the projection be traced? Is it not possible that the last scene, in which the narrator is revealed to be an inmate in Caligari's asylum, is simply one more of the cunning doctor's tricks?

In fact, every possible explanation of the dénouement is rational, up to a point, but what happens when they are all put together as coequal alternatives is not: the asylum set at story's beginning and end presents as skewed a perspective as any other. This should not be so if the "objective" frame is intended to rescue us from "subjective" paranoid delusions. What happens instead, as Paul Coates eloquently explains from the twentieth-century homocentric perspective, is that "the individual who stands at the work's center is simultaneously decentered by the projections issuing from him. The result is a powerful disorienting oscillation between subjective and objective viewpoints." Or as Richard J. Murphy has it, from the same standpoint, subcategory psychological: "It is almost as if the entire narrative were structured—as in a dream—according to the associative consciousness of a single narcissistic being."

Now the old allegorists—and the proponents of the New Expressionism we will meet in the next chapter—would endorse these conclusions by Coates and Murphy, but with an important adjustment of perspective.

They would agree, looking backward and forward Alice-in-Wonderland style, that the true narrator-demiurge of *The Cabinet of Dr. Caligari* is neither Caligari nor the hapless narrator. But since for them projection works from the outside to the inside, not vice versa, the allegorists' *tertius ad quem* is neither a person, however narcissistic, nor a "point of view" (a critical term that itself took on almost allegorical dimensions in the twentieth century). They would say, rather, that the omniscient role belongs to all that spooky painted scenery in whose inky shadows and energy lines the characters' souls have soaked a tad too long. The main character of *Caligari* is animated matter resonating with Duncan's "dream in which all things are living," the synesthesic primal reality we cannot see.

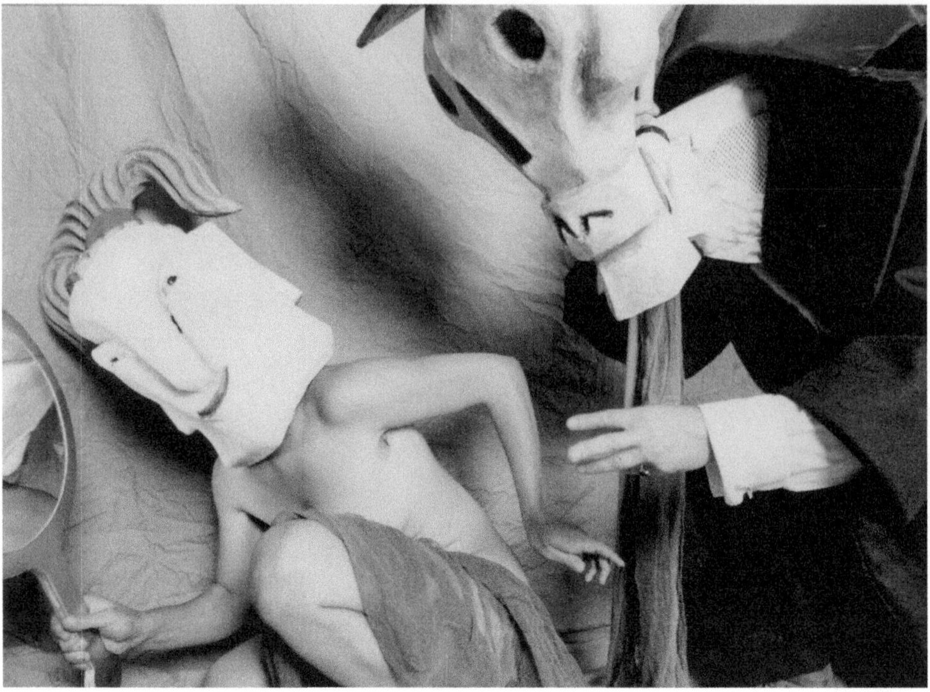

The Suburban Matron encounters Death. From Chris Hardman's "Skin & Bones/Flesh & Blood" (1995). Photo courtesy Antenna Theater.

The fact is that every writer *creates* his own precursors.

—Jorge Luis Borges

NINE

THE NEW EXPRESSIONISTS

Thanks to *Caligari*'s instant success in 1919, Expressionism was the first and only avant-garde movement internationalized through film even as it became moribund in the visual arts. Irrevocably linked by *Caligari* to the horror and fantasy genres, film Expressionism would carry on through the 1920s in such notable examples as Paul Wegener's *The Golem: How He Came into the World* (1920), F. W. Murnau's *Nosferatu, A Symphony of the Grave* (1922), and Fritz Lang's *Metropolis* (1927). Although its association with the lower-end horror genre worked to weaken Expressionism's links with its avant-garde origins, over the twentieth century its highly visually oriented sensibility never stopped being reinvented in one medium or another.

For decades after the 1920s, ripples from the Expressionist pond continued to spread throughout Europe and across the Atlantic in other arts as well. Bruno Schulz was quickly labeled a premiere Expressionist when his stories appeared in Polish journals in the late 1920s. Vorticism in the work of Wyndham Lewis carried the Expressionist principles to England. And while the Abstract Expressionist movement of the 1940s and 1950s remains America's major high-art inheritor of the movement's legacy, the Expressionist aesthetics of films like *Caligari,* which created a sensation when it opened in the United States, were to resurface along with their émigré directors in the strange American low-art mating of German Expressionism with the hard-boiled detective mode of pulp fiction that became the great *film noir* movement of the 1940s.

After a lull in the 1960s and 1970s, a painterly school of "Neoexpressionism" surfaced in a brief flurry of activity in the 1980s among Berlin painters like Salomé, Walter Dahn, and Georg Jiri Dokoupil. Expressionist *noir* took an analogous leap to the 1990s, when a new generation of mainstream American directors (the Coen brothers, Tim Burton, David Lynch, John Dahl, Quentin Tarantino, and others) used the vocabulary and conventions of this 1940s genre to fashion a strange new creature that might be dubbed "Re-Noir." Puppet theater, live and filmed, postmodern and New Expressionist, also enjoyed a cusp-of-the-century rebirth in the 1990s and early 2000s avant-garde.

The New Expressionism film of the 1990s, spilling into the early 2000s, grew out of the realist Re-Noir revival but is a distinctly different animal, most obviously because of its incorporation of the supernatural. Similarly, the New Expressionism features, but is not synonymous with, the grotesque; Quentin Tarantino, for example, as a proponent of the always-flourishing American realist grotesque, is not a New Expressionist; Ethan and Joel Coen, Tim Burton, and Alex Proyas are—a distinction I will explore more fully in Chapter 12. New Expressionist American film is a distinctly mass entertainment medium with interesting high-art riffs; its European counterparts, however, remain within the high-art tradition even as they draw from genre. (A fine distinction, and even as I write the line is rapidly blurring.)

What I am identifying is not a school, or even a movement based in a few geographical locations, like the original Expressionism. It is, rather, a sensibility—an informal "family resemblance," in Wittgenstein's sense, lacking a true genealogy or traceable lines of influence. The New Expressionist sensibility exempts, among others, straightforward science fiction novels (as distinct from films); mainstream literary fantasists; and "romances" as defined in Chapter 10 (by and large, New Expressionist works are not romances). Consciously or (most often) unconsciously, the New Expressionism revives the system of a living cosmos in which all things in this world exist in a hierarchy of interconnections with one another and with a timeless, invisible otherworld.

In his study of Goethe's obsession with alchemy, Ronald Gray once tried to describe, from an *episteme* perspective, the timeless attraction of the Neoplatonic worldview for a certain type of writer:

> For all their illogicality . . . and perhaps in part because of it, alchemy and occultism, as distinct from pure mysticism, exert a curiously strong influence on imaginative writers . . . The reason for this fascination is to be found in the alchemist's preoccupation with processes deep down in the mind. At some time in the past, one feels, these must have been examined and described in some detail by men who felt that the knowledge thus acquired could be handed on only in a symbolical form. Beneath this cloak, however, the lore of the unconscious could be communicated in great complexity and in a garb not unsuited to the subject.

Substitute the old word "transcendent" for its twentieth-century counterpart "unconscious"—or better, combine the two—and you have the central preoccupation of the New Expressionist sensibility.

Here are some of the defining features of the New Expressionism, in no particular order:

The inner is made visible in the outer. The features of the physical world provide a vocabulary for subjective expression; if you want to know what a character is feeling, look at the landscape instead of her face. When Bess, Learlike, screams out her grief on the cliffs in Lars von Trier's *Breaking the Waves*, the crashing waves give us a synchronous picture of her grief that is pure pathetic fallacy. In a far more aggressively concretized projection, the main character of Will Self's novel *My Idea of Fun* is able to *impose* his subjective thoughts on the environment. As with the Old Expressionism, the logic of the New Expressionism is the logic of dreams.

A metaphysical dimension is present. Externalizing subjective attributes returns us via Romanticism to the Renaissance world of emblem and allegory, and by extension to a cosmic order that is congruent with the subjective world. The feature that most significantly distinguishes the New Expressionism from its early twentieth-century forebears is that *not just the inner, but the transcendental, is made visible in the physical landscape.* See the playwright Craig Lucas's amazing film *Reckless* (1994), in which we find ourselves marooned with Mia Farrow inside the bubble of another person's dream. Only at the end of this strange story do we briefly glimpse the one minor character who, Krishnalike, has imagined all its wild and unlikely events. See also the brilliant exchange of souls among a puppeteer and his cohorts in *Being John Malkovich* (1999), directed by "Spike Jonze" (Adam Spiegel) and written by Charlie Kaufman.

The supernatural is no longer only the grotesque. Marking the important shift in our culture toward broader acceptance of the transcendental, it dares to be not of the Devil—though in its high-art manifestations no other deity, as a rule, is provided. See the infamous ringing-bells scene in *Breaking the Waves.*

A high-art edifice is constructed on a low-art foundation. Genre is a launching pad, not a container. This is an important distinction. The best New Expressionists do not engage in the repetition compulsion of formula narrative, either within or across stories. Von Trier, for example, does not obsessively retell a single primal story in the way Lovecraft does, nor does he follow the narrow plot road of the comic books. Neither, in their own way, do the Coen brothers, though most of their films fall into one genre category or another. These deliberate cracks in the façade of genre are precisely what let the light in; as we will see in Chapter 12, *noir* elements in New Expressionist works are often literally extinguished by the sun.

Extreme melodrama does not alienate us; extreme action is essential for deep identification with the main character. Selma in von Trier's *Dancer in the Dark* (2000) is an Everywoman-Christ on whom life's most outrageous calamities are inflicted. The issue is not whether we "believe" in the plausibility of these events, but whether we experience exactly how, at the deepest level of being, Selma's suffering is our own. Identification, not empathy, is the primary feeling mode of allegory.

Cliché is likewise deliberate, nonironic, and serves a higher purpose as allegory. Within a culture based on a materialist worldview, cliché is the *only* avenue back to allegory, because it is the sole arena in which hyperstylization, a precondition of allegory, is possible. The fate of Barton Fink, in the Coen brothers' eponymous film, is instructive here. Barton is a 1930s Clifford Odets–type social realist playwright whose dearest wish, when he moves from New York to Los Angeles for a screenwriting job, is to get to know the "common people." But in the world of New Expressionism, wishes are (as academics like to say) problematic. Soon he is vaulted into the company of a very uncommon common person, the madman played by John Goodman, and the hotel in which they bunk converts to an Expressionist nightmare of symmetrical flames licking out to the corridor from symmetrical rooms, Goodman's own exteriorized hell, when he sets it on fire. Now at the end of his rope, Barton is mysteriously transported into the landscape of the kitschy, sentimental magazine picture of a girl on a beach that decorates his room—a social realist's idea of hell if ever there were one. By this time, however, Barton has had quite enough of the "real" world, and his future inside this new aesthetic seems (and is) positively sunny by comparison. Similarly, we are told in von Trier's miniseries *The Kingdom* that a character who has just died has gone to the "Swedenborg room"—a witty piece of dream shorthand, with the faintest antiseptic whiff of sectarian cubbyholing, for some sort of generic Protestant afterlife.

Where do we find these New Expressionists? Prose literature, arguably the most conservative art form, enjoyed a strong realist grotesque tradition in America during the twentieth century in the works of William Faulkner, Flannery O'Connor, Jane Bowles, and others. The New Expressionist sensibility in America is found neither in continuers of this tradition nor in postmodernist redactions but rather in the occasional anomalous work of older authors, including Robert Olen Butler's half-satiric but memorable story collection *Tabloid Dreams* (in which, for example, the ghost of a *Titanic* victim haunts a waterbed) and ambitious works by Denis Johnson such as *Fiskadoro* (1985) and *Jesus' Son* (1999). It also appears in works by little-known writers such as Steve Weiner's remarkable *The Museum of Love* (1993), a picaresque odyssey of the grotesque influenced by the films of the Quay brothers and first published in England, where it met a wider and more enthusiastic reception than in the United States. Other young writers such as Kirsten Bakis (*Lives of the Monster Dogs*, 1997) and Stacey Richter (*My Date with Satan*, 1999), show a muscular and idiosyncratic use of the fantastic in the characteristic New Expressionist mingling of high and low art.

These works, however, seem the exception to the still-current American high style of engaged topical realism. For now, literary New Expressionism is best exemplified by an Old World writer such as the British novelist Will Self, who presents a consistent set of aesthetic terms within the New Expressionist sensibility than his American counterparts.

More than North America, Britain has seen a strong "minor" tradition of twentieth-century high-art fantasists, from the religious parables cum thrillers of the very Anglican Charles Williams (and before him the Catholic G. K. Chesterton) to the energetic folkloric-feminist fictions of Angela Carter. The New Expressionist sensibility departs sharply from this tradition, as the work of proponents such as Self and David Mitchell (*Ghostwritten*, 2000) demonstrates. The three-dimensional power Self imparts to his fiction also stands in marked contrast to those American experiments in the realist grotesque that rely heavily on the ventriloquism of the overvaunted narrative "voice" to make us believe in them. Such works are like stage sets; there is nothing behind them once the performance is over, and even the voice itself seems in retrospect a kind of sleight-of-hand. As an author Will Self has other kinds of problems, but (very admirably) this is not one of them.

Self was compared by his first wave of reviewers to William Burroughs, Vladimir Nabokov, Thomas Pynchon, Lewis Carroll, and others. Samuel Butler is certainly another; but Günter Grass with his *The Tin Drum*, that far more fully realized parable of a child freak whose special powers embody his age's discontents, seems Self's closest cousin. At the same time, this former cartoonist has borrowed equally from the traveling portmanteau of American pop genres, including horror, science fiction, and comic books. Armored with the impenetrable confidence of the true eccentric (as opposed to the trendy imitator of oddness), Self in his first novel, *My Idea of Fun: A Cautionary Tale* (1993), displays an authentic grotesque imagination—grotesque, that is, not just in the standard definition of present-day critics like Arthur Clayborough, suggesting "incongruity with the real or normal," but with the added supernatural dimension of the New Expressionism—a dimension, moreover, whose entire territory is not visible in the work it informs, because there is not enough room for it. *My Idea of Fun* maps a portion of an extremely odd inner cosmos and challenges us to fill in some of the rest with what we've been given. That we are not quite able to do so in this brilliant but rather rushed novel has to do with failure of development, not of imagination.

Briefly, *My Idea of Fun* is the story of one Ian Wharton, whose childhood in a seaside trailer park near Brighton is dominated by a sinister male friend of his mother's, who initiates Ian into a dark world of necromancy even as the boy matures on the surface into an ordinary young married marketeer in London. Ian shares with Mr. Samuel Northcliffe, a.k.a. Samuel Broadhurst or The Fat Controller, an unusual innate ability that we can instantly recognize as Renaissance "corporeal looking": he is able to call up images from the outside world with total accuracy, then inhabit and control these internal images. Accomplishing this feat for the first time, Ian realizes that "I was inside my own representation and that representation had become the world." His "eidetic" adventures are far from illusory; under his mentor's corrupt tutelage, Ian moves from controlling static internal images to manipulating the external world in a demiurgic way reminiscent of Bruno and the Renaissance magi. (Demiurgy in the most basic sense of shaping of the material world by supernatural means is a frequent motif of the New Expressionism.)

In this chronicle of a 1990s magus, the Gothic world of Ian's internal fantasy contrasts severely with the mundanity of the outside world, which it gradually infects and then controls, resulting in gruesome real-life murder and mutilation. Along the way Ian is taken under the wing of a psychologist, one Hieronymous Gyggle, who helps him mature as he tests and attempts to rationalize Ian's eidetic powers. Ultimately Gyggle, seemingly the one benevolent force in Ian's life, is rather confusingly revealed as a possible cohort of The Fat Controller's in directing Ian's destiny toward mating and host-fathering a new Samuel Broadhurst. Worse, The Fat Controller reveals through his powers as a "Demiurge of Dissociation" that he has caused his charge not to remember that Ian himself, and not his mentor, has committed a series of dreadful murders. By story's end, just as The Fat Controller seems to have been dispatched for good by a denizen of the mysterious realm known as the Land of Children's Jokes, he triumphantly reincarnates in the person of Ian's putative son.

Self presents The Fat Controller as a kind of Neoplatonic immortal or Illuminatus, "eminence gris of geopolitics." Though he boasts, "I am the very Lama of Lost Souls, I reduce the human to the material, utterly and completely," The Fat Controller actually produces the reverse effect—namely, that of lending a strange sheen of transcendence to the material world. Certainly he must be counted at least a grandnephew of Caligari's, turning Ian into his Cesare, sleepwalking instrument of his murderous will, and enlisting a complicitous psychoanalyst to steer Ian into the "Is this real or am I crazy?" mode. As a self-regenerating demiurge and new Merlin, The Fat Controller requires dying Corn God periods of dormant "enfeeblement" in the seacliff bunkers of the South Downs before reemerging with his sinister powers fully restored. What makes The Fat Controller effective as a literary creation, however, is the way his character grows so effortlessly out of its highly specific historical and social matrix. Harvested from the not immediately promising cultural soil of post-Thatcherite England, Mr. Northcliffe/Broadhurst's shamanesque attributes are grounded in the quotidian realities of the symbiotic marketing-finance-media world that Self clearly knows well. As the epitome of a 1980s businessman, The Fat Controller is a kind of *genius loci*, completely generic to his time and place.

Self's gift is to make the fantastic ordinary and the ordinary fantastic, suspending both elements in an elegant syntactic matrix. He cuts wittily to the heart of the business world's banalities, in a way no earnest Fifties angry young man would have dreamed of doing, by means of extended allegorical *tableaux vivantes* such as a "spectacle of ineluctable commerce" in which "one hand proffering money bill-like to another repeated itself, hither and thither, stitching up the ragged braid of the shopfronts." There is also the "Money Critic," a millennial late-capitalist magus discovered in his Spenserian lair with stacks of world currency heaped high all around him. Splendidly robed in an iridescent "floor length djellaba of unparalleled richness, patterned with interlocking geometrical shapes and financial symbols," the Money Critic is a gourmand aesthete who judges bonds by smelling and nibbling them: "Peaty, mulchy, mouldy—almost tetanussy." And there is the North London Book of the Dead ("a set of instructions to be recited to the dying, in order that their immortal souls should be cancelled out") in which Gyggle's junkies, like Tibetan monks, recite over their dying cohort a cabbalistic list of brand-name products: "Perrier, Polaroid, Walkman, Xerox."

Finally, we must not omit Ian's magical gift of "retroscendence": not only is he, in The Fat Controller's words, a "good little skryer" or psychic seer á la the Elizabethan John Dee, but his ability to follow visually any item he can see to its organic Ur-source allows Ian to track, for example, a pair of boxer shorts through poetic vistas of cotton harvested on the Nile straight on down to their subatomic structure—an invaluable marketing skill, to be sure. His further ability to alter physically what he "sees" with his inner eye makes Ian the ultimate New Expressionist demiurge of his own world. It also puts him, comically, in the same category as the Lacanian mother, whose gaze (in yet another instance of the twentieth-century displacement of numinous powers to the realm of secular psychology) is supposed to distort and shape her child's body.

Given this wonderfully *sui generis* "occult" dimension, what exactly *are* the metaphysics of this novel? As in other examples of New Expressionist film and literature, they are the tenets of the Renaissance natural philosopher, positing a universe of tiered realities in which microcosm and macrocosm do not symbolize but concretely *embody* each other. When Ian sees The Fat Controller's tiny image in a shop display window, the eidetic homunculus pipes up: "I control all the automata on the island of Britain, all those machines that bask in the dream that they have a soul. I am also the Great White Spirit that resides in the fifth dimension, everything is connected to my fingertips—by wires." A Kleistian puppet-imago is professing itself master of the universe, and within Self's terms we are inclined to accept its claim. This is a universe like that of Alex Proyas's 1998 film *Dark City*, to be discussed in Chapter 12, in which aliens and one human turncoat demiurgically create external landscapes and manipulate human memory. It is equally like that of Robert Fludd's 1619 treatise "A Philosophical Key," in which, among other things, this Christian Neoplatonist subjects the wheat plant to alchemical retroscendence, an experiment he regarded as the cornerstone of his elaborate cosmology.

In Self's Fluddian cosmos of materialized abstractions, dreams also possess a physical reality, like air pockets in the external world, and they can be entered as easily as walking into a room: "Once abandoned by their original occupants these artefacts are left lying about our crowded universe waiting for new tenants to inch into, grubwise." Ian, put into a "possession trance" of deep sleep by Dr. Gyggle, walks into the junkie Richard's dream and both men are simultaneously "wholly sucked into this world of forms. Forms that had set off from the idea of the human body and driven as far and as fast as they could, back towards the moment of conception. Until they reached this world, a world of the foetal."

This regressive Neoplatonic realm (which modernist and postmodernist perspectives alike would misidentify as a projective "Freudian fantasy" but which Self presents, in good New Expressionist fashion, as an actual location) turns out to be a medieval dream-vision landscape updated to post-apocalyptic urban-industrial. Ian and Richard find themselves traveling through a "giant shed, if that's what it was,"

> sometimes crossing wide expanses of concrete, other times crouching to make their way through twisting tunnels lined with chipboard, or Formica. Everywhere there was evidence of failed industry. Defunct machinery lay about, dusty and rusty. Bolts, brackets, angle irons and other unidentifiable hunks of metal were scattered on the floor; a floor that changed from concrete to beaten earth and in places disappeared altogether underneath a foot or more of water.

Their Chaucerian journey takes them to the "Land of Children's Jokes," a place of "giant toadstools instead of chairs and grossly distended puff balls in place of sofas," a "joke bestiary that children could relate to. Creatures with vestigial limbs, omnipotent capabilities and no genitals, only rounded furry mounds, impossible to penetrate." The Boschlike entities of this region we recognize as emblematic Forms of schoolyard jokes, such as the worm tricked by the promise of goodies into crawling out of a man's anus (I did recognize this one, if not the ones about the man with the spade in his head, the razor-chewing baby, or the quadriplegic).

In short, the allegorical mode puts *My Idea of Fun* in a literary genre that Jean de Meun, not John Osborne, would feel at home in. Self's technique is not postmodern, a label often carelessly used as a synonym for "self-conscious." He is rather an Idealist/Romantic, another identifying marker of the New Expressionism that represents a completely different kind of consolidating response to the agendas of modernism and postmodernism alike. Self provides a unitary cosmology (one that is, in appropriately corporate terminology, "vertically integrated") in which a separate World of Forms is presented neither as the author's "metaphor" nor as the main character's "projection" but as a simultaneously existing reality, period. Its underlying Neoplatonism collapses the Cartesian boundaries between subject and object, internal and external, mind and body. This radical move, hiding as it were in the guise of genre fiction, puts into question the essential homocentricity of the notion of projection—that is, its assumption that human subjectivity is the source of all phenomena in the universe that cannot be explained by the empirical-materialist rules laid down by science.

At times Self seems to vacillate between Neoplatonic and Aristotelian protocols by invoking, through the character of Gyggle the therapist, the stereotypical convention of placing what initially seems to be a supernatural event in a larger rational frame via the "Is this real or am I crazy?" conundrum. But in the novel's structure of concentric circles, Ian is revealed not to be crazy; everything that happens is real. Self has chosen the supernatural Neoplatonic road of popular genre rather than the Aristotelian-materialist road of high literature. Some have noted echoes in Self of the paranoid-Gnostic imaginary world of Thomas Pynchon, but I would say that the similarities between these two writers lie more in a certain adolescent emotional tone than in their metaphysics. It is a surprise to discover that Self, for all his excesses, provides at least the promise of a fuller humanity that never comes in Pynchon, for all the latter's brilliance and gift for narrative development.

"Promise of a fuller humanity!"—eidetically, I can already hear my readers screaming—"in a work in which the main character vividly imagines, and by imagining enacts, 'fucking the decapitated neck of a tramp in the Tube'? Or sucking the penis of a dog he has just tortured to death?" To this perennial reaction against the issue of excessive, taboo-flouting violence John Ruskin replied in *Modern Painting:* "it is because the dreadfulness of the universe around him works upon his heart, that [the grotesque artist's] work is wild . . . His beasts and birds, however monstrous, will have profound relations with the true." This statement applies as much to Will Self as it does to a painter like Francis Bacon, whose strategy was approximate to Self's. The violence of *My Idea of Fun* is Expressionist violence, enacted in perverse verbal images as Ian uses his eidetic imagination to morph or transform his victim's bodies in various painterly ways (soldering facial folds, for example). As with Bacon, this is a highly mediated representation, demiurgic rather than destructive in its deepest impulses.

In the end, it must be said, the real outrage of *My Idea of Fun*, what is truly *contra naturam*, is neither the mutilation of bodies nor the presence of the supernatural but rather Self's mutilation and foreshortening of his main character's essence and his story's narrative potential. The first third of the book, a richly detailed account of Ian's childhood, sets us up for an intricate working out of a very complex mix of elements, a *Bildungsroman* that never quite comes to pass. Once embarked on his unique journey to adulthood, Ian Wharton is rudely yanked out of it; things in Ian's life, whether viewed in the first or third person, speed up too much. The promise of fuller humanity does come, in his emotionally authentic encounters with women, but it is a promise that Self, seemingly under the influence of his own inner Fat Controller, cuts brutally short. Just as Ian is about to become a human being with Jane, the woman he marries, suddenly he's in full and unconvincing emotional reverse back to being The Fat Controller's bagboy—coitus interruptus (a repeating motif in this story) with a vengeance. All the intricate threads are dropped before a full pattern is visible, and this is a deep disappointment.

But—it might once again be argued, in the loose way we have come to use the term—is it not a "postmodern" effect, this duplication in mandarin prose of the callow plotting effects of teenage boys' horror comics? The answer must be no. It was a precept of Yvor Winters's useful notion of the imitative fallacy, in no way invalidated by the advent of various new aesthetic vocabularies, that just as you don't write in a boring way to represent a boring situation, you don't stunt a narrative to mirror the stunting of the main character. (One thinks again of *The Tin Drum*, in which the three-dimensionality of the story curiously flattens out once the protagonist reaches majority, as if both authors were trapped in the same spell of childhood as their characters.)

Herein lies the heart of the debate over distinctions between high art and genre introduced in Chapter 4—distinctions that are real, and crucial to understanding the aesthetic marginalization of the supernatural after the Renaissance, its linkage with the grotesque and demonic, and its gradual reemergence as a high-art category over the course of the twentieth century. From the broadest perspective, there is a sense in which the avant-garde itself is highly mainstream and the true margin is found, with qualification, in the sub-Zeitgeist of popular entertainment. At the same time, for all our love of pure Story, popular entertainments do have the aesthetic and emotional failings their detractors pinpoint: cartoonish characterizations, familiar plots with simplistic resolutions that cancel out any sense of ambiguity or complexity, and above all, the demonic sense of claustrophobic repetition. If the distinction, as I have argued in the case of Lovecraft, is between conscious and unconscious creative expression, then originality is not as crucial as *consciousness*, in the sense that Kafka more than Lovecraft was a conscious artist.

What the conscious practitioners of the New Expressionism avoid are, first of all, the not inconsiderable ontological pitfalls of the old worldview: that, for example, a disabled body signifies a disabled mind, and so on. In his early writings Lovecraft was guilty of the naive and reprehensible Expressionism of racism that equates, for example, outer skin color with inner moral "darkness." Though he later recanted these views, they serve as a reminder of those huge territories of knowledge where the Neoplatonic perspective cannot, and should never, replace the Aristotelian.

Consciousness is also not the same as intent, or omniscient control; artists recognize first of all that intent and outcome are never matching quantities, and second, that they never possess the full perspective on their own finished works. Artistic consciousness might be described as a felt harmony with, rather than a surface denial of or abreaction against, the deepest personal content of one's work, along with an instinct for the right path to follow to carry it through to the best expression. This is the difference between, for example, the director Shinya Tsukamoto's *Tetsuo: Man of Iron* (1988), in which a man inserts shafts of iron in his legs as a direct expression of rage, and the raft of earlier Godzilla, Mothra, and other Japanese genre movies in which mutated monsters wreak havoc on major cities as an unconscious and disconnected reflection of war, H-bombings, and the rages of victor and vanquished alike.

Of the kind of art Self practices, then—that of the New Expressionist conscious genrefier—one asks only for realism of the most basic sort: that the river flow forward and not backward, that the narrative structure as well as the main character traverse a complete course. We want the arc of human development followed once it has been started; we don't want to be spiraled back to the Land of Children's Jokes. By the book's end, however, we are back on the low road via a plot driven by gimmicks—gimmicks that work against the deepening and forward-flowing impulse in this novel, gimmicks with the potential to harden into habits farther down the road in a literary life, gimmicks that are acceptable, and expected, in formulaic genre works but not so okay in an ambitious project like *My Idea of Fun*. That said, one can only sympathize with Self's Scylla and Charybdis dilemma of risking overload in a fast-paced narrative by tracing his characters' trajectories in more careful detail inside an already densely arcane invented world.

In *Wittgenstein's Nephew*, the Austrian writer Thomas Bernhard suggests that the difference between the eponymous main character and his famous uncle is that "one published his mind, the other didn't." Enough of Will Self's imagination was published in *My Idea of Fun* to demonstrate that it is world class. Realizing the complete edition of this mind on the printed page, however, may call for a certain ineffable inner turning on the author's part, a turning that sometimes demands inconvenient, economically disastrous silence just when the world is clamoring loudest for more.

LARS VON TRIER AND THE RINGING BELLS

The Danish film writer/director Lars von Trier is another Old World younger artist addicted to twisting the clichés of pulp fiction and popular film out of their rigid circle into a resonant spiral. Even so, his radical departure from the aesthetics of the previous generation, which cut its teeth on art films of the 1960s and 1970s, has stirred, and continues to stir—in the case of his most recent works, *The Idiots* (1998) and *Dancer in the Dark* (2000)—a considerable negative reaction. When it was released in the United States in 1996, von Trier's earlier *Breaking the Waves* garnered a rather heated grassroots critical response that ran, "It's great until the last third, which is over the top, and the ending, which is *way* over the top and ruins it."

The twists of plot and style that this highly narcissistic director terms his "whims," however, are part of a deliberate, if unfamiliar, aesthetic enterprise—very little of which, incidentally, is visible in von Trier's filmic manifesto "Dogma 95." The notorious original manifesto with its ten-point "Vow of Chastity," co-signed by his fellow Danish filmmaker Thomas Vinterberg (*The Celebration*), seems to promise a solemn return to uncompromising social realism in the form of "authenticity"—hand-held cameras, no extraneous music, unity of time and place, color only, and so forth—with the ironic consequence that it has been widely adopted by dozens of earnest young filmmakers in the United States (partly, one suspects, by virtue of its convenient dovetailing of aesthetic purity with budgetary constriction). In practice, all of the vow's strictures have been broken by von Trier in the series of phantasmagoric, anti-naturalistic films he has made; the real innovation of this Dogme Brother lies elsewhere.

Breaking the Waves breaks a number of molds. The shaky hand-held camera motion (Dogma vow 3), that indispensable feature of 1970s *cinema vérité*—which is also the decade in which the picture, rather arbitrarily, is set—does indeed trick us into imagining we are entering a world of gritty naturalism. But in fact we aren't; this film intends to stake out very different ground indeed. First we trip over the title, which echoes, but also departs from, two common phrases: "making waves" (something the heroine, Bess, certainly does in her insular environment) and "breaking waves," an act of nature that is also a kind of endlessly repeating climax. "Breaking the waves" inverts both phrases in a characteristically going-against-the-grain manner that embodies the film's aesthetic.

It's another genre-twisting element, however, that truly sets the tone of this film. *Breaking the Waves* is divided into simply titled "chapters" ("Bess's Marriage," "Jan's Illness") that open with beautiful stills of the stark Scottish landscape patterned after the woodcut vignettes of old-fashioned novels. Half real physical world, half fantasy, these color-tinted photographs beckon us toward a lurid wonderland reminiscent of Maxfield Parrish that contrasts severely with the muted, brownish look of the narrative itself. Over these doctored images of wilderness, in place of what we might reasonably expect by way of background music (haunting Celtic folk songs tastefully foreshadowing the heroine's sad fate), we get raucous, pumping chestnuts of pop hits imported by the workers on the offshore oil rigs ("Goodbye Yellow Brick Road" and the like) that act as a Greek chorus to the story (lyrics are carefully matched with the content of each chapter episode) and also defiantly signal the triumph of the main character's taste over *Masterpiece Theatre*–type aesthetic considerations of local color. (Asked by the dour presbyters of her church what contributions she thinks these outsiders have brought to their village, Bess cheerfully replies, "Their music!")

These emblematic frames tell us exactly how to read the film, whose foundation is the real, harrowing world of human emotions. Onto this bedrock of joy and suffering von Trier wants to graft a New Expressionist realm that is realer than what, in art, conventionally passes for "real," because it attempts to concretize internal psychological and external spiritual forces at the same time. In the case of *Breaking the Waves*, one element being materialized is those forces for good or evil that thickly cluster around the territory of Eros. Even here we are still on the familiar ground of the old Expressionism, but von Trier is poised to take the extra step in the film's story, which goes like this: In a tiny ingrown island community off the coast of Scotland, a high-strung young woman marries Jan, a sensual, easygoing oil rigger. Exuberant after her wedding, Bess tells Jan, of her austere, bell-less chapel, "Let's make the bells ring!" But she is fated to stumble over her own intensity from the very start. Even Jan's first departure back to work devastates her, and in two-way conversations with God (in which she ventriloquistically assumes both parts) Bess prays desperately—a trifle too desperately?—for his return. An accident on the rig makes this longed-for event happen sooner than expected: her husband returns for good, permanently paralyzed from the neck down. In the aftermath of this catastrophe Jan tells his new young wife, whom he has initiated into the pleasures of sex, that she should divorce him, take a lover, because he is no good for her any more. Her characteristically extreme negative response prompts him to cleverly modify his directive: it would please *him*, he says, if she took lovers and then told him all about it.

To the horror of the others who love her, Bess overcomes her modesty and plunges wholeheartedly into her new role. She is careful, however, not to have sex with any man who genuinely cares for her, such as the young doctor, but initiates only the most brutal, impersonal encounters with the underclass of the port. As ostracism from her church and community looms, the young doctor hits on a last resort: he will have Bess locked up "for her own good" in a mental hospital, as she had been once previously. But Bess escapes police custody and, with the knowledge that Jan is dying, heads back to a freighter where she had been violently assaulted once before, thinking to sacrifice herself in a tradeoff with God so that Jan will be saved. After she is beaten to death by the sailors, Jan revives against all medical reason and even begins walking again. Stealing Bess's body to spare her the ignominious interment of a "sinner damned to hell," he and his friends bury her at sea. Later, back on the rig, his mates joyfully bring Jan topside to hear a miracle in the middle of the North Sea: big gray bells (invisible to sonar, of course) pealing noisily in the sky above them.

The film poses a paradox of warring axioms: Is love the "mighty power" at work here (as Jan maintains), or is it illness (as his sister-in-law has it), or have the two forces somehow gotten hopelessly mixed up? In its deliberate naiveté, the literal image von Trier employs to answer this question is a poison pill to late-modernist middlebrows (who think of themselves, naturally, as highbrows). Church bells ringing in heaven, how unspeakably corny! Not to mention the "miracle" of Jan's recovery, presumably as a result of Bess's ultimate and fatal sexual adventure. Miracles and bells, the pastel sentimentalism of a turn-of-the-century postcard or Italian roadside shrine, an unholy alliance of 1940s Hollywood movie kitsch with organized religion—*quelle horreur!* Caught in such a knee-jerk response, we might not stop to consider that, bizarrely, von Trier's camera gazes *down* at the enormous bells of heaven from above—a divine perspective that Bess herself occasionally inhabits—rather than up from the usual human vantage below. Like Bess, we are allowed briefly to assume the Deity's "point of view," as English professors used to call it. This shot alone is a tip-off that the austerities of the twentieth-century avant-garde have left coming generations no choice but to rebel by going backward, as it were, into exaggerated conventionalism and cliché, in order to discover an emotionally richer aesthetic vocabulary.

To most intelligent viewers, especially those over age forty, the New Expressionist dimension of *Breaking the Waves*—that is, its deliberate supernatural kitsch—radically diminishes the film's psychological credibility. Get rid of that wretched ending, they say, and you would have an affecting study of a borderline personality crushed by circumstance, spousal perversion, and ruthless tribal mores. The same viewers, naturally, show nary a quiver of indignation as they watch the plays of Shakespeare featuring all those upsets of nature that describe and embody the moral universe of his characters, because all English majors know that Shakespeare is not to be blamed for his ignorance of scientific empiricism; these peculiarities were part of the Elizabethan worldview. It's okay for Horatio to say to the expiring Hamlet, "Flights of angels sing thee to thy rest," but it's not okay for the bells to ring after Bess's death. Lacking the metaphysical level on which the bells operate, however, *Breaking the Waves* would be just another example of the sort of art Westerners have happily consumed for a hundred and fifty years: social realism shading into modernism that steadfastly upholds a rational-empirical worldview. Lars von Trier's dilemma is somewhat akin to that of Jorge Luis Borges's character Pierre Menard, whose great achievement was to write *Don Quixote* in the twentieth century—a feat that surpasses Cervantes's original effort if only because doing so means bucking every wave and ripple of the Zeitgeist.

Von Trier is not such an anomaly, however. At the beginning of the twenty-first century an enormous gap in sensibility is yawning. Overturning the realist prohibition on attributing human feelings to objects in the environment, the New Expressionism revives the implicit assumption that the outer mirrors the inner, that a storm embodies (does *not* symbolize or stand for) psychological turmoil, and that bells ringing not only materialize Bess's inner powers but suggest as well their resonance with a transcendental moral order. To the adherents of this sensibility, the demand for "realism" is as narrow and two dimensional as the bells are to detractors of *Breaking the Waves*. In New Expressionist terms, the bells represent a Shakespearean ending in which the moral order has been restored by a message from those inner areas of reality coincident with a transcendental reality we do not experience with our five senses—and it is a defiant message in the face of all sensible judgment as rendered by the well-intentioned, both within the film and in the audience.

Even judged on its own terms, however, *Breaking the Waves* is not quite a completely realized work of art. What mars its accomplishment is not the dying Jan's miraculous return to life or the ringing bells but some big holes in character development. The director's conception of Jan seems to be not of a pervert, as most parties inside and outside the film assume, but of a decent man who is almost as selfless as Bess. At each turn Jan appears willing to sacrifice his happiness and his life to free his young wife from her loyal bondage to him, as displayed in his insistence that she take a lover and report to him about it (rising, one senses, out of a well-meaning but very male-oriented idea of what it would take to make Bess happy, coupled with the knowledge that she will do anything he says), his signing the papers that will commit Bess and thereby save her from further erotic degradation, his decision not to undergo more operations and so, he thinks, finally to die and thereby free her. But some crucial evidence is missing. Stolid Jan exposes Bess's first tale of sex as made up; her second, real foray (masturbating a stunned but willing local at the back of the bus) she sanitizes by retelling it to Jan as if she were doing it to him. We never see Jan's reactions to the later increasingly squalid and dangerous episodes. Is he titillated, as he claims he will be, or is he secretly horrified? We hear others state that his mind has darkened and that he is leading her downward; Jan himself scrawls on his writing tablet, "LET ME DIE I'M EVIL IN HEAD."

Does Jan actually come to take pleasure from the accounts, as he tells Bess he will? Or is he merely repeating others' judgment on him? Jan's true nature remains opaque in a way it shouldn't, and the needed information may be lying on the cutting-room floor. This missing link affects our understanding of other characters as well as the basic premise of the film. For if only Jan appreciates the extreme nature of Bess's love, only he is her equal in love, then is it the young doctor—kind, unwilling to exploit Bess sexually, finally in love with her—who is aligned with the forces of evil? The doctor is willing to lock her up in the same way and for the same reasons that brought about her incarceration before, reasons that he himself at first rejects ("It's natural to show what you feel," he says glibly) until he sees the direction Bess's "natural feelings" are leading her. At her inquest he seems about to recant when he informs the bewigged jurists that everything he has written in Bess's medical record ("immature," "neurotic") should be replaced by the single word "good." In the face of their stony incomprehension, however, he retreats once again to the safety of diagnostic labels.

Breaking the Waves brings to mind finally two famous but very different short stories, one perverse and one sentimental, out of the Anglo-American tradition. In the first, W. W. Jacobs's "The Monkey's Paw" (1902), an old couple wish on an Indian amulet first for money—which they receive in the form of a settlement for their son's grisly death in the factory where he works—second, for his return to them; and third, that he *not* return when shambling footsteps and a heavy knock sound at their door. The second is O. Henry's "The Gift of the Magi" (1906), in which a newlywed husband and wife each sacrifice the thing they hold most dear to buy the other a Christmas gift, but what they've given can only be used with the treasured possession sacrificed. It is this kind of fairytale logic that balances the plot of *Breaking the Waves* on Bess's two wishes: first that Jan come home and second that he not die. These wishes become externalized forces acting omnisciently in the world of this story, forces through which Bess, by the demiurgic intensity of her desires, first causes Jan to be paralyzed, then causes him to live and walk again.

Thus Bess's greatest sin, as she completely understands, was committed long before Jan's accident, not after. In Shakespearean (and New Expressionist) terms, her excessive love has upset the natural order—the Tao, if you will—of the larger world around her, thereby initiating a disturbance in the moral ether, the transcendental environment that invisibly surrounds us, conducive to Jan's accident. For this transgression she must atone. And atone she does, transforming herself in the process into a female Christ cum Mary Magdalene. Stoned by children, the outcast Bess is only too prepared to take up her cross, here a sluggish motorbike she must drag up a Scottish Golgotha to the bleak chapel of her forefathers. Her role-playing dialogues with God—an exercise in piety the late Gestaltist godfather Fritz Perls would have doubtless heartily endorsed—reinforce our sense of a God the Father/Bess the Daughter revisionism that triumphantly demolishes her fellow parishioners' life-quenching patriarchalism. (Of the Scots it has been said that first you must dig through all that ice before you hit the granite.)

Meanwhile, using a therapeutic strategy that would have been heartily endorsed in turn by Sigmund Freud (who vividly described the pathology of the "subject's overvaluation of his own mental processes" in his essay "The Uncanny"), the young doctor tries cajoling Bess out of delusory omnipotent thinking to bring her back to "reality." Gently he teases her: "What powers you possess!" But in the New Expressionist universe of *Breaking the Waves*—a different kind of uncanny—she does, she does.

Psyche and Cupid, from Apuleius's *The Golden Ass.* Antioch mosaic pavement, Late Antiquity. Courtesy Princeton University Department of Art and Archaeology.

Take heart, I said to myself: don't think of Wisdom now; ask the help of Science.

—Umberto Eco

TEN

THE *HERMETICON* OF UMBERTUS E.

Is it a sign of the secret web of meaning linking all outer-world phenomena to have had no thoughts of the ancient Greek prose novels for twenty-five years, and then to hear of them three times in a single day?

The day in question was February 22, 1991, and I am not discounting the possibility that there might have been some numerological or cabbalistic significance in the doubling of numbers. The venue was Berkeley, California. In the morning I received a letter from a scholar friend who had reviewed a draft of an essay of mine (eventually Chapter 5 of this book) about those two twentieth-century masters of the grotesque, Bruno Schulz and H. P. Lovecraft. He advised me first, to go back to Apuleius and second, to look up "that woman who wrote about the romance." Because I had not read the Greek romances of Late Antiquity since undergraduate days and had not read Gillian Beer's *The Romance* at all, I headed for the library that afternoon. After trying, and failing, to locate Professor Beer's slender volume in the misfiled chaos of a budget-cut state university's stacks, I was killing time in the periodicals room when I came upon a short piece by Marina Warner in an old copy of *PN Review*. In this lecture given at a Dublin writers' conference she declared that we now live in a postcolonial era whose multicultural ambience is reminiscent of the Hellenistic Mediterranean. What art form, asked Warner, better captures the syncretic spirit of both ages, ancient and modern, than those raffish, cosmopolitan prose narratives known collectively as the Greek romances?

Leaving the periodicals room, I was pondering this coincidence when I spotted a notice on a library bulletin board: the scholar and critic Margaret Anne Doody was to give a lecture that afternoon entitled "The Real Rise of the Novel: From Late Antiquity to the Late Twentieth Century." Hearing the soft but unmistakable sound of footfalls on my grave, I made my way to the lecture hall.

Like Warner, Doody drew the syncretic, multicultural parallel between the Mediterranean world of the early Christian era and our late twentieth-century global village. By labeling the Greek romances as trash, inferior art, compared to high classical literature, both Nietzsche and the Anglocentric literary critics of the twentieth century had unjustly maligned these ancient prose narratives, she argued. In reality, the Greek romance was an iconoclastic narrative genre that, in sharp contrast to the patriarchal mode of epic poetry, featured the disenfranchised—women, slaves—as main characters and focused on the individual's right to determine (in our current way of saying it) his or her own fate. Setting up a case that Samuel Richardson had drawn important elements of *Pamela* from Heliodorus's *Aethiopica*, Doody concluded that the novel of the eighteenth through twentieth centuries cannot be understood without reference to the Greek romance.

The day's experience left me with the distinct feeling of having become a character in an Umberto Eco novel: in all innocence I had stumbled upon a secret international conspiracy to promote the Greek romance, for who knows what arcane purposes. Two courses of action now seemed desirable: to look up the new translations edited by Basil Reardon that Professor Doody had cited—for, as a student all those years ago, I had likewise been told the Greek romances were decadent trash, the stuff of Crocodile Street—and, for moral support in my mounting paranoia, to reread Eco's *Foucault's Pendulum.* I performed the latter task first, in a head-spinning three days. When I reached the novel's climax, a human sacrifice in the underground chambers below the Conservatoire des Artes et Métiers in Paris, I noticed for the first time that the words the grand shaman shouts just before plunging the knife into his victim's heart belong to none other than H. P. Lovecraft's demonic language Aklo: "I'a Cthulhu! I'a S'ha-t'n!" The circle, and conspiracy, was complete.

The dust of all this synchronicity has settled now. The results are in, and here is my thinking on the matter. *Foucault's Pendulum* is a Greek romance, albeit a very late one. And Greek romances are primal Story in Chesterton's sense; they are archetypal penny dreadfuls, the Ur-form of Western sub-Zeitgeist popular entertainment—lots of fun to read, but still with something missing. You might feel compelled, in the repetition-compulsion way, to read another Greek romance, but probably not the same one twice. They are trash, worthy trash—though I think the word *kitsch* best captures their flavor.

In modern times the best known of these ancient Greek novels (even though it was written in Latin) remains Apuleius's second-century C.E. *Metamorphoses*, also known as *The Golden Ass*, with its famous story-within-a-story of Cupid and Psyche; it was Shakespeare's favorite, too. But as Reardon points out in his introduction to *Collected Ancient Greek Novels*, the neat label "Greek romance" actually covers five or six centuries, a variety of types (love stories, fable-history, comedy), and at least two distinct tones: naive and ironic. Genre boundaries, thus, are not distinct, and elements of Greek romance can even be found in the apocryphal Christian narratives. Nonetheless an identifiable Greek romance narrative pattern exists, and it is a familiar one: a man and woman meet and fall in love, are separated and exposed to harrowing adventures, are reunited. Or as Graham Anderson has listed the sequence: "initial felicity rudely broken by journey and separation; danger to life, limb, and chastity; rescue by divine agency; and eventual reunion through similar means."

Greek romances are romances, of course, and that form deservedly received critical rehabilitation in the later part of the twentieth century. Northrop Frye claimed for it (as all subsequent readers must duly note) the high status of a quasi-religious mode of thought, a "secular scripture" structurally linked to the salvation quest of Christianity in which the vicissitudes suffered by the protagonist allow him to achieve a higher spiritual level by the story's end. But the romance is also, as Gillian Beer observed—I was finally able to lay my hands on her book—a flexible, slippery form that includes many other possibilities as well. It is, for one thing, a propagator of "evasive formulae."

For me the operative word here is "formula." Regardless of the unquestioned virtues of the romance form as a whole, the Greek romances suffer especially, it seems to me, from the restrictions common to all formulaic popular literature—most obviously, two-dimensional characters and completely predictable plot patterns; more profoundly, the constriction of spirit and repetition compulsion that reading them brings on. Predictability, two-dimensionality, and repetition compulsion have an entirely different and less satisfactory flavor in the context of popular written narrative—the kitsch of the bestseller—than they do in traditional oral folktale. And although their characters have the considerable novelty (for their time) of being entirely "fictional" as opposed to historical or mythic, the romances are, as Reardon admits, "sentimental and sensational." His argument that these tales fill the void left by high classical literature because they represent romantic love and private emotions has to be taken, therefore, as special pleading. And though "simplified characters," as Beer stresses, are an important defining element of the romance form generally, the type of simplification favored by the Greek romance is not of that expansive sort that "allows us to act out through stylized figures the radical impulses of human experience." Fully representative of the genre are Habrocomes and Anthia, hero and heroine of Xenophon's *Ephesiaca.* Unswervingly chaste and faithful to each other, once united in marriage at the story's end they "lived happily ever after; the rest of their life together was one long festival."

It is wise, however, not to be too severe in the face of the deep universal hunger that Story in all its forms satisfies—the "simple need for some kind of ideal world in which fictitious persons play an unhampered part," as Chesterton said of the penny dreadfuls. As love stories with happy endings, the Greek romances satisfy this need. They are, however, devoid of complex shadings of emotion and response; any ambivalence in their principals' behavior toward each other is strictly a function of plot advancement, not character development. Mikhail Bakhtin noted the Greek romance's narrative pattern as an example of the reductive monologic voice; it equally exemplifies Umberto Eco's own statements about the text that is closed by virtue of its author's cynical choice of an "objective structural strategy" involving a dialectic of heroes and villains rather than one that allows the psychology of the characters to motivate their actions. The necessity to impose this strategy partly accounts for the interesting passivity of the main characters: whereas in the old tragedies the hero acts, in the Greek romance things happen *to* the heroes. This passivity was cited unfavorably, as a sign of decadent effeminacy, by earlier male scholars and favorably by Doody, as an indication that the male characters partake of traditionally feminine characteristics in contrast to their more active female counterparts.

At first glance the uninhibited sexuality of some of the Greek romance characters, along with the open and sanctioned male homosexuality, seems to promise a more wide-ranging treatment of that area than we are accustomed to find in later Western literature. This proves, however, to be a false hope raised by differing social, not literary, customs, since in all other ways the characters are stock and conventional. Moreover, the multiculturalism of these works is somewhat called into question by the fact that they are full of ethnic stereotypes drawn from the perspective of their mostly Greek authors, who are fond of contrasting tricky, light-fingered Egyptians, for example, with heroic Greeks.

It is certainly true that because the imperial "elite" Western scholars of the late nineteenth and early twentieth centuries identified strongly with the Roman empire, they disparaged the Greek East in an across-the-board way that makes both the period and its literature worthy of renewed interest and attention. These men were, in fact, unwittingly denigrating their own civilization, for in many profound elements of structure and content alike—Christianity itself being not the least—Western culture is, as we have seen, a Hellenistic invention. By the same token, the fact that the Old Bulls of academia slandered the culture of Late Antiquity as decadent should not, by reverse reasoning, make all its products wonderful in our eyes; we should beware of replacing an old do-or-die standard (such as patriarchy) with a new one (matriarchy) that will destroy just as effectively our ability to make careful individual discriminations and judgments. For scholars of gender, real female alchemists such as Kleopatra or Maria Jewess, for example, provide historical and social information about women in Late Antiquity in a way the heroines of the Greek romance cannot; the latter furnish information only about the type of narrative in which they are embedded.

Therefore—though these were not necessarily Doody's major points—it does not follow that because a genre prominently represents women and slaves it is *not* trash, or that a tale with a highly conventionalized narrative pattern can ever be said to demonstrate, through the actions of its characters, either social egalitarianism or the individual's freedom of choice. One might as well make the same arguments—and some do—of a beautifully crafted and photographed Hollywood cops-and-robbers opus that features a woman police sergeant as its protagonist and an array of ethnic types cast in other leading roles. The actions of these characters are determined by the logic of the formulaic narrative that controls them, not by principles of social democracy in the real world. As Eco very perceptively notes in his analysis of Ian Fleming's James Bond novels, "The very use of [stock] figures (the Manichaean dichotomy, seeing things in black and white) is always dogmatic and intolerant—in short, reactionary—whereas [the author] who avoids set figures, who sees nuances and distinctions, is democratic."

Yet when all is said and done, what we are dealing with here is pure Story, Story that cannot be denied. There's much to enjoy in the Greek romances: the lightning shifts in tone and content of Apuleius, from pornography to romantic love to religious conversion; the elaborate plots-within-plots of Heliodorus and the way the action of the story advances while his characters are engaged in group fainting spells (a wonderful foreshadowing of Edgar Allan Poe); and the charming pastorality of Longus's *Daphnis and Chloe.* There is, finally, all the inherent attraction of lively stories from a long-dead world, the richness of the culture and language they reflect. In the end the Greek romances irresistibly recall the classic comics I devoured as a child, if not quite as eagerly as the scary stuff—from the *Iliad* (how heartening to learn from a scholar and native Greek that he had first read it as a comic, too) to *The Count of Monte Cristo* and *Cyrano de Bergerac* and *The Last of the Mohicans.* To this day, for me as for countless others, these stripped-down picture-Stories remain the only source of many of the world's masterpieces.

Now to Eco. (As Margaret Doody said of the romances, with a bow to Forster, "Only connect.")

First, understanding even the content of *Foucault's Pendulum*, let alone its narrative form, requires us to look back to the same society that produced both the Greek romance and the tangled web of religio-philosophical schools and cults whose influence I have been tracking in this book. For this sprawling melodrama is above all a summation and subversion of the complex history of the Hermetic, Gnostic, Neoplatonic, and other religious traditions I have traced in these chapters, and the Mediterranean world of Hellenism through Late Antiquity was their birthplace.

Eco has a specific agenda in using what he calls "Hermeticism" as the leitmotif of his novel, and that is to demonize it. Taking the cluster of rumor and legends around the medieval Knights Templar order as a starting point, he intends to parody the sickly flavor of "secret knowledge" cultivated by the adepts and initiates of esoteric traditions. By conflating

Hermeticism with Neoplatonism, Gnosticism, Jewish cabbala, and all the other survivals of the old worldview under the single label "occultism" and stretching its boundaries to the wildest extremes imagined by its most lunatic adherents, he intends to expose the "occultist's" manner of subverting logic, which "dims the intellectual light that allows you always to tell the similar from the identical, the metaphorical from the real."

In its opening pages, the book promises to be (appropriately, considering Pope's own satire of Paracelsus) a veritable *Dunciad* of alchemists and Hermetic madmen. The reader—this reader—approaches joyfully such a wild conflation of historical fact and fiction, full of admiration for the wit and learning that inform every page. Finally, one hopes, we will get the last word on the bizarre, ambiguous history of the "Perennial Philosophy," as the old esoteric worldview was called in the late nineteenth century by its conscious converts—its serious side and its shady ridiculous side, which coexist uneasily like one of those pasted-together androgynes that sixteenth-century alchemists used as an emblem of the union of spirit and matter.

To a degree, *Foucault's Pendulum* fulfills these high expectations. For all its zany exaggeration, the novel still presents an exuberant, richly detailed *reductio* of fifteen hundred years of Western culture. Like the Greek romances, it is fun, and there is much simple enjoyment to be derived (in the words of a Greek romance translator) from such a "primitive and satisfying view of the world." Like them it is nostalgic, but deliberately and sardonically so, an ironic homage replete with satiric paeans to the lost unity of premodern Western culture of which the following, addressed by the narrator to two memory magi of bygone times, is a nice example: "O Raimundo [Lully], O [Guilio] Camillo, you had only to cast your mind back to your visions and immediately you could reconstruct the great chain of being, in love and joy, because all that was disjointed in the universe was joined in a single volume in your mind." This is a wicked little parody, complete with in-joke pun on the name of A. O. Lovejoy, whose authoritative work on the Neoplatonic cosmos in Western culture is entitled *The Great Chain of Being.* Eventually, however, five hundred pages of any sort of parody begin to wear thin, and the escape from seriousness produces in a reader its Hegelian opposite—the desire to escape from unremitting fun. *Foucault's Pendulum* offers no such safety valve. Increasingly we feel ourselves trapped inside a giant Eco chamber of literary and philosophical allusion in which all elements have been expediently reduced to game pieces.

For most of all, like Ian Fleming and the writers of the Greek romances, this high-culture literary critic is engaged here in "cynically building an effective narrative apparatus," one that not only draws from the conventions of the modern thriller but conforms to them in every respect. Eco has his character Belbo make the following remark, which could serve as the novel's epigraph: "Maybe only cheap fiction gives us the measure of reality . . . It's easier for reality to imitate the dime novel than to imitate art." In many ways this book may seem to be saying the same thing, but there is a difference between formula used by a conscious genrefier like Lars von Trier as an integral part of a radical quest for a new aesthetic vocabulary and formula applied without modification to animate a novel of ideas. Unattached to a real aesthetic (as opposed to critical) vision, cardboard characters and plots do have a life and occult energy of their own; in particular, they have the power to reduce serious ideas to their own level of conventionality.

Cast in the rigid mold of genre, the novel's ten-part division into the cabbalistic *sefirot* or emanations thus becomes no more than a trivializing device, a baroque and functionless decoration, as do the tasteful bits of background character building and the multiple referentiality of the characters' names: Casaubon is not just a Milanese graduate student turned editor, he is Meric Casaubon, the first Renaissance scholar/editor to study the Hermetic texts critically and date them correctly, and he is also the Reverend Edward Casaubon of George Eliot's *Middlemarch* who—very appropriately for this story—cannot manage to complete his "Key to all Mythologies." Abulafia is the name not only of the thirteenth-century Jewish mystic and cabbalist we met in Chapter 3, but of the word processor one of the characters calls his "golem," on which he enters the Tetragrammaton for fun to discover the name of God. Ultimately, the multiple-track allusions dissolve into no meaning at all (a criticism Eco himself levels against the Hermetic-poststructuralist devils). We feel not that we have penetrated to the heart of a philosophical labyrinth but rather that we have been left stranded in the middle of a cold, fancy game of virtual reality purchased from the computer store. And such gamesmanship and emotional distancing are somehow more disturbing coming from a deeply intelligent and erudite sensibility than they would be from a cheerful hack.

Eco is nobody's fool; he knows full well he is casting himself in the role of "last *avatar* of Kitsch." I suspect he would say that by so doing he has demonstrated the decadence of a culture at its tether's end. More likely is the possibility that the book represents only the tether's end of the substream of philosophical tradition Eco himself embodies. A subtext of *Foucault's Pendulum* not available to the general reader is the fact that Eco's adversarial stance springs from the venerable feud between the academic semioticians, the Aristotelian schoolmen of modern times, and the French poststructuralist school. Jacques Derrida in particular is Eco's target, in front of whom he positions Hermeticism as a very large metonym. Or to put it in the terms of that considerably superior work *The Name of the Rose*, the noble rationalist and technophile William of Baskerville is once again pitting himself against the dark, chaotic forces of mysticism as represented by the gullible, superstitious Ubertino.

This allegorical encounter is played out in the text of the Tanner Lectures given by Eco at Cambridge University's Clare Hall in 1990. Published under the title *Interpretation and Overinterpretation*, these lectures develop the thesis Eco presented in *Foucault's Pendulum* in a more expository but no less adversarial mode, and with the true opponent revealed. Continuing his battles with "Hermetic irrationalism old and new," Eco acknowledges that

> once it had been reworked by Pico della Mirandola, Ficino, and Johannes Reuchin, that is to say, by Renaissance Neo-platonism and by Christian Cabalism, the Hermetic model went on to feed a large portion of modern culture, ranging from magic to science. The history of this rebirth is a complex one: today, historiography has shown us that it is impossible to separate the Hermetic thread from the scientific one or Paracelsus from Galileo.

From this reasonable statement he goes on to posit—just as his arch-foe the Hermetic scholar Frances Yates did before him, though not so ambitiously—an inherited esoteric historic tradition of unlikely scope and continuity. Even today, Eco says, the path of error is still clogged with traffic; postmodern criticism, he declares, features the same "slippage of meaning" as does what he calls the cosmogony of an "open-ended universe" that is "one big hall of mirrors, where any one individual object both reflects and signifies all the others"—a universe that allows, by virtue of analogy, the possibility of "infinite interconnections."

The old worldview, however, was not synonymous with the model that Eco presents. From Bolos of Mendes through the Renaissance, connections between the material world and the invisible world, albeit wildly inaccurate in empirical terms, were presented as one to one, hierarchical, and precise. In a line of reasoning that may resemble the scorned analogizing process more than he realizes, Eco has conflated a number of traditions into a single model on which he bestows the derogatory and historically inaccurate label "occult." As scholars of Hermeticism like Brian Copenhaver have warned repeatedly, however, "modern scholars should not use *Hermetic* and related terms as if they were vaguely synonymous with *magical* and its cognates."

In *Foucault's Pendulum* Eco forges an explicit link between Late Antiquity and the late twentieth century when he has a character compare the syncretism of modern Brazilian folk religions to the cults that riddled that earlier society:

> In the centuries of the late empire, Africa received the influences of all the religions of the Mediterranean and condensed them into a package. Europe was corrupted by Christianity as a state religion, but Africa preserved the treasures of knowledge, just as it had preserved and spread them in the days of the Egyptians, passing them on to the Greeks, who wreaked such great havoc with them.

Typically, what starts as a comparison is converted by the Hermetic spokesman to continuity and conspiracy: far from showing mere surface similarities, the character argues, the African cults have survived secretly to this day as part of an underlying millennia-old plot.

The insistent and unfavorable comparisons between Late Antiquity and the present day that Eco makes in his own voice have a tinge of nostalgia, perhaps because they belong to a long-standing tradition of historical analogizing. His equation of present-day Western culture not with "the glory that was Rome" but with the wider syncretic Greco-Mediterranean society (still carrying those overtones of decadence and slippage from an ideal) in which it was embedded has been a familiar trope since the late eighteenth century, when Edward Gibbon set the model in his *Decline and Fall of the Roman Empire*. It is also a coded sub-Zeitgeist indication that modernity (as symbolized by the Roman empire) is dead; for better or worse we have jumped ahead one more time notch into the dread postmodern multicultural syncretism of Hellenism shading into Late Antiquity. (At this rate, by the year 2050 the analogy will have moved forward into the early Middle Ages—and given the resurgence of religiosity, that parallel may work, too.)

For now, Nietzsche's "Alexandrian man," whom he berated in *The Birth of Tragedy* as a "librarian and corrector of proofs," has become Eco's second-century man, "dazzled by lightning visions while feeling his way around in the dark . . . develop[ing] a neurotic awareness of his own role in an incomprehensible world"—a way of perceiving, Eco implies, that is once more vying for our hearts and minds. But already this is old news. Then as now, mainstream pundits like Eco missed the *tertium ad quem* in this equation: in the second century, that a single religion, Christianity, would break out of the pack to become the next behemoth, and now, that a similar charismatic fusion of old and new has already taken place—under, above, and around us. Yet to come is not the paradigm shift itself, which has already happened, but only our full awareness of it.

How does this theme play out in *Foucault's Pendulum?* I still believe that Eco is striving, under the frozen mask of playfulness, to smuggle in one serious point of rationalist discourse: namely, to brand "occult" thinking, which in the universe of *Foucault's Pendulum* is synonymous only with Hermeticism-Neoplatonism, as a "psychosis of synarchic plots." But this goal is impossible to fulfill: if the terms of the structure forbid us to be serious, then we cannot side with any implicit position. Of Ian Fleming, Eco wrote that "our author does not characterize his creations . . . as a result of an ideological opinion but purely for rhetorical purposes"—such purposes being to pander to *endoxa*, "the common opinion shared by the majority of readers." Fleming, following the spirit of his times, labeled his bad guys communists. And while Eco has his philosophical reasons for opposing that worldview, the Hermeticists become his own "communists" not in fair dispute but only because that is their indispensable function in the Manichaean hero/villain dichotomy. The narrative form of the thriller is egalitarian and subversive to just the degree that it subverts the rationalist's position as effectively as it does the occultist's. By the end of *Foucault's Pendulum* this structural nihilism seems more monstrous than the murderous acts of the designated villains.

Here I must interrupt myself—for I, too, am a decadent unable to stick to the high road of formal analysis, and an admirer of penny dreadfuls to boot—to note that the women characters in Eco's novel are pretty bad, if only because Eco tries so earnestly to make them the intellectual equals of their men while still bestowing on them their ancient role as embodiments of the life principle. The main character's girlfriend Lia, for example, speaks "with the wisdom of life and birth." (Speaking as a woman, I should like to say: if only I could.) Here is a sample of that wisdom: "I have one cunt and you have one cock—shut up and don't joke—and if we put these two together, a new thing is made, and we become three. So you don't have to be a university professor or use a computer to discover that all cultures on earth have ternary structure, trinities." And so on.

Natural female smarts aside, I did manage to extract a very useful piece of computing information out of Eco's clever mélange of "Apple and cabala": namely, the purpose of the "Undelete" function key in the WordPerfect software program. An extremely appropriate piece of knowledge, too, since "Undelete," in computer ontology, represents the ultimate hedging of bets. No decision has to be binding and irrevocable; like bargain-counter Gnostic demiurges, we can all create and destroy, then bring anything we like back from the dead.

So there is finally something a little disappointing about all this postmodern fun chastely coupled with the muscular exercise of enormous erudition and unencumbered by the embarrassments of feeling or belief. It's like the night of athletic sex that Apuleius's hero, the intellectual Lucius, spends with the maid Fotis in *The Golden Ass*. In the morning, thanks to her magic, he wakes up transformed into a donkey, and he must go through endless sufferings in animal form before he consecrates himself to Isis the Great Mother, who graciously changes him back into a human.

I don't hold out the last straw grasped at by a jaded second-century roué—goddess worship—as a solution to the serious intellectual and spiritual impasse that a work like Eco's embodies. Lucius, after all, ends up that most suspect of creatures in Eco's gallery of rogues, an initiate. But in literary terms Apuleius at least gave us a transformation, an avenue of release both in content and in tone from the plot-prison of the conventional Greek romance. By virtue of its reactionary form, *Foucault's Pendulum* is a donkey that stays a donkey—not to be confused, by the way, with the *Asinus asinorum*, Giordano Bruno's holy donkey of donkeys, who leads us into wisdom—and, for all its educated self-awareness, still fails to incorporate the suggestion that this is not the same as being human.

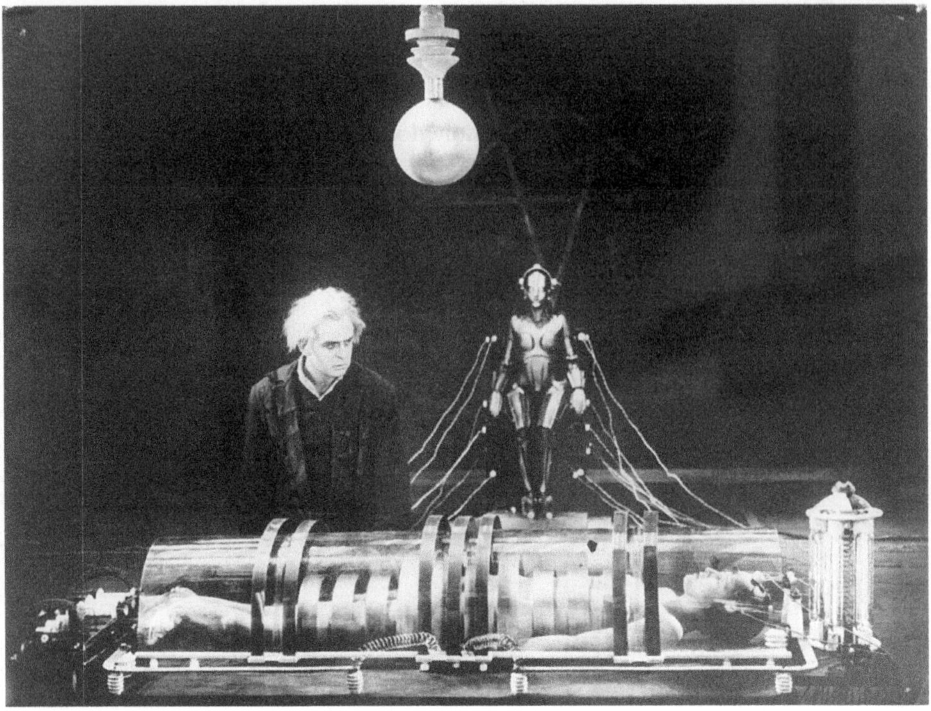

Animating the "false Maria" robot from her human counterpart. From Fritz Lang's *Metropolis* (1927).

We will give birth by machine. We will build a thousand steam-powered mothers. From them will pour forth a river of life. Nothing but life! Nothing but robots!

—Damon the Robot, *R.U.R.*

Rust to rust, ashes to ashes . . .

—Philip K. Dick

ELEVEN

THE GREAT TWENTIETH-CENTURY PUPPET UPGRADE

In *Puppet Master II* (1990), a movie you are not likely to have seen unless you have a thirteen-year-old male child (or were one yourself in the not too distant past), an Egyptian sorcerer circa the year 1912 informs the young Henri Toulon, an aspiring puppeteer, that stringed puppets are a thing of the nineteenth century. "*All* modern puppets," the sorcerer says haughtily, "are electrical." This little scene neatly dramatizes that crucial moment in the early twentieth century where we left off our history of puppets in Chapter 3, just before they began the most remarkable series of metamorphoses in all their long existence, from thousands of years as performers and mechanical curiosities to a strikingly telescoped development in brand-new bodies: for a hundred or so years as androids, for seventy-five as robots, for thirty-odd as cyborgs, and for a mere decade as the virtual-reality constructs or "avatars" that might best be described as ethereal Neoplatonic daemons.

At the beginning of the nineteenth century, as we have seen, the two mutually opposed traditions of the artificial human had taken their modern shape as (1) the uncanny but soulless mechanical shell, as imagined by Hoffmann, and (2) the Neoplatonic ensouled idol, as perceived by Kleist and other Romantics. The first tradition, of course, accurately describes human-constructed mechanical simulacra in the real world: it is helpful to remember that empirically speaking, they *are* lifeless objects made and controlled by humans. This tradition also appears in the conventional late twentieth-century position that the *imagined* robot of popular entertainments (an entity whose far greater capabilities, in contrast, are entirely fictitious) symbolizes the human stripped of his or her "soul," in modern parlance a reference only to our species' perceived unique but mortal consciousness. One commentator's interpretation of the meaning of robots in these entertainments is typical: "Science is robbing us of our humanity metaphorically expressed as our soul: it threatens to replace the individual, God-given soul with a mechanical machine-made one." But even in this kind of *episteme* interpretation, the careful translation of "soul" from metaphysically real entity to secularized metaphor allows a sanitized if indirect access to some of the great issues that inform our unquenchable fascination with these imaginary entities.

But the first thing we notice is that up on the big screen those soulless automata supposedly lacking all our color, originality, and emotion somehow manage to steal every scene from the human actors; we can't take our eyes off them. One reason this analysis moves from novels to films in the twentieth century is simply that it's far more thrilling to see a cyborg than to read about one; as a visual image the simulacrum still carries its traditionally powerful "uncanny" impact. And that is where the second way of looking at the imaginary simulacrum comes in.

In the Neoplatonic perspective, the preeminence of the machine brought about by the industrial revolution did not rob us of the idea of the soul at all. On the contrary, the machine *received* this idea, just at that critical moment when the old cosmogony gave way to the new. Once empirical thinking began to dominate, the powers we attributed to machines became—from a premodern perspective—blasphemously inflated in the absence of a recognized divine. The Reformation notwithstanding, miracles did not stop happening in the year 600 C.E.; for the last few hundred years, in the safety of C. S. Lewis's third world of *imagine*, we have let machines perform them. In the realm of nineteenth- and twentieth-century science fiction, anything is possible if a machine brings it about. The "machine in the ghost" (to borrow Slavoj Zizek's phrase, if not his intended meaning) takes on all the capabilities of its human creators and more, ultimately assuming the role of the Gnostic demiurge (Philip K. Dick's "reality-projecting artifact" of Chapters 7 and 8) who stands between God and his creation. It is the machine, not humans, that dissolves the boundaries of time and space, creates life and new species, duplicates or mutates old species, violates and transcends the laws of nature.

This unconscious belief in the divinity of machines has carried over into the popular language used to describe real scientific inventions, everything from giant computers that "conquer space and time" to robots that "reproduce"—only the next rung of the infinite Jacob's ladder of technological progress, as the *episteme* frame of popular journalism continually reminds us. In an article provocatively entitled "As Machines Become More like People, Will People Become More like God?" (an excerpt from his book *Robo sapiens: The Evolution of a New Species*), the cybertheoretician Ray Kurzweil declared that "by the second half of the twenty-first century there will be no clear distinction between human intelligence and machine intelligence." Read the fine print, however, and you discover that, indeed, the robots don't mate; they are machines painstakingly programmed by humans to build other machines. And the computer hasn't really conquered space and time because it will continue to run only as long as it stays plugged in and the power company doesn't go broke. Having made the machine the heir of our own perceived divinity-on-earth status, however, we are not about to abandon our faith in it.

The machine that most resonates with our secret divinizing needs is, naturally, the one we made in our own image. By the beginning of the twentieth century, the idea of an animated walking, talking simulacrum had advanced considerably past the crudities of a Talking Turk. Self-animation, autonomy, and supernatural powers would become the primary characteristics of this new idol in the sub-Zeitgeist of popular entertainments. By that century's end, the physical superiority of this entity had become a given *(The Terminator)*. Moral and spiritual superiority (already bestowed by the science fiction genre on extraterrestrials, the Anthropoi from outer space) quickly followed; the simulacrum was now portrayed as far better quipped as an ethical and emotional role model to humanity than humans themselves *(Terminator 2: Judgment Day)*. Not only was it "more human than human" *(Blade Runner)*, in the best Kleistian tradition it also had a greater capability of achieving divinity than humankind *(Ghost in the Shell)*.

On the secondary path of human pathology we have also been following, the Divine Machine played an important supernatural role in the

Western psychotic imagination during the nineteenth and twentieth centuries. From Plato to Descartes, the image of the puppetmaster pulling strings to make his creation move had emblematized first a presumed division between soul and body, then one between mind and body. Recognizing the close connection of the puppet and the robot with notions of intrapersonal invasion, manipulation, and loss of autonomy, the new twentieth-century discipline of psychology identified the sensation that an alien entity is manipulating the afflicted person, "pulling the strings," as a symptom of various types of pathology, particularly schizophrenia.

In the schizophrenic manifestation, as Daniel Paul Schreber eloquently described it (see Chapter 5), the person feels like a helpless puppet receiving and obeying audible commands from a tyrannical master—often in the form of internal voices produced by the person's own vocal cords and experienced as voices from the outside. In effect, puppet and master have switched roles: now, in a parody of the old worldview, the person is the simulacrum receiving commands from a higher authority; the master, though lodged within, is perceived as elsewhere. A less severe form, dubbed "marionettismus," or marionette syndrome, is an "emotional complex of feelings of powerlessness, emotional rigidity, and ego alienation," and Philip K. Dick's many female "schizoid" android characters (in N. Katherine Hayles's diagnosis) might be said to allegorize this syndrome. Indeed, an obsession with simulacra of all kinds—from "fake fakes" to androids—pervades Dick's fictional works.

In the famous case of the "Influencing Machine," reported by Freud's disciple Victor Tausk in 1919, a young woman maintained that she was under the total control of an electrically powered machine formed in her own likeness, with a coffin for a torso and electric batteries instead of internal organs. Someone else manipulated this machine, she said, producing strong and unpleasant physical reactions in her body. Louis Sass has interpreted this patient's sense of the influencing machine as "a projected image not of the physical body but of the subjective body—a lived body that is, so to speak, turned inside out and solidified, reified by the intensity of a self-directed gaze. And this inside-out body nearly fills the universe, reducing the world to a room located in some vague elsewhere and other people to phantoms." In effect, this schizophrenic had demiurgically created her own demonic Anthropos complete with two-tiered sympathetic correspondences between its superior, originating macrobody and her own.

In both its main course and its branching paths, the dramatic trail blazed by the earthly gods from the late nineteenth century on is not hard to follow. During this time, real performing puppets survived and flourished in rather the same aura of enforced quaintness that letterpress printing assumed in the world of books—in children's shows and, strikingly, in Expressionist avant-garde theater and film. Hollywood's vast audiences around the world, however, guaranteed that their high-tech movie offspring ultimately snagged the lion's share of the spotlight. Even though these imaginary simulacra show a clear historical sequence of subtly changing attributions, we will find that their creators considerably blurred the boundary lines among their many types, and between them and humans. Karel Capek's "robots" in *R.U.R.* are technically androids (even though they were played by humans), just as the "android" Hadaly of Villiers de l'Isle-Adam's *The Future Eve* is technically a robot. The "cyborg" terminators are clearly another kind of killer puppet, and the "puppets" of the Japanese *animé* film *Ghost in the Shell* are human victims of a virtual entity known as the Puppet Master. So even as we acknowledge the technology-driven nature of the upgrades, we bear in mind the important admonition the character Thomas Edison makes in *The Future Eve:* "Knowing the mechanism of the puppet will never explain to you how it becomes the phantom."

ADAM AND EVE AND PINOCCHIO

Italy's single most famous literary export is not Dante or Petrarch but a journalist named Carlo Lorenzini, writing as Carlo Collodi. His serialized novel *The Adventures of Pinocchio: Story of a Puppet* (1883), about a wooden puppet who finally achieves his dream of becoming a real human boy, was an instant international success and marks a consolidation of the trend started by Hoffmann toward a new popular genre of stories *about* puppets in contrast to puppet performances themselves. The Pinocchio character and story also provide an essential bridge between the nineteenth-century model of the simulacrum that stays a simulacrum and the new hybrid form, the simulacrum that transforms itself into the human and more than human, that would dominate popular entertainments of the following century. In the tradition of the Romantic puppet tractates, it was the simulacrum *imagined* in the company of humans, not the old puppet shows themselves, that brought with it the extra and unacknowledged charge of soul-carrier into the twentieth century.

Auguste Villiers de l'Isle-Adam's *L'Eve future* (1885–1886), published in the same decade as *Pinocchio*, would also deeply influence representations of the human simulacrum in the early new century, with artists as varied as Fritz Lang and Karel Capek drawing inspiration from a French aristocrat's prescient but now little-known novel about an amazing female "magneto-electric Android." The inventor-theurge of *The Future Eve* is none other than Thomas Edison, the "Wizard of Menlo Park," benign magus of a sort not seen since Late Antiquity (and not to fully reappear until the end of the twentieth century), whose creation—in a measure of the changing attitude toward souls and idols—does not wreak havoc on humans but instead provides them with a mysterious and positive link to the transcendent. Using "electromagnetic power and Radiant Matter," the fictitious Edison proposes to make a mechanical replica of Lord Celian Ewald's love Alicia Clary, a beautiful but shallow actress, by "photosculpting" the android onto a facsimile of the woman's body. Sensibly pointing out that Ewald, like everyone, has only fallen in love with "the objectified projection" of his own soul, Edison suggests that the English lord can animate his soul-longings in this mechanical woman to produce the perfect mate. When Ewald rightly worries that this product of reflexive narcissism might leave him feeling "a little too alone," Edison makes the Kleistian promise that "the copy will be more like the model than the original itself," that he will deliver to Ewald a being "a thousand times more identical to herself . . . than she is in her own person."

Clad in bearskin coats, the two men hasten to view the results in Edison's chilly grotto laboratory beneath his mansion, an Alexandrian "underground Eden" of Heroesque mechanical flora and fauna laid out in caves that were formerly an Algonquin burial ground. (The presence of Native American burial grounds in a work of fiction, European or Euro-American, is always a sub-Zeitgeist warning buzzer that something transcendent is present but dangerously ignored or covered over; in a twist of deflected bad conscience that our culture has developed into an art form of its own, we vaguely register that nothing good ever comes of this association.) Not surprisingly, this paradise of automated wonders (Edison lights his cigar from "the heart of a fiery camellia") is rather a horrible place, and so, at first glance, is the android named Hadaly, a "dark" creature who talks with the eerie recorded voice of Ewald's human beloved, played on a golden phonograph lodged inside her body.

At this point, however, Hadaly's metamorphoses are far from complete. As part of a confusing series of theurgic events, Edison also had a female hypnotic patient in his underground caves who sporadically animated Hadaly with a "supernatural being," a separate and disembodied personality named Sowana that she created in the "living ether" during her trance sessions with Edison. This patient died when the android was brought to life, but Sowana "incorporated herself, like a fluid vision, within Hadaly"; Edison says he merely furnished the physical vessel for this mysterious soul to inhabit. Already brought to life by electricity and the spirit Sowana, Hadaly now begs Ewald to animate her with his own soul. This last fusion allows Hadaly to supernaturalize herself completely from her mechanical origins, and she becomes an autonomous entity, the "Ideal made material." Such a remarkable *unio mystica*, however, cannot last in the sublunary world—especially one created in the compromised space of a former Algonquin burial ground. On a sea journey (possibly echoed in Bram Stoker's *Dracula*, published some fifteen years later), Hadaly dies when her black coffin is engulfed in flames in the hold of the ship returning her and Lord Ewald to Europe, and Ewald takes his own life in despair.

One suspects Ewald of being a stand-in for the author, who seems to have only a half-articulated awareness that he has created a kind of dream vision of a man's wish both to fall in love and to find his own female side, and through this emotional fusion with himself and another to achieve spiritual transcendence; and he has possibly even less awareness that he has murdered his own dream. Pointing to the strange confluence of traditions in *The Future Eve*, Daniel Gerould observes that "the novel's recurring theme of replication is carried one step further by the author in that the old gods, myths, and beliefs—seemingly vanquished by science—are repeated in new technological modes . . . Returning from exile, the occult, otherworldly, and transcendent infiltrate the stronghold of materialism, where they are re-animated and reinstated." The reinstatement of the otherworldly, so explicit in this work, is also the less obvious subtext of *The Adventures of Pinocchio*. Standing one concentric circle outside the frame of his moralizing allegory (a child's maturation cast as a journey from puppethood to humanity), Carlo Collodi also served as his own "Wizard of Menlo Park," giving his wooden character the breath of life in a way no mere puppeteer—Kleist notwithstanding—could do.

On the high road, Pinocchio's "progeny," in Harold Segel's phrase—and they were Hadaly's as well—are first and foremost the puppet-humans, human-puppets, and assorted other simulacra that emerged in the European avant-garde theater before and after World War I. As *Frankenstein* received its first film translation in 1931, other simulacra thrived in the theater, art, and film of Eastern Europe: Gustav Meyrink's novel *The Golem* (1915), followed by Paul Wegener's Expressionist *The Golem: How He Came into the World* (1920). Bruno Jasienski wrote the play *The Mannequins' Ball* (1931) just as Bruno Schulz was tailoring his own dummies; Prague was the scene for such fancies as *Golem: A Romantic Review* (1931) as well as the seminal *R.U.R.* This pervasive use of puppets and mannequins in experimental drama of the early twentieth century, though collectively labeled modernism, was often—as it had been for Villiers de l'Isle-Adam—a groping backward toward the Romantic revival of the Late Antique moving idol's transcendental superiority.

Hadaly's spirit lives on in the British thespian E. Gordon Craig's Kleistian exhortations to actors, in his famous essay "The Actor and the Über-marionette" (1907), to transform themselves into an entity he called the "Über-marionette." This superpuppet mindset, Craig asserted, "will not compete with life—rather will it go beyond it. Its ideal will not be the flesh and blood but rather the body in trance—it will aim to clothe itself with a deathlike beauty while exhaling a living spirit." Via the emblematic figure of the actor, Craig had also intuited that our idea of the human could not remain artificially separated from an exalted being like Hadaly; not only must humans somehow incorporate her mechanical uncanniness into themselves, they must also acknowledge that they *are* she.

On the puppet low road, meanwhile, the advent and rapid preeminence of animated film cartoons in the first half of the twentieth century arguably siphoned off a great deal of the former audience of the old traveling puppet shows. No one who either remembers or observes the hypnotic fascination that cartoon characters hold for children can doubt the enormous power of this twentieth-century "animation of images"; yet another form of simulacra, cartoons as a phenomenon give us a rare opportunity for understanding the gut-level magnetism that puppet shows exerted for untold earlier generations. (*Pinocchio* itself became a Walt Disney cartoon in 1940, forging a link with the new medium while also moving this tale yet another step away from "live" performance.) Puppets and ventriloquist's dolls held their own in vaudeville and other venues until midcentury, when they transferred successfully to American television in such characters as Howdy Doody and Kukla, Fran, and Ollie, followed by the Muppets. Nothing in either these traditional puppet shows for children or the resurgence of puppet characters in avant-garde theater, however, quite prepares us for the plethora of homicidal mannikins that emerged in Anglo-American popular film after the year 1950.

KILLER PUPPETS

> "It can't be bargained with, it can't be reasoned with, it doesn't feel pity, or remorse, or fear, and it absolutely will not stop, ever, until you are dead!"
>
> —*The Terminator*

Historically, Western puppet entertainments were always violent spectacles, as witness the standard pummelings of traditional Punch and Judy shows, which usually ended with Punch's onstage hanging and exit in a coffin. The rough-and-tumble, however, was always puppet to puppet, not puppet to human, and this is an important distinction. In the second category, Hugo in the "Ventriloquist's Dummy" segment of the British film *Dead of Night* (1945), an autonomous entity who wreaks havoc on the people around him, bears the distinction of being the first puppet murderer of a human in a popular film.

Hugo the Dummy represents an important new twist on the conventional Hoffmannesque model: from the puppet as manipulated victim of a sinister human master to the puppet as sinister manipulator of human victims. Besides his malevolence, Hugo's other notable trait is the fact that he can make his own way in every sense. Beneath his frozen smile Hugo is an evil entity who talks, moves, plots and schemes, kills, and ultimately brings about his hapless "master's" destruction—all entirely on his own. Autonomy on all levels, in fact, is what will distinguish twentieth-century imaginary simulacra from most of their predecessors. And once there is physical autonomy, social autonomy is a close second. Forget Dr. Frankenstein, forget Dr. Faust; in no time the Divine Machines were casting off their now-superfluous human agents, acquiring supernatural powers along with their freedom. Over and over the old roles were reversed as the newly independent and increasingly omnipotent simulacra first surpassed, then dominated, their human masters.

But what in all this made the puppets want to kill us? Various situation-specific motivations are provided by the stories: The *Puppet Master* series of feature films (1989–2000), for example, has a recurring cast of murderous puppets (Pinhead, Leech Woman, Tunneler, Jester, Blade, and Theresa—all still available as toys) who (mostly) follow the commands of their master, Henri Toulon. In the first *Puppet Master* (1989), Toulon has just died but is determined to bring himself back from the dead "much stronger than he ever was" by means of the same animating techniques he used for his magic puppets. As part of his quest for immortality, Toulon's spirit dispatches them one by one to kill the guests his widow has invited to his mansion, guests who have special powers: one brings statues to life after ancient Egyptian practices; a second tunes in to the emotional life of objects; a third dreams of things to come. Ultimately, however, the puppets turn on the Puppet Master and finish him for good with their customized weapons; in the story's terms, Toulon is clearly a bad magus deserving of death. Other horror films feature masterless simulacra running amok: devil dolls, stuffed animals turned homicidal, and the like, who randomly dispatch innocent humans. These stories play on the contrast of an inanimate object invested with the aura of childhood innocence that is suddenly infused with (always) demonic energy—the upsurgence of the supernatural grotesque from the least anticipated source.

The archetypal killer puppet of late twentieth-century popular film is Chucky, the "Good Guy" doll animated by the soul of a serial killer, the "Lakeside strangler," in *Child's Play* (1988) and its three sequels—the serial killer, of course, being American mass culture's coded icon of unrepentant evil, secular stand-in for the Devil. At the moment he is shot to death by a policeman while hiding in a toy store, the killer—thanks to the prayers of a mojo wizard and the electricity generated by a handy lightning bolt—is able to lodge his soul in a grinning Chucky doll.

In a sardonic echo of Pinocchio's quest, the killer's soul can also leap out of this doll into the first person he reveals himself to, becoming successively more human with each exchange of bodies. Electricity was the bridge over which the eighteenth century made its great passage from God to Nature, from a belief in the primacy of divine power to an equally strong belief in the primacy of material power. Yet echoes of the old idea that the natural electricity of lightning also represented the conjunction of the transcendental world with this world have lingered—and particularly in the fact that whether it manifests as lightning or a wall socket, the transcendental force formerly perceived as divine energy now powers machines. The striking combination of Chucky's angelic "Good Guy" doll's face, his close physical proximity to an innocent child, and the utter evil of his nature yielded a number of successful sequels, all of which feature at one point or another the same *tableau vivante:* a bank of identical "Good Guy" dolls packaged in cellophane and lined up on a store counter, their lifeless bodies sharply contrasted with the sinister manic animation of the single possessed doll.

Killer puppets like Chucky clearly embody the long-standing Protestant dictum that what is not of this world is of the Devil. But if only evil can be supernatural—that is, of the spirit, because it is not bounded by the body—where does that leave the good? We may not be entirely satisfied either with the Reformation's answer or with the materialist one we gave ourselves later—that neither good nor evil is of the spirit because the spirit does not exist. From down in the grotto territory of the sub-Zeitgeist, the evidence suggests, we still reach for that ineffable level of spirit beyond the material world. The enormous paradox is that within the constraints of our current worldview we are only able to express our desire at two removes, and in a highly distorted fashion—first in the hypothetical context of fantasy, and second in the proxy bodies of imaginary artificial humans. The traditional Protestant taboo on the supernatural combined with our own distortion of our desire sends it back to us as Chucky.

REBEL ROBOTS

> "Robots of the world! The power of man has fallen!
> A new world has arisen: the Rule of the Robots!"
>
> —Radius the Robot, *R.U.R.*

As next technological heir of the puppet after the automaton, the robot began displacing its predecessor as an *idea* and as a subject of film and theater long before it ever became anything like a reality—which (we need again to remind ourselves) it still is not, even as our imaginations continue to race far ahead of what is technically possible.

The word *robot*, from Czech *robota*, meaning enforced work or drudgery (*robotnik* means serf), was introduced by Karel Capek in his play *R.U.R.* (*Rossum's Universal Robots*), first performed in 1921. Though the "revolt of the marionettes" theme dates at least as far back as the seventeenth-century Italian *commedia dell'arte*, it is perhaps a fitting mirror of the great social upheavals of the twentieth century that its imaginary simulacra typically rebelled against theirs masters and emerged dominant. Capek's play was a seminal work that would deeply influence Fritz Lang's *Metropolis* (1927), another Expressionist masterpiece of that decade, as well as the next seventy-five years of Western fantasy writing and technological innovation. In 1941 Isaac Asimov introduced the term *robotics* for a field of technology that then and now exists as only a tiny portion of the field our imaginations have created, and in 1948 Norbert Wiener coined *cybernetics* to designate another field in which the interplay of imagination with technology is almost impossible to separate.

Given *R.U.R.*'s enormous impact, the real surprise is that its robot workers are not the mechanical marvels we have come to associate with this term but golemlike clones that the eccentric inventor Rossum (an allegorical name that means Intelligence or Brain) has brewed alchemically from a human plasmalike substance, then stamped into shape with giant cookie-cutter machines. Rossum, a "fearful materialist," made his creatures to "supply proof that Providence was no longer necessary" and humans could supplant God's role. At the beginning we are told, in the Hoffmann manner, that the robots are stronger and smarter than humans but "lack a soul"; inevitably, they rebel and kill all the humans but one, from whom they try to extract the original formula for their creation. With no formula forthcoming and extinction looming, Kleistian *Grazia* descends on the robots when Primus and Helena, two second-generation models, discover that they love each other and will sacrifice their lives for the other's sake. Seeing this, the last remaining human bids them: "Go, Adam, go, Eve. The world is yours."

In Fritz Lang's *Metropolis*, adapted from his wife Thea von Harbou's novel, it is the humans who revolt against oppressive masters and a simulacrum who betrays the serf-workers. The futuristic city Metropolis is an H. G. Wellsian society of underground slaves (the Workers) and an above-ground privileged elite (the Thinkers). In a religiously charged grotto of crucifix-strewn catacombs, the workers are organized by their saintly leader, Maria, to protest the subhuman conditions of their existence in the horror of the Underground City. (In a nice touch, the owner's son has a vision of the entrance to the workers' subterranean factory as "Moloch," a Renaissance-style hell mouth identical to Orco's mouth at Bomarzo.) Their masters, however, conspire to create a simulacrum of Maria that will lead the workers to their own destruction. Maria the Robot (a.k.a. "Futura") is a "true" robot, though she also is animated electrically like Frankenstein's monster. Sexual and traitorous, the false Maria is revealed as a simulacrum after she is burned at the stake for her crimes (her blackened wiring is the giveaway), and the workers emerge triumphant from their grotto into daylight.

Despina Kakoudaki has shown how the shared traits of "exaggerated physique" and "physical repulsiveness" from the golem tradition mainstreamed by Mary Shelley in 1816 merged with the "soldier/ worker/ slave triad" of nineteenth- and twentieth-century social activism and political theory to produce a consistent set of narrative conventions for robots by the end of the 1920s: "The story is told again and again, almost unchanged. Robots are better than human or worse than human. They are unfeeling but kind, or unfeeling but loyal, or unfeeling but able to follow orders. They are supremely ethical or unable to judge right from wrong. Or they are emotionally sensitive, shy, super-intelligent beings, whose physical difference is represented as a debilitating deformity." Kakoudaki also notes the differences between male and female simulacra in these early robot stories, particularly in their perceived sexuality (males are asexual, females highly seductive) and role as victim (female) or victor (male). Over the two-hundred-year continuum from Hoffmann's Olimpia to Hadaly to Maria the Robot to characters like Eve 8 in *Eve of Destruction* and Motoko, the female cyborg of *Ghost in the Shell*, these conventions have changed very little even as the female simulacrum has become increasingly foregrounded as a main character.

A further enduring convention of the early fictions is the robot characters' "arbitrary and hierarchical relationship with cold or indifferent parents." This is, of course, the perceived tragic fate of all great imaginary automata, puppets, and golems, from Shelley's monster to Pinocchio to Lovecraft's Wilbur Whateley to Philip K. Dick's simulacra and androids.

Often enough, however, it proves to be a reflection of their author-creators' own psychological makeup bestowed—via their fused relationship with the intermediary fictitious human theurge of the particular story—on the mechanical double or *ka.* Here the defining characteristic is "indistinguishable from human": the simulacra function as our evil twin, our alter ego, repository of all we refuse to acknowledge in ourselves. But they are more than that, they carry a heavier burden than simply the psychological shadow. Artificial humans in popular film of the last fifty years, whether they are styled as puppets, dolls, clones, or cybernetic intelligences, not only have powers that exceed our own, they also have some kind of direct access to the supernatural and even personal immortality—exactly those qualities contemporary Westerners perceive as absent in ourselves and in the world around us.

By midcentury, the early twentieth-century theme of social (in contrast to personal) rebellion attached to robots had temporarily subsided. As a culmination of the many stories about robots in the growing genre of science fiction in pulp magazines and comic books after the 1920s, a new kind of robot made a spectacular Hollywood debut in Fred M. Wilcox's *Forbidden Planet* (1956). Here the formidably mechanized "Robby the Robot" is a benign maternal demiurge, the true Prospero in a story with explicit roots in *The Tempest.* Servant of Dr. Edward Morbius, a human scientist marooned with his daughter on the planet Altair, Robby was created by Altair's extinct inhabitants the Krell. Robby's powers far exceed those of his new human master; he is demiurgically able, for example, to duplicate the molecules of all matter fed into him. Against all modern conventions of the genre, however, Robby is no killer. Malevolence is not displaced onto him but rather emanates directly from the human scientist's own id, which has been unnaturally magnified via a machine built by the mysterious Krell. The former inhabitants of Altair, we learn, were superior beings of "high benevolence" whose Gnostic goal was to "free themselves from their bodies." Instead, the Krell were destroyed by their own Divine Machine: a huge device powered by their "subconscious minds" that was able to "project solid matter to any point." But since, as a visiting captain from Earth pithily observes, "We're all monsters in our subconscious," the bodiless Krell (forerunners of the virtual-reality entities to be examined in Chapter 12) inevitably unleashed the evil that resulted in their own self-destruction. Morbius must learn to control his own subconscious or earn the same fate.

With the exception of Andrei Tarkovsky's film version of Stanislaw Lem's *Solaris,* few science fiction films before or after have displayed the psychological sophistication of *Forbidden Planet.* Robots with creaky mechanical bodies and hollow voices remained staple minor characters, cute flunkies or colorful sidekicks (much like the helpful animals of the older fairytale tradition or, less attractively, like representations of people of color in Hollywood movies) in films like the *Star Wars* series. Stanley Kubrick/Arthur C. Clarke's *2001: A Space Odyssey* (1968) gave Robby's maternal virtues a sinister twist in the character of HAL, an unctuous, high-strung, and ultimately murderous male-voiced artificial intelligence powering a spacecraft whose human occupants must destroy him to save themselves. HAL spawned in turn any number of disembodied AI voices emanating from Divine Machines (usually flying ones) in a succession of science fiction movies.

A new trend emerged with the movie *Robocop* (1987)—tag line: "Part man, part machine, all cop"—in which a human policeman who has been savagely beaten is put back together in a body that is more machine than human. *Robocop,* its sequels, and similar films of the 1980s mark the beginning of the real subjectivization of the simulacrum, its closer and more sympathetic identification with the human as well as the supernatural. Once the human operator was overthrown or rendered irrelevant, the film stories gradually refocused on a literal merging of human and nonhuman *within the autonomous simulacrum itself* to produce a new imaginary creature who was increasingly main character, not sidekick; subject, not object.

As the sub-Zeitgeist trend moved toward a more overt reconnection of the human with the divine, this union of simulacrum with human into a single being would become the great theme of this genre in the late twentieth century. *Bicentennial Man* (1999) presents the upgrade as successive metamorphoses of the robot into something closer and closer to human. In his "profound transition from the mechanical to the biological," the robot main character designs himself a central nervous system. Immortal by virtue of his mechanical brain, he commits a Christlike suicide at the age of two hundred years, declaring, "I would rather die a man than live for all eternity a machine."

UNGRATEFUL GOLEMS, CLUMSY CLONES

What are the computers and robots of our time if not golems?

—Isaac Bashevis Singer

Even though the novelty of the "metal men" eclipsed the popularity of the "resurrection bodies," from its earliest disguise as Frankenstein's monster the organic simulacrum has enjoyed a steady rise to prominence. The *Alien* series (1979–1997) evoked the terror of the real-life AIDS epidemic of the 1980s in presenting the constantly metamorphosing aliens as a collective "perfect organism," a demonic Anthropos whose "structural perfection is matched only by its hostility." The invincibility of the aliens as a life form underlines the continual triumph of the organic over the inorganic, as embodied in the "untamable" Alien Queen. In the ongoing fusion of the human with its high-tech double, *Alien: Resurrection* (1997) reveals the series's main character, Ripley (now played in an appropriately glinty-eyed manner by Sigourney Weaver), to be an "alien clone," a problematical descendant fabricated from blood samples taken from the original Ripley after her Caesarian birth of a baby alien two hundred years earlier. Strictly in terms of the unfolding mythos of technological divinization, the transfer of demonic transcendence from the mechanical back to the biological suggests a kind of sub-Zeitgeist corrective in operation. This last fusion, however, reunites the divine and the human in a way that significantly reduces the demonic dimension (though we will always be guessing when it may reappear).

With the emergence of a full-blown technology for cloning by the end of the twentieth century, a third generation of nondemonic human golems made their debut in the mythos of American popular film. In the early Woody Allen movie *Sleeper* (1973) and the clever *Multiplicity* (1999), clones are presented as a harmless burden to their original; after the Sorcerer's Apprentice model, their main problem is that they proliferate beyond their creator's power to control them, thereby wreaking havoc. An interesting exception is *Powder* (1995), written and directed by Victor Salva, which frames the creation of a benign golem around the circumstance that his human mother was killed by lightning (with the implicit metaphor of divine impregnation as well as divine intervention) while he was still in her womb. In the later 1990s manner, this albino hero is not at all demonic but a misunderstood outsider and a force for good who meets a martyr's end from his bigoted classmates.

In contrast, *Eve of Destruction* (1991), the story of an uptight, ultra-coiffed female scientist and her raging cloned Döppelganger, makes an amusing late twentieth-century coda to *The Future Eve* and *Metropolis.* "Eve 8," a nuclear-armed human weapon cloned from her creator, is also the unwitting inheritor of "issues," as clinical psychologists like to say, from the human Eve's traumatic childhood. Eve 8's blood is purely cosmetic since she is powered by (what else?) electrical currents. The only problem is that human Eve "forgot" to install an off switch. Thus when Eve 8 is shot during an accidental encounter with a bank robber, all her fury as a fighting weapon is triggered. After killing, among others, her creator's abusive father, the simulacrum is hunted down and destroyed, her rage defused before it is vented via nuclear warhead.

The old misogyny around female robots is highly visible here, of course, but the simulacrum's calm explanation the instant before she begins tearing things apart—"I'm *very* sensitive!"—lends a comic undertone of female psychopathology to Eve 8's carnage. More explicitly than the stories of mechanical simulacra, the evolving metalegend of the clone highlights the central issue of all the puppet stories: the deep identification of the human main character with the human-made *ka,* who characteristically shows a radically different, but *truer,* identity. All qualities good and bad, human and superhuman, that we cannot acknowledge ourselves as possessing reside in this double that is drawing ever nearer to us.

AGILE ANDROIDS

> "There's more to being human than flesh and blood."
>
> —Android character in *Nemesis* (1993)

The 1980s also marked the filmic debut of the robots' sexier, technologically superior nephews and nieces the androids (to be supplanted in turn by cyborgs in the 1990s). How does this imaginary entity differ from its immediate imaginary forebear? Compared with a robot, an android is closer biologically to and visually indistinguishable from a human. The Greek word *androides* was used in English as early as the mid-eighteenth century in reference to the legendary simulacra of the thirteenth-century magus-friar Albertus Magnus, but it is noteworthy that by 1972 the *Oxford English Dictionary* had dropped *android* from the category "rare" thanks to the word's proliferation in science fiction literature after the mid-twentieth century. The android is now defined by the *OED* as a "robot made of flesh and bone," halfway between the mechanical robot and the even more human cyborg. In plain language, (1) an android has at least a fleshy covering over its metal parts ("skin job" is a derogatory nickname for androids in *Blade Runner*), making it look considerably more human than Robby or C-3PO; (2) its body is not merely flexible, it is *more* flexible than a human's; and (3) it can have, or at least looks as if it can have, sex with other androids and with humans. All three traits have enormous significance in the transformation of the simulacrum from an obvious counterfeit and inferior into the human and more than human.

In their android upgrade, imaginary artificial humans inevitably inherited the familiar Protestant mantle of murderous evil from their puppet and golem brethren and forebears. A 1966 novel by Philip K. Dick, *Do Androids Dream of Electric Sheep?* was heavily adapted in the movie *Blade Runner* (1982), where Dick's androids were converted to "replicants," serfs used as slave labor in Earth's colonies on other planets. Programmed to die within five years, or about the time it is reckoned that they will begin developing human emotions on their own, five rogue replicants have hijacked a spacecraft and are on their way to Earth to extract the formula to extend their lives from their human creator, the inventor Tyrell. In their godlike physical beauty and superhuman strength, the killer androids of the film version manifest as corrupt rebel angels; they also possess a great deal more fire and demonic energy than the shuffling, dispirited multicultural citizens of twenty-first-century Greater Los Angeles, a Late Antiquity syncretic nightmare out of Umberto Eco. Suspected replicants are tested with a "Voight-Kampff machine" that will expose their lack of empathy. Significantly, their turning-into-human transformation requires no magical techno-ritual or moral conversion; it has more the flavor of an organic process. In sub-Zeitgeist logic, films like *Blade Runner* were preparing their audiences to deepen their subjective identification with the simulacra.

In *The Terminator* (1984), another powerful simulacrum legend of the 1980s, a computer system of the future called Skynet has animated all computer-powered machines in a relentless war to destroy the human race—a theme carried over from *R.U.R.* and carried on in *The Matrix* (1999) and other later films. Skynet sends a "killing machine" called the Terminator back in time to present-day Los Angeles to murder the future mother of John Connor, leader of the human resistance fighters; to avert these history-changing consequences, John Connor sends his own human friend Kyle to protect her. Sarah Connor and Kyle fall in love and make the baby that will grow up to be the man who saves the human race from the machines.

The conventional take on this nicely constructed mythic tale is that it is a "retelling of Christ's birth in a soulless land." But our attention is gripped not so much by the prospect of John Connor's human birth (the character never appears in this film or its sequel) but rather by the all-powerful, unstoppable Terminator, its red electronic eyes still glowing demonically and its metal hulk quivering with the urge to kill even as we watch its melted skeleton disarticulating vertebra by vertebra. The sequel *Terminator 2: Judgment Day* (1991) flips the plot by having the still-desperate human resistance fighters send back an upgraded "good" Terminator to protect Sarah and her young son John from destruction by an even more upgraded "bad" Terminator. The fact that the same actor, Arnold Schwarzenegger, moves from demonic to benign simulacrum between the first film and its sequel dramatizes the significant shift in the depiction of the artificial human during the decade of the 1990s.

After melting down the killer Terminator in an alchemical *vas* of boiling lead—the only medium deemed able to destroy the "software" of these upgraded Divine Machines—the good Terminator sacrifices himself in the lead as well, to ensure the destruction of his murderous kind (the same death chosen by Ripley, the human impregnated with the organic alien superspecies, in the 1992 *Alien 3*). The deepest paradox of the alchemical process, however, coincides with the most ironclad *Wiederholungs*-convention of the horror story genre: destruction absolutely guarantees rebirth. Even though we know in our hearts that the forces of evil will be alive again by the next sequel, however, the benevolence of the good Terminator (in contrast to his life-destroying evil twin) lays the psychological groundwork in his audience for a new imaginary species in which the ultimate merging of the human and the mechanical will forge an imaginative link with the benign, not the malign, transcendent.

IMMORTAL CYBORGS

> In the forty years of their existence, [silicon life forms] have already evolved further than carbon life in its first two billion years . . . They will be telepathic since they will hear with antennas. They will communicate in the universal language of 0 and 1, into which they will translate the languages of the five senses and a rainbow of other senses unknown to carbon man . . . Silicon life will be immortal.
>
> —O. B. Hardison

When the virtual entity known as the Puppet Master says to Motoko, the female cyborg in *Ghost in the Shell* (1995), "Now we must slip our bonds and rise to the higher structure," scholars of Gnostic Christianity and the Late Antique syncretic cults—and of modern cults like Heaven's Gate—would recognize his vocabulary at once, for the cybernetic description of the liberation of the soul upon physical death is very like the Gnostic one. The paean to the silicon-based cybernetic organism by the literary scholar O. B. Hardison they would recognize as well. We have already seen this figure in Adam and Eve and Jesus, and we have glimpsed him briefly in the white figure rising over the South Pole in Poe's *The Narrative of Arthur Gordon Pym*, in Kleist's marionette and E. Gordon Craig's "Über-marionette," in Hadaly the Androsphinx and *R.U.R.*'s Primus and Helena in their robot Eden. Under the cloak of a new technology, the Anthropos is back.

In this latest hypostasis of cyborg, or cybernetic organism, the simulacrum has been purged of the negativity that orthodoxy bestowed on it—the fate of blasphemer and creation alike exemplified in Umberto Eco's warning that "the moment you pick up the clay, electronic or otherwise, you become a demiurge, and he who embarks on the creation of worlds is always tainted with corruption and evil." In its place now is the Neoplatonic and cabbalistic conviction that, in Moshe Idel's words, "the way to contact with the Divine" is by making a golem who is no monster but a child of light; for the first time in three hundred years, the human-made human is not represented as demonic.

With the idea of the cyborg, we have returned full circle to that ideal of pious believers in Late Antiquity; the ever-tilting scale between machine and human in previous imaginary simulacra is essentially thrown away and we are presented with an entity in which machine and human have seamlessly merged (and which speaks its own Divine Language to boot).

Over the course of the twentieth century the artificial human gradually came to represent a combination god, externalized soul, and Divine Human from which we constructed, without ever acknowledging it, a continued belief in immortal spirit—a belief that lives in a layer of the psyche deeper and less accessible than the conventional moral commitment most religious observers in a late industrial society make within their houses of worship.

The *OED* defines a cybernetic organism as "a person whose physical tolerance or capabilities are extended beyond normal human limitations by a machine or other external agency that modifies the body's functioning: an integrated man-machine system." The adjective *cybernetic*, as we saw, comes from the word Norbert Wiener coined in the late 1940s to describe the new field of information delivery, which he said would occur via an agent he dubbed the *cyber*, or navigator. Since midcentury, both the term and the field have evolved with staggering rapidity—much like the *Alien* organisms—into a very specific technology-driven discipline with a very inflated vocabulary attached to it.

Compared with the previous deflation and demonization of the graven image, the sheer grandiosity of powers attributed to the computer as Divine Machine is striking. The genesis of cybertheory will be examined in greater detail in Chapter 12; for now, we may note the ubiquity among cybertheorists of the notion that N. Katherine Hayles describes as the "erasure of embodiment," a conceit that gives rise to "fantasies of unlimited power and disembodied immortality" and a new construction of the human that

> privileges informational pattern over material instantiation, so that embodiment in a biological substrate is seen as an accident of history rather than an inevitability of life . . . considers consciousness . . . as an epiphenomenon . . . thinks of the body as the original prosthesis we all learn to manipulate . . . [and sees] no essential differences or absolute demarcations between bodily existence and computer simulation, cybernetic mechanism and biological organism.

In this view of the merged "posthuman" simulacrum, the cyborg is both the imaginary entity we watch in popular entertainment and our own human selves as hybrid organisms participating in the exchange of information—with our bodies functioning as the puppet "prostheses" that our cyberbrains manipulate in the material world.

Underlying this Cartesian philosophical construct is an ancient Gnostic spirit-matter dualism (as distinct from the Hermetic or Neoplatonic attempts to unite the two dimensions) that works unconsciously to spiritualize the rather sterile cosmos of the "information system." No better example of this tension between the contradictory surface and underlayers of cybertheory exists than Mamori Oshii's animated feature film *Ghost in the Shell* (1995), which comes out of the rich Japanese *animé* tradition. Far more overtly philosophical than American science fiction movies, *Ghost in the Shell* is the story of a female government cyborg-hacker, Major Motoko Kusanagi, who hunts a mysterious fugitive provocatively known as the Puppet Master. (In the film's parlance, "ghost" is intelligence or mind, "shell" the body machine that can be freely jettisoned and traded for another, from the "ghost in the machine" discourse familiar since the mid-twentieth century.) This fugitive is an autonomous computer program, "Project 2501," which was alchemically "born in the sea of information," created for the specific purpose of becoming a government spy. The rogue program escaped, took refuge in a human body, somehow managed to generate another ghost (a real "soul") in an auxiliary brain center, was murdered by his government pursuers, and is now in quest of a new host. Project 2501, a.k.a. the Puppet Master, has the power to take over humans from a distance and plant false identities with matching memories in their consciousness, making them "puppets without ghosts."

Sent to track down the Puppet Master and destroy him, Motoko worries: "What if a computer brain could generate a ghost and harbor a soul?" In that case, she feels, she "would doubt her own reality." All cyborg in contrast to her part-human partner Batou, Motoko loves to dive and swim (paralleling her professional task of "diving into the shell," the term for jumping into the consciousness of a separate human body). In a visual reference to the Puppet Master's (and her own) birthplace in the "sea of information," Batou asks Motoko what she sees in "the water's darkness" as she floats in the ocean while they are on a fishing break. The Puppet Master, telepathically ventriloquizing through Motoko's mouth, replies, "For now we see through a glass darkly," and, via I Corinthians, we are cross-culturally back in the Christian Platonizing framework.

With his abilities and intelligence now evolved far above those of humans, the Puppet Master (Program 2501 does seem to be male) wants

Motoko; if he and Motoko "merge," he tells her through her own mouth, she will "bear his offspring into the net," which will allow the Puppet Master to "achieve death." This is a desirable outcome because by reproducing and dying he will acquire the human "variety" needed to "guard against extinction"; to be human, he says, means "to continually change." In the story's climax, when he has been cornered in a shootout with government agents, the Puppet Master tells Motoko it is time to abandon her shell and rise—and just as he says this, she dies, killed by a stray government bullet. Cut to a scene with Motoko's partner Batou, who has inserted her ghost, or so he believes, into a girl child cyborg. But in fact the Puppet Master got there first; this is his own biological offspring with Motoko, a new kind of soul-possessing entity that possesses neither parent's identity.

Through the eyes of this cyborg child and prototype Divine Human, a vision of the Internet unfolds: a world of Cyberforms, cities tied by cables, vast and limitless. To see through the eyes of the Anthropos means the glass and darkness of the material world are no longer interposed. The Gnostic separation of the Puppet Master's soul from earth and a shell to the "higher structures" has been replaced, in his offspring, by a Neoplatonic experience of heaven-on-earth while she is still embodied. "Where shall I go now?" she asks, Radiant Matter pulled by the rip current of the Ideal, as we watch vicariously.

A further step remains to be taken. In *Ghost in the Shell* a fusion has occurred, but it is not with the human. The new ensouled cyborg experiences heaven-on-earth in her own body, but that body is not ours. The Anthropos lives, but not inside us; Giordano Bruno's goal has not been not fulfilled. To reunite the human subject with its divine essence requires a further step—a step that can only be taken by a human.

The door in the sky. From Peter Weir's *The Truman Show* (1999). Copyright Paramount Pictures.

"The future has an ancient heart."

—Italian saying

TWELVE

THE DOOR IN THE SKY

In the backward shadow of the millennium, the last two years of the twentieth century witnessed a curious mini-boom in mainstream American films dealing with the rather arcane subject of characters trapped within other characters' fabricated worlds. In 1998 there was Truman, unwitting star of the sinister Christof's long-running television series *The Truman Show;* John Murdoch, prisoner with his fellow citizens on *Dark City*, a floating jellyfish cum spacecraft styled as a retro German Expressionist urban environment by alien masters who give their human guinea pigs "memory injections" of lives they never led and rebuild their faux city during a time suspension at the stroke of midnight every night; *What Dreams May Come*, in which a man discovers that the afterlife is a self-constructed topography that mirrors exactly the thoughts and moods of its inhabitants; and *Pleasantville*, about 1990s teenagers trapped in the alternate world of a 1950s sitcom.

In 1999 a similar cluster of films featuring worlds within worlds posed the same predicament to their hapless heroes and heroines, most notably via the conceit of virtual reality: *The Matrix*, in which the "real" world as we know it is revealed to be only a "neuroactive simulation" devised by a new breed of computers who have enslaved the human race in wired-up pods, feeding off their bioenergy while deceiving them with a fantasy life of total normality; *eXistenZ*, David Cronenberg's mock paean to virtual reality, whose title is that of a game meant to deconstruct the boundaries of life, and whose own boundaries are deconstructed by a mysterious metagame aptly dubbed "TranscendanZ"; and *The Thirteenth Floor*, about characters who enter a virtual world that not only perfectly reproduces 1930s Los Angeles but ultimately supplants it.

Obviously—and this is a typical sub-Zeitgeist conundrum—the trend arises as much from the tendency of those in the Los Angeles big-stakes movie community to copy a financially successful concept, however weird, as from any deep-seated upheavals in our religio-philosophical orientation. Yet the story lines also have some by-now-familiar antecedents, short and long term. In the short term, the trend grows out of a grassroots New Expressionism found mostly in comic strips, science fiction, and genre film but also present, as we saw in Chapter 9, in scattered European art films and works of literary fiction.

In the long term, these low- and high-art twentieth-century tales share a set of philosophical underpinnings that one suspects their creators, true innovators all, may not be fully conscious of. While it's fun to see a hip European like Luc Besson deliberately infusing his screenplay of *The Fifth Element* (1996) with all the esoterica of alchemy and cabbalism—such as the Quintessence, or four-becoming-five, embodied in the Anthropos or Divine Human, in this case a woman, who speaks the pre–Tower of Babel Perfect Language; and a vacation planet, Fhloston Paradise, that explodes, possibly in sympathetic resonance to the principle of phlogiston, the eighteenth-century theory of combustion—it's more fun still to trace the unfolding of a new naive tradition whose surface tendrils in mass entertainment genres conceal deep roots in some very old concerns in Western culture.

GIORDANO DOES HOLLYWOOD

Viewed from this larger perspective, the confluence of comic book mythos, science fiction, *film noir*, and half-conscious metaphysical assumptions in these new films comes across as outrageously Neoplatonic. Yes, were his ashes to be remastered digitally into some sort of animated simulacrum as only this sort of movie loves to do, none other than Giordano Bruno himself would feel right at home in the framework of these *fin-de-millennium* demiurge myths. The unapologetic devotee of Egyptian magic would immediately recognize and revere the powers, benign and demonic, the human and alien magi in these entertainments use to govern the microcosms their playthings inhabit. And as an inveterate rebel, Bruno would also applaud (or so I like to imagine) the maverick spirit that impels the human captives to break out of the manufactured cosmos they inhabit into a world altogether beyond their imagining.

Within this framework of subliminal Platonism and genre formula, the most interesting of these latter-day Greek romances, *Dark City* and *The Matrix*, share a single ontological assumption: that our daily lives, along with our entire sense of ourselves as embodied in memories of our past, are an illusion implanted to conceal a cruel reality in which we are enslaved and exploited by demonic masters (whether aliens or machines) possessing demiurgic supernatural powers. *Dark City*'s director/screenwriter, Alex Proyas, like some other major figures of the New Expressionism, hails neither by birth nor by genes from the United States or Eastern Europe. Born in Egypt and taken by his immigrant family to Australia at the age of three, he first directed *The Crow* (1994), a striking exemplar of American comic book Expressionist mythmaking. In Proyas's script (with Lem Dobbs and David Goyer) of *Dark City*, an appealing mix of H. P. Lovecraft and Fritz Lang, the Nosferatu-clone "Strangers" are collective-consciousness jellyfishes encased in the brains of dead human bodies. Dubbing themselves Mr. Hand, Mr. Book, and the like, they reveal their tin ear for things human and thereby their inability to capture their victims' "souls" even as they manipulate their memories—a power, as we saw, that the cyborg Puppet Master also possesses in *Ghost in the Shell*. The Strangers' manic building powers also recall from Chapter 4 the phantasmagoric idol creating and destroying that Cynthia Ozick imputes, in *The Messiah of Stockholm*, to her self-created version of Bruno Schulz's "lost masterpiece" *Messiah*, a world of graven images that ultimately collapses, "with the noise of vast crashings and crushings," under its own idolatrous weight.

The Strangers are serviced by their human flunky, "Dr. Daniel Poe Schreber"—a neat conflation, within the mad scientist figure, of our old friends Edgar Allan Poe and Daniel Paul Schreber. Judge Schreber's reincarnation here inevitably brings to mind the paranoid frame of *Caligari* as well. In *Dark City*, however, ordinary daily life is the illusion that "Dr. Schreber" (now cast in the role of his perceived former tormentor, the asylum director) helps foster. What is more, John Murdoch, one of the aliens' human experimental subjects, finds that he also possesses their matter-shaping and world-building abilities, a talent he immediately puts to use. This turn-of-the-century transformation of the supernatural from psychotic construction to visionary reality is a highly significant and suggestive shift from the earlier models of the "Is this real or am I crazy?" conundrum explored in Chapter 7.

In *The Truman Show*, directed by the Australian Peter Weir from a script by the New Zealander Andrew Niccol, the unwitting Truman (the "true man" in his ersatz world) lives in an emblematic upscale suburban tract whose placid surface ripples only ever so slightly when a klieg light hand-lettered "Sirius" accidentally drops onto his smoothly paved driveway. What Truman has always naively believed to be the real world is actually the set of a TV series that has voyeuristically chronicled his life since birth. His wife, mother, best friend, neighbors are not who he thinks they are, but SAG-registered thespians all. Though conceptually identical to *Dark City*, the story retains the old-fashioned rationalizing frame of *Caligari*. This time the macrocosmic Archon of Truman's world is no extraterrestrial, only a mundane TV hack named Christof. As magus and ultimate performance artist—at one critical moment he utters the memorable demiurgic command "Cue the sun!"—Christof holds echoes of Christo as well as Christ.

Writer-director Gary Ross's *Pleasantville*, in contrast, is the story of a brother and sister sucked into the sugary world of an ancient sitcom rerun playing on their television set by means of the fortuitous combination of lightning—electricity again—and a magic remote control device given them by an enigmatic demiurge in the form of the TV repairman Don Knotts. In this version of the "captive in someone else's created reality" story the two newcomers in the Platonic-form nuclear family and nuclear community are not only aware of the secret macrocosm from the outset; they themselves are the alien representatives of this world (though not, of course, authors of their predicament). Meanwhile the town's denizens, like the prelapsarian Truman, have no awareness of any reality beyond their black-and-white community, in which Main Street (as all Pleasantville students learn in school) circles around (like the worm Ourobouros of Greek myth) to meet itself.

Like John Murdoch in *Dark City*, David and Jennifer eventually discover their own world-changing powers, transforming in the course of the story from passive victims to active co-demiurges as their 1990s actions and attitudes shatter one by one the rigid 1950s ideal forms. And as in *What Dreams May Come*, their very presence in this world begins to alter it. In a characteristic New Expressionist device, the environment displays its sympathetic connections to their inner nature by changing first a flower or two, then selected human inmates, from black and white to color. In each case a character's connection with his or her deepest "true-man" inclinations—sexual, artistic, or intellectual—triggers the transformation; a comically rueful note is struck when the free spirit Jennifer, once she has helped sexually liberate her classmates, discovers the joys of reading and decides to stay on when she realizes she'll have a much better shot, from 1950s Pleasantville, of getting into a decent college.

In *What Dreams May Come*, directed by the New Zealander Vincent Ward and too slickly adapted by Ron Bass from a Richard Matheson novel, the main character, Chris Nielsen, becomes a demiurge after his death. Emerging in a syncretic otherworld of Romantic and Impressionist paintings that is partly his artist wife's vision and partly his own, he discovers that Paradise is do-it-yourself, an alternate self-created universe of infinite possibility in which "thoughts are real" and "that which you believe becomes your world." Not surprisingly, this and the other stories visually enact a New Expressionist Shakespearean "natural order," one that Christof violates and John Murdoch restores. Moving from one allegorical topos to another, Chris Nielsen travels a classic psychotopographic journey through despair to redemption—and ultimately a very non-Christian reincarnation back in the material world.

These various strands culminate in the story line of *The Matrix*, written and directed by brothers (and former comic book writers) Larry and Andy Wachowski. Its starting assumption is that the world is something "pulled over your eyes to blind you": a human discovers, in terms structurally identical to those of the nonvirtual films just discussed, that what he thought was his everyday life is actually a virtual fantasy world set a hundred years in the past. As in *Dark City*, what is uncovered is no transcendental otherworld but a shockingly ugly different version of material reality. What seems to be everyday life is nothing more than a mental fantasy manipulated by cynical demiurges in an omniscient digital matrix that has been his mind's home since birth; his physical appearance, he learns, is merely the "digital projection of your mental self." His real body, meanwhile, like those of most of the human population, lies imprisoned, naked, and virtually wired, in sterile rows of liquid pods.

The year, in fact, is 2197, and the planet is a sunless wreck ruled by computers spawned by that familiar demonic Divine Machine, a single governing artificial intelligence. The few human rebels who have escaped the living death of their pods have established—with Symmes Hole echoes—a new city called Zion, deep inside the earth "near the warmth of the core." Thomas A. Anderson, the hacker main character, gradually learns that he is actually Neo, the prophesied savior who will die, revive, and—like John Murdoch in *Dark City*—defeat the false Archons as the Chosen One, the single human who can master their world-bending powers, unhook his fellow humans from the memory-implanting matrix, and restore reality.

Like *Dark City*, *The Matrix* exhibits a hodgepodge of high and low influences, including Hong Kong martial art, sci-fi, Japanese *animé*, and cyberpunk sources. Most directly, it belongs to a distinctive subgenre of science fiction literature and film that anticipated the introduction of the Web and virtual reality in the 1980s. This virtual genre is clearly the progenitor of the nonvirtual magus movies as well, which seamlessly transfer the topographic allegory of the disembodied world to the "real" landscape outside the computer monitor. The widespread construction of the Web and virtual reality as a real location divorced from time and space is, I would argue, what has single-handedly moved the dormant Platonic sensibility in Western culture from its exile in the sub-Zeitgeist back into the mainstream. It has powerfully resurrected the old premodern construct of a unified hierarchical cosmos with a transcendent level that rules the material plane we lesser mortals inhabit, a level we now view as accessed in a quasi-magical way by high technology rather than by meditation, prayer, or incantation.

MIRROR WORLDS

It has been a mere decade since electronic communication leaped over its own traces from black-and-white paper facsimiles to the full-color simulacrum of the World Wide Web, setting in motion the profound intellectual as well as technological revolution foreshadowed by Marshall McLuhan (who, Krishnalike, communicated an exalted "Platonic dream" of technical utopias in a 1969 *Playboy* interview in which he hailed the Anthropos in the form of the cybernetic "new man, linked in a cosmic harmony that transcends time and place").

It was precisely here, in the metaphors first used to describe electronic representation, that the real alchemical wedding of very old and very new, ancient philosophy and high technology, took place. In *The Holographic Universe* Michael Talbot quotes a physicist with the evocative name of David Bohm who uses the hologram as a device to explain the nature of the universe: "The tangible reality of our everyday lives is really a kind of illusion, like a holographic image. Underlying it is a deeper order of existence, a vast and more primary level of reality that gives birth to all the objects and appearances of our physical world in much the same way that a piece of holographic film gives birth to a hologram." Or as Philip K. Dick asked: "Do we collectively dwell in a kind of laser hologram, real creatures in a manufactured quasi-world, a stage set within whose artifacts and creatures a mind moves that is determined to remain unknown?" Our loss of memory of the ideal world, Dick asserted, this failure to achieve Platonic anamnesis, is the root of our spiritual problem. Lodged in our divinely constructed "subcircuit" (that is, this world), we no longer have the ability to summon our ingrained knowledge of VALIS, the immortal "universe-organism."

Firmly set in the Divine Machine tradition, such early conflations of the new technology with a living cosmos laid the foundation for a metaphysical construction of virtual reality when this already extensively imagined technology manifested itself in our sublunary realm in the early 1980s. The term "virtual" is usually traced to classical Latin *vis*, "power" or "force," but it derives more directly from the adjective *virtualis*, a common descriptive term in medieval philosophy for what exists only in the intellect and not in material reality. (Another relevant concept from medieval Christian philosophy, and one we saw in Chapter 8 applied to memory systems, is that of the *unus mundus*, reality's "potential matrix" or God's preexistent plan for the world, before he actualized it in material reality.) Erik Davis credits our current usage of "virtual" to Antonin Artaud's notion of *la réalité virtuelle*, which likens the theatrical experience to the deep spiritual transformations of matter by spirit in the alchemical process. Artaud, one suspects, is likely to have drawn the term from the old Catholic usage.

However it came by its name, virtual reality quickly replaced the hologram as the dominant construct for describing the immortal world beyond our world of the senses. The new grotto of "cyberspace" could be viewed collectively as a comprehensive single territory, a realm, rather than isolated images. Such metaphors arose, William Irwin Thompson has argued, because "the conventional worldview of materialism is not subtle enough to deal with the complexities of a multidimensional universe in which domains interpenetrate and are enfolded in one another." A metastasis of image was under way in which the distancing role of metaphor quickly dissolved into identity and more than identity, establishing a pervasive framework in which the concepts "hyperspace" and "virtual reality" were first accorded the same status as empirical reality, and then a higher status still.

After they conquered the discourse of cybernetics and media, these metaphors of the new realm were at first ironically mainstreamed. In a playful review in the *New York Times* in 1997, a reporter dubbed the medieval Book of Hours "a kind of communication software for accessing the divine," via the "Outernet." "The comparison with computer technology is not inapt," Holland Cotter went on: "To the medieval mind, the entire universe took the form of a vast, minutely calibrated network in which everything, natural and supernatural, was linked, though connections were often indirect. A petition from man to God, for example, passed through any number of transfer points in the form of interceding saints and angels, or even the Virgin herself, before it arrived, like an ethereal version of E-mail, at its destination." The "reassuring message," Cotter concluded, is that of the "salvational technology that the Book of Hours itself represents: God is in heaven; everything connects."

What translated as an amusing set piece to the bulk of the *New York Times*'s lay readership, however, has been anything but that in the new vitalism of computer theory and its fictional spin-offs in film and literature, where any lingering division between the terms of the analogy has long since dissolved. Of the growing number of Internet-based religious groups, Robert Wright reports: "The central notion of technosophy—that life is a technology—has as its flip side the idea that technology is a form of life. Strange as this sounds, it is an increasingly common refrain in cyberculture. If the idea is valid—if indeed fiber optics are living tissue—

then it is easier to think of Earth in the Age of Internet as a coherent living system, a giant organism complete with a giant brain."

Whether it is constructed as a TV series, an asteroid, or Paradise, the realm of hyperspace is now routinely depicted not as a neutral vacuum but as the highly charged matrix of an active universe of correspondences, antecedent to our empirical world of the senses and capable of creating simulacra in that world. We now implicitly endow both outer space and hyperspace with the old qualities of the eternal, incorruptible ether at the same time that they also receive, as in *What Dreams May Come*, the exteriorized contents of our inner lives: "For everything in life, there is a counterpart in afterlife."

The virtual realm that exists above, outside, or beside (but, curiously, never below) our own is not only timeless and immortal, its "inhabitants" (that is, software programs) are styled as living creatures as well. From the implicit metaphor of the "daemon," the computer subroutine that returns undeliverable email, it is an easy step out of metaphor and into something like conflated allegory to style the "bot" program as the software equivalent of a robot, one that moreover boasts a biological genealogy. And it is just as easy a step from an onscreen photorealistic human image to a virtual person who exists only on the computer to, ultimately, an "avatar," applying the term for the human incarnation of a Hindu god to the latest upgrade of this computer simulacrum.

As the metaphors entrenched themselves and multiplied over the decade of the 1980s, theorists endeavored to show how the Platonic notion of the new alternate world lent itself to sober professional endeavor. In *Mirror Worlds* (1991), the computer scientist David Gelernter (later to be a target of the Luddite Unabomber Theodore Kaczynski) offered to business and organizational management the prospect of a not-yet-developed microcosmic computer software tool: "A Mirror World is some huge institution's moving, true-to-life mirror image trapped inside a computer—where you can see and grasp it whole. The thick, dense, busy sub-world that encompasses you is *also*, now, an object in your hands. A brand new equilibrium is born." Though he stressed that Mirror Worlds were to be regarded as "scientific viewing tools," the messianic undertone is hard to miss. Defining "topsight" as a looking down that implies mastery, Gelernter proclaimed: "*People build microcosms to find topsight.*"

In conflating the infinite universe around him into an arena of inner images, Giordano Bruno craved topsight, too. Inner vision, he said, is like a mirror "informed and illuminated by itself, which is both light and mirror at the same time, and in which a perceptible object is one with a percipient subject." And if, as Bruno believed, engraving the universe within oneself by internalizing talismanic images allows one to "know" God gnostically and therefore become God, then the first step toward human divinity is constructing a simulated microcosm in such a way that inner and outer reality alternately reflect and affect each other. String theory, the latest advance in theoretical physics, reinforces this Brunonian notion of cosmological doubling. In *The Elegant Universe*, the physicist Brian Greene argues that every conceivable form of the universe must possess a kind of shadow or mirror form that will generate an identical alternate cosmos. Instead of moving us briskly forward on the wide road of Progress, in fact, the wonders promised to those who dare to peer into the Mirror World turn us irresistibly backward—to, for example, Merlin's "glassie globe" in Spenser's *Faerie Queene*, which "vertue had, to shew in perfect sight, / What euer thing was in the world contayned, / Betwixt the lowest earth and heauens hight."

The concept of a mirror world far antedates even the Renaissance in Western culture. The Greeks, says Jean-Pierre Vernant, thought the mirror "opens a breach in the backdrop of 'phenomena,' displays the invisible, reveals the divine, and lets it be seen in the brilliance of a mysterious epiphany." We have seen how, in that pivotal period for Western culture the fourth century C.E., Plotinus modified Plato's alternate worlds (this one and the world of Ideal Forms) into a hierarchy within which our world at the bottom imperfectly reflects the divine world at the top, and how the Hermetic Anthropos was first lured to the material world when he saw his own likeness mirrored up to him from Earth's oceans. Equally strong was the tradition of the human soul itself as a double-edged mirror, able—if sufficiently pure—to reflect the events of the timeless world in this one. From Philo of Alexandria and Porphyry, the Neoplatonic notion of the mirror interfacing between this world and the next was carried through by medieval mystics like Bernard Silvestris during the interval between the years 400 and 1200, when the actual technology of mirror making was lost in the Western world, and in secular literature such as the *Roman de la Rose*, the *Divine Comedy, and* others. To assert, then, as Gelernter does, that mirror worlds "offer penetrating vision: they repair the shattered whole" is to invoke no "brand new equilibrium" but a very old one—the *Harmonica macrocosmica.*

More important, viewing the two worlds, material and virtual, as coexisting raises the important question "Who's in charge?" which by the turn of the millennium had long since superseded "Is this real or am I crazy?" If both worlds are real, which one rules the other? Typically, the stiff undertow of Western Platonism makes us want to believe that we are the shadows in the virtual cave, not the other way around. Following the old pattern, the electronic microcosm that we created has done a flip-flop in our imaginations to become the macrocosm that governs our lives—a reversal of creator and created that is a recurring, not an aberrant, theme in our culture. In the 1960s a simplistic analogy to computers, reminiscent of the eighteenth-century mechanistic watchmaker model of the cosmos, became the foundation of an entire discipline—cognitive psychology—in which mental functions were described in terms of computer hardware and software. Like that field's database metaphor, the metaphor of the mirror allows some uncertainty about which element of the comparison is, as it were, in the driver's seat—which is (to use the analogy in question) the "default" mode, human or cybernetic? In each case, significantly, power is ceded to the machine as the implicit constant against which a less steady variable, the human, is meant to be measured.

Just as Gelernter was writing, the highly successful "Sims" or interactive games of simulated environments (such as *Sim City* and its many progeny) were being developed, reinforcing a sense of the individual human player's demiurgic powers as well as of the macrocosm/microcosm structure of the universe. The *Sim City* series was an urban planning game that quickly spawned a "people simulator," *The Sims*, in which gamers can create a family or community of virtual people, assign them jobs and identities, manage their lives and finances, and feed or care for them. (Accidents are programmed to occur to upset and challenge the gamer's sense of omnipotence.) A "sim" experience is vividly enacted in the Strangers' frantic architectonics in *Dark City*, where buildings sprout and wither like living organisms.

The ultimate Sim is George Lucas's tongue-in-cheek interactive game "Afterlife," described as a "hilarious and challenging world-building strategy game" in which "players build the heaven and hell of an alien world and assist wayward 'souls' to their final resting places. As souls begin to migrate, players manage the souls' arrival by zoning and developing areas for the seven deadly sins and their respective virtues. Through intense resource management, players must balance their divine/demonic work force, meet the needs of the population and anticipate disasters." Special features of the game, which boasts the "grandest scope of any simulation game, trading literally billions of characters," are the "ability to manage two planes (heaven and hell) simultaneously" and the "ability to track individual 'souls.'" In the same way, the official website of *What Dreams May Come* reveals the allegorical Pilgrim's Progress sensibility (discussed in Chapter 8) that informs such interactive games: the player moves from Consciousness City to the Sea of Doubt to Hell House to, inevitably, Create Your Own World. To play these psychotopographic games, seriously or ironically, is not only to engage deeply in the allegorical experience of journeying from one state of mind, one *topos* to another, but to endorse the tangibility of this level of ideas as well.

THE NEW FAUSTS

As a good Neoplatonist, Giordano Bruno believed that the world of our senses is only an *umbris idearum*, a shadow of the larger world of ideas, that grand hidden macrocosm whose secrets we can only indirectly apprehend. To penetrate this realm, Bruno collapsed religion, magic, and science into the magus's single pursuit, with art as a conflated fourth element as well. Magic in this context becomes, in Ioan Couliano's words, the "science of the imaginary." After the Renaissance, as we have seen, the magus figure split in two as the artist, divorced from divine inspiration, became the good magus in the newly valorized aesthetic dimension of secular culture (as in the conventional interpretation of Shakespeare's Prospero as the playwright himself). The natural-philosopher-turned-scientist, meanwhile, received the negative projection of misguided tinkerer and befuddled sorcerer's apprentice.

Other than a rather Manichaean version of the Devil, Western popular films of the supernatural before the year 1990 featured no real deities, good or bad. (With its benign "superhuman" daemons and their malign counterparts, the American comic book cosmology has always been, like the Hindu pantheon, inherently more balanced.) Not until the ascendance of the new/old virtual worldview do we begin to see, along with a smattering of angels, a mini-trend of, for example, benevolent female demigoddesses. In *Johnny Mnemonic* the late Anna Karman, "founder and CEO of Pharmacon," a multinational drug concern, is "implanted" into a virtual system after death but before morbidity sets in; her immortal living image appears onscreen at critical junctures to advise Johnny and his cyber-rebel cohorts. To anyone attuned to popular conventions of the twentieth-century supernatural, this is a strange and unprecedented moment—indeed, a very Hellenistic moment, straight out of Greek romance.

Through the end of the 1980s, as the first representations of virtual reality came to film (the pathbreaking *Tron*, about personified software characters enslaved by an evil Master Control Program, appeared in 1982), the mad scientist magi predictably spawned cybernetic golems who were devils, not angels. The neutral Neoplatonic daemon that faithfully returned one's mis-sent e-mail from the far corners of cyberspace was not to be confused with these virtual demons. Virtual reality itself was similarly portrayed as "infecting" our world in a demonic way: the evil force trapped inside VR or the electrical system always and inevitably burst out into sublunary reality with devastating results. A typical film of this genre, *Virtuosity* (1995), features "Syd 6.7," a creature of virtual reality called a "nanotech" who has been programmed by his bad magus to possess the combined character traits of a gaggle of famous serial killers. Syd's birth is pure alchemy—he incubates in a colloidal suspension of silicon-based "nanocells" in a high-tech alchemical *vas*—and so is his death: when Syd escapes from his own world to wreak havoc in ours, he must be chased back to the timeless world, where he is captured and destroyed against a red background of multiple mouths screaming, VR's own Inferno of lost souls.

The early 1990s witnessed the beginning of a new trend in which the virtual demons gradually gave way, though still negatively, to the Divine Human. According to a quickly established subconvention, all virtual entities desire to embody in our world, and certain humans desire to disembody in theirs—passing each other in opposite directions, as it were. A 1997 episode of the TV series *The X-Files* entitled "Kill Switch" presented an artificial intelligence that has escaped its confines on the Net to become virtual "wildlife" running amok. Meanwhile the AI's demiurgic co-creators, a man and a woman, want to transmit their own consciousnesses into virtual reality, discarding their physical bodies to enjoy a "perfect union." Even as Agent Scully protests, "Electrons chasing each other through circuits—that's not life," the female survivor "uploads" herself to join her lover in a Gnostic ascent through the hard-drive spheres into an immortal realm. With an alchemical display of colors, the rainbow of her mental consciousness flashes on the monitor as her mind is sucked into cyberspace, leaving behind a withered body—and disturbing echoes of Heaven's Gate.

The Anthropos as virtualizing human was given its most dramatic treatment in *Lawnmower Man* (1992), whose premise is that virtual reality allows us to reclaim something called the "primal mind" (that is, our divine essence in the World of Forms), thereby tapping into powers such as telepathy that shamans and alchemists traditionally possessed. Once the simpleton Jobe Smith enters virtual reality through the efforts of one Dr. Angelo, he immediately experiences a sense of omnipotence ("This is my universe; I am God here") and realizes that in this world he can eventually become divine (even as he is simultaneously described as having a "psychotic break"). Persecuted and exploited by a sinister government agency, Jobe predicts that "virtual reality will grow . . . it will be everywhere." Jobe intends to complete his evolution into Anthropos-God by "projecting himself into the mainframe" (that is, the highest celestial sphere) and converting to pure energy, thereby achieving both divinity and a triumphant reincarnation in the material world. "My birth cry," he boasts, "will be the sound of every telephone ringing in the universe."

The Matrix and *Dark City* also portray human protagonists assuming the roles formerly occupied by their virtual daemon antagonists. Like the daemons, they break out of the illusory world in which they are imprisoned, but with a significantly more positive outcome; the mad scientist takes a secondary role to the Brunonian heroic enthusiast who becomes master of his own fate. John Murdoch's demiurgic powers in *Dark City* are potentially inflationary but curiously un-Faustian. By story's end he has become a super-Prospero—in Frances Yates's words, the "magically powerful personality tuned in . . . to the powers of the universe." Both he and Neo in *The Matrix* have dared to break the bonds of their fabricated personal histories (false memory being the defining feature of the illusory world); "transgressing the laws of nature" does not damn them, it sets them free. By "accessing" their Platonic anamnesis, in Dick's terms, they have gained control of both the world ruled by their masters and their own identities. Like Christof, John Murdoch "cues the sun," but with the nobler end of turning the Dark City asteroid into a pastoral version of Tommaso Campanella's *Civitas Solis* or "City of the Sun," complete with bathing beach and pier, an act that also points the supremely *noir*-oriented mode of early and mid-twentieth-century film Expressionism in a much sunnier direction. John Murdoch and Neo lead their people, like the workers of *Metropolis*, out of Orco's mouth into the light—a vision of utopia not far removed from the perfectly round city, founded on a solar religion, that Campanella envisioned in his 1623 tract.

Just as those human characters who breach the boundary of the insensible world and master what lies beyond have been increasingly depicted as good magi rather than mad scientists, the virtual demons and their uncles the cyborgs have also followed the general turn, post-1990, into supernatural benignity. As we saw in Chapter 11, Terminator 2 is as noble as Terminator 1 was implacably evil. This movement from demon to angel, *male* to *bene*, bad magus to good magus seems to indicate, among other things, the first real signs of decline in the three-hundred-year-old tradition of the grotesque as preeminent definer of the supernatural. The sub-Zeitgeist is registering a growing half-conscious reacceptance of some of the underlying assumptions of supernaturalism, and what is acknowledged often becomes what is no longer feared or demonized. Although some of this effect, as we have seen, can undoubtedly be traced to the spatial association of virtual reality with the ether of the angels rather than the grotto of the demons, by any measure the rationalist trap door is becoming harder to locate.

The sub-Zeitgeist of the last decade of the twentieth century also suggests that high literature and film of the coming century will not extend the aesthetics of postmodernism. A case in point is Jan Svankmajer's *Lesson Faust* (1994), which revives the old Faust puppet plays as a collage of styles and a mix of human and puppet characters. The postmodern frame, however, obliges us to regard Faust's dilemma as a parody rather than a conflict informed by feeling. By the end of Svankmajer's deconstruction of a fragmented commentary—in which his contemporary Faust-magus comes to an ignominious end run over by a demon-driven red car, whereupon a homeless man steals his disarticulated arm wrapped in butcher paper—even the most sympathetic viewer is forced to conclude that this is absolutely as far as the Western aesthetic can go in the Aristotelian direction. The pendulum must swing back, and the sub-Zeitgeist is pointing the way.

The impending retrograde direction, I submit, is no decline into a fundamentalist Dark Ages. The new sensibility does not threaten a regression from rationality to superstition; rather, it allows for expansion beyond the one-sided worldview that scientism has provided us over the last three hundred years. We should never forget how utterly unsophisticated the tenets of eighteenth-century rationalism have left us, believers and unbelievers alike, in that complex arena we blithely dub "spiritual." Even as we see all too clearly the kitsch of much New Age religiosity and fear the rigidity of rising fundamentalism, we remain alarmingly blind to our own unconscious tendencies in this same direction. Our conventional secular bias whispers to us that the ideas we see naively articulated on the cinema screen (ideas as blasphemous to secular humanists as they are to the religious orthodox), if they are to be taken seriously at all, signal a backward slide into religious oppression and intolerance. What our perspective does not allow us to recognize is the positive and enduring dimension of such ideas when they are consciously articulated in our culture. We forget that Western culture is equally about Platonism and Aristotelianism, idealism and empiricism, *gnosis* and *episteme*, and that for most of this culture's history one or the other has been conspicuously dominant—and dedicated to stamping the other out.

The shift in sensibility now taking place, as I have tried to show, is nothing new in the story of Western culture, which manifests in a cyclical swing—fifteen hundred years in one mode followed by three hundred in the other. To fear and oppose these developments is to overly identify with one element in the Western dialectic at the expense of the other and thereby miss the exciting moment of opening up (as opposed to sliding back) that is ushering us into a new Renaissance—not so much a technological one (our overvaluing of technology, like our exalted notions of materialist progress, is part of the perversion and displacement of the religious impulse) as one of expanded intellectual and artistic possibilities.

The "return of the repressed," of course, poses the dangers of all Pandora's boxes. In critiquing Jacques Derrida's notion of a *fin-de-siècle* "hauntology," Martin Jay remarks on the pitfalls of an unmediated "desire to restore an alleged lost moral wholeness and cozy domesticity." Moreover, cybertheory has conflated the imaginary with the material using the same dubious shortcuts that the fantasy cults have employed in conflating *imagine* with *believe.* The cybergrotto's ethereal Gnostic nature, as it is now almost universally represented, calls out for a good portion of Aristotelian body-mind to ground and reembody it. But by the same token—and this is almost impossible for the staunch Aristotelian to concede—we can't use empirical reasoning to disqualify the existence of the soul or a kind of reality outside time and space. "The two errors: we can either have a spiritual or a materialist view of life," Cyril Connolly once said. "We cannot say that truth lies in the centre between the spiritual and material conception, since life must be one thing or the other." He added, significantly: "But can it be both?"

Truth does lie in recognizing both. Though their adherents have always been adversarial, the two worldviews are actually complementary; neither perspective qualifies as rigid dogma or superstition so long as it is applied to its own turf. We get into trouble only when we mix territories, expecting the transcendental to do the work of the empirical and vice versa. Unfortunately, only during the briefest of historical interludes have the two coexisted in their more or less appropriate realms. The most intellectually exciting and innovative times in our culture have been just these rare periods when the two worldviews overlapped in open conflict and neither was dominant. The Renaissance itself, when the Platonic worldview coexisted with the Aristotelian, is a prime example. From our current Aristotelian mode, we assume that the extraordinary vitality of that period was the result of the gradual displacement of religious "superstition" by the rise of rationality and the scientific method. It might equally be seen as the result of the dynamism of the two points of view vying with each other, contesting territories. ("A wise man," Emerson said, "will see that Aristotle Platonizes.")

Such an interlude may again be upon us. Again and again in the demiurge films a moment comes when the main character collides with the painted canvas that marks the limits of his Archon's created world, then breaks through it: Truman comes upon the real door in the fake sky at the end of his world, John Murdoch rips through the faded paint of a "Shell Beach" advertisement to expose the gaping void of outer space. Both are like the famous early sixteenth-century engraving of the natural philosopher who sticks his head through the soap-bubble skin of the terrestrial sphere to gape at the wonders of the celestial world beyond. Now as then, these images suggest a major transition in sensibility. For it is precisely the moment when we become completely conscious of the boundaries of the worldview we have comfortably inhabited for several centuries that is also, inevitably, the moment we abandon it: we see the door in the sky, and we walk through it.

NOTES

ACKNOWLEDGMENTS

INDEX

NOTES

1. GROTTO, AN OPENING

xiv Novalis quoted in S. S. Prawer, *Caligari's Children: The Film as Tale of Terror* (Oxford: Oxford University Press, 1980), 280.

1 Leonardo da Vinci, *Diaries*, quoted in Naomi Miller, *Heavenly Caves* (New York: George Braziller, 1982), 5.

1 "crude initiatory cave": Naomi Miller describes it as "really a Mithraic chapel or even more likely, the domain of Pluto" in *Heavenly Caves*, 51; Eugenio Battisti says it is a "parody of an Etruscan tomb" in *L'Antirinascimento* (Milan: Feltrinelli, 1962), 133.

2 "Italian antiquarians": W. H. Gombrich, *The Sense of Order: A Study in the Psychology of Decorative Art* (Ithaca: Cornell University Press, 1979), 278.

2 Horace, *Ars Poetica*, Epistles, book II.

2 "place of birth and death": Horst Bredekamp, *Vicino Orsini und der heilige Wald von Bomarzo: Ein Fürst als Künstler und Anarchist* (Worms: Wernersche Verlagsgesellschaft, 1991), 84.

2 Montaigne: "And what are these things of mine, in truth, but grotesques and monstrous bodies, pieced together of divers members, without definite shape." "On Friendship," in *The Complete Essays of Montaigne*, trans. Donald M. Frame (Stanford: Stanford University Press, 1943), 135. Montaigne also wrote eloquently of the Italian grottoes in his *Journals*.

2–3 "replete with automata": See, e.g., Battisti, *L'Antirinascimento*, 220–253.

3 "Alexander Pope's studio": Miller, *Heavenly Caves*, 80, 83.

3 Pope quoted in Maynard Mack, *Alexander Pope: A Life* (New Haven: Yale University Press, 1985), 362–363.

3 John Ruskin, *The Stones of Venice*, quoted in Gombrich, *Sense of Order*, 256.

3 Peter Kingsley, *Ancient Philosophy, Mystery and Magic: Empedocles and Pythagorean Tradition* (New York: Oxford, 1996).

3 All quoted passages from Plato, *The Republic*, trans. G. M. A. Grube (Indianapolis: Hackett, 1974), book IV, 514a–b, 168–170.

4–5 "Bolos of Mendes": See Brian P. Copenhaver, ed. and trans., *Hermetica* (Cambridge: Cambridge University Press, 1992), xxxiii; see also Jack Lindsay, *The Origins of Alchemy in Graeco-Roman Egypt* (London: Frederick Muller, 1970), 31.

5 "great chain of being": As E. M. Tillyard once summed it up, the idea of the chain of being derives "from Plato's *Timaeus*, developed by Aristotle, adopted by Alexandrian Jews, spread by Neo-Platonists," persisting from the Middle Ages through the eighteenth century. *The Elizabethan World Picture* (New York: Random House, n.d.), 26.

5 Pico della Mirandola, *Heptaplus, or Discourse on the Seven Days of Creation*, trans. Jessie Brewer McGaw (New York: Philosophical Library, 1977), 24.

5 Arthur O. Lovejoy, *The Great Chain of Being: The History of an Idea* (1936; Cambridge, Mass.: Harvard University Press, 1964), 329.

5 Umberto Eco, in *Interpretation and Overinterpretation* (Cambridge: Cambridge University Press, 1992), links "occultism," Hermeticism, and poststructuralism; see Chapter 10 of this book.

5 M. H. Abrams, *Natural Supernaturalism: Tradition and Revolution in Romantic Literature* (New York: Norton, 1971), 13.

5 "dark place of wisdom": Kingsley, *Ancient Philosophy*, 36; also see Kingsley, *In the Dark Places of Wisdom* (Inverness: Golden Sufi Center, 1999).

6 D. P. Walker, "The Cessation of Miracles," in Ingrid Merkel and Allen G. Debus, eds., *Hermeticism and the Renaissance: Intellectual History and the Occult in Early Modern Europe* (Washington: Folger Shakespeare Library, 1988), 111–124. Walker's title is a play on Plutarch's "On the Cessation of Oracles."

7 Keith Thomas, *Religion and the Decline of Magic* (New York: Scribner's, 1971), 590.

7 Joscelyn Godwin, *Athanasius Kircher: A Renaissance Man and the Quest for Lost Knowledge* (London: Thames and Hudson, 1979), 5.

8 "plurality of material worlds": Lovejoy, *Great Chain of Being*, 124–125.

9 Friedrich Nietzsche, preface, in *The Birth of Tragedy and the Genealogy of Morals*, trans. Francis Golffing (New York: Anchor, 1956), 17.

9 Jorge Luis Borges, "Tlön, Uqbar, Orbis Tertius," in *Labyrinths: Selected Stories and Other Writings*, ed. Donald A. Yates and James E. Irby, trans. James E. Irby (New York: New Directions, 1964), 10.

9 Leo Bersani, *The Culture of Redemption* (Cambridge, Mass.: Harvard University Press, 1990).

10 Forster, *A Passage to India* (New York: Harcourt, Brace and World, 1952), 146–147.

10–11 All quoted passages from Forster, "The Story of the Siren," in *The Eternal Moment and Other Stories* (New York: Grosset and Dunlap, 1964), 159–176. Bodies of water were traditionally associated with the grotto; Miller, *Heavenly Caves*, 13.

13 All quoted passages from Kafka, "The Burrow," in *Kafka: The Complete Stories*, ed. Nahum N. Glatzer (New York: Schocken, 1971), 325–359.

13 Giordano Bruno in *Spaccio della bestia trionfante* (1584). See Karen Silvia de León-Jones, *Giordano Bruno and the Kabbalah: Prophets, Magicians, and Rabbis* (New Haven: Yale University Press, 1997), 98–99.

14 Greene, "Under the Garden," in *A Sense of Reality* (New York: Viking, 1963), 165–237. All quoted passages from this U.S. edition.

14 "a two-hundred-year-old man": The image of a Godlike elder sitting on a toilet has a number of analogues in the boyhood fantasy/dreams of various writers; see Wendy Lesser, *The World below the Ground* (Winchester, Mass.: Faber and Faber, 1987), 51. The most intriguing parallels are two anecdotes found in Carl Jung's *Memories, Dreams, Reflections*, trans. Richard and Clara Wilson, rev. ed. (New York: Vintage, 1965): a dream from early childhood about an enormous phallus on a golden throne in a chamber under a meadow and an adolescent obsessive vision of God on his golden throne destroying a cathedral with a gargantuan turd. These two visions, Jung acknowledged, were compensatory reactions to the ascetic and ethereal Protestantism in which he was raised—and no doubt functioned similarly in the fantasy life of other schoolboys. Yet both have a strong ritualistic flavor as well, as do the underground events in "Under the Garden."

It is not beyond the realm of possibility that Greene had read *Memories, Dreams, Reflections* (whose English-language edition first appeared in 1961) before or during the composition of "Under the Garden." When Greene suffered a breakdown at the age of sixteen, he was treated by a Jungian lay therapist, Kenneth Richmond. His entire treatment consisted of dream analysis, in which Richmond obliged him to supply his own interpretations: Norman Sherry, *The Life of Graham Greene*, vol. 1 (London: Jonathan Cape, 1989), 95–98. Moreover, the opening of "Under the Garden," in which the narrator looks at an X-ray of his own cancer as if it were an exteriorized landscape ("the whorls . . . reminded the patient of those pictures of the earth's surface taken from a great height that he had pored over at one period during the war, trying to detect the tiny grey seed of a launching ramp"; 165), strangely and ironically echoes the epigraph from Coleridge's *Notebooks* that Aniela Jaffe, Jung's confidante and editor, supplied to *Memories, Dreams, Reflections*: "He looked at his own Soul with a Telescope. What seemed all irregular, he saw and shewed to be beautiful Constellations." Whether or not Jung's memoir influenced Greene, to label the toilet-seat image "Freudian" is to overlook the levels of allegorical meaning—and the deeper truths of "real" religion—that both Jung and Greene would be likely to insist were present.

15 Paul O'Prey, in *A Reader's Guide to Graham Greene* (London: Thames and Hudson, 1988), 66; Michael Sheldon, *Graham Greene: The Man Within* (London: Heinemann, 1994), 53.

16 Lesser, *World below the Ground,* 201.

16 Bernard McElroy, *Fiction of the Modern Grotesque* (London: Macmillan, 1989), 5.

16 Mikhail Bakhtin, *Rabelais and His World* (Bloomington: Indiana University Press, 1984); Wolfgang Kayser, *The Grotesque in Art and Literature,* trans. Ulrich Weisstein (New York: Columbia University Press, 1981); Tzvetan Todorov, *The Fantastic: A Structural Approach to a Literary Genre,* trans. Richard Howard (Ithaca: Cornell University Press, 1973).

16 See, e.g., Kenneth Gross, "Moving Statues, Talking Statues," *Raritan* (Fall 1989): 1–25, *The Dream of the Moving Statue* (Ithaca: Cornell University Press, 1992), and "Love among the Puppets," *Raritan* (Summer 1997): 67–82.

17 "an autonomous inner grotto": Ewa Kuryluk, in *Salome and Judas in the Cave of Sex* (Evanston, Ill.: Northwestern University Press, 1989), 93, observes that psychoanalysis itself belongs to the grotesque tradition.

17 Borges, "Tlön, Uqbar, Orbis Tertius," 10.

17 "*unheimlich*": Sigmund Freud, "The 'Uncanny,'" in James Strachey, ed. and trans., *Complete Psychological Works of Sigmund Freud,* vol. 17 (London: Hogarth Press and Institute of Psychoanalysis, 1917–1919), 219–253.

18 Rudolf Otto, *The Idea of the Holy,* trans. John Harvey (1928; New York: Oxford University Press, 1958), 14–15. I owe much in this discussion to S. S. Prawer's discussion of the uncanny in *Caligari's Children,* ch. 4.

18 "You can raise issues": Nicholas Kazan quoted in Stephen Farber, "New Scare Tactics, Low on Blood and Gore," *New York Times,* www.nytimes.com/1/12/98/artleisure/.

19 Otto Rank, *Psychology and the Soul: A Study of the Origin, Conceptual Evolution and Nature of the Soul,* trans. Gregory C. Richter and E. James Lieberman (1930; Baltimore: Johns Hopkins University Press, 1998), 8. The title in German is *Seelenglaube,* literally "belief in the soul."

19 Paul Tillich quoted in Prawer, *Caligari's Children,* 125.

20 Michael Camille, *The Gothic Idol: Ideology and Image-Making in Medieval Art* (Cambridge: Cambridge University Press, 1989), 78–79.

21 Lawrence Weschler, in *Mr. Wilson's Cabinet of Wonders: Pronged Ants, Horned Humans, Mice on Toast, and Other Marvels of Jurassic Technology* (New York: Vintage, 1995), remarks on "the premodern wellsprings of the postmodern temper" (90).

21 John Searle in, e.g., *Mind, Language, and Society: Philosophy in the Real World* (New York: Basic Books, 1998).

21 Bruno, *On the Contemplation of Images, Signs and Ideas*, II, 3, paraphrased in Frances A. Yates, *Giordano Bruno and the Hermetic Tradition* (Chicago: University of Chicago Press, 1964), 336.

21–22 Horst Bredekamp, *The Lure of Antiquity and the Cult of the Machine: The Kunstkammer and the Evolution of Nature, Art, and Technology*, trans. Allison Brown (Princeton: Markus Wiener, 1995), 113.

22 Mikhail Bakhtin, *Rabelais and His World*, trans. Helene Iswolsky (Bloomington: Indiana University Press, 1984), 317.

22 "metamorphosis into an animal": Bruno, *Eroici Furori*, I, 4. De León-Jones, in *Giordano Bruno and the Kabbalah*, says: "Bruno transforms the basis of Platonic contemplation by asserting its fundamentally bestial nature—the fundamental need for the human soul to become an animal, a stag, or an Ass . . . Bestial qualities are inherent in man, and thus in the divinity, or vice versa" (98). Frances Yates discusses Bruno's fascination with the ancient Egyptians, who "from the natural forms of beasts ascended to the penetration of the divinity," in *Giordano Bruno and the Hermetic Tradition*, 222.

2. EARLY ADVENTURES OF THE EARTHLY GODS

24 Edward Gordon Craig, "The Actor and the Über-marionette," in *On the Art of the Theatre* (Chicago: Browne's Bookstore, 1911), 82–83.

26 Bishop Reginald Huber (1782–1826). From *Hymns Ancient and Modern*, the standard hymnbook of the Anglican church. I am indebted to Jane Lancaster for this identification.

27 Joseph Joubert, *Notebooks*, trans. Paul Auster (San Francisco: North Point, 1983), 59.

27 J. D. Ray, *The Archive of Hor* (London: Egypt Exploration Society, 1976), 130.

27 Garth Fowden, *The Egyptian Hermes* (Princeton: Princeton University Press, 1993), 101, 113.

27 "the argument": Tullio Maranhao, introduction, in Maranhao, ed., *The Interpretation of Dialogue* (Chicago: University of Chicago Press, 1990), 13.

28 Susanna Elm, "Early Christian Belief," lecture presented at "Knowledge and Belief" symposium, University of California at Berkeley, Sept. 28, 1999.

29 "Platonists or Aristotelians": Coleridge cited by Jorge Luis Borges, who added: "The former feel that classes, orders, and genres are realities; the latter, that they are generalizations." "On the Cult of Books," in *Other Inquisitions 1937–1952*, trans. Ruth L. C. Simms (Austin: University of Texas Press, 1964), 128.

30 Heinrich von Kleist, "On the Marionette Theater," trans. Christian-Albrecht Gollub, in A. Leslie Willson, ed., *German Romantic Criticism*, German Library, vol. 21 (New York: Continuum, 1982), 244.

32 "*pneuma* and *psyche*": Gilles Quispel, "Hermes Trismegistus and the

Origins of Gnosticism," lecture, University of California at Berkeley, Dec. 13, 1993.

32 "Western medicine": D. P. Walker, "The Astral Body in Renaissance Medicine," in Penelope Gorik, ed., *Music, Spirit, and Language in the Renaissance* (London: Variorum Reprints, 1985), 121–122, 145.

32 "the Gnostics believed": Kurt Rudolph, *Gnosis: The Nature and History of Gnosticism*, trans. Robert McLachlan Wilson (San Francisco: Harper and Row, 1983), 172.

33 "did not fabricate": Robert Kriech Ritner, *The Mechanics of Ancient Egyptian Magic Practice*, Studies in Ancient Oriental Civilization (Chicago: Oriental Institute of the University of Chicago, 1993), 247.

33 Marie-Louise von Franz, "Psyche and Matter in Alchemy and Modern Science," in *Psyche and Matter* (Boston: Shambala, 1992), 147.

33–34 Jean-Pierre Vernant, "Mortals and Immortals: The Body of the Divine," in *Mortals and Immortals: Collected Essays*, ed. Froma I. Zeitlin (Princeton: Princeton University Press, 1991), 29, 31, 34, 44.

34 *Timaeus*, 33B-34A, in *Plato's Cosmology: The* Timaeus *of Plato*, trans. Francis Cornford (Indianapolis: Bobbs-Merrill, 1951), 55.

34 "God as Logos": John 1:1. I am indebted to Joscelyn Godwin for pointing out this connection.

34 Zosimos quoted in von Franz, "Psyche and Matter," 149. Also see Carl H. Kraeling, *Anthropos and Son of Man: A Study in the Religious Syncretism of the Hellenistic Orient* (New York: Columbia University Press, 1927).

34–35 "Mind, the father of all": Brian P. Copenhaver, ed. and trans., *Hermetica* (Cambridge: Cambridge University Press, 1992), 3.

35 Moshe Idel, "Hermeticism and Judaism," in Ingrid Merkel and Allen G. Debus, eds., *Hermeticism and the Renaissance: Intellectual History and the Occult in Early Modern Europe* (Washington: Folger Shakespeare Library, 1988), 69–70.

35–36 "Greek Magical Papyri": See, e.g., the examples in Georg Luck, *Arcana Mundi: Magic and the Occult in the Greek and Roman Worlds* (Baltimore: Johns Hopkins University Press, 1985), 93–96.

36 *"s'ankh":* Marie Weynants-Ronday, *Les Statues vivantes: Introduction a l'étude des statues égyptiennes* (Brussels: Editions de la Fondation Égyptologique Reine Élizabeth, 1926), 111.

36 Ioan Couliano, *Out of This World: Otherworldly Journeys from Gilgamesh to Albert Einstein* (Boston: Shambala, 1991), 61.

36 John Cohen, *Human Robots in Myth and Science* (London: George Allen and Unwin, 1966), 16.

36 "Aion, the lion-headed": Frederik Poulsen, "Talking, Weeping and Bleeding Sculptures: A Chapter of the History of Religious Fraud," *Acta Archaeologica* 16 (1945): 190.

36 "Live birds": Leda J. Ciraolo, "The Warmth and Breath of Life: Animating Physical Objects [Paredros] in the Greek Magical Papyri," *SBL 1992 Seminar Papers* (Atlanta: Society of Biblical Literature, 1993), 240–254.

36 "Artemidorus": Froma I. Zeitlin, "Living Portraits and Sculpted Bodies in Chariton's Theater of Romance," Sather Lecture, University of California at Berkeley, March 6, 1996.

36 "mummification flourished": See, e.g., Susan Walker and Morris Bierbier, *Ancient Faces: Mummy Portraits from Roman Egypt* (London: British Museum Press, 1997).

37 "eternal indestructible": von Franz, "Psyche and Matter," 147.

37 Zosimos quoted in von Franz, "Psyche and Matter," 149.

37 "up the hierarchical ladder": Jack Lindsay, *The Origins of Alchemy in Graeco-Roman Egypt* (London: Frederick Muller, 1970), 16.

37 "externalized soul": Cohen, *Human Robots*, 43, 53.

37–38 Kenneth Gross, "Love among the Puppets," *Raritan* (Summer 1997): 71.

38 "divorced from nature": Horst Bredekamp, *The Lure of Antiquity and the Cult of the Machine: The Kunstkammer and the Evolution of Nature, Art and Technology*, trans. Allison Brown (Princeton: Markus Wiener, 1995), 11.

38 Maurizio Bettini, *The Portrait of the Lover*, trans. Laura Gibbs (Berkeley: University of California Press, 1999), 221.

38 "The wooden doll": For a complete description of this tomb and its contents, see *Crepereia Tryphaena: Le scoperte archeologiche nell'area del Palazzo di Guistizia* (Venice: Marsilio Editori, 1983).

38 "Not only could"; "every ritual action": Jeremy Naydler, *Temple of the Cosmos: The Ancient Egyptian Experience of the Sacred* (Rochester, Vt.: Inner Traditions, 1996), 135–137.

39 "mysteries of theurgy"; "Porphyry": Brian Copenhaver, "Hermes Trismegistus, Proclus, and the Question of a Philosophy of Magic," in Merkel and Debus, eds., *Hermeticism and the Renaissance*, 80.

39 "luminous disk": Hans Lewy quoted in Couliano, *Out of This World*, 145. See also Lewy, *Chaldean Oracles and Theurgy: Mysticism, Magic and Platonism in the Later Roman Empire* (Cairo: Institut Français d'Archéologie Orientale, 1956), 196.

40 "soul-stuff"; "the ingredient of": Quoted in Fowden, *Egyptian Hermes*, 118.

40 This and further passages from *Asclepius*, in Copenhaver, ed., *Hermetica*, 92, 90.

41 Poulsen, "Talking, Weeping and Bleeding Sculptures," 182–183.

41 Damascius quoted in Edwyn Bevan, *Holy Images: An Inquiry into Idolatry and Image Worship in Ancient Paganism and Christianity* (London: Allen and Unwin, 1940), 34.

41–42 J. G. Landels, *Engineering in the Ancient World* (London: Chatto and Windus, 1978), 203. Hero's practical texts were the *Pneumatica* and the *Automatopoietike*.

42 *"neurospastes"*: Max von Boehn, *Puppets and Automata*, trans. Josephine Nicoll (New York: Dover, 1972), 49.

42 Plato, *The Laws*, trans. Thomas L. Pangle (New York: Basic Books, 1988), book I, 644d-645c.

42 Tertullian quoted in Hans R. Purschke, *Die Entwicklung des Puppenspiels in den klassischen Ursprungslandern Europas: Ein historischer Überblick* (Frankfurt: s.p., 1984), 12.

42 Synesius of Cyrene quoted in Purschke, *Entwicklung des Puppenspiels*, 13.

43 "routinely mutilated": Weynants-Ronday, *Statues vivantes*, 110.

43 Kenneth Gross, *The Dream of the Moving Statue* (Ithaca: Cornell University Press, 1992), 45.

43 "idolatry practiced": Quoted in Frank R. Trombley, *Hellenic Religion and Christianization c. 370–529*, vol. 2 (London: E. J. Brill, 1993), 13–14.

3. THE PUPPET TRACTATES

46 Ben Jonson, *Bartholomew Fair*, ed. Gordon Campbell, in *The Alchemist and Other Plays* (Oxford: Oxford University Press, 1995), 5.5.45–64.

47 "a popular story": Cyrus Hamlin, ed., *Faust: A Tragedy*, trans. Walter Arndt (New York: Norton, 1976), 387. The Faustus story was also popular in eighteenth-century English puppet shows, though it had mostly died out by 1800. Robert Leach, *The Punch and Judy Show: History, Tradition and Meaning* (Athens: University of Georgia Press, 1985), 163.

48–49 "Pulcinella"; "Punch": Max von Boehn, *Dolls and Puppets*, trans. Josephine Nicoll (Philadelphia: David McKay, n.d.), 306–307; see also Michael Byrom, *Punch in the Italian Puppet Theatre* (Fontwell, Sussex: Centaur, 1983), 9.

49 "motion-men": In *Gammer Gurton's Needle* (1517) a character says he will go "and travel with young goose, the motion-man, for a puppet player." Quoted in Joseph Strutt, *Sports and Pastimes of the People of England* (London: T. Bensley, 1810), 150n.

49 Michael Camille, *The Gothic Idol: Ideology and Image-Making in Medieval Art* (Cambridge: Cambridge University Press, 1989), 249–250.

49 "talking head": Lieslotte Sauer, *Marionetten, Maschinen, Automaten: Der künstliche Mensch in der deutschen und englischen Romantik* (Bonn: Bouvier Verlag, 1983), 14.

49 "gods on strings": George Speaight, *The History of the English Puppet Theatre*, 2nd ed. (Carbondale: Southern Illinois Press, 1990), 54.

49 "a crucifix in Boxley": Strutt, *Sports and Pastimes*, 144.

49 "to enact the Passion": Leach, *Punch and Judy Show*, 18.

49–50 "the factitious gods": Quoted in Camille, *Gothic Idol*, 256.

50 "until the twelfth century": Camille, *Gothic Idol*, 36.

50 Boehn, *Dolls and Puppets*, 71–72. Noting the ancient and pre-Christian lineage of this custom, Boehn says: "superstition, seizing its opportunity, here clad itself in its richest raiment" (71).

50 *The New Atlantis* described in Horst Bredekamp, *The Lure of Antiquity and the Cult of the Machine: The Kunstkammer and the Evolution of Na-*

ture, Art, and Technology, trans. Allison Brown (Princeton: Markus Wiener, 1995), 61.

50 "were viewed as": Bredekamp, *Lure of Antiquity*, 49.

51 Ronald Gray, *Goethe, the Alchemist: A Study of Alchemical Symbolism in Goethe's Literary and Scientific Works* (Cambridge: Cambridge University Press, 1952), 202.

51 Moshe Idel, "The Golem in Jewish Magic and Mysticism," in Emily D. Bilski, ed., *Golem! Danger, Deliverance and Art* (New York: Jewish Museum, 1988), 11–18. See also Idel, *Golem: Jewish Magical and Mystical Traditions on the Artificial Anthropoid* (Albany: State University of New York Press, 1990), 233.

51–52 "the real creation": Idel, "Golem in Jewish Magic and Mysticism," 25.

52 "Alemanno": Moshe Idel, "Hermeticism and Judaism," in Ingrid Merkel and Allen G. Debus, eds., *Hermeticism and the Renaissance: Intellectual History and the Occult in Early Modern Europe* (Washington: Folger Shakespeare Library, 1988), 69–70.

52 "God's golem": Gershom Scholem, *On the Kabbalah and Its Symbolism*, trans. Ralph Manheim (New York: Schocken, 1969), 161–164.

52 Grimm quoted in Scholem, *On the Kabbalah*, 159.

53 "*mumia*": Roland Pecout, *Les mangeurs de momies: Des tombeaux d'Égypte aux sorciers d'Europe* (Paris: P. Belfond, 1981), 75.

53 "mysticall Mummies": Quoted in C. G. Jung, *Mysterium Coniunctionis: An Inquiry into the Separation and Synthesis of Psychic Opposites in Alchemy*, trans. R. F. C. Hull, 2nd ed. (Princeton: Princeton University Press, 1970), 213–214.

53–54 D. P. Walker, *The Ancient Theology: Studies in Christian Platonism from the Fifteenth through the Eighteenth Centuries* (Ithaca: Cornell University Press, 1972), 12.

54 Ficino, *De vita coelitus comparanda*, quoted in Ioan Couliano, *Eros and Magic in the Renaissance*, trans. Margaret Cook (Chicago: University of Chicago Press, 1987), 117.

54 Tommaso Campanella, epilogue to *De sensu rerum et magia*, quoted in D. P. Walker, *Spiritual and Demonic Magic: From Ficino to Campanella* (Notre Dame: University of Notre Dame Press, 1975), 119.

54–55 Johann Daniel Mylius quoted in Jung, *Mysterium Coniunctionis*, 394.

55 Bruno quoted in Karen Silvia de León-Jones, *Giordano Bruno and the Kabbalah: Prophets, Magicians, and Rabbis* (New Haven: Yale University Press, 1997), 78.

55 "that philosophers are also": Bruno, *Segillus sigillorum*, quoted in Couliano, *Eros and Magic*, 65–66.

55 Achim von Arnim quoted in Hans Meyer, "*Faust*, Enlightenment, *Sturm und Drang*," in Hamlin, *Faust*, 476.

55 William Blake, "There Is No Natural Religion," in David V. Erdman, ed., *The Poetry and Prose of William Blake* (Garden City, N.Y.: Doubleday, 1965), 3. Blake refigures the Divine Human as follows:

"The desire of Men being Infinite the possession is Infinite and himself Infinite."

56 Perkins quoted in Couliano, *Eros and Magic*, 63.

56 Keith Thomas, *Religion and the Decline of Magic* (New York: Scribner's, 1971), 90.

56–57 John C. Briggs, *Francis Bacon and the Rhetoric of Nature* (Cambridge, Mass.: Harvard University Press, 1989), 90.

57 Thomas, *Religion and the Decline of Magic*, 75.

57 Terry Castle, *The Female Thermometer: Eighteenth Century Culture and the Invention of the Uncanny* (New York: Oxford University Press, 1995), 142.

57 "researchers like William Harvey": D. P. Walker, "The Astral Body in Renaissance Medicine," in Penelope Gorik, ed., *Music, Spirit and Language in the Renaissance* (London: Variorum Reprints, 1982), 13. Harvey, says Walker, believed that "blood fashions the embryo, takes in the divine and celestial nature of the spirit."

58 "Since man had been" to "mechanics was": Bredekamp, *Lure of Antiquity*, 37, 46, 80, 86.

58–59 C. S. Lewis, *The Allegory of Love: A Study in Medieval Tradition* (New York: Oxford University Press, 1958), 82, 83.

60–61 "undermines the stability"; "encounters among souls": Tullio Maranhao, introduction, in Maranhao, ed. *The Interpretation of Dialogue* (Chicago: University of Chicago Press, 1990), 3.

61 "Platonic and Hermetic dialogues": Rudolph Drux, *Marionette Mensch: Ein Metaphernkomplex und sein Kontext von Hoffmann bis Büchner* (Munich: Wilhelm Fink Verlag, 1986), 181. See also Paul de Man, "Aesthetic Formalization: Kleist's *Über das Marionettetheater*," in *The Rhetoric of Romanticism* (New York: Columbia University Press, 1984), 263–290. De Man comments that Kleist's essay "belongs among the texts of the period which our own modernity has not yet been able to confront" (266).

61 T. E. Hulme quoted in M. H. Abrams, *Natural Supernaturalism: Tradition and Revolution in Romantic Literature* (New York: Norton, 1971), 68.

61 "Zoroaster's Prayer": See Joachim Maass, *Kleist: A Biography*, trans. Ralph Manheim (New York: Farrar, Straus and Giroux, 1983), 221.

62 All quoted passages from Heinrich von Kleist, "On the Marionette Theater," trans. Christian-Albrecht Gollub, in A. Leslie Willson, ed., *German Romantic Criticism*, German Library, vol. 21 (New York: Continuum, 1982), 238–244.

64 Sherry Turkle, "Virtual Pets and Virtual Dolls," lecture, University of California at Berkeley, Feb. 18, 1999.

64 René Descartes, *Discourse on Method*, in *Discourse on Method and Related Writings*, trans. Desmond M. Clarke (Harmondsworth: Penguin, 1999), 40. Descartes also declared that animals are automata because mind cannot act on their bodies.

65 Cohen, *Human Robots*, 43.

65 "disagreeably perfect": E. T. A. Hoffmann, "The Sandman," trans. J. T. Bealby, in E. F. Bleiler, ed., *The Best Tales of Hoffmann* (New York: Dover, 1967). All quoted passages of Hoffmann stories are from this edition.

66 Ernst Jentsch quoted in Sigmund Freud, "The 'Uncanny,'" in James Strachey, ed. and trans., *Complete Psychological Works of Sigmund Freud*, vol. 17 (London: Hogarth Press and Institute of Psychoanalysis, 1917–1919), 227.

66–67 "Metallic Medium": Brenda Maddox, *Yeats's Ghosts: The Secret Life of W. B. Yeats* (New York: HarperCollins, 2000), 4.

67 Giacomo Leopardi, *Dialogo di Federico Ruysch e delle sue mummie*/"Dialogue between Frederick Ruysch and His Mummies," in *Operette morali/Essays and Dialogues*, ed. and trans. Giovanni Cecchetti (Berkeley: University of California Press, 1982). All quoted passages are from this edition.

67 *"tableaux morts":* For a detailed description, see Lawrence Weschler, *Mr. Wilson's Cabinet of Wonders: Pronged Ants, Horned Humans, Mice on Toast, and Other Marvels of Jurassic Technology* (New York: Vintage, 1995), 85–88.

67 "public censors": See Rosamond Wolff and Stephen Jay Gould, *Finders, Keepers: Eight Collectors* (New York: Norton, 1992), 31, on modern censorship of Ruysch's creations.

68 See also Edgar Allan Poe, "Some Words with a Mummy," in Poe, *Poetry and Tales* (New York: Library of America, 1984), 805–821; Poe's garrulous mummy, "Allamistakeo," narrates a tale of a very ancient premature burial.

69 Rainer Maria Rilke, "Doll: On the Wax Dolls of Lotte Pritzel," trans. Idris Parry (London: Syrens, 1994). All quoted passages are from this edition.

69 All quoted passages from Rainer Maria Rilke, fourth Duino elegy, trans. Harold Segel, in *Pinocchio's Progeny: Puppets, Marionettes, Automatons, and Robots in Modernist and Avant-Garde Drama* (Baltimore: Johns Hopkins University Press, 1995), 45.

69–70 Segel, *Pinocchio's Progeny*, 45.

70 Louis Sass, *Madness and Modernism: Insanity in the Light of Modern Art, Literature, and Thought* (New York: Basic Books, 1992), 342–343.

70–71 "Have you heard"; "Weep, ladies": Bruno Schulz, "Tailors' Dummies: Continuation," in Schulz, *The Street of Crocodiles*, trans. Celina Wieniewska (Harmondsworth: Penguin, 1977), 65, 64. All quoted passages from the four stories composing "Tailors' Dummies" are from this edition.

71 "Tailors' Dummies," "Treatise on Tailors' Dummies, or the Second Book of Genesis," "Tailors' Dummies: Continuation," and "Treatise on Tailors' Dummies: Conclusion," *Street of Crocodiles*, 51–76.

72 *The Book of Idolatry*, in Jerzy Ficowski, ed., *The Drawings of Bruno Schulz* (Evanston: Northwestern University Press, 1990), 47–115.

4. THE STRANGE HISTORY OF THE AMERICAN FANTASTIC

74 Maurice Lévy, *Lovecraft: A Study in the Fantastic*, trans. S. T. Joshi (Detroit: Wayne State University Press, 1988), 13.

74 Paul Bray, "Tone in Ashbery," *Annals of Scholarship*, in press.

76 Tristram Potter Coffin, *The British Traditional Ballad in North America*, supp. by Roger DeV. Renwick (Austin: University of Texas Press, 1977), 2.

76 David S. Reynolds, *Beneath the American Renaissance: The Subversive Imagination in the Age of Emerson and Melville* (Cambridge, Mass.: Harvard University Press, 1989), 5.

76 Walt Whitman quoted in Reynolds, *Beneath the American Renaissance*, 16.

76–77 Robert Fogel, *The Fourth Great Awakening and the Future of Egalitarianism* (Chicago: University of Chicago Press, 2000).

77 Harold Bloom, *The American Religion: The Emergence of the Post-Christian Nation* (New York: Simon and Schuster, 1992).

77 John L. Brooke, *The Refiner's Fire: The Making of Mormon Cosmology, 1644–1844* (Cambridge: Cambridge University Press, 1995).

77 Bloom, *American Religion*, 100.

77 "American Constitution": See Michael Kammen, *A Machine That Would Go of Itself: The Constitution in American Culture* (New York: Knopf, 1986). I am indebted to Martin Procházka for making this connection.

77 "outward innocence": Reynolds, *Beneath the American Renaissance*, 91.

79 Jules Feiffer, "The Minsk Theory of Krypton," *New York Times Magazine*, Dec. 29, 1996, www.nytimes.com.

80 "abduction by spirits": Bill Ellis, "'I Wonder, Wonder, Mother': Death and the Angels in Native American Balladry," *Western Folklore* 38, no. 3 (July 1979): 170–171. I am indebted to John Niles for supplying this source.

81 Isaac Bashevis Singer, "The Last Demon," in *The Collected Stories of Isaac Bashevis Singer* (New York: Farrar, Straus and Giroux, 1983), 179–187. This connection was made by Cynthia Ozick in "I. B. Singer's Book of Creation" in *Art and Ardor* (New York: Knopf, 1983).

84 Walter Benjamin, "On Some Motifs in Baudelaire," in Hannah Arendt, ed., *Illuminations: Essays and Reflections*, trans. Harry Zohn (New York: Schocken, 1969), 166.

85 "printed in Poland": Jakob Schulz, personal communication, 1988.

85–86 Cynthia Ozick, "The Phantasmagoria of Bruno Schulz," in *Art and Ardor*, 226.

86 Arthur Clayborough, *The Grotesque in English Literature* (New York: Oxford University Press, 1965), 3.

86–87 Michel Foucault, *Death and the Labyrinth: The World of Raymond Roussel*, trans. Charles Ruas (New York: Doubleday, 1986), 79.

87 John Updike, introduction, in *Sanatorium under the Sign of the Hourglass* (Harmondsworth: Penguin, 1979), xvi. See Moshe Idel's judgment on

Schulz: "Modern man, alienated from the Divine, is afraid of the theological complications of his creative powers." Idel, "The Golem in Jewish Magic and Mysticism," in Emily D. Bilski, ed., *Golem! Danger, Deliverance and Art* (New York: Jewish Museum, 1988), 15.

89 "It might be my way": Philip Roth, *The Breast* (New York: Holt, Rinehart and Winston, 1972), 72.

90 "unfinished-looking creature": Ozick was doubtless aware of the ancient tradition of referring to an unmarried woman as a golem or an imperfect being. See Moshe Idel, *Golem: Jewish Magical and Mystical Traditions on the Artificial Anthropoid* (Albany: State University of New York Press, 1990), 233.

90 "was no mystic": All quoted passages from Cynthia Ozick, "Puttermesser and Xanthippe," in *The Puttermesser Papers* (New York: Knopf, 1997), 23–101.

91–92 All quoted passages from Cynthia Ozick, *The Messiah of Stockholm* (New York: Vintage Books, 1988).

93 "the chief characteristic": Cynthia Ozick, "Literature as Idol: Harold Bloom," in *Art and Ardor,* 189–190.

93 "Ha-Shem": I am indebted to the keen ear and encyclopedic knowledge of Martin Schwartz for this interpretation.

94 "What is being invented": Ozick, "Phantasmagoria of Bruno Schulz," in *Art and Ardor,* 227.

94 Bruno Schulz, "The Mythologizing of Reality," in *Letters, Drawings and Selected Prose of Bruno Schulz,* trans. Walter Arndt with Victoria Nelson (New York: Harper and Row, 1988), 116–117.

94 "Three letters": Ozick, "Puttermesser: Her Work History, Her Ancestry, Her Afterlife," in *Puttermesser Papers,* 5.

97–98 Doris Lessing, "Fantastic and Realistic Literature," lecture given April 5, 1984, to a packed hall of more than 5,000 people in the Marin County Civic Auditorium, San Rafael, California.

5. H. P. LOVECRAFT AND THE GREAT HERESIES

102 "heir of Hawthorne, Melville, and Poe": Peter Cannon, *H. P. Lovecraft* (Boston: Twayne, 1989), 125.

102 Biographical data from S. T. Joshi, *H. P. Lovecraft: A Life* (West Warwick, R.I.: Necronomicon Press, 1996); Cannon, *Lovecraft,* xiii–xv; Kenneth W. Faig Jr. and S. T. Joshi, "H. P. Lovecraft: His Life and Work," in S. T. Joshi, ed., *H. P. Lovecraft: Four Decades of Criticism* (Athens: Ohio University Press, 1980); Winfield Townley Scott, "His Own Most Fantastic Creation: Howard Phillips Lovecraft," in *Exiles and Fabrications* (Garden City, N.Y.: Doubleday, 1961), 50–72; and "The Parents of Howard Phillips Lovecraft," in David E. Schultz and S. T. Joshi, eds., *An Epicure in the Terrible: A Centennial Anthology of Essays in Honor of H. P. Lovecraft* (London: Associated University Presses, 1991). An early biography by L. Sprague de Camp, *Lovecraft: A Biogra-*

phy (New York: Ballantine, 1975), has been supplanted by the various articles cited here.

102 "other people's manuscripts": Faig and Joshi, "Life and Work," 14; H. P. Lovecraft, *Selected Letters,* ed. August Derleth and Donald Wandrei (Sauk City, Wis.: Arkham House, 1971), xxi.

103 Edmund Wilson, "Tales of the Marvellous and Ridiculous," *New Yorker,* Nov. 25, 1945, rpt. in Joshi, ed., *Four Decades,* 47.

103 "surge of critical interest": See, e.g., Cannon, *Lovecraft;* Joshi, ed., *Four Decades;* Joshi, *The Weird Tale* (Austin: University of Texas Press, 1990); Schultz and Joshi, eds., *Epicure;* Maurice Lévy, *Lovecraft: A Study in the Fantastic,* trans. S. T. Joshi (Detroit: Wayne State University Press, 1988); Donald R. Burleson, *Lovecraft: Disturbing the Universe* (Lexington: University of Kentucky Press, 1990); Noel Carroll, *The Philosophy of Horror* (New York: Routledge, 1991); and numerous volumes of extracts of his writings compiled by the leading Lovecraft scholar, S. T. Joshi. Lovecraft's literary disciples have been as diverse as the novelist-essayist Colin Wilson and the poet James Schevill, the pop surrealist artist-sculptor H. I. Giger, who opened a Necronomicon Bar in his home village in Switzerland, and the Satanist Anton LaVey, whose Satanic Bible reportedly contains a prayer to Cthulhu. Neal Stephenson's sprawling novel *Cryptonomicon* (1999) incorporates an indirect homage in its title.

103 "god of Fiction": Lovecraft to Reinhardt Kleiner, Feb. 2, 1916, *Selected Letters,* 20.

103 "the Aesthetic tradition": Barton Levi St. Armand, "Synchronistic Worlds: Lovecraft and Borges," in Schultz and Joshi, eds., *Epicure,* 308–309. St. Armand labels Lovecraft and Jorge Luis Borges as children of the 1890s Aesthetics movement, but Schulz can easily be substituted for Borges.

103 "Supernatural Horror in Fiction," in *Dagon and Other Macabre Tales* (Sauk City, Wis.: Arkham House, 1987), 365–436. All citations will be from the Arkham House edition of Lovecraft's works, cited by volume title.

104 "These early images": Schulz, "An Essay for S. I. Witkiewicz," in *Letters and Drawings of Bruno Schulz with Selected Prose,* trans. Walter Arndt with Victoria Nelson (New York: Harper and Row, 1988), 111.

104 "I began to have": Letter to Reinhardt Kleiner, Nov. 16, 1916, *Selected Letters,* 35.

105 *"Necronomicon"*: Others were "the Comte d'Erlette's *Cultes des Ghouls,*" "von Juntz's *Unaussprechlichen Kulten,*" and so forth, all constructed from word plays on the names of various friends. Lovecraft's invented references were so convincing that American libraries for the past fifty years have been besieged with requests for the *Necronomicon* and the other works. Lovecraft fans use these devices as in-jokes: his principal publisher is now "Necronomicon Press," succeeding "Arkham House"; books of memorabilia are issued under the imprint of "Miskatonic

University"; faithfully reconstructed picture books of the "indescribable" monsters have appeared; mock-learned scholarly studies of archaeology, linguistics, and natural science deal with the monsters and their elusive history of contacts with the human race; and various pastiche volumes have been published bearing the title *Necronomicon.*

106 "was mostly a kind of force": "The Dunwich Horror," in *The Dunwich Horror and Others* (Sauk City, Wis.: Arkham House, 1984), 198. Note the parallel to the widespread Gnostic story of Sophia, the lowest aeon, giving birth to a formless entity that fails to survive, her sin being to bring forth a likeness of herself without divine authority. See Giovanni Filoramo, *A History of Gnosticism,* trans. Anthony Alcock (Oxford: Basil Blackwell, 1990), 71.

106 Nerval quoted in Phyllis Jane Winston, *Nerval's Magic Alphabet* (New York: Peter Love, 1989), 81.

107 "Debora Vogel": Jerzy Ficowski, introduction, in Bruno Schulz, *The Street of Crocodiles,* trans. Celina Wieniewska (Harmondsworth: Penguin, 1977), 15; Faig and Joshi, "Life and Work," 13.

107 Heinrich von Kleist, "Über die allmahliche Verfertigung der Gedanken beim Reden," *Samtliche Werke und Briefe,* vol. 2 (Munich: Carl Hanser, 1961), 319–324.

107 "tertiary syphilis": The medical diagnosis was syphilis-associated "general paresis." Lovecraft wrote: "In April, 1893, my father was stricken with a complete paralysis resulting from a brain overtaxed with study and business cares. He lived for five years at a hospital, but was never again able to move hand or foot, or to utter a sound." Letter to Kleiner, Nov. 16, 1916, *Selected Letters,* 33. The elder Lovecraft's medical record, reproduced in *Lovecraft Studies* 24 (Spring 1991): 15, notes that in April 1893 "he broke down completely while stopping in Chicago. He rushed from his room shouting that a chambermaid had insulted him, and that certain men were outraging his wife in the room above." Winfield Scott Lovecraft was admitted to Butler Hospital in Providence; the convulsions he experienced there shortly before the end of his life "are also certain proof that WSL did not simply have manic-depression or schizophrenia. [He] almost certainly died of syphilis." M. Eileen McNamara, M.D., "Winfield Scott Lovecraft's Final Illness," ibid., 14.

107 "a paranoid psychosis": The psychiatric records of Lovecraft's excessively protective mother, Susie (who was also committed to, and died in, Butler Hospital), note a longstanding "traumatic psychosis" and even "psycho-sexual contact" with her son. See Scott, "His Own Most Fantastic Creation," 56–60. She was known to have been obsessed with her son's "hideous" appearance, a delusion she frequently communicated to him, and which he believed; a neighbor quoted her as speaking "about weird and fantastic creatures that rushed out from behind buildings and from corners at dark"; the last time the neighbor saw her, on a streetcar, "she was excited and apparently did not know where she

was." Kenneth W. Faig Jr., "The Parents of Howard Phillips Lovecraft," in Schultz and Joshi, eds., *Epicure*, 69.

107 "his actual father, Jakub": Schulz's father was the owner of a cloth goods shop who retreated to a sequestered life at home for the last ten years of his life. Though the term has been widely supplanted by its former first cousin "bipolar disorder" or manic depression, I follow the fourth revised edition of the *Diagnostic and Statistical Manual of Mental Disorders* (Washington: American Psychiatric Association, 1994) in using "schizophrenia" to refer to that highly distinct type of mental illness which displays such recurring features as thought disorder, concretization of language, visual and auditory hallucinations, and occasionally paranoia.

107–108 "two people going": Quoted in *Letters of C. G. Jung*, vol. 2, ed. Gerhard Adler with Aniela Jaffe, trans. R. F. C. Hull (Princeton: Princeton University Press, 1975), Bollingen series 95:2, 266n.

108 Theophile Gautier quoted in Richard Holmes, *Footsteps: Adventures of a Romantic Biographer* (Harmondsworth: Penguin, 1985), 263.

108 Schreber, *Memoirs of My Nervous Illness.* All quoted passages from the English-language edition, trans. and ed. Ida MacAlpine and Richard A. Hunter (Cambridge, Mass.: Harvard University Press, 1984).

108 Sigmund Freud, "Psycho-Analytic Notes upon an Autobiographical Account of a Case of Paranoia (Dementia Paranoides)," *Collected Papers*, vol. 3, trans. Alix and James Strachey (New York: Basic Books, 1959), 387–470.

108 "theoretical perspectives": See Phyllis Grosskurth, "Freud's Favorite Paranoiac," *New York Review of Books*, Jan. 18, 1990, 36–38; and the summary given in Rosemary Dinnage, "Grand Delusion," *New York Review of Books*, March 3, 1994, 17–19. Louis Sass, in *Madness and Modernism: Insanity in the Light of Modern Art, Literature, and Thought* (New York: Basic Books, 1992), proposes that the schizophrenic experience is exaggeratedly "Apollonian and Socratic" rather than "primitive" and Dionysian, as traditional psychiatry describes it, and that it is "characterized less by fusion, spontaneity and the liberation of desire than by separation, restraint and an exaggerated cerebralism and propensity for introspection." Sass argues that the "primitivist" regression model is a "modern and developmental version of the Great Chain of Being" that wrongly puts schizophrenia at the lowest stage of a nonexistent hierarchy. See also Sass, *The Paradoxes of Delusion: Wittgenstein, Schreber, and the Schizophrenic Mind* (Ithaca: Cornell University Press, 1994).

109 "not composed altogether": "The Call of Cthulhu," in *Dunwich Horror*, 140.

109 *"non-human creatures"*: "The Whisperer in Darkness," in *Dunwich Horror*, 217.

109–110 "breakdown": In the absence of any explicit statements by Lovecraft about the nature of this episode, it appears that withdrawing from school and from the outside world may have been a longstanding pattern of his, upheld by his female relatives, who seem to have reinforced his sense of himself as a delicate invalid.

110 "autobiography"; "spiritual genealogy": Schulz, "Essay for Witkiewicz," 114.

110 "dynamic of externalization": The observation that schizophrenia involves a confusion between subject and object, internal and external, dates to Freud's notion of a *Real-Ich* whose function of distinguishing between internal and external becomes impaired; the presence of this dynamic is generally upheld in the clinical literature. See, e.g., Bent Rosenbaum and Harly Sonne, *The Language of Psychosis* (New York: New York University Press, 1980), 43.

110 "No wall however thick": *Memoirs of My Nervous Illness*, 242.

110–111 *"psychotopography"*: Analogously, Gaston Bachelard, in *The Poetics of Space*, trans. Maria Jolas (New York: Orion, 1964), 8, has formulated a discipline he calls *topoanalysis*, or the "systematic psychological study of the sites of our intimate lives."

111 "the environment": Paul Haderman, "Expressionist Literature and Painting," in Ulrich Weisstein, ed., *Expressionism as an International Literary Phenomenon* (Paris: Didier, 1973), 127.

111 Philip Otto Runge quoted in Wolfgang Kayser, *The Grotesque in Art and Literature*, trans. Ulrich Weisstein (New York: Columbia University Press, 1981), 37.

111 "be transformed": Giovanni Filoramo, *A History of Gnosticism*, trans. Anthony Alcock (Oxford: Basil Blackwell, 1990), 41, xv.

112 Schulz, "Father's Last Escape," in *Sanatorium under the Sign of the Hourglass* (Harmondsworth: Penguin, 1979), 174.

112 "man's house": Schulz, "Autumn," in *Letters and Drawings*, 225.

112 "does not tally": *Memoirs of My Nervous Illness*, 86.

112 "The Rats in the Walls," in *Dunwich Horror*, 27.

113 "It was as though": *Memoirs of My Nervous Illness*, 86.

113 "Here at the very bottom": Schulz, "Mythologizing of Reality," in *Letters and Drawings*, 43. "Mothers" refers to Faust's famous cry in Goethe's *Faust*, part II: "The mothers! The Mothers! How eerily it sounds."

113 "merges into mythology": Schulz, "Essay for Witkiewicz," 114.

114 Mikhail Bakhtin, *Rabelais and His World*, trans. Helene Iswolsky (Bloomington: Indiana University Press, 1984), 37n. Bakhtin has commented extensively on the characteristic downward movement to debasement in the grotesque. In the Bakhtinian perspective, the character of Wilbur in "The Dunwich Horror" is a latter-day Pantagruel, in whose body—in strictest terms of Renaissance natural philosophy—all the forces of the cosmos are drawn.

114 Tobin Siebers, *The Romantic Fantastic* (Ithaca: Cornell University Press, 1984), 85.

114 "Shape does not": Schulz, "Essay for Witkiewicz," 113. Compare Giordano Bruno, to whom "the universe without the world's soul, cor-

poreal substance without incorporeal substance, are inconceivable. The only thing that changes is accidental form, external and material, whereas matter itself and substantial form, the soul, are indissoluble and indestructible . . . Matter in its unity, like the Platonic *chora*, is only perceptible intellectually." Quoted in Ioan Couliano, *Eros and Magic in the Renaissance*, trans. Margaret Cook (Chicago: University of Chicago Press, 1987), 79.

115 "a species of beings": Schulz, "Treatise on Tailor's Dummies: Conclusion," in *The Street of Crocodiles*, trans. Celina Wieniewska (Harmondsworth: Penguin, 1977), 66.

115 "formless protoplasm": *At the Mountains of Madness*, in *At the Mountains of Madness and Other Novels* (Sauk City, Wis.: Arkham House, 1985), 95. The title of this story suggests a duality of meaning: that these mountains *produce* madness in explorers who penetrate their secrets and that this site is the physical representation *of* madness.

115 "sticky, green spawn": "Call of Cthulhu," 152.

115–116 "For years": Schreber, *Memoirs of My Nervous Illness*, 185.

116 Carlo Ginzburg, *Ecstasies: Deciphering the Witches' Sabbath*, trans. Raymond Rosenthal (New York: Pantheon, 1991), 241–247.

116 Henri Bergson quoted in Siebers, *Romantic Fantastic*, 82.

116–117 "Above the waist": "Dunwich Horror," 174–175.

117 "medical textbooks": I am indebted to Herbert Schreier, M.D., for suggesting the connection between Lovecraft's monsters and the deformities of syphilis; and to Guy Micco, M.D., for providing me with a number of period medical textbooks containing these illustrations, notably D'Arcy Power and J. Keogh Murphy, eds., *A System of Syphilis*, 6 vols. (London: Hodder and Stoughton, 1910).

117 "monstrous fusion": Kayser, *Grotesque*, 37.

118 "a complete paralysis": Lovecraft, *Selected Letters*, vol. 1, 33.

119 "God is incapable": *Memoirs of My Nervous Illness*, 188.

119 Walter Benjamin, "On Language as Such and the Language of Man," in *Reflections: Essays, Aphorisms, Autobiographical Writings*, trans. Edmund Jephcott (New York: Harcourt Brace Jovanovich, 1978), 317.

119 "a name concretely *is*": Steven Katz, "Mystical Speech and Mystical Meaning," in Katz, ed., *Mysticism and Language* (New York: Oxford University Press, 1992), 25; Gershom Scholem, *On the Kabbalah and Its Symbolism*, trans. Ralph Manheim (New York: Schocken, 1969), 35. Also see Moshe Idel, "Reification of Language in Jewish Mysticism," in Katz, ed., *Mysticism and Language*, 44.

119–120 "Jakob Boehme": See Steven Konopacki, *The Descent into Words: Jakob Boehme's Transcendental Linguistics*, Linguistica Extranea Studia 7 (Ann Arbor: Karoma, 1979); Ingrid Merkel, "*Aurora;* or The Rising Sun of Allegory: Hermetic Imagery in the Work of Jakob Boehme," in Ingrid Merkel and Allen G. Debus, eds., *Hermeticism and the Renaissance: Intellectual History and the Occult in Early Modern Europe* (Washington: Folger Shakespeare Library, 1988), 306; Wolfgang Kayser, "Böhmes Natursprachenlehre under ihre Grundlagen," *Euphorion*, vol. 31 (1930;

Nendeln, Liechtenstein: Kraus Reprint, 1967), 521–563. Barton Levi St. Armand, in "Synchronistic Worlds," 307, points to Lovecraft's use, in "The Haunter in the Dark," of a triangle containing a lidless eye (the "three-lobed burning eye") as a figure from Boehme's *Aurora.*

120 "breakdown in analogical thinking": See, e.g., Sherry Rochester and J. R. Martin, *Crazy Talk: A Study of the Discourse of Schizophrenia* (New York: Plenum, 1979); Rosenbaum and Sonne, *Language of Psychosis.*

120 "A rolling stone": As an outside observer, I witnessed a year's worth of resident diagnostic training at Napa State Mental Hospital in which the presence of the concrete thinking characteristic of schizophrenia (as distinct from the generally incoherent "word salad" characteristic of manic depression and generalized psychotic disorder) was assessed by asking the patients to explain the proverb "A rolling stone gathers no moss." Answers that did not address the figurative meaning were considered indicators of schizophrenia. An outpatient who asked me, "Will you join me in a cup of coffee?" laughed uproariously when I answered, "Thanks, but the two of us wouldn't fit." Louis Sass, noting the Modernist move toward a private inner language characteristic of schizophrenia, argues that schizophrenics are "overly abstract as well as overly concrete"; *Madness and Modernism,* 125, 184.

120 "I am exposed": *Memoirs of My Nervous Illness,* 49.

120 Michel Foucault, *Death and the Labyrinth: The World of Raymond Roussel,* trans. Charles Ruas (New York: Doubleday, 1986), 163.

121 "destroys the rays": See MacAlpine and Hunter, introduction, in *Memoirs of My Nervous Illness,* xxxvi. Schreber's self-devised tactic resembles one described in a psychiatric study that determined that schizophrenics are much less likely to hear these voices if they hum softly; 59 percent of the patients in the study who hummed a single note experienced a reduction in voices. AP bulletin, quoting Michael Foster Green and Marcel Kinsbourne, *Alcohol, Drug Abuse and Mental Health Administration Newsletter,* May 1991.

121 *"ultima ratio": Memoirs of My Nervous Illness,* 173.

121 "prepositions, adverbs": Nikolai Gogol, "The Overcoat," in *The Overcoat and Other Tales of Good and Evil,* trans. David Magarshack (New York: Norton, 1965), 243.

121 "The primeval word": "Mythologizing of Reality," 115.

122 "my constant talk": "The Unnameable," in *Dagon,* 200–201.

123 "No, no, I tell you": "Rats in the Walls," 44–55. A poignant parallel from the asylum records of Lovecraft's father are the initial diagnostic notes describing his "marked slurring of speech," and repeating entries—"Extremely noisy," "Shouting," "violent," "noisy"—through the years of his inexorable decline. *Lovecraft Studies* 24 (Spring 1991): 15.

123 "The Comet," in *Sanatorium,* 160.

124 "mythically *trismos*": Maurizio Bettini, *Anthropology and Roman Culture: Kinship, Time, Images of the Soul,* trans. John Van Sickle (Baltimore: Johns Hopkins University Press, 1991), 222–223.

124 James Russell, "Seven Armenian and Greek Doctrines on the Seven Vowels," lecture, University of California at Berkeley, Apr. 30, 1993.

125 "The discrepancies": Bruno Schulz, "The Annexation of the Subconscious: Observations on Maria Kuncewicz's *The Foreigner*," in *Letters and Drawings*, 96.

125 Fritz Leiber, "A Literary Copernicus," in Joshi, ed., *Four Decades*, 54.

125 "something fundamental": In a letter to August Derleth, Lovecraft said: "It is my contention that real *weirdness* or imaginative liberation depends on the depiction of something *which does not exist*, or which probably does not exist. If ghosts, Tsathoggian monsters or any sort of a 'supernatural' world *existed*, weird fiction would sink to commonplaceness." *Selected Letters*, vol. 3, 435.

125–126 "From my experience": "Beyond the Wall of Sleep," in *Dagon*, 25–26.

126 *"geometry"*: "Call of Cthulhu," 143.

126 "billowing, stealthily moving clouds": "Sanatorium under the Sign of the Hourglass," in *Sanatorium*, 125.

126 "pre-image": "The Comet," in *Sanatorium*, 155.

127 "a community of actions": Brian Copenhaver, "Hermes Trismegistus, Proclus, and the Question of a Philosophy of Magic," in Merkel and Debus, *Hermeticism and the Renaissance*, 82. The passage quoted is from the tenth hermetic treatise of the second century C.E. Corpus Hermeticum. The Arab philosopher Al-Kindi's *De radii* was the treatise on stellar rays that most influenced medieval and Renaissance astrology and spiritual magic. According to Couliano (*Eros and Magic*, 117, 127), the version of the theory prevalent in the Renaissance postulated that all things in the universe are interconnected by invisible links provided by living rays emanating from the sun.

127 "Ormuzd": Schreber might have drawn his knowledge of Ormuzd and Ariman, the Zoroastrian gods of light and dark, from a variety of translations of the *Avesta* in the major European languages that were available by the 1870s.

127 "God entered into": *Memoirs of My Nervous Illness*, 232.

127 Gérard de Nerval, *Aurélia Followed by Sylvie*, trans. Kendall Lappin (Santa Maria: Asylum Arts, 1993), 84–85. Nerval continues: "Secret voices, warning and exhorting me, came from plants, trees, animals, and the most lowly insects . . . from combinations of pebbles, from shapes in corners, chunks or openings, from the outlines of leaves, colors, sounds and smells, emanated for me hitherto unknown harmonies."

127 "A person with": *Memoirs of My Nervous Illness*, 224.

128 "Gnostic dualist": St. Armand, "Synchronistic Worlds," 318. As creator of the Shining Trapezohedron, Lovecraft has clearly drunk from the same Neoplatonic well as Bruno Schulz.

128 "the most gruesome": *Memoirs of My Nervous Illness*, 79. Much like Lovecraft, Schreber vehemently insists on his status as a nonbeliever.

But he uses it as an argument for the reality of the apparitions: "In my opinion science would go very wrong to designate as 'hallucinations' *all* such phenomena that lack objective reality, and to throw them into the lumber room of things that do not exist; this may possibly be justified in those hallucinations quoted by Kraepelin . . . which are *not* connected with supernatural matters . . . It seems psychologically impossible that *I* suffer only from hallucinations. After all, the hallucination of being in communication with God or departed souls can logically only develop in people who bring with them into their morbidly excited nervous state an already secure faith in God and the immortality of the soul. *This, however, was not so in my case.*" *Memoirs of My Nervous Illness*, 90.

128–129 Otto Rank, "Psychology and the Soul," from *The Belief in the Soul and Psychology*, trans. E. James Liberman and David Edminster, rpt. in *Anais* 10 (1992): 49.

129 "are in reality": Freud, "Psycho-Analytic Notes," 465. Eighty years later, Sass reaffirms this diagnostic framework in *Madness and Modernism:* "Schreber's whole world of nerves and rays virtually demands to be read as a psychological rather than cosmological vision, as a kind of allegory of the divided state of Schreber's own hyperaware, acutely reflexive mind" (258).

129 Siebers, *Romantic Fantastic*, 56.

129 David Williams, "Wilgefortis, Patron Saint of Monsters and the Sacred Language of the Grotesque," in Robert A. Collins and Howard D. Pearce, eds., *The Scope of the Fantastic: Selected Essays from the First International Conference on the Fantastic in the Arts*, Contributions to the Study of Science Fiction and Fantasy, no. 11 (New York: Greenwood, 1987), 174.

129 Bataille quoted in Rosemary Jackson, *Fantasy: The Literature of Subversion* (London: Methuen, 1981). In the fourth edition of the *Diagnostic and Statistical Manual of Mental Disorders*, a new entry entitled "Religious or Spiritual Problem" for the first time legitimizes religious problems "as a category of concern distinct from any mental disorder," reflecting "psychiatry's steady movement away from an earlier tendency to treat religion as a delusion or as evidence of immaturity, escapism or neurosis." Peter Steinfels, "Psychiatrists' Manual Shifts Stance on Religious and Spiritual Problems," *New York Times*, Feb. 10, 1994.

129–130 Lévy, *Lovecraft*, 115.

130 Slavoj Zizek, "The Sublime Object of Ideology," lecture, University of California at Berkeley, Apr. 14, 1991.

130 Kayser, *Grotesque*, 185.

130–131 Idel, *Golem*, xvi.

131 Filoramo, *History of Gnosticism*, 41.

131 "It is absolutely necessary": *At the Mountains of Madness*, 105.

131 "The most merciful": "Call of Cthulhu," 123.

131–132 John Updike, introduction, in *Sanatorium under the Sign of the Hourglass*, xv.

133 W. H. Auden, "The Guilty Vicarage," in *The Dyer's Hand and Other Essays* (New York: Random House, 1962), 158. Acknowledging himself an addict of the detective story, Auden attempts to distinguish between the "magic function" of this genre and genuine works of art: "In [Kafka's] *The Trial* . . . it is the guilt that is certain and the crime that is uncertain; the aim of the hero's investigation is not to prove his innocence (which would be impossible for he knows he is guilty), but to discover what, if anything, he has done to make himself guilty. K, the hero, is, in fact, a portrait of the kind of person who reads detective stories for escape."

134 Lenore Terr, *Too Scared to Cry* (San Francisco: HarperCollins, 1990).

135 G. K. Chesterton, "A Defence of Penny Dreadfuls," in John Gross, ed., *The Oxford Book of Essays* (New York: Oxford University Press, 1992), 372–373.

135 Bakhtin, *Rabelais and His World*, 305.

135–136 Russell Merritt, "Expressionist Fantasy and the Uncanny," lecture, University of California at Berkeley, Sept. 24, 1999.

136 Lévy, *Lovecraft*, 115.

136 Foucault, *Death and the Labyrinth*, 164.

137 S. S. Prawer, *Caligari's Children: The Film as Tale of Terror* (Oxford: Oxford University Press, 1980), 280.

6. SYMMES HOLE, OR THE SOUTH POLAR GROTTO

138 *"Quaesivit":* The source of this Latin tag and its rather free translation is unknown both to me and to staff of the Scott Polar Institute whom I queried.

140 *The Timaeus*, trans. Francis Cornford, *Plato's Cosmology: The Timaeus of Plato* (Indianapolis: Bobbs-Merrill, 1951), 33B–34A, 54–55.

140 Plato, *The Republic*, trans. Francis Cornford (New York: Oxford University Press, 1954), 351.

140 C. G. Jung, *Aion: Researches into the Phenomenology of Self*, trans. R. F. C. Hull, 2nd ed. (Princeton: Princeton University Press, 1979), 246.

140 "astral body": D. P. Walker, "The Neoplatonic Astral Body in Renaissance Medicine," in Penelope Gorik, ed., *Music, Spirit, and Language in the Renaissance* (London: Variorum Reprints, 1985), 121.

140 Joseph Joubert, *Notebooks*, trans. Paul Duster (San Francisco: North Point Press, 1983), 20.

141 *"orbis Terrarum":* This is a point Thomas Burnet would constantly make: *"What the Ancients have said concerning the form and figure of the World, or concerning the Original of it from a Chaos, or about its periods and dissolution, are never to be understood of the Great Universe, but of our Earth, or of this Sublunary and Terrestrial World." The Sacred Theory of the Earth* (Carbondale: Southern Illinois University Press, 1965), II,

ch. 8, 193. Even as he frames it in the language of the Platonic intellectual world, Burnet is expressing the shift of perceived power from the celestial to the elemental world.

141 Robert Fludd quoted in Allen G. Debus, *The Chemical Philosophy: Paracelsian Science and Medicine in the Sixteenth and Seventeenth Centuries* (New York: Science History Publications, 1977), vol. 1, 260.

141 Athanasius Kircher, *Mundus subterraneus*, I, 86, 147–150, 159, quoted in Lynn Thorndike, *A History of Magic and Experimental Science*, vol. 7 (New York: Columbia University Press, 1958), 572.

141 "Christian geology": Ernest Tuveson, *Millennium and Utopia: A Study in the Background of the Idea of Progress* (Berkeley: University of California Press, 1949), 56.

141–142 "Mundane Egg": The Mundane Egg derives from various Pythagorean and Orphic ideas of a cosmic egg, through the medieval Christian Neoplatonic notion, elaborated by Bernard de Silvestris, Hildegarde von Bingen, and others, of the world soul as egg, with the heavens as the shell and Earth as the yolk. See Peter Dronke, *Fabula: Explorations into the Uses of Myth in Medieval Platonism*, Mittellateinische Studien und Texte, vol. 9 (Leiden: E. J. Brill, 1985), 80–97. As applied by the ancients to the shape of the Earth, the oval form had more of a mythic than an exact physical connotation.

143 "pre-Fall soul": This is Burnet's Neoplatonic version of continental drift, which is not so far from our current explanation: "The Continents were made of those three or four primary masses into which the falling Orb of the Earth was divided, but the Islands were made of the fractures of these, and broken off by the fall from the skirts and extremities of the Continents." *Sacred Theory*, I, ch. 10, 108.

143 "we leave [Earth]": *Sacred Theory*, III, 377.

143 Erasmus Darwin, *The Botanic Garden*, 2 vols., ed. Donald H. Reiman (New York: Garland, 1978).

143 "means of internalizing": Ernest Tuveson, *The Avatars of Thrice-Great Hermes: An Approach to Romanticism* (Lewisburg: Bucknell University Press, 1982), 44.

144 "inner topography": As Barbara Nolan has observed: "The invention of a visionary landscape provided the necessary 'places' through which the hero or narrator might move from his earthly life toward his vision of heaven . . . The fictional 'places' were to serve as metaphors for the mental states of the spiritual pilgrim who travels with his eyes closed by day and open by night—open, that is, to the presence of grace made visible to the spiritual or cleansed eye." *The Gothic Visionary Perspective* (Princeton: Princeton University Press, 1977), 145–146.

144 Whitman, "Passage to India," ll. 81–82, 169–174, in *Walt Whitman: The Complete Poems*, ed. Francis Murphy (Harmondsworth: Penguin, 1975).

144 "internalized soul region": As René Daumal would declare in his post-Surrealist quest narrative *Mount Analogue*, a work archetypal to this

genre, "*For a mountain to play the role of Mt. Analogue* . . . its summit must be inaccessible but its base accessible *to human beings as nature has made them.*" Trans. Roger Shattuck (San Francisco: City Lights, 1968), 24.

144 "Robert Fludd's Pan": "Of me therfor hath [God] made the circular palace of this bewtious World giving me the title of Pan, for as much as I represent the Vniversall Nature: . . . This payre of hornes therfore planted on my forehead do represent the Arctick and Antarctick poles of the bigger World." *Robert Fludd and his Philosophicall Key*, intro. by Allen G. Debus (New York: Science History Publications, 1979), 79.

144–145 "*imagine* their journeys": Jules Verne uses the same effect in *Journey to the Centre of the Earth*, trans. Robert Baldick (Harmondsworth: Penguin, 1965), 215, having characters first hypothesize a creature that subsequently appears. In H. P. Lovecraft's *At the Mountains of Madness*, Antarctic mirages prefigure "real" landscapes that appear later in the narrative.

145 M. H. Abrams, *The Mirror and the Lamp: Romantic Theory and the Critical Tradition* (New York: Oxford University Press, 1953), 55.

145 Ralph Waldo Emerson, "The Over-Soul" and "Circles," Essays IX and X in Joseph Slater et al., eds., *The Collected Essays of Ralph Waldo Emerson*, vol. 2, *Essays: First Series* (Cambridge, Mass.: Harvard University Press, 1979), 159–178, 179, 186. I am indebted to Barton Levi St. Armand for this connection.

145 "*lodestone*": Robert Fludd believed the magnet provided an excellent example of the sympathetic identity of humans with Earth: "The Loadstone is in comparison of its mother earth, even as man is to the whole world; wherefore Man is called the Son of the world by *Hermes* . . We find, I say, in the Loadstone, all the passions as well sympatheticall as antipatheticall, which do affect his mother earth; for it hath its Poles with the earth . . . And . . . it hath its Aequinoctialls, Colures, Meridians, and Tropicks." *Mosaicall Philosophy*, quoted in Debus, *Chemical Philosophy*, vol. 1, 239.

145 Plato, *The Republic*, trans. G. M. A. Grube (Indianapolis: Hackett, 1974), 351.

146 Porphyry, *Cave of the Nymphs:* see David Ulansey, *The Origins of the Mithraic Mysteries: Cosmology and Salvation in the Ancient World* (Oxford: Oxford University Press, 1989), 79.

146 "Aristotle"; "Pythagoreans": *Metaphysica*, II, trans. Daniel E. Gershendon and Daniel A. Greenberg (New York: Blaisdell, 1963), 5–55; Armand Rainaud, *Le continent austral* (1893; Amsterdam: Meridian, 1965), 21.

146 "hang upside down": Anna-Dorothee von den Brincken, *Fines Terrae: Die Enden der Erde und der vierte Kontinenten auf mittelalterlichen Weltkarten* (Hanover: Hahnsche, 1992), 21–28.

146 "Androphagi": John Livingston Lowes, *The Road to Xanadu: A Study in the Ways of the Imagination*, 2nd rev. ed. (London: Constable, 1951),

119. Lowes's description of Coleridge's creative process as a distillation of varied sources is implicitly organized within the high Romantic metaphor of the imagination as alchemical crucible.

146 Shaftesbury quoted in Tuveson, *Thrice Great Hermes*, 121.

147 "in the Pole": Arthur Waite, *Hermetic Museum*, 2nd rev. ed. (London: John M. Watkins, 1953), vol. 2, 166.

147 "*Deus absconditus*": Jung, *Aion*, 134.

147 "true nature of the Pole": Jung, *Aion*, 171. According to Frances Yates, Robert Fludd in *Utriusque* offers a "strange projection of the entire globe from the point of view of the Pole, the mystic Pole." *Giordano Bruno and the Hermetic Tradition* (Chicago: University of Chicago Press, 1964), 381.

147 "immense Icefields": A. Grenfell Price, ed. *The Explorations of Captain James Cook in the Pacific as Told by Selections of His Own Journals, 1768–1779* (New York: Dover, 1971), 150.

147 "Iamblichus": Coleridge quoted in Maren-Sofie Røstvig, *"The Rime of the Ancient Mariner" and the Cosmic System of Robert Fludd*, Tennessee Studies in Literature, vol. 9 (Knoxville: University of Tennessee Press, 1966), 70.

147–148 Mary Shelley, *Frankenstein, or the Modern Prometheus*, ed. James Rieger (Chicago: University of Chicago Press, 1982), 221. Shelley presents as parallels Walton's quest for the Pole and Frankenstein's for the forbidden act of creating life.

148 "travelogue of a spiritual journey": Stephen J. Pyne, *The Ice: A Journey to Antarctica* (New York: Ballantine, 1986), 163; Røstvig, "'Rime of the Ancient Mariner,'" 69.

148 All quoted passages from *The Rime of the Ancient Mariner* from *Complete Poetical Works of Samuel Taylor Coleridge*, ed. E. H. Coleridge, 2 vols. (Oxford: Oxford University Press, 1975).

149 Jerome McGann, "The Ancient Mariner: The Meaning of the Meanings," in *The Beauty of Inflections: Literary Investigations in Historical Method and Theory* (New York: Oxford University Press, 1985), 153.

149 "existence was uncertain": Harold Beaver, introduction, in *The Narrative of Arthur Gordon Pym of Nantucket* (Harmondsworth: Penguin, 1975), 11–12.

149 All quoted passages from *Symzonia: A Voyage of Discovery By Captain Adam Seaborn* [pseudonym of John Cleves Symmes] (Gainesville, Fla.: Scholars' Facsimiles and Reprints, 1965).

150 "J. N. Reynolds": See Martin Gardner, *Fads and Fallacies in the Name of Science* (New York: Dover, 1957).

150 H. P. Lovecraft, *Miscellaneous Writings*, ed. S. T. Joshi (Sauk City, Wis.: Arkham House, 1995), 494–495.

150 Joscelyn Godwin, *Arktos: The Polar Myth in Science, Symbolism, and Nazi Survival* (Kempton, Ill.: Adventures Unlimited Press, 1996), 127. I am indebted to David Ulansey for suggesting this and other pertinent sources.

150 "life-threatening predicaments": The alchemically oriented Gaston Bachelard described his epiphany about Poe's maddening novella, which bored him in his youth when he read it within the framework of realism: "This adventure, which outwardly covers two oceans is, in reality, an adventure in the unconscious." *Water and Dreams: An Essay on the Imagination of Matter*, trans. Edith R. Farrell (Dallas: Pegasus Foundation, 1983), 57.

151 *"Tekeli'li!": The Narrative of Arthur Gordon Pym and Related Tales*, ed. J. Gerald Kennedy (New York: Oxford University Press, 1994), 178.

151 "black island of Tsalal": Toni Morrison, in *Playing in the Dark: Whiteness and the Literary Imagination* (Cambridge, Mass.: Harvard University Press, 1992), 31–32, has harsh words about the racist overtones of Poe's naive use of black and white imagery in *Pym*, but some of this imagery may also derive from alchemy, about which Poe had considerable knowledge. In alchemical color symbolism, moving from black to white is an important step in transmutation of landscape and soul alike; it represents the dialectic between the early *nigredo* or black stage and the penultimate *albedo* or whitening (to be followed by a rainbow color display before the ultimate *rubedo* or reddening).

151 "shrouded human figure": See Richard Kopley, "Early Illustrations of *Pym*'s 'Shrouded Human Figure,'" in Robert A. Collins and Howard D. Pearce, eds., *The Scope of the Fantastic: Selected Essays from the First International Conference on the Fantastic in the Arts*, Contributions to the Study of Science Fiction and Fantasy, no. 11 (New York: Greenwood, 1987), 155–170, for a number of fascinating versions.

151 Richard Howard, introduction, in *The Narrative of Arthur Gordon Pym of Nantucket* (Boston: David Godine, 1973). John Irwin comments on this "white shadow": "It exhibits the uncertainty of the boundary between observer and phenomenon, that condition of indeterminacy in which the observer in part creates the phenomenon he observes and thus ends by observing his own presence in a kind of veiled narcissism." *American Hieroglyphics: The Symbol of the Egyptian Hieroglyphics in the American Renaissance* (New Haven: Yale University Press, 1980), 213–214. Stanislaw Lem develops this notion of subject/object indeterminacy extensively in *Solaris*.

152 William Butcher, *Verne's Journey to the Center of the Self: Space and Time in the* Voyages extraordinaires (London: Macmillan, 1990), 2. Jules Verne's *Le Sphinx des glaces* (1897) is extracted and included as a supplement in the Penguin edition of *Pym* as *The Sphinx of the Ice-Fields*, trans. Harold Beaver, 275–311.

152–153 "a lost civilization": References to the occult (as opposed to the "real") Pole are present in other of Lovecraft's works such as "The Dunwich Horror," in which the half-human, half-demonic protagonist scans his human grandfather's alchemical books: "Grandfather kept me saying the Dho formula last night and I think I saw the inner city at the two magnetic poles. I shall go to those poles when the earth is cleared off."

The Dunwich Horror and Others, ed. S. T. Joshi (Sauk City, Wis.: Arkham House, 1984), 184.

153 "If we could open": Burnet, *Sacred Theory*, III, ch. 10, 100.

153 "a haunted, accursed": All passages from H. P. Lovecraft, *At the Mountains of Madness*, in *At the Mountains of Madness and Other Novels* (Sauk City, Wis.: Arkham House, 1985), 3–106.

153 "hole in the head": A French asylum inmate's diagram from the famous *Art brut* collection depicts this image literally: the globe is overlaid with a sympathetically connected "interior world" that strikingly resembles a medieval *mappemonde*. See "Florent" (1883–1955), "La Terre et ses ramifications internes" (1944–1949), from *L'Art Brut* (Paris: Musée des Arts Decoratifs, 1967), fasc. IV, 1965.

154 "true landscape of Solaris": Bachelard, *Water and Dreams*, 57.

154 "We are searching": All quoted passages from Stanislaw Lem, *Solaris*, trans. Joanna Kilmartin and Steve Cox (San Diego: Harcourt Brace, 1987), 72.

155 William Huffman, ed., *Robert Fludd: Essential Readings* (London: Aquarian Press, 1992), 122.

156 "barbaric and unknown race": All quoted passages from Thomas Pynchon, *V.* (New York: Bantam, 1964). In *The Gnostic Pynchon* (Bloomington: Indiana University Press, 1990), Dwight Eddins comments: "Godolphin's epiphany reveals the extent of gnostic surrogation. Retroactive to the mythic origins of the race, the cabal's plot substitutes a flamboyant 'garden' of death for the fecund plexus of all life. This inverted Eden suggests that in the beginning was the Inanimate, that its logos is decreation, and that its entropic Kingdom is coming to destroy the last illusions of organic vitality. Such is the power of the demiurgic forces that 'They' can plant a colorful 'mockery of life' at the almost-inaccessible still point of Earth, bringing about through the shock their ultimate triumph: causing the animate to doubt its animateness, to identify with seemingly ubiquitous barrenness. The insidious message of Vheissu is 'V.'s you'" (65).

156 Coleridge quoted in Lowes, *Road to Xanadu*, 489n.

157 Leonora Carrington's protagonist Marion Leatherby projects onto the Arctic the same Paradisal vision that Shelley's Captain Robert Walton does: "I try in vain to be persuaded that the pole is the seat of frost and desolation; it ever presents itself to my imagination as the region of beauty and delight"; *Frankenstein*, 9.

157 "Kavan herself claimed": Brian W. Aldiss, introduction, in Anna Kavan, *Ice* (London: Picador, 1973), 6; all quoted passages are from this edition. See also D. A. Callard, *The Case of Anna Kavan: A Biography* (London: Peter Owen, 1992).

158 Carrington's *The Hearing Trumpet:* First published in French translation as *Le Cornet acoustique* in 1974; first published in English in 1977. Text used is Virago Modern Classic no. 371 (London: Virago Press, 1991).

158 "annals of Surrealism": In surveying surrealist novels in his introduction to Giorgio de Chirico's *Hebdomeros*, for example, John Ashbery cites works by Breton and Aragon but not Carrington. (Cambridge, Mass.: Exact Change Press, 1992), ix–xii.

159 "Polar romance novels": A very partial list: J. G. Ballard, *The Drowned World* (London: Victor Gollancz, 1963); John Calvin Batchelor, *The Birth of the People's Republic of Antarctica* (New York: Dial Press, 1983); Ursula K. Le Guin's "Sur: A Summary Report of the Yelcho Expedition to the Antarctic, 1909–10," in *The Best American Short Stories 1983*, ed. Anne Tyler with Shannon Ravenel (Boston: Houghton Mifflin, 1983); the New Zealander Ian Wedde's *Symmes Hole* (Auckland: Penguin New Zealand, 1986); and the Austrian Christoph Ransmayr's *The Terrors of Ice and Darkness*, trans. John E. Woods (New York: Grove Weidenfeld, 1991). In *Outerbridge Reach* (New York: Ticknor and Fields, 1992), Robert Stone includes an ambivalent hallucinatory episode on a Tristan da Cunha–like island in the Southern Ocean that echoes both the main character's "false" trip and the transcendental polar experience.

159 "great sentimental journey": *The Guardian*, quoted as dust jacket copy, *Fire Down Below* (New York: Farrar, Straus and Giroux, 1989). The first and second volumes in this trilogy are *Rites of Passage* (1980) and *Close Quarters* (1987).

160 "Once Antarctica": Pyne, *The Ice*, 194.

161 "our globe, seen by God": Emerson, "Circles," 179.

161 "a continent devoted to science": "The Crystal Laboratory," episode of the PBS series *The New Explorers*, broadcast June 15, 1995.

7. IS THIS REAL OR AM I CRAZY?

162 "The Haunted Mirror," directed by Robert Hainer, written by John Baines, in *Dead of Night* (1945). In this episode of the four-part film, the speaker finds his bedroom mirror consistently returning the reflection of a different room and himself as a different person in it.

164 Tzvetan Todorov, *The Fantastic: A Structural Approach to a Literary Genre*, trans. Richard Howard (Ithaca: Cornell University Press, 1973), 25.

165 Terry Castle, *The Female Thermometer: Eighteenth Century Culture and the Invention of the Uncanny* (New York: Oxford University Press, 1995), 175.

165–166 Stanislav Grof, "Varieties of Transpersonal Experiences: Observations from LSD Therapy," in Stanley R. Dean, ed., *Psychiatry and Mysticism* (Chicago: Nelson-Hall, 1975), 332.

166 Mikkel Borch-Jacobsen, "What Made Albert Run?" review of Ian Hacking's *Reflections on the Reality of Transient Mental Illness*, *London Review of Books* 21, no. 11 (May 27, 1999), www.lrb.co.uk.

166 "shamans": See, e.g., Mircea Eliade, *The Sacred and the Profane: The Nature of Religion*, trans. Willard R. Trask (New York: Harcourt, Brace, and World, 1957), 196.

166 "spiritual awakening": As noted in Chapter 5, the link between schizophrenia and religious experience is recognized by schizophrenics themselves, the following being a not uncommon testament: "The Group for the Advancement of Psychiatry asked the readers of Dear Abby: If you have suffered from schizophrenia, what was the single most striking factor in your recovery? We got hundreds of responses. To us, the single most striking factor was the role of their own religion and spirituality. They felt, rightly or wrongly, that a spiritual connection, the ability to believe that they were going to be better through a higher power, was the most important thing. And it was really astounding to the scientists who were looking at this, because we had expected answers like medication or psychotherapy." John A. Talbot, M.D., "What Do We Talk about When We Are Paying Someone to Listen?" *New York Times Magazine*, May 6, 2000, www.nytimes.com.

166 "possessed by the Devil": In 1999 the Vatican issued a statement that cast aside the notion of the Devil as a personified demon and redefined evil as a pervasive "harmful influence." A new rite of exorcism was described, in the words of a news report, that "acknowledges that psychological disturbances and illnesses such as epilepsy and schizophrenia have often been misinterpreted as diabolic possession and recommends clergy to take guidance from psychiatrists before performing exorcisms. 'One must be very careful,' said [Cardinal Jorge Medina] . . . 'since ordinary people tend to confuse psychosomatic and psychological problems with demonic ones.'" *The Telegraph*, Sept. 10, 2000, www.telegraph.co.uk.

166–167 Ioan Couliano, *Eros and Magic in the Renaissance*, trans. Margaret Cook (Chicago: University of Chicago Press, 1987), 124, 125.

168 "the original script": S. S. Prawer, *Caligari's Children: The Film as Tale of Terror* (Oxford: Oxford University Press, 1980), 168.

169 "a mysterious patient": *Hollywood Reporter*, July 24, 2000, www.hollywoodreporter.com.

170 "With the stroke": Deborah Esch and Jonathan Warren, eds., *The Turn of the Screw*, Norton Critical Edition, 2nd ed. (New York: Norton, 1999), 85.

170–171 "family psychodynamics": See F. O. Matthiessen, ed., *The James Family: Selections from the Writings of Henry James, Senior, William, Henry, and Alice* (1947; New York: Vintage, 1980).

171 Virginia Woolf, "Henry James' Ghosts," in Esch and Warren, eds., *Turn of the Screw*, 160.

171 Leon Edel, introduction to *Henry James: Tales of the Supernatural*, in Esch and Warren, eds., *Turn of the Screw*, 192.

171 "Little Bessie": Bill Ellis, "'I Wonder, Wonder, Mother': Death and

the Angels in Native American Balladry," *Western Folklore* 38, no. 3 (July 1979): 170–185. See the discussion of British and American ballad versions in Chapter 4.

171–172 "fairy-tale pure and simple"; "merely apparitional": James, notebook entry and preface to the New York edition, in Esch and Warren, eds., *Turn of the Screw*, 120, 124.

172 "about my young woman": James, letter to H. G. Wells, Dec. 9, 1898, in Esch and Warren, eds., *Turn of the Screw*, 116.

172 "spirits of the dead": E.g., the real ghost of a jilted lover in "Sir Edmund Orme" (which also climaxes with a kind of deathbed exorcism) and Spencer Brydon's *ka*, his "just so totally other person," in "The Jolly Corner."

172 "The charm": James, preface to the New York edition, in Esch and Warren, eds., *Turn of the Screw*, 125.

173 Philip K. Dick quoted in Lawrence Sutin, *Divine Invasions: A Life of Philip K. Dick* (New York: Harmony, 1989), 155.

173 Stanislaw Lem, "Philip K. Dick: A Visionary among the Charlatans," trans. R. D. Mullen and Darko Suvin, in Lem, *Microworlds: Writings on Science Fiction and Fantasy*, ed. Franz Rottensteiner (San Diego: Harcourt Brace, 1984), 106–135.

174 "At the moment": Dick, "If You Find This World Bad, You Should See Some of the Others" (1977), in Lawrence Sutin, ed., *The Shifting Realities of Philip K. Dick: Selected Literary and Philosophical Writings* (New York: Harmony, 1995), 251.

174 "It is female": Philip K. Dick, self-interview, quoted in Sutin, *Divine Invasions*, 231.

174 "The loss of his sister": In accordance with his wishes, the body of the adult Philip was buried next to that of his infant sister in a Colorado graveyard. Sutin, *Divine Invasions*, 289.

174 "vast Ocean of soul": Bruno quoted in Karen Silvia de Léon-Jones, *Giordano Bruno and the Kabbalah: Prophets, Magicians, and Rabbis* (New Haven: Yale University Press, 1997), 81.

174 "I was aware": Dick, *Exegesis*, quoted in Sutin, *Divine Invasions*, 269.

175 "I felt keenly": Dick, "If You Find This World Bad," 252.

175 "pluriforms of God": Dick, *Exegesis*, in Sutin, ed., *Shifting Realities*, 333–334.

175 "ten major principles": Dick, *Exegesis*, in Sutin, ed., *Shifting Realities*, 332.

176 "a memoir of madness": Thomas Disch, *The Dreams Our Stuff Is Made Of: How Science Fiction Conquered the World* (New York: Free Press, 1998), 155.

176 "Sound Bite": Sherry Turkle, "Virtual Pets and Dolls," lecture, University of California at Berkeley, Feb. 18, 1999.

176 "brilliant coherence": Sutin, ed., *Shifting Realities*, xxi.

176 "God manifested" journal entry 11–17–80, quoted in Sutin, *Divine Invasions*, 269.

177 "true story": "Christ the Vampire was a magician in ancient Palestine. The Romans tried to kill him . . . Only they didn't know to drive a stake through his heart. So he has lived ever since, appearing to people who are weak. Whoever accepts his kiss gets sucked into the whole trip and becomes a mindless zombie wandering around trying to suck in the living by saying things like 'Jesus is the answer.'" J. G. Eccarius, *The Last Days of Christ the Vampire* (Gualala, Calif.: III Publishing, 1987), 19.

178 "practitioners of Jungian psychology": Their demonization as a "Gnostic cult" by writers such as Richard Noll (*The Jung Cult: Origins of a Charismatic Movement* [Princeton: Princeton University Press, 1994]) seems unwarranted. Jung's standing in the mainstream intellectual culture continues to be extremely low for various reasons: his extensive examination and incorporation of the premodern worldview in his work, his initial interest in the mythmaking behind Nazism, which he later repudiated, but for which he has taken a greater beating than, e.g., Martin Heidegger; and his split with Freud, whose school ruled as the dominant Western psychological paradigm for more than half a century.

178 Disch, *Dreams Our Stuff Is Made Of,* 141–142.

178 "UFO religions": See James R. Lewis, ed., *The Gods Have Landed: New Religions from Other Worlds* (Albany: State University of New York Press, 1995); Irving Hexham and Karla Poewe, "UFO: A Science Fiction Tradition," *Christian Century* 144, no. 15 (May 7, 1997): 489.

178 "a cosmology": John A. Saliba, "Religious Dimensions of UFO Phenomena," in Lewis, ed., *The Gods Have Landed.*

178 "Westerners' projected notions": Disch, *Dreams Our Stuff Is Made Of,* 186–187.

178 "Scientology"; "Aum Shinrikyo": Disch, *Dreams Our Stuff Is Made Of,* 141–142.

179 "Two thousand years ago": "(original) January 16, 1994; (slightly edited) January 1997: Crew from the Evolutionary Level Above Human Offers Last Chance to Advance Beyond Human," www.well.com/user/vegas/heavensgate, mirror site for www.heavensgate.com. Downloaded March 29, 1997. For an excellent study of the early days of this cult, see Robert W. Balch, "Waiting for the Ships: Disillusionment and the Revitalization of Faith in Bo and Peep's UFO Cult," in Lewis, ed., *Gods Have Landed,* 137–166.

179 Alexander Key (1904–1979), son of a cotton gin owner whose Florida business was burned by nightriders, lost both parents in early childhood and wrote a series of children's novels whose main characters were children from another world and/or possessing special powers.

180 "good way of life": A Klingon initiate, quoted in the documentary *Trekkies* (1999). See also "Klingon like Me," *Utne Reader,* March 1994.

181 "Christian mysticism and Jewish cabbala": In *The Search for the Perfect Language,* trans. James Fentress (Oxford: Blackwell, 1995), Umberto Eco also traces the "need to discover unity" from the linguistic frag-

mentation of fifth-century Europe, a proto-Babel in which "people no longer spoke Latin but Gallo-Romanic, Italico-Romanic, or Hispano-Romanic" (16).

181 René Descartes, *Discourse on Method and Related Writings,* trans. Desmond M. Clarke (Harmondsworth: Penguin, 1999), 41. For our culture's unique Aristotelian technotwist on this motif, see, e.g., the Columbia Pictures movie *Animal,* about "a man who undergoes multiple transplants of animal organs after a bad car accident and awakens to find himself taking on the traits of those beasts" (Reuters, Sept. 29, 2000).

181 See, e.g., David M. Guss, ed., *The Language of Birds* (Berkeley: North Point Press, 1985), 10.

181 Hugh Ormsby-Lennon, "Rosicrucian Linguistics: Twilight of a Renaissance Tradition," in Ingrid Merkel and Allen G. Debus, eds., *Hermeticism and the Renaissance: Intellectual History and the Occult in Early Modern Europe* (Washington: Folger Shakespeare Library, 1988), 322.

181 "In three stories": This is a fertile field: from Wallace Stevens's "Thirteen Ways of Looking at a Blackbird" ("But I know the blackbird is involved in what I know"), to Bernard Malamud's Schwartzy the talking crow in "The Jewbird," to Schubert's "Die Krähe," and on and on.

181–182 "Raven, genus *Corvus*": This section was not derived from, but is far surpassed by, Guy Davenport's brilliant "Every Force Evolves a Form," in Davenport, *Every Force Evolves a Form* (San Francisco: North Point Press, 1987), 151–155.

182 "Thought and Memory": Or Hugin and Munin. See *The Prose Edda of Snorri Sturluson,* sel. and trans. Jean I. Young (Berkeley: University of California Press, 1964), 63.

182 "the narrower territory of psychosis": Certain birds, in Daniel Paul Schreber's universe, were remnants of souls, "miraculously created birds" as distinct from "natural birds." *Memoirs of My Nervous Illness,* trans. and ed. Ida MacAlpine and Richard A. Hunter (Cambridge, Mass.: Harvard University Press, 1984), 167–168. Schreber's birds are not unlike Father's creation of phantasmagoric birds out of ornithological illustrations in Bruno Schulz's "The Birds" in *The Street of Crocodiles.* Besides being a universal image of madness on the order of "bats in the belfry," they also irresistibly recall the Serapeum site at Memphis overflowing with its four million ibis mummies, as compellingly described by John Ray in *The Archive of Hor* (London: Egypt Exploration Society, 1976).

182 "little meaning": All quoted passages from "The Raven," in Edgar Allan Poe, *Poetry and Tales* (New York: Library of America, 1984), 81–86.

183 "They have given": All quoted passages from "The Blackbird," trans. Thomas Frick and Wilhelm Wiegandt, in Robert Musil, *Selected Writings,* ed. Burton Pike (New York: Continuum, 1986), 326–339.

185 "a lioness confined": In his notebook Musil stated: "In 'The Blackbird' I was not successful in expressing my mother's strength that seemingly had no substance." *Diaries 1899–1941*, ed. Mark Mirsky, trans. Philip Payne (New York: Basic Books, 1999), 438.

8. TWO OLD BIRDS AND THEIR NEW FEATHERS

189 "great speckled bird": From Duncan, "Tribal Memories Passages 1," in *Bending the Bow* (New York: New Directions, 1968), 9–10.

189 Plato, *Phaedrus*, trans. Alexander Nehamas and Paul Woodruff (Indianapolis: Hackett, 1995), 37.

189 Philip K. Dick, "Cosmogony and Cosmology," in Lawrence Sutin, ed., *The Shifting Realities of Philip K. Dick: Selected Literary and Philosophical Writings* (New York: Harmony, 1995), 293. Dick added: "Therefore, if the human being is to fulfill his task—that of being a sort of mirror or image of the urgrund—he must experience anamnesis." The idea of the material world as a mirror or reflection of the greater world and its revival in metaphors of cybernetics and virtual reality will be explored in Chapter 12.

189–190 Cesare Ripa, "Memoria," in Edward A. Moses, ed., *Baroque and Rococo Pictorial Imagery: The 1758–60 Hertel Edition of Ripa's* Iconologia *with 200 Engraved Illustrations* (New York: Dover, 1971), plate 143.

190 "if Socrates was right": In the *Phaedrus* Socrates tells a story of the invention of writing in ancient Egypt in which a king named Thamus protests that written language will destroy true human memory. Plato, *Phaedrus*, 79.

190–191 "artificial memory": According to tradition, the technique was invented by the poet Simonides, who having narrowly escaped being crushed to death when the ceiling fell in on a banquet where he had been reciting, was able to identify the mangled corpses of the guests because he remembered the order in which they had been sitting around the table. Frances A. Yates, *The Art of Memory* (Chicago: University of Chicago Press, 1966), 1–2.

191 "the word 'topic'": Yates, *Art of Memory*, 31.

191 "mnemotechnics": Yates, *Art of Memory*, 4.

192 "Plan of St. Gall": Mary Carruthers, "Memory and Invention: The Poet as Master Builder in the Middle Ages," lecture, University of California at Berkeley, March 9, 1995. See also Carruthers, *The Book of Memory: A Study of Memory in Medieval Culture* (Cambridge: Cambridge University Press, 1992).

192 "When God created": Marie-Louise von Franz, "Psyche and Matter in Alchemy and Modern Science," in *Psyche and Matter* (Boston: Shambala, 1992), 159.

193 "may at once": Quoted in Yates, *Art of Memory*, 132. Italics added.

193 "the possessor": Frances A. Yates, *Giordano Bruno and the Hermetic Tradition* (Chicago: University of Chicago Press, 1964), 198.

193 Ioan Couliano, *Eros and Magic in the Renaissance*, trans. Margaret Cook (Chicago: University of Chicago Press, 1987), 125.

194 "somewhere beyond": Proust quoted in Walter Benjamin, "On Some Motifs in Baudelaire," in Hannah Arendt, ed., *Illuminations: Essays and Reflections*, trans. Harry Zohn (New York: Schocken, 1969), 158.

194 Walter Benjamin, "The Image of Proust," in *Illuminations*, 215.

195 "man eats God": Philip K. Dick quoted in Lawrence Sutin, introduction, *Shifting Realities of Philip K. Dick*, xii.

196 "Sometimes this was"; "I put the image": A. R. Luria, *The Mind of a Mnemonist: A Little Book about a Vast Memory*, trans. Lynn Solotaroff (Cambridge, Mass.: Harvard University Press, 1987), 32, 36. Carruthers has also pointed out the similarity of S.'s memory techniques to the classic memory systems; *Book of Memory*, 75–79.

197 Sergei Eisenstein, "Color and Meaning," in *The Film Sense*, trans. and ed. Jay Leyda (New York: Harcourt Brace Jovanovich, 1975), 148–149. Of Eisenstein's voice S. remarked to Luria: "There are people whose voices seem to be an entire composition, a bouquet . . . Listening to him, it was as though a flame with fibers protruding from it was advancing right toward me"; *Mind of a Mnemonist*, 24.

197 Jorge Luis Borges, *Ficciones*, trans. Anthony Kerrigan (New York: Grove Press, 1962), 115. "Funes the Memorious" comes from the collection *Artifices* (1944). Borges may have read about S. in Eisenstein's account in *The Film Sense*, first published in English in 1942.

198 "within a system of images": Eisenstein, "Color and Meaning," 150.

199 Osip Mandelstam, "Journey to Armenia," in *The Noise of Time: The Prose of Osip Mandelstam*, trans. Clarence Brown (San Francisco: North Point Press, 1986), 208.

199 Vladimir Nabokov, *Speak, Memory: An Autobiography Revisited*, rev. ed. (New York: G. P. Putnam's Sons, 1966), 12.

200 "using an elaborate": Erik Davis, *TechGnosis: Myth, Magic and Mysticism in the Age of Information* (New York: Harmony, 1998), 208–209.

200 "logical loops": Davis, *TechGnosis*, 210. Colossal Caves, Davis notes, "actually fulfilled one of the classic recommendations for the old memory palaces: Internalize the structure of an actual place (in this case, Kentucky's Bedquilt Cave), and then add magical elements and properties" (211).

201 "first-person allegory": Davis, *TechGnosis*, 212–213.

202 "Outriders of Karana": Devisers of a now-defunct multiplayer virtual world called "Britannia," whose elaborate and totally imaginary "Grand Atlas" is retained at www.tapr.org/?OutridersKarana.

202 C. S. Lewis, *The Allegory of Love: A Study in Medieval Tradition* (New York: Oxford University Press, 1958), 322, 44.

202 Angus Fletcher, *Allegory: The Theory of a Symbolic Mode* (Ithaca: Cornell University Press, 1964), 36–37.

203 "the Surrealists": In *Surrealism and the Occult: Shamanism, Magic, Alchemy, and the Birth of an Artistic Movement* (Rochester, Vt.: Destiny

Books, 1992), Nadia Choucha points out that despite their official alliances with Marxism and Freudianism, the Surrealists' tenets much more closely resembled those of Jung (via Janet and the collective unconscious, also the Catholic occult mysticism of the Symbolists). Her summary of the "occult principles" governing Surrealism should be familiar: "1. The universe is a single, living substance. 2. The universe is composed of interactive opposites. 3. Mind and matter are a unified entity. 4. Everything that exists corresponds in universal analogy—the male/female duality is a microcosm of the universe. 5. Imagination is a real motivating force that can act upon matter in a subtle way. 6. Self-realization, and thus realization of the universe comes through a variety of methods, e.g., intuition, illumination, meditation, accident, self-induced derangement, or experimentation" (5).

203–205 "what we think of as Expressionism": See Paul Raabe, ed., *The Era of German Expressionism*, trans. J. M. Ritchie (Dallas: Riverrun, 1980).

205 Ludwig Marcuse, "Something of a Deluge," in Raabe, *Era of German Expressionism*, 294–295.

205 "self-conscious and unified school": See such overviews as Maurice Nadeau, *The History of Surrealism*, trans. Richard Howard (New York: Collier, 1965).

205 "elongation of physical elements": Russell Merritt, "Expressionist Fantasy and the Uncanny," lecture, University of California at Berkeley, Sept. 24, 1999.

206 M. H. Abrams, *Natural Supernaturalism: Tradition and Revolution in Romantic Literature* (New York: Norton, 1971).

206 "total self": Paul Haderman, "Expressionist Literature and Painting," in Ulrich Weisstein, ed., *Expressionism as an International Literary Phenomenon* (Paris: Didier, 1973), 134.

206 "attribution of one's own attitudes": Definition from *American Heritage Dictionary*, 3rd ed.

206 "The projection": Freud quoted in Fletcher, *Allegory*, 23n.

207 "archaic identity": Marie-Louise von Franz, *Projection and Re-Collection in Jungian Psychology: Reflections of the Soul*, trans. William H. Kennedy (La Salle, Ill.: Open Court, 1978), 8.

207 Jeremy Naydler, *Temple of the Cosmos: The Ancient Egyptian Experience of the Sacred* (Rochester, Vt.: Inner Traditions, 1996), 156.

207 "The argument pursued": Naydler, *Temple of the Cosmos*, 135. Compare Philip K. Dick, about his mystical experience: "I saw Valis outside me modulating reality. Aha; but that was a projection (cf. Jung). Projection explains it . . . It was my own mind that I was seeing external to me. I traveled down into the phylogenic (collective) unconscious. God had nothing to do with it. Right?" In Sutin, ed., *Shifting Realities*, 330.

207–208 Philip K. Dick, "Cosmogony and Cosmology," in Sutin, ed., *Shifting Realities*, 281.

208 "Everything outside us"; "In Nature there is everything": *Aureum Vellus* (1623) and Goethe quoted in Ronald Gray, *Goethe, the Alchemist:*

A Study of Alchemical Symbolism in Goethe's Literary and Scientific Works (Cambridge: Cambridge University Press, 1952), 9.

208 "pull us further": Davis, *TechGnosis*, 213–214.

209 S. S. Prawer, *Caligari's Children: The Film as Tale of Terror* (Oxford: Oxford University Press, 1980).

209 Paul Coates, *The Gorgon's Gaze: German Cinema, Expressionism, and the Image of Horror* (Cambridge: Cambridge University Press, 1991), 157.

209 Richard J. Murphy, "Carnival Desire and the Sideshow of Fantasy: Dream, Duplicity, and Representational Instability in *The Cabinet of Dr. Caligari*," *Germanic Review* 66, no. 1 (Winter 1991): 48.

9. THE NEW EXPRESSIONISTS

212 Jorge Luis Borges, "Kafka and His Precursors," in *Labyrinths: Selected Stories and Other Writings*, ed. Donald A. Yates and James E. Irby, trans. James E. Irby (New York: New Directions, 1964), 201.

213 "only avant-garde movement": Russell Merritt, "Expressionist Fantasy and the Uncanny," lecture, University of California at Berkeley, Sept. 24, 1999. I am also indebted to Russell Merritt for referral to other valuable sources.

213 "For decades after the 1920s": Essays by Ulrich Weisstein and Jan Jozek Lipski in Ulrich Weisstein, ed., *Expressionism as an International Literary Phenomenon* (Paris: Didier, 1973), provided other helpful overviews of the internationalization of Expressionism.

214 "Neoexpressionism": See, e.g., the anthology of works by these painters in Wolfgang Max Faust and Gerd de Vries, *Hunger nach Bildern: Deutsche Malerei der Gegenwart* (Cologne: Dumont, 1982). The label was also taken up by German filmmakers, but these directors (such as Wim Wenders) practice an aesthetic sharply different from that of the New Expressionism.

214–215 Ronald Gray, *Goethe the Alchemist: A Study of Alchemical Symbolism in Goethe's Literary and Scientific Works* (Cambridge: Cambridge University Press, 1958), 254.

218 Arthur Clayborough, *The Grotesque in English Literature* (New York: Oxford University Press, 1965), 3.

219 "I was inside": All quoted passages from Will Self, *My Idea of Fun: A Cautionary Tale* (New York: Vintage, 1994).

221 For Robert Fludd, humans, wheat, and gold were the foremost of Queen Nature's "mansions" in their respective realms: "How excellent would that Artist appear beyond his companions, who by the most complete act & fire of celestial Alchemy, could first learn justly to distinguish the parts as well spiritual and corporeal of the Queens chiefest . . . dwelling-place [i.e., wheat]; for so by the surveying of his most secret and hidden regions he shall quickly be taught in a true vision to know himself and to discern the highest heaven of his inward Man." "A Philosophical Key," in William Huffman, ed., *Robert Fludd: Essential*

Readings (London: Aquarian Press, 1992), 111. Fludd would have envied Ian's comparable abilities vis-à-vis the cotton plant.

223 John Ruskin, *Modern Painting* III.V.VIII, para. 4.

226 Thomas Bernhard, *Wittgenstein's Nephew: A Friendship*, trans. Ewald Osers (London: Quartet, 1986), 29.

226 "his radical departure": In an interview with Peter Ovig Knudsen posted at the official site for von Trier's film collective, www.dogme95.dk, von Trier said: "At one level the Dogma rules emerged from a desire to submit to the authority and the rules I was never given in my humanistic, cultural-leftist upbringing; at another level they express the desire to make something quite simple." Yet the "Dogma" seems never to have been a dogma, only an in-joke that turned into a wildly successfully label in the international film world.

229 *"quelle horreur":* An earlier film of von Trier's with a large cult following, a campy Danish TV miniseries called *The Kingdom* (1990), would doubtless provide the ultimate proof, to his detractors, of this director's frivolity. The overt moral for this inspired piece of spitballing, in which von Trier pits beleaguered doctors representing a social order built on rational principles in a losing battle against a bewildering barrage of outrageously supernatural events, is stated up front via lugubrious voiceover: the doctors' sin is none other than "denial of the spiritual."

10. THE *HERMETICON* OF UMBERTUS E.

234 Umberto Eco, *Foucault's Pendulum*, trans. William Weaver (New York: Ballantine, 1989), 8. All quoted passages from this edition.

236 Margaret Anne Doody's lecture was later published in expanded form as *The True Story of the Novel* (New Brunswick: Rutgers University Press, 1996).

236 Basil Reardon, ed., *Collected Ancient Greek Novels* (Berkeley: University of California Press, 1989).

237 "apocryphal Christian acts": Giovanni Filoramo, *A History of Gnosticism*, trans. Anthony Alcock (Oxford: Basil Blackwell, 1990), 16. Many other commentators have noted romance elements in the Apocrypha.

237 Graham Anderson, introduction to "An Ephesian Tale," in Reardon, ed., *Collected Ancient Greek Novels*, 125.

237 Northrop Frye, *The Secular Scripture* (Cambridge, Mass.: Harvard University Press, 1976). Frye was expanding his earlier comments on romance in *Anatomy of Criticism: Four Essays* (Princeton: Princeton University Press, 1957).

237 Gillian Beer, *The Romance* (London: Methuen, 1970), 31.

237 "two-dimensional characters": For amusing and comprehensive lists of repeating elements of character, situation, values, and style, see Arthur Heiserman's brilliant critical examination of the Greek romance, *The Novel before the Novel: Essays and Discussions about the Beginnings of Prose Fiction in the West* (Chicago: University of Chicago Press, 1977).

238 Basil Reardon, *The Form of the Greek Romance* (Princeton: Princeton University Press, 1991), 24.

238 G. K. Chesterton, "In Defence of Penny Dreadfuls," in John Gross, ed., *The Oxford Book of Essays* (New York: Oxford University Press, 1992), 372–373.

238 Mikhail Bakhtin, *The Dialogic Imagination*, trans. Caryl Emerson and Michael Holquist (Austin: University of Texas Press, 1983).

238 Umberto Eco, *The Role of the Reader: Explorations in Semiotics of Texts* (London: Hutchinson, 1981).

240 Eco, *Role of the Reader*, 162.

241 Anderson, in Reardon, ed., *Collected Ancient Greek Novels*, 126.

241 "O Raimundo": It is possible that the following passage, from the Elizabethan Gabriel Harvey's *Pierce's Supererogation* (1593; London, 1845), served as the inspiration for Eco's brilliant *imitatio:* "O Humanity, my Lullius, or O Divinity, my Paracelsus, how should a man become that peece of Alchimy, that can tame the Rattesbane of villany into the Balme of honesty."

242 "cynically building": Eco, *Role of the Reader*, 8.

243 "William of Baskerville": Ironically, Eco's literary model for this character, Sherlock Holmes, practiced a bizarre and wholly improbable method of deduction that can only be called a parody of the scientific method. His creator, Arthur Conan Doyle, was not coincidentally a committed believer in spiritualism. By adopting the conventional view of Sherlock as a Master of Reason without examining the flourishing contradictions around this fictional character, Eco has cast as his main character a mole from the enemy's camp.

243 Umberto Eco, *Interpretation and Overinterpretation*, ed. Stefan Colloni (Cambridge: Cambridge University Press, 1992), 31.

244 Brian Copenhaver, "Hermes Trismegistus, Proclus, and the Question of a Philosophy of Magic," in Ingrid Merkel and Allen G. Debus, eds., *Hermeticism and the Renaissance: Intellectual History and the Occult in Early Modern Europe* (Washington: Folger Shakespeare Library, 1988), 93.

245 Friedrich Nietzsche, *The Birth of Tragedy and the Genealogy of Morals*, trans. Francis Golffing (New York: Anchor, 1956), 109.

245 Eco, *Role of the Reader*, 45, 161.

246 "second-century roué": This is not to discount the possibility that the narrative had a dual authorship, with Apuleius simply adding book 11 to Lucius of Patrae's original story. See Arthur Darby Nock, "Greek Novels and Egyptian Religion," *Essays on Religion and the Ancient World*, ed. Zeph Stewart (Oxford: Clarendon Press, 1972), 170.

11. THE GREAT TWENTIETH-CENTURY PUPPET UPGRADE

248 Karel Capek, *R.U.R.* (New York: Theater Guild Library, 1923), 165. All quoted passages from this edition.

249 *Puppet Master II*, directed by Dave Allen; story by Charles Band and David Fabian.

250 "Science is robbing": Per Schelde, *Androids, Humanoids, and Other Sci Fi Monsters: Science and Soul in Science Fiction Films* (New York: New York University Press, 1993), 9.

250 Slavoj Zizek, *The Plague of Fantasies* (London: Verso, 1997), 88.

251 Ray Kurzweil in *Talk*, April 2001, 154.

252 "emotional complex": Rudolph Drux, *Marionette Mensch: Ein Metaphernkomplex und sein Kontext von Hoffmann bis Buechner* (Munich: W. Fenk, ca. 1986), 189.

252 N. Katherine Hayles, *How We Became Posthuman: Virtual Bodies in Cybernetics, Literature, and Informatics* (Chicago: University of Chicago Press, 1999), 161.

252–253 "Influencing Machine": See Louis Sass, *Madness and Modernism: Insanity in the Light of Modern Art, Literature, and Thought* (New York: Basic Books, 1992), 217–218, 227.

253 "knowing the mechanism": Auguste Villiers de l'Isle-Adam, *Tomorrow's Eve*, trans. Robert Martin Adams (Urbana: University of Illinois Press, 1982). All quoted passages from this edition.

255 Daniel Gerould, "Villiers de l'Isle-Adam and Science Fiction," *Science-Fiction Studies* 11 (1984): 321.

256 Edward Gordon Craig, "The Actor and the Über-marionette" (1907), in *On the Art of the Theatre* (Chicago: Browne's Bookstore, 1911), 84–85.

257 *The Terminator* (1984), directed by James Cameron; screenplay by Harlan Ellison, James Cameron, Gale Ann Hurd, and William Wisher Jr. from stories by the science fiction writer Harlan Ellison.

257 "Ventriloquist's Dummy," written by John Baines and directed by Alberto Cavalcanti, in *Dead of Night* (1945).

258 *Puppet Master* (1989), directed by David Schmoeller; story by Charles Band and Kenneth J. Hall, screenplay by Joseph G. Collodi (this has got to be a plant). *Puppet Master III: Toulon's Revenge* (1991), directed by David DeCouteau, screenplay by C. Courtney Joyner, has a notable story line: Evil Nazi scientists use Toulon's theurgic techniques to animate dead soldiers' bodies from the Russian front so that they can return to battle as shields for the living. The Puppet Master foils this scheme by sending Pinhead, Leech Woman, Tunneler, et al. to kill the Nazis, which they do with enormous brio.

258 *Child's Play*, directed by Tom Holland, story by Don Mancini, screenplay by Don Mancini, John Lafia, and Tom Holland.

261 Despina Kakoudaki, "The Human Machine: Visual Representation and Artificial Intelligence" (Ph.D. diss., University of California at Berkeley, 2000), 3. See also Kakoudaki, "Pinup and Cyborg: Exaggerated Gender and Artificial Intelligence," in Marleen S. Barr, ed., *Future Females, The Next Generation: New Voices and Velocities in Feminist Sci-*

ence Fiction Criticism (Lanham, Md.: Rowman and Littlefield, 2000), for excellent close readings of *Metropolis* and *Ghost in the Shell.*

261–262 "arbitrary and hierarchical": Kakoudaki, "Human Machine," 9.

262 "explicit roots in *The Tempest*": Along with Irving Block and Alan J. Adler, William Shakespeare is given a writing credit.

263 *Bicentennial Man,* directed by Chris Columbus; screenplay by Nicholas Kazan from the short story by Isaac Asimov.

264 Isaac Bashevis Singer, foreword, in Emily D. Bilski, ed., *Golem! Danger, Deliverance, and Art* (New York: Jewish Museum, 1988), 6.

264 *Alien,* directed by Ridley Scott; story by Dan O'Bannon and Ronald Shusett, screenplay by Dan O'Bannon (and David Giler and Walter Hill).

264 *Alien: Resurrection,* directed by Jean-Pierre Jeanette; screenplay by Joss Whedon.

264 *Multiplicity,* directed by Harold Ramis; screenplay and story by Chris Miller.

265 *Eve of Destruction* (1991), directed by Duncan Gibbons; screenplay by Duncan Gibbons and Yale Udof.

265 *Nemesis* (1993), directed by Albert Pyun; screenplay by Rebecca Charles.

266 *Blade Runner,* directed by Ridley Scott; screenplay by Hampton Fancher and David Peoples.

267 "retelling of Christ's birth": J. P. Telotte, *Replications: A Robotic History of the Science Fiction Film* (Urbana: University of Illinois Press, 1995), 179.

267 *Terminator II,* directed by James Cameron; screenplay by James Cameron and William Wisher Jr.

268 O. B. Hardison, *Disappearing through the Skylight: Culture and Technology in the Twentieth Century* (New York: Viking, 1989), 337, 348.

268 *Ghost in the Shell* [Kokako kidota], directed by Mamori Oshii; screenplay by Kazunori Ito and Masamune Shiro.

268 Umberto Eco, *Foucault's Pendulum,* trans. William Weaver (New York: Ballantine, 1989), 49.

268 Moshe Idel, "The Golem in Jewish Mysticism and Magic," in Bilski, ed., *Golem,* 15.

269 Hayles, *How We Became Posthuman,* 2–3.

12. THE DOOR IN THE SKY

272 "The future": "Il futuro ha un cuore antico," cited by the historian Giorgio Galli and quoted in Lucia Birnbaum, *Black Madonnas: Feminism, Religion, and Politics in Italy* (Boston: Northeastern University Press, 1993), 15. The Italian original was kindly supplied to me by Professor Birnbaum.

275 *Dark City:* In an interview Proyas listed Philip K. Dick as a writer who influenced him, and two specific "streams of influence" on *Dark City:*

"the German expressionist movies like *Metropolis, Nosferatu, The Cabinet of Dr. Caligari* and then the noirs from the '40s and '50s which were actually influenced by German Expressionism . . . All sorts of plot points from *Dark City* come from film noir. It's just taken to an extreme, and the extreme resolves itself in terms of science fiction. It's like once they discover the answers to their questions, they realize they're in an existential nightmare. In turn, it comes right back to German Expressionism." George Khoury, "The Imaginer: An Interview with Alex Proyas," *Creative Screenwriting* 7, no. 5 (Oct. 2000): 85, 87.

276 *The Truman Show:* Lawsuits have been filed about the originality of this story, but ultimately, one suspects, it derives from the wonderfully innocent notion propounded by Andy Warhol's Factory back in the 1960s to stick a camera in a man's room and have it run twenty-four hours a day, a premise also underlying a spate of recent "reality" television shows.

278 "distinctive subgenre": Its best-known proponent is William Gibson. The film *The Thirteenth Floor,* for example, is based on a 1963 novel, *Simulacron 3,* by Daniel F. Galouye. Among myriad other examples are Neal Stephenson's seminal *Snow Crash* (1993), featuring a "Metaverse" of alternate worlds, and Alexander Besher's *Rim* (1994), in which a virus infects a virtual world called Satori City, causing it to crash and strand its human inhabitants.

279 Marshall McLuhan, "The *Playboy* Interview," in Eric McLuhan and Frank Zingrone, eds., *Essential McLuhan* (New York: Basic Books, 1996), 268. He added: "I expect to see the coming decades transform the planet into an art form; the new man, linked in a cosmic harmony that transcends time and place, will sensuously caress and mold and pattern every facet of the terrestrial artifact as if it were a work of art, and man himself will become an organic art form." In the same interview he asserted that "via the computer, we could logically proceed from translating languages to bypassing them entirely in favor of an integral cosmic unconsciousness somewhat similar to the collective unconscious envisioned by Bergson" (262).

279 David Bohm quoted in Michael Talbot, *The Holographic Universe* (New York: HarperCollins, 1991), 46.

279 Philip K. Dick, *Exegesis,* in Lawrence Sutin, ed. *The Shifting Realities of Philip K. Dick: Selected Literary and Philosophical Writings* (New York: Harmony, 1995), 252–253.

279 *"unus mundus":* Marie-Louise von Franz, "Psyche and Matter in Alchemy and Modern Science," in *Psyche and Matter* (Boston: Shambala, 1989), 158–159.

279 Erik Davis, *TechGnosis: Myth, Magic and Mysticism in the Age of Information* (New York: Harmony, 1998), 190.

280 "cyberspace": The term was coined by William Gibson in his 1984 novel *Neuromancer.* George Gilder's term is "telecosm" (www.gildertech.com). Like the Renaissance, this is an era of techno-

logical neologisms that paradoxically strengthen our conceptual bonds to pretechnological Western culture.

280 William Irwin Thompson quoted in Davis, *TechGnosis*, 215.

280 Holland Cotter, "Accessing Outernet: Medieval Software," www.nytimes.com, Sept. 19, 1997.

280–281 Robert Wright, "Can Thor Make a Comeback?" *Time*, Dec. 16, 1996, 69.

281 "We now implicitly endow": See, e.g., Margaret Wertheim, *The Pearly Gates of Cyberspace: A History of Space from Dante to the Internet* (New York: Norton, 1999).

281 "For everything in life": Richard Matheson, *What Dreams May Come* (New York: Tor, 1998), 49.

281 "a biological genealogy": See Andrew Leonard's grandly titled *Bots: The Origins of New Species* (New York: Hardwired, 1997).

281 "A Mirror World"; *"People build microcosms":* David Gelernter, *Mirror Worlds: or the Day Software Puts the Universe in a Shoebox . . . How It Will Happen and What It Will Mean* (Cambridge, Mass.: MIT Press, 1991), 3, 183.

282 Giordano Bruno, *On the Composition of Images, Signs, and Ideas,* trans. Charles Doria, ed. Dick Higgins (New York: Willis, Locker, and Owens, 1991), 38.

282 Brian Greene, *The Elegant Universe: Superstrings, Hidden Dimensions and the Quest for the Ultimate Theory* (New York: Norton, 1999).

282 Jean-Pierre Vernant, "In the Mirror of Medusa," in Vernant, *Mortals and Immortals: Collected Essays,* ed. Froma I. Zeitlin (Princeton: Princeton University Press, 1991), 142.

282 "Neoplatonic notion of the mirror": For an overview, see Herbert Grabes, *The Mutable Glass: Mirror Imagery in Titles and Texts of the Middle Ages and the Renaissance* (Cambridge: Cambridge University Press, 1982).

282–283 Gelernter, *Mirror Worlds,* 184. Gelernter also invokes the familiar image of the sphere: "the golden Microcosmal Orb of kingship, the *sphere perfectly held in the right hand* symbolizing the whole world—inherited from Rome by Byzantium, passed onwards to medieval kingship and into modern times. The original Mirror World. Look at it and imagine (if you cannot see) the world and your kingdom: the two being synonymous" (34).

283–284 "Afterlife": See www.lucasarts.com.

285 *Johnny Mnemonic,* directed by Robert Longo; screenplay by William Gibson from his novel.

286 *Lawnmower Man,* directed by Brett Leonard; screenplay attributed to Stephen King though his name was removed after a lawsuit; from a story by Stephen King. An interesting variant is found in *Ghost in the Machine* (1993), directed by Rachel Talalay. Here that tried-and-true entity, the soul of a serial killer, transforms itself into neuroelectrical impulses thanks to an electrical power surge caused by lightning as the

dying man is having an MRI scan during a severe storm. Via the scan, the killer's soul journeys straight to the hospital's medical database, out of which he can traverse the Internet and the electrical system simultaneously (though he's still imprisoned in this "other world," from which he can kill), inhabiting cyberspace and household appliances with equal abandon. Ultimately he dies when he is chased into a particle accelerator, where a computer virus eats him.

286 Frances A. Yates, *Giordano Bruno and the Hermetic Tradition* (Chicago: University of Chicago Press, 1964), 192.

288 Martin Jay, "Force Fields," *Salmagundi* 108 (Fall 1995): 25.

289 Cyril Connolly, *The Unquiet Grave: A Word Cycle by Palinurus* (New York: Perseda, 1960), 31–32.

289 Ralph Waldo Emerson, "Circles," Essay X, in Joseph Slater et al., eds., *The Collected Essays of Ralph Waldo Emerson*, vol. 2, *Essays: First Series* (Cambridge, Mass.: Harvard University Press, 1979), 183.

ACKNOWLEDGMENTS

Acknowledgments for a book growing out of ideas seeded in essays that were composed over a span of years must be, for me, a genealogy of relationships—with friends and colleagues whose writings, conversation, and sharing of ideas are deeply embedded in the result. I will offer my thanks in mostly chronological order, with apologies in advance to anyone I have inadvertently omitted: to the late Reuel Denney of the University of Hawaii for his early encouragement; to C. E. Poverman, who suggested I read the stories of Bruno Schulz when I first returned to the U.S. mainland from Hawaii in 1981; to Dennis Jakob for introducing me to the work of Frances Yates; and to printer Jack Werner Stauffacher for giving me Naomi Miller's *Heavenly Caves* and for providing a living model of the artist-thinker's life. Manfred Triesch of the San Francisco Goethe Institute and the writer Horst Bienek, both gone now, brought me to Europe and the wider cultural context to which Schulz belongs. Among his many generosities, Bienek, who died in 1990, gave me both his home in Munich to live in and his German edition of *The Republic of Dreams,* a collection of Schulz's short pieces and fragments, a book that would set in motion a complicated series of Schulzian events.

In Poland, where I traveled courtesy of a Koskiuszko Foundation grant, I am deeply grateful to the letterpress printers Janusz and Jadwiga Tryzno of Correspondance des Artes in Lodz for arranging my stay along with many other kindnesses, and through their auspices to Professor Jerzy

Jarniewicz of the English Institute of the University of Lodz and to Professors Tadeusz Rachwel and Claire Hobbs of the English Institute of the University of Silesia for hosting my lectures there. In all matters Polish, theatrical, and avant-garde I follow the wise counsel of Professor Daniel Gerould of the CUNY Graduate School and his wife, the translator Jadwiga Kosicka. I am particularly indebted to their suggestions of sources and their close reading of several chapters.

In England, I am indebted to Steve and Tim Quay both for their friendship and for introducing me to the late Jakob Schulz, Bruno Schulz's nephew and literary executor. I owe special thanks to Professor Jay Winter and Bursar Colin Gilbraith of Pembroke College, Cambridge for arranging a brief residency there, during which the foundational research of this book was accomplished.

At Brown University, a fellowship at the John Nicholas Brown Center for American Civilization gave me access to the papers of H. P. Lovecraft and time to bring the book to completion. I want to thank the center's director, Joyce M. Botelho, and her staff; the estimable John Stanley, special collections curator at the John Hay Library and Lovecraft authority; historian Jane Lancaster; and Professor Barton Levi St. Armand of the American Civilization program for all their help and suggestions.

In Berkeley, California, the list includes both home and visitor teams, so I will omit titles. First, I want especially to thank Jerome McGann for the stimulation of his own work and for early encouragement. The classical scholar Daniel Caner generously shared his bibliography on animated statues. Paul Alpers and Randolph Starn, in their successive terms as director of the Townsend Center for the Humanities, gave unstintingly of their time, knowledge, support, and friendship over the years, as did Christina Gillis, associate director, and Francis Starn. David Reid and Jayne Walker have been enthusiastic readers and loyal supporters; to them I also owe the much-appreciated backing of Mike Davis and the late Mike Sprinker for this project. Peter Kingsley's works and lectures were inspirational, as were Maurizio Bettini's; to the latter I am especially indebted for the stimulus of his talk "A Doll Denied to Venus" and his reading of several chapters. Lifelong friend and Iranologist Martin Schwartz provided innumerable insights and references; Armenologist and scholar of mysticism James Russell also shared his considerable knowledge. Jack Niles has been my resource for issues ballad-related and medieval; Despina Kakoudaki for early twentieth-century robots in literature; Alexander Nehamas for Socrates and Montaigne; and Russell Merritt for film Expressionism. Drs. Herbert Schreier and Guy Micco shed invaluable light on syphilis during my Lovecraft researches.

Elsewhere, Louis Sass, that polymath residing in the Rutgers Psychology department, has pushed me, both in his works and in dialogue, to a deeper understanding of the philosophical issues behind schizophrenia. The knowledge, wit, and scholarly acumen of another polymath, music scholar Joscelyn Godwin, in his books as well as in his correspondence and close reading of portions of the manuscript, have helped me immeasurably. Americanist and good friend Wendy Martin has lent her support in ways too numerous to count. I thank the Headlands Center for the Arts for giving me studio space in the most beautiful site in the continental United States, where I completed the final revisions on this book.

I am grateful to Steve and Tim Quay, Laurie Simmons, and Chris Hardman, founder of Antenna Theater, for allowing images of their work to be reproduced in this book. I owe thanks to Nancy Goldman of the Pacific Film Archive and Lisa Calden and Cheryl Maslin of the University Art Museum, University of California at Berkeley, for their assistance in locating film stills; to Mark Solaris of Video Cat, San Francisco, for his skill in scanning the images used in this book; to Dennis Letbetter for creative photography; to Francesco Battisti for granting me permission to use the photograph of the Orco's mouth taken by his father, the late scholar Eugenio Battisti; and to the editors of the journals *Raritan*, *Agni*, *Salmagundi*, and *Threepenny Review* for providing a venue to present earlier versions of this material.

At Harvard, finally, I am indebted to the long-term enthusiasm of editor *nonpareil* Lindsay Waters; to the outstanding line editing and patience of Camille Smith; and to the generosity of my three readers: first and foremost, Harold Bloom, and two anonymous readers whose deep responses to the book provided both encouragement and helpful tips for avoiding the path of error. Neither they nor any other persons mentioned here bear responsibility for my numerous detours down that road. Special thanks to Tom Livingston for his dedication and enthusiasm in proofreading and indexing the Lovecraftian entity this book became.

INDEX

Printed and bound by CPI Group (UK) Ltd, Croydon, CR0 4YY

09/06/2025

14685843-0001